IMMIGRATION DETENTION
LAW, HISTORY, POLITICS

The liberal legal ideal of protection of the individual against administrative detention without trial is embodied in the habeas corpus tradition. However, the use of detention to control immigration has gone from a wartime exception to normal practice, thus calling into question modern states' adherence to the rule of law.

Daniel Wilsher traces how modern states have come to use long-term detention of immigrants without judicial control. He examines the wider emerging international human rights challenge presented by detention based upon protecting 'national sovereignty' in an age of global migration. He explores the vulnerable political status of immigrants and shows how attempts to close liberal societies can create 'unwanted persons' who are denied fundamental rights. To conclude, he proposes a set of standards to ensure that efforts to control migration, including the use of detention, conform to principles of law and uphold basic rights regardless of immigration status.

DANIEL WILSHER is a senior lecturer in law at City Law School, London, and a part-time immigration judge in the Immigration and Asylum Chamber, First Tier Tribunal.

IMMIGRATION DETENTION
LAW, HISTORY, POLITICS

DANIEL WILSHER

CAMBRIDGE
UNIVERSITY PRESS

CAMBRIDGE UNIVERSITY PRESS
Cambridge, New York, Melbourne, Madrid, Cape Town,
Singapore, São Paulo, Delhi, Mexico City

Cambridge University Press
The Edinburgh Building, Cambridge CB2 8RU, UK

Published in the United States of America by Cambridge University Press, New York

www.cambridge.org
Information on this title: www.cambridge.org/9781107005761

First published 2012

A catalogue record for this publication is available from the British Library

ISBN 978-1-107-00576-1 Hardback

CONTENTS

ACKNOWLEDGEMENTS

This book was written between 2006 and 2010, but began life much earlier prompted by my experiences as a lawyer visiting long-term immigration detainees in prisons and holding facilities. I was struck by the fact that often neither detainees nor the authorities clearly understood why they were being held. Often their release would follow from sending a simple fax setting out the reasons why continued detention made little sense. The absence of robust judicial oversight meant, however, that such releases were left to the vagaries of chance meetings with the right lawyers. This seemed to me a strange situation given the centrality of habeas corpus and personal liberty within liberal legal systems. Years later I wanted to bring together into one place a text which might better explain the historical development of the law in this area. This volume is an expanded and developed version of what became my Ph.D. thesis. I am very grateful to my supervisor, Professor Elspeth Guild. She has been a wonderful adviser, coach and friend throughout the process. With her on hand to inspire me, I was able to continue to believe in the value of this project even when my spirit sank a little or time ran short.

At Radbout University, Nijmegen, I was always welcomed by Professor Kees Van Groendijk, who provided me with a strong sense that everything would be all right in the end. Evelien Brouwer, Galina Cornelisse and Ricky van Owers were constantly supportive and welcoming. I also would like to thank City Law School, City University, London for giving me a term sabbatical in which I was able to do some of the large-scale research free from teaching obligations. I would also like to thank the reviewers of my thesis, Professor Roel Fernhout, Professor Kees Van Groendijk and Professor Dan Kanstroom. The latter was particularly kind to help me by travelling so far. I also gained very helpful insights from anonymous reviewers of the draft book. The result is much better than the draft.

I had considerable help from Professor Daniele Lochak, University of Paris, on the French material. She was always thorough and prompt in responding to my rather hesitant French emails. Marc Bernardot was also a good source of material on French history. In the United States, I received great help from Jack Wallace at Florida Immigrant Advocacy Center, Archi Pyati at Lawyers Committee for Human Rights, Professor Margaret Taylor of Wake Forest University School of Law and Professor David Cole of Georgetown Law School. At the London School of Economics library, Clive Lawson was a wonderful teacher on the intricacies of US government papers before they were finally digitized. I thank the staff at Rheidol Rooms cafe for all the carbs. Ella Singleton worked with great speed and skill on the bibliography. Holly Buick provided me with excellent research assistance on the conditions of detention material for which I am very grateful.

To my mother and step-father, Lesley and Len Doyal, I owe a great deal. They have always been there to inspire and challenge me, qualities that must run deep in this book. I am glad that the writing of this book coincided with the part-time return to Europe of Ken Wilsher and Avril Hodges and the chance to spend more time together. My sister Hannah has been a great motivator when I have been too self-deprecating. I appreciate it. From my family Julia, Grace and Hal Bennett I have had the best resource of all – a place that I can truly call home. I love them very much and am very lucky to be able to share my life with them.

INTRODUCTION AND OVERVIEW:
FREE MOVEMENT OF PERSONS AND
LIBERTY OF THE PERSON

The detention of foreigners under the auspices of immigration powers has grown enormously in both its scope and scale during the last thirty years. In a pattern repeated throughout developed nations, and increasingly copied by others, unauthorized or rejected foreigners are being held in prison-like facilities for extended periods without serious legal controls or accountability. The causes of this rise in immigration-related detention are many, but the results are clear; imprisonment of individuals without the normal due process safeguards commonly demanded in liberal democracies is now taking place on a vast scale. This process of 'warehousing' immigrants, outside the mainstream of the law, has entailed much that is arbitrary or inhumane. We can see this as part of a more general trend towards 'politicizing' the treatment of unauthorized migrants. This book is an attempt to explain the historical development of this phenomenon and to explore the underlying legal and political challenges that it exposes for societies ostensibly committed to a public policy based upon liberal reason and the rule of law.

From free movement to border controls: the alien as liberal subject in the nineteenth century

The 'alien' was not always so alien. The impetus towards free trade that prevailed during most of the nineteenth century encompassed labour migration. For a time, the development of liberal principles of economics and constitutionalism marched together to enhance the status of aliens. The increasing recognition of equality to act on the market, stripping away old restrictions based upon privileges and status, extended to aliens' protection within the economic order of liberalized economies. This was mirrored in the liberal protection of the alien's person. The habeas corpus tradition within Anglo-American law drew no clear distinction between citizen and alien. We see a growing juridical separation of the economic sphere (that of freedom and equality) from that of inter-state power relations (the sphere of war).[1] As a result, aliens were marked out mainly in relation to the state of war: alien enemies and alien friends became the key distinction. Absent the state of war, the alien was free to move within and across borders.

This era of classical free movement began to end when new forms of economic autarky emerged towards the end of the nineteenth century. After great waves of settlement and the emergence of nation-states with stable populations, the border began to emerge more clearly as a site of politics and regulation. This reflected a range of domestic concerns: the conflict between labour and capital, with workers seeking to protect wages from cheaper migrants; race- or religious-based exclusionary tendencies linked to claims about national identity, and sometimes moral panics about alien disease or criminal deviance. In the rhetoric of international relations, unwanted migration was said to be akin to invasion by foreign powers. The formal state of war, with its enemy/friendly alien divide, was superseded as the important legal and political category. This first era of globalization ended with aliens being seen both as bearing industry, skills and labour power but also as potentially disruptive of economic and social security, deviant or dangerous agents of foreign powers. Free movement became a threat as well as an opportunity.

The emergence and development of permanent immigration detention laws: from war powers to aliens powers

Although the huge expansion in detention facilities and detainee numbers is relatively recent, restrictions on migrants' liberty first emerged during these earliest forms of migration control in the late nineteenth century. Such control initially took place at ports of entry in order to separate out aliens viewed as 'undesirable'. As noted, this was mainly on economic and racial grounds. Detention was viewed in largely bureaucratic terms, being seen as a necessary part of the process of selection and care of aliens arriving at the border. It was generally brief and did not attract jurisprudential

---

1 Schmitt speaks of '[t]he general movement to freedom, a termination of traditional orientations and, in this sense, a total mobility of the most intensive sort'. C. Schmitt, *The Nomos of the Earth in the International Law of the Jus Publicum Europaeum*, New York: Telos Press, 2006, 236.

attention. Its use was later extended to serve as a means to deport aliens convicted of crimes or political activists pursuing troublesome causes. In these cases detention itself moved more centre-stage, becoming linked to national security policy and thus bearing analogy with war-time tools like preventive internment of enemy aliens. Indeed, during World War One we shall see that detention of aliens began to fall under both war powers and immigration powers.

The line between security measures and immigration measures has remained blurred ever since. Thus in recent years we have seen resort to detention under immigration powers to tackle terrorism. This is not surprising given that, in its infancy, the aliens' power was conceived of as a descendant of the war power. Gradually, however, it has mutated into a free-standing and open-ended tool used to justify wide-ranging government action against aliens.

The modern era: normalizing administrative detention of unauthorized or deportable foreigners

The greatest growth in immigration detention in modern times has been that applied to a new category – those who are unauthorized. They are termed variously 'irregular', 'undocumented' or 'illegal' in different contexts, but usually share a lack of immigration authorization to enter or remain in a state. This hides the underlying diversity of such persons who are motivated by a wide range of social, economic and political factors. Throughout history migration has primarily been fuelled by such incentives. Demand for migrant labour has remained strong both from public and private sectors, but nations have placed limits on the lawful volume or types of labour migration. With lawful channels constrained amidst persisting push and pull factors, unauthorized entry has increased. 'Unauthorized' immigration has thus come into being in large part because of the proliferation of regimes which mandate the securing of prior permission to enter developed states.

Similarly, asylum seekers have been subject to restrictions on accessing Western nations. They have therefore been unable to obtain permission to enter before arrival. Arriving without prior permission or entering unlawfully they find themselves vulnerable to detention by reason of their immigration status. They can be held as 'illegal immigrants' pending permission to enter or remain. Detention of these unauthorized migrants (whether seeking asylum or economic improvement) has thus become widespread and is no longer confined to Western nations where the practice began.[2] This process was driven by a complex mixture of 'security' concerns associated with loss of control over borders. Detention was part of a general 'fight' against unauthorized immigration, but one which was rarely based on the danger posed by individual criminal deportees or suspected terrorists.

Enemies or friends? The ambiguous contemporary moral and political status of foreigners

We can thus see that detention has now become a technique of control used in a great many different situations to a wide variety of different categories of foreigners, a few alleged to be individually dangerous, most not. Both numbers of detainees and periods of detention have also risen substantially in recent years. These new legal categories not only bring persons under the panoply of detention powers, but also suggest that they occupy a lower political or moral status than citizens or lawful immigrants. They are deemed 'illegal', which has come to contain its own hostile implications. The legal categories thus both reflect and reinforce developing political and cultural norms about irregular migrants as deviants. This suggests a threat to be repelled and appears to legitimate (and even demand) more draconian detention policies. Such stereotypes do not accord with important aspects of liberal legal and moral theory, in particular the commitment to demonstrate respect for the equality and liberty of each person.

This contrasts sharply with the position of Western nations towards lawful migrants. Legal economic migration, although allowed selectively, has not been closed off. Skilled migrants' status has been enhanced to the point where there is often a high degree of equality between them and citizens. This is most obvious for lawful resident migrants, who are given the same access to most economic and social rights as citizens. This has been driven by high levels of competition to attract particularly valuable migrants and pressure to admit them from industry and public service providers. This been an important driver towards rising

---

2 Report of the UN Working Group on Arbitrary Detention (WGAD), 13th Session, A/HRC/13/30, 15 Jan. 2010, para. 54. This notes that since the 1997 extension of the WGAD's mandate to cover administrative detention of asylum seekers and immigrants, all country mission reports contain a chapter on administrative immigration detention.

equality in the membership status of migrants. The same trend can be seen in more generous naturalization rules for long-term residents. Given that migration and migrants are not *per se* the subject of restrictive policies, it might appear paradoxical that the fight against 'unauthorized' migration, including the use of detention, has grown so fierce. In fact, the authorized/unauthorized line has, in important respects, replaced the citizen/alien divide.

Constitutionalism and the problem of unauthorized persons

Whilst charting the development and expansion in the detention of immigrants, the study also seeks to critically examine this from the perspective of law and human rights. Migration policy, control over borders and the right to determine which categories of persons can be permitted to remain part of a community are intensely controversial issues. Historically their resolution has taken place through the democratic and bureaucratic processes, not the courts. Indeed, by the early twentieth century courts officially ceded most power over such questions to the other branches of government. Building, shaping and protecting nations through migration policy were political questions not within the courts' jurisdiction or competence. International law was also reinterpreted to fit this model so that territorial sovereignty could be asserted to deny any obligation to admit even friendly aliens. This permitted governments to engage in, for example, deliberately racist migration controls without legal review. The political calculations of the democratic process trumped any constitutional or rule of law considerations.

Immigration detention, however, appears to be an exceptional case because it interferes with one of the most fundamental rights within democratic states, a right that the liberal legal order has staked much of its legitimacy upon defending. Despite this, we shall see that such detention is now governed largely by political and bureaucratic imperatives. Given political assertions of the nexus between 'security' and migration control, courts have been reluctant to question executive detention of aliens. More fundamentally, courts have been confronted with a deeper constitutional question: what residual rights, if any, do immigrants have if the government has declared that they are not unauthorized to be members of the community? To conclude that non-membership ousts the constitution permits an unbridled executive power, even an *imperium*, over such persons. The constitutional status in domestic law of unwanted and unauthorized migrants is a crucial question in determining the ambit of detention powers.

The absence of a modern international law and politics of migration

The doubtful status of aliens under domestic legal orders is mirrored in the absence of an international law framework regulating migration and migrants' rights. Whilst the mobility of persons across borders has remained vibrant, there has been a failure to regulate this process by sending and receiving nations. Whilst the modern era of globalization has mirrored that of the nineteenth century in witnessing massive trade liberalization protected by elaborate treaty mechanisms, this has been confined to goods, services and capital. Trade in labour, between developed and developing nations at least, is still largely controlled by national law. Since World War One, legal and political rhetoric has viewed the exercise of the aliens power as closer in nature to that of war powers than trade relations.[3] Given the lack of bargaining power between sending and receiving countries, there has been no pressure to agree mutual standards of treatment. As a result, maximal discretion over migration law has been retained by developed countries in their relations with developing countries' nationals. The status of the latter therefore remains heavily exposed to mercurial domestic political calculations in the receiving state and the ebb and flow of pro- and anti-immigrant lobbies.

The treaties relating to refugees and stateless persons that were signed after World War Two have not been followed or updated to manage modern migrations. These earlier treaties gave an international status to persons who had no state or whose state would not protect them. This helped safeguard international order by integrating them into new states upon specified terms. In the modern world, formal recognition of migrants as stateless or refugees is the exception. Most unauthorized migrants fall outside any formal treaty regime and as such present a destabilizing factor to international society.[4] They are often difficult to

---

3 Indeed, increasingly, one area where Western states have developed cooperation is over restrictions on migration. See G. Lahav, *Immigration Politics in the New Europe*, New York: Cambridge University Press, 2004, who argues that 'co-operation on migration has existed predominantly in the form of prevention'. He concludes that 'in so far as convergence is based on compatible interests to secure effective state control over migration, co-operation may bolster – not compromise – state sovereignty', 228.

4 E. Haddad, *The Refugee in International Society: Between Sovereigns*, Cambridge University Press, 2008, who argues that even refugee law is 'more a communitarian security issue than

actually expel due to practical or legal reasons, but have been declared to be 'expelled' under domestic law. Even states that wish to, do not find it easy to protect their migrant citizens who have chosen to leave. In such circumstances, unauthorized migrants assume the position of international outcasts. We see an international society that sometimes does not have any legal or geographical 'space' left for those who have been rejected by all states. They do not fit anywhere. Executive detention is one result of this exile.[5]

Increasing detention arising from gaps in the international migration regime has led to concern about the problem amongst many groups. International courts, tribunals, monitors and human rights institutions are beginning to recognize that the practice of detaining migrants under the banner of protecting 'territorial sovereignty' has led to practices which are arbitrary, inhumane, expensive and sometimes unnecessary. Apparently fundamental principles like that of the right of states to control their borders may look less fundamental in the light of the actual practices that they entail. Such experience has led one leading human rights body to go as far as to argue that whilst 'fully aware of the sovereign right of States to regulate migration... immigration detention should gradually be abolished'.[6] In the absence of explicit treaty mechanisms designed to protect nationals who are overseas however, only the provisions of general human rights instruments may be invoked. The relationship between these general norms and border control is subject to ongoing legal and political debate.

A residual role for international human rights: the inalienable rights of unauthorized persons?

We have identified two important ways in which unauthorized aliens are vulnerable to arbitrary state action. First, they can fall outside the scope of domestic constitutions that protect only citizens and, perhaps, authorized

---

a cosmopolitan humanitarian concern, it follows that refugees are perceived and controlled more as a matter of national and international security than a matter of human security', 91.

5 For a detailed discussion of the position of the stateless, see *Unravelling Anomaly: Detention, Discrimination and the Protection Needs of Stateless Persons*, London: Equal Rights Trust, 2010.

6 Report of the UN Working Group on Arbitrary Detention, 13th Session, A/HRC/13/30, 15 Jan. 2010, para. 58.

foreigners. Second, there is no clear set of international obligations giving a status to aliens in general. The specific group of refugees under the 1951 Refugee Convention is the main exception. Perhaps because of these two legal gaps, the modern period has seen increased recourse to the use of general human rights treaties by aliens. These are mainly drafted in terms which do not depend on immigration status or authorization. Nevertheless, 'border' control policies have increasingly turned inward as modern states have stripped away many 'fundamental' rights to liberty, work, healthcare, social security, and even marriage and family life, of unauthorized foreigners as part of their 'immigration control' strategies.

International tribunal case-law has thus far mainly decided that these treaties create important obligations on states to refrain from expelling even unwanted foreigners where this would lead to certain types of serious harm.[7] This does not amount to 'authorization' to be a 'member' of that society with a package of civil, economic and social rights. Such persons are merely unremovable. They do not thereby acquire 'membership' in any wider sense. Could they be detained for life and thereby, whilst not subject to expulsion, physically segregated from the wider society? The answer depends on how far international human rights law may go in recognizing a kind of regularization right.[8] This raises the general cosmopolitan question at its height: are there inalienable rights that all persons can assert against whichever state they are presently in, regardless of their formal membership status? Of course, to the extent that there are such rights, this may amount to a guarantee of 'membership' of the global human society. Human rights treaties guarantee all the rights contained therein to all *persons* unless they explicitly or impliedly permit derogation. Immigration status is usually irrelevant.[9] *Border control* is an important derogating interest, but it cannot support *unconstrained* measures against unauthorized foreigners. To do so puts membership of a nation (or at least immigration status) above personhood as the precondition for fundamental human rights.

---

7 For a strong example, see *Chahal* v. *United Kingdom* 23 EHRR 413, in which even national security interests could not prevail where a deportee faced a threat of torture in his home country.

8 For a right of membership derived from the prohibition on expulsion, see D. Thym, 'Respect for Private and Family Life under Article 8 ECHR in Immigration Cases: a Human Right to Regularise Illegal Stay?' (2008) *ICLQ* 57 87–112.

9 There are obviously fundamental political rights that are unique privileges of citizenship. Limitations on basic civil rights based upon immigration status appear to be less obviously justifiable. Most modern legislation seeks to focus its restrictions on unauthorized aliens' access to social and economic rights.

Nevertheless, despite the tendency towards 'absolutist' rhetoric within human rights talk, the real issue is one of *balance*. There is no doubt that foreigners can rightly be discriminated against in relation to some interests. That is the corollary of citizenship. Despite this inherent inferiority, foreigners need not be denied *respect* as individuals. In fact, I shall argue that the most important 'right' is the right of every foreigner subjected to state power to be governed by a system of law and practice that promotes migration policy whilst adequately taking into account those individuals it actually affects. This allows continued scope for criticism of measures that are arbitrary or harsh when set against this yardstick.

Detained foreigners as enemies, criminals, emergency internees or outlaws

Against the background of the issues set out above, this book examines the history and law relating to immigration detention against some basic themes. The most important is to ask how we should see the legal status, in either international or domestic law, of those detained. There are four possibilities that present themselves. First, analysis might reveal that the alien has been viewed as an enemy with whom the state is at war. This has its roots in the prevalent view that the entry and stay of foreigners engages the war, foreign affairs and national security powers of the state. In this case, action may be taken to deal with a threat posed by migrants that could not be contemplated in 'peacetime'. As we shall see, whilst governments have used the language of conflict metaphorically, they have not made formal declarations of war against migrant-producing nations.

If the war analogy is inappropriate, detained aliens might be closer to criminal suspects in status. Although held without a formal criminal process, jurisprudence might have provided a shadow set of guarantees as regards timely expulsion processes, risk assessments and rights to bail. This approach would set up procedural processes that put the state seeking to detain to a burden of proof on key issues. Increasingly the most important of these issues is whether deportation is really likely to be achieved promptly and whether alternative, less invasive, measures might be adequate to ensure compliance with immigration rules.

Where detainees are treated neither as formal enemies nor criminal suspects, another description that seems appropriate for some periods in history is that of 'emergency detainees'. This arises in situations falling short of war but where a crisis may have arisen in that, for example, the border has been vulnerable to large volumes of unauthorized migrants. In modern times, however, although there has been a perception of permanent crisis in relation to migration, formal declarations to this effect have not been made. Instead, 'normal' immigration powers have been adapted and found adequate to meet particularly large migrations.

Finally we may consider detainees to be simply 'unauthorized persons'. By this we mean simply that they have not established any clear legal status under domestic or international law. This presents a legal 'non-status' to the extent that no formal set of principles, international or national, regulates their treatment. We will consider how far this is a true representation of the methods used by states to detain aliens. If in fact they may truly be considered 'outlaws', this situation reveals perhaps most clearly the potential vulnerability of detainees to abuse. The idea of the 'outlaw' suggests both that the law does not provide proper safeguards against arbitrariness, but also that the law positively legitimates harsh measures.

Detention centres as extra-legal spaces and virtual borders

The second theme relates to the legal and physical nature of immigration detention centres. The camp, particularly for refugees or displaced persons, has been a feature of migration throughout the past hundred years. Resettlement of such persons to new countries was often determined by negotiation and consent. The resettling state authorized migrants' entry prior to them leaving the camps and travelling. Similarly, early migrants arriving spontaneously on ships were held on board until authorized to enter or expelled. Vessels were considered special zones beyond the reach of the law. Gradually remote control developed through visa restrictions and carrier sanctions. Crossing borders thereby became subject to extensive prior authorization procedures.[10]

In the modern era, those who do nevertheless arrive or enter without authorization are often held in immigration detention centres until they are authorized or expelled. How far do these places – transit zones, jails,

---

10 For a discussion of the importance of territory to the development of international law and society, see Schmitt, *The Nomos of the Earth*: 'Thus, in some form, the constitutive process of a land-appropriation is found at the beginning of the history of every settled people, every commonwealth, every empire. This is true as well for the beginning of every historical epoch. Not only logically, but also historically, land-appropriation precedes the order that follows from it. It constitutes the original spatial order, the source of all further concrete order and all further law', 48.

holding centres and prisons – amount to special zones which are neither fully within nor without any existing state?[11] In such spaces, the jurisdiction of courts may be limited or extinguished altogether as detainees find themselves held in the name of a law which the government determines the limits of. Furthermore, many persons in detention have no country that will take them back and nowhere to go. This often stems from *de jure* or *de facto* statelessness. In these cases the detention centre may amount to a permanent 'border within borders', a hollowed out space for these unreturnables. We consider the extent to which this is an accurate picture of the law and practice of detention.

Political and legal reasoning over membership within liberal societies: detention as the residue of arbitrary power

We also consider some questions of jurisprudence that flow from these first two questions. If we consider unauthorized foreigners in detention to be 'outlaws', is this based upon their non-member status and/or their 'extra-territoriality'? If they are not strictly outlaws, then we must consider what principles of law have come to regulate their detention and whether these are defensible. One point that emerges clearly is a paradox. The classical idea that exercise of the 'aliens power' was beyond judicial reasoning has now been swept away. Courts now routinely subject government decisions over rights of entry and stay to close scrutiny using principles of due process, human rights and communitarian ideals of integration.[12] Those found to be without rights to stay after such scrutiny have thus been ruled to be outside even this extended, judicially protected 'community'. Modern liberal states thus exhibit a highly developed political and legal process for determining membership and exclusion.[13]

---

11 G.L. Neuman, 'Anomalous Zones' (1995–6) 48 *Stan. L. Rev.* 1198.

12 P.H. Schuck, 'The Transformation of Immigration Law' (1984) 84 *Colum. L. Rev.* 1, which sets out the argument that the development of constitutional and judicial review of migration decisions moved the law decisively away from the traditional idea of a wide legislative plenary power over migration. Also see Joppke, who argues that in Europe strong constitutional courts have been able to protect migration rights from legislative restrictions: C. Joppke, 'Why Liberal States Accept Unwanted Immigration' in A. Messina and G. Lahav (eds), *The Migration Reader: Exploring Politics and Policies*, London: Lynne Rienner Publishers, 2006, 526.

13 Note that attempts by liberal governments to exclude judicial review of immigration decisions have been subject to fierce resistance by constitutional courts. See for example, D. Dyzenhaus, *The Constitution of Law: Legality in a Time of Emergency*, Cambridge

'Unauthorized' migrants in liberal societies may therefore have been found to be non-members after (1) *political* debate on the general categories for membership within a democratic forum (in which migrants' interest groups *may* have participated); (2) *executive* consideration of their case in terms of administrative rules; and (3) *judicial* analysis of their particular immigration claims and ties to the nation. Detention in such cases expresses the residue of truly arbitrary power after this expanded liberal political and forensic process has been exhausted (or has not been completed favourably yet). It is the physical and legal expression of their exclusion from the community. Detainees have fallen outside the limits of the internal legal order and yet they are not protected by an external legal order agreed upon by states. Such a person may be truly said to be an 'outlaw' as regards their capacity to lead an autonomous life governed by law. Their lives may be seen as essentially worthless to themselves and to the states of the international community. This might suggest that '[t]he exclusionary device of making people illegal is so complete that those so labelled scarcely even have human rights'.[14]

Democracy, security, detention and authorization

There has indeed been an increasing tendency in contemporary Western states' rhetoric towards politically and morally de-legitimating all aliens not authorized by government to be present. These unauthorized persons are described as worthless at best or hostile at worst. Immigration authorization and border control have been made into a 'security' issue. The expansion and normalization of detention camps has only been possible through this political process. This widespread cultural and political phenomenon has, however, always been in tension with the actual fact that there are many millions of unauthorized persons, often engaged in complex and valuable relationships with their host societies. There have for political, practical and humanitarian reasons therefore always been methods of 'reauthorizing' such persons. There is a spectrum of such modes, from highly political amnesties for thousands to more 'hard' legalistic rules on long-term over-stayers or more flexible legal standards giving non-expulsion rights derived from international human rights law.

University Press, 2006, who examines the courts' restriction of ouster clauses in Australia and the United States of America.

14 C. Dauvergne, *Making People Illegal: Migration Laws for Global Times*, Cambridge University Press, 2008, 28.

Whilst usually leading to permanent residence, this need not be the only type of reauthorization. For detainees, release on bail amounts to a more limited form of authorization; to be at large subject to reporting conditions. For many years, governments recognized the benefits of flexible bail powers. Indeed, where expulsion proved impossible legislation sometimes provided both for bail and more expansive 'reauthorization' rules allowing rights to work, for example. Modern politics and legislation has, however, moved away from temporary authorization and bail in favour of a binary choice between full authorization and expulsion. Given the assertion that migration control is a security issue, release from detention prior to full authorization has become politically illegitimate. Governments have thus normalized detention to an extent only previously seen in wartime.

Increasingly the 'political' branches of government have been driven towards hollowing out the legal status of unauthorized migrants. The broad notion of 'security' adopted has meant that such persons constitute an 'enemy' against whom strict measures are justified.[15] Again the spectre of the 'outlaw' beckons. Where are the appropriate limits upon such state action to be found? Even detainees must surely be 'authorized' to have access to basics such as toiletries, food and bedding, otherwise they could be starved or made ill. Yet much of the practice of modern immigration politics, particularly in liberal democracies, has tested the limits of law, morality, reason, utility and internationalism. Democracies, in which aliens cannot vote, appear to have developed a strong tendency towards ever-increasing levels of harshness in immigration enforcement measures. Legislatures have been reluctant to provide *legal* entitlements for persons who are unauthorized, preferring to remove rights or leave matters to executive discretion. In principle, judicial review has an important role in closely scrutinizing immigration enforcement policy which, lacking strong democratic safeguards, may inherently favour marginal benefits to citizens over serious harms to aliens.[16]

15 For the argument that the definition of 'friend' and 'enemy' is the ultimate 'political' decision which must be logically prior to the operation of any legal order, see C. Schmitt, *Political Theology: Four Chapters on the Concept of Sovereignty*, 2nd edn (trans. G. Schwab), Cambridge, MA: MIT Press, 1985.

16 Even strong republicans, who wish in general to limit judicial review in favour of democratic processes which they see as more likely to be protective of citizens, appear to accept that there may be a small number of groups who are particularly vulnerable to moral panics and hostility leading to harsh laws. See Bellamy, who seems to accept that in the case of asylum seekers, courts may have a role if 'even their rights to a fair hearing and a humanitarian regards for their safety and well-being are ignored'. R. Bellamy, *Political*

The rule of law and the limits of the aliens power: beyond authorization

Jurisprudence was nevertheless for many years quite passive in the face of the political claims of governments to hold monopoly control over migration policy. However, as noted above, the liberal constitution has increasingly begun to assert itself through judicial adjudication of membership claims. The political branches no longer have the final word on authorization. Can we move beyond a jurisprudence that simply seeks to provide extended judicial assessment of membership claims? Detention cases demand that even those not found to be worthy of membership at all (or whose membership is not yet established) are afforded protection under law. The nature of this protection raises some important questions about the central liberal doctrine of the rule of law.

In the end, a truly *liberal* state's assertion of a monopoly of force over all persons physically under its control during peacetime generates a tension within law. On the one hand, law sees the distinction between insiders and outsiders as fundamental to its purpose; the constitution must exist to protect the nation from outside threats. On the other hand, law must adequately regulate the state's use of force, even for the benefit of outsiders who are present. This tension asks, in essence, whether the rule of law is more constitutive of liberal democracies than regulation of membership and borders.[17]

We shall see that immigration detention has usually conformed to 'thin' versions of the rule of law. Governments have usually been able to point to a basic legal power to detain. However, as detention has become longer, more widespread and with increasingly harsh effects on detainees, it has conflicted with 'thicker' versions of the rule of law. Detention has increasingly become unstuck from its ostensible function of

---

Constitutionalism, Cambridge University Press, 2007, 256–8. He recalls here Stone J's opinion in *United States* v. *Carolene Products* 304 US 144 152–3, n4 (1938), which is often said to mark the germ of the idea with its reference to more searching judicial review where 'prejudice against discrete and insular minorities may be a special condition, which tends seriously to curtail the operation of those political processes ordinarily to be relied upon to protect minorities'.

17 See Dyzenhaus discussing Hans Kelsen's idea that 'all state power, even at international level, is subject to the rule of law is a moral milestone, an expression of the liberal hope that, as Carl Schmidt understood it, the exception could be banished from the world'. D. Dyzenhaus, 'The Rule of (Administrative) Law in International Law' (2004–5) 68 *Law and Contemp. Probs.* 127, 162. Also see D. Dyzenhaus, 'Now the Machine Runs Itself: Carl Schmitt on Hobbes and Kelsen' (1994–5) 16 *Cardozo L. Rev.* 1–19.

selecting who to admit or enforcing the speedy and efficient physical return of unwanted immigrants. It has mutated into a more general form of executive and political control over unauthorized aliens, capable of arbitrariness, oppression and disproportion.

Do such practices offend the 'rule of law'? Here we can see a convergence between modern jurisprudence, which has argued for a richer notion of the rule of law, and emerging judicial practice, which has attached renewed importance to the rule of law in cases concerning aliens.[18] Liberal constitutions must closely regulate the deployment of state violence over all 'persons' subject to its power – even when they have not been authorized to be members of the community. To find otherwise ultimately pushes liberal states in the direction of slave societies in which the majority (or the government) can render non-members' lives devoid of intrinsic worth, subject to the unbridled power of the state. This requires a reappraisal of the unruly and protean aliens power with its tendency to expand to meet political exigencies of the day. Whilst law may influence such a reappraisal, real progress depends, in the end, on a political recognition that the aliens power is deployed in time of peace not war. Most foreigners do not come bearing arms. Actions of doubtful necessity, even in war, should not be deployed against aliens in the less pressing circumstances of peace.

---

18 See T. Bingham, *The Rule of Law*, London: Allen and Lane, 2010 for a 'thick' version of the rule of law from a leading judge who sat in a number of important contemporary cases involving alien detention and restriction.

The creation of immigration detention: from free movement to regulated borders in America and the United Kingdom

Alien friends and alien enemies in the early modern period: libertarian equality and open borders

Until there was immigration control, there could be no immigration detention. Looking at liberal states in the mid-nineteenth century, we can see a relative lack of concern about 'the border' as a site of regulation.[1] The crucial distinction was between 'enemy' and 'friend'. Wars created 'enemy aliens' who were dealt with under the government's war powers and according to customary international law with its reciprocal arrangements for prisoner exchange. Thus, outside wars, aliens were not generally subject to controls on movement. As regards internal law relating to friendly aliens, there was a trend towards repealing former protectionist restrictions on their economic activities.[2] The emerging global capitalist economy sought to find the highest rates of return and the commercial

---

1 Indeed, as early as 1215 Magna Carta, the Great Charter of King John of England, had proclaimed that 'All merchants may enter or leave England unharmed and without fear, and may stay or travel within it . . . for purposes of trade . . . This however does not apply in time of war to merchants from a country that is at war with us. Any such merchants found in our country at the outbreak of war shall be detained without injury to their persons or property, until we or our chief justice shall have discovered how our own merchants are being treated in the country at war with us. If our own merchants are safe they shall be safe too' (Art. 41).
2 In Britain, growing equal civil status was not without reverses. 'In Tudor times the position of aliens was that they could not own land but could own chattels. They were encouraged to come but measures were taken to limit them taking in alien lodgers, apprentices and entering certain trades. There were no general Acts but by the royal proclamation of 1554 all were required to leave save for merchants and ambassadors servants. They numbered several thousand in London . . . They were not deemed to be "freeman" for Magna Carta purposes but they were able to bring personal actions and were protected by criminal law.' J. Baker, *The Oxford History of the Laws of England 1483–1558*, vol. VI, Oxford University Press, 2003, 611–17.

rights to trade became the new basis for international law.[3] Free labour migration, within and between friendly nations, based upon wage competition, was a crucial element in supporting capital formation and this underpinned the 'right' of movement for aliens.[4] Furthermore, in the new revolutionary governments of America and France, this was underpinned by the emerging idea of 'inalienable' Rights of Man, stripping away the former distinctions based upon rank or religion. Alienage appeared as another such arbitrary characteristic too.

These cosmopolitan times were reflected in significant juristic and public opinion disparaging discrimination against aliens.[5] The libertarianism of the era was also suspicious of executive interference with civil rights, regardless of nationality. The distinction between alien friends and alien enemies was, however, fragile. As we shall see, the birth of the idea of immigration control largely destroyed this division; war powers in respect of enemy aliens mutated, sometimes through emergency powers, into a new general power over all aliens.

Early debates on expulsion and exclusion of aliens: habeas corpus, banishment and denial of asylum

The remedy of habeas corpus was the central guarantee against arbitrary arrest and detention within the common law world.[6] Importantly, it was

3 Schmitt notes: '[t]he prevailing concept of a global universalism lacking any spatial sense certainly expressed a reality in the economy distinct from the state – an economy of free world trade and a free work market, with the free movement of money, capital and labor. Liberal economic thinking and global commercialism had become hallmarks of European thinking since the Cobden Treaty of 1860, and were now the common currency of thought . . . In short: over, under, and beside the state-political borders of what appeared to be a purely political international law between states spread a free i.e., non-state sphere of economy permeating everything: a global economy.' C. Schmitt, *The Nomos of the Earth in the International Law of the Jus Publicum Europaeum*, New York: Telos Press, 2006, 235.

4 L.P. Moch, *Moving Europeans: Migration in Western Europe since 1650*, Bloomington: Indiana University Press, 1992.

5 Indeed, the great English scholar, Holdsworth, went so far as to say that due to 'this closer connection between the nations, arising mainly from the growth of international trade, and the social changes which have come in its train, have set in motion a course of legal development which has in relation to civil rights and liabilities substituted for the old lines of division between subjects and aliens and alien friends and alien enemies . . . a new line of division which is based on enemy character'. W.S. Holdsworth, *A History of English Law*, vol. IX, London: Methuen, 1926, 99. As one prescient judge put it in an early case: 'Commerce has taught the world humanity.' *Per Wells* v. *Williams* (1697) 1 Ld. Raym. 282.

6 See Holdsworth, *A History of English Law*, at 104–25. For the position in the United States, see W.F. Duker, *A Constitutional History of Habeas Corpus*, Westport, CT: Greenwood

also, for many years, the main safeguard against unlawful immigration measures. As late as 1890, a leading liberal English scholar could say '[t]he Crown has no prerogative to interfere with the free ingress or exit of any alien friend . . . any attempt at such interference can be stopped by Habeas Corpus or action of false imprisonment'.[7] Physical control over the body of aliens was a precondition to availability of the remedy, even though the main object was to challenge the legality of any immigration decision behind it.

With no concept of a wide power to control the entry and stay of friendly aliens, perhaps there were 'constitutional' limits on their treatment? In the United States, an important illustration of this was the debate over the Alien Act 1798, enacted in a climate of fear over European, particularly French Jacobin, radicalism and justified as a measure to protect national security.[8] It gave power to the president to order aliens to depart where he judged them to be treasonable or dangerous to peace or safety.[9] A person convicted of remaining in breach or returning after removal could be detained for as long as, in the president's opinion, public safety required.[10] This excited considerable disquiet at the time. The government had contended that expulsion was not a punishment, but rather preventive and required no trial. No less an eminent constitutional architect and jurist than James Madison replied that 'if a banishment of this sort be not a punishment, and among the severest punishments, it would be difficult to imagine a doom to which the name can be applied'.[11]

Press, 1980. For a comparative examination of commonwealth countries, see D. Clark and G. McCoy, *The Most Fundamental Right*, Oxford: Clarendon, 2000. See for a modern review R.J. Sharpe, *The Law of Habeas Corpus*, 2nd edn, Oxford: Clarendon, 1989, 97.

7 W.F. Craies, 'The Right of Aliens to Enter British Territory' (1890) 6 *LQR* 28, 39.

8 The historical context and political debate is set out in D. Kanstroom, *Deportation Nation*, Cambridge, MA: Harvard University Press, 2007, Ch. 2.

9 Section 1.

10 Section 2. This first appearance in American federal law of executive detention specifically aimed at friendly aliens revealed a doctrinal uncertainty with its unhappy mixture of criminal and executive elements. The courts were to determine if the crime of remaining in breach of the deportation order had been committed, whilst the government assessed if deportation was justified and how long detention should last after conviction (a kind of internment). Whilst nowadays the criminal and executive powers are distinct, in 1798 the idea of wholly administrative detention powers allied to border control had not yet been conceived of.

11 Madison spoke of the 'banishment of an alien from a country into which he has been invited as the asylum most auspicious to his happiness, – a country where he may have formed the most tender connections; where he may have invested his entire property, and

Madison's view reflected the contemporary view that friendly resident aliens had a right to stay that should not be revoked without due process. Although he grounded this in banishment amounting to 'punishment', this was not essential. Denial of personal liberty would have been sufficient to trigger due process concerns. The government's case was anyway unconvincing, as the same logic might support preventive detention of seditious citizens. A further argument was required – that aliens had an inherent, if ill-defined, lesser status – to support their expulsion without trial. One suggestion was that aliens were not parties to the constitution and therefore derived no protection from it. Madison replied that if that were so 'they might not only be banished, but even capitally punished, without a jury, or the other incidents to a fair trial'.[12] This is a central question that will recur throughout this study. What limits are there on the state's powers over aliens?

Neuman argues that there were in fact profound contradictions in the early American jurists' ideas, influenced as they were by social contract theories when framing the US Constitution. They conceived of a contract between pre-existing members of a society – apparently not encompassing outsiders. Nevertheless, they also believed that any government so created was constrained by adherence to fundamental laws derived from natural rights theory, rights that belonged to every human being regardless of the social contract.[13] Madison had raised fundamental issues which, as Kanstroom notes, 'illustrate a major unresolved tension in U.S. constitutional history: between a robust rule-of-law version of the nation of immigrants ideal... and the categorical, status-based distinctions that legitimize government action against non-citizens that would be unacceptable if applied to citizens'.[14]

---

acquired property of the real and permanent as well as the movable and temporary kind; where he enjoys, under the laws, a greater share of the blessing of personal security and personal liberty than he can elsewhere hope for...' J. Madison, *Report on the Virginia Resolutions*, 4 Elliot's Debates, 544, 555.

12 *Ibid.*
13 G. Neuman, *Strangers to the Constitution*, Princeton University Press, 1996, Ch. 1, 9–15. He shows that Vattel's writings on the nature of the social contract was a strong influence upon the framers of the US Constitution. Writing about the law of nations, Vattel was ambiguous on the position of aliens, saying that they were bound by the laws of territory upon which they entered, but the sovereign was only bound 'internally' (morally) to respect their natural rights. States had a right to select whom to admit in its own interests except in cases of 'absolute necessity'. Violation was not something that 'externally' could generate a right to take action by the alien's state of nationality unless it concerned a clear case of injustice or discrimination for persons already admitted.
14 Kanstroom, *Deportation Nation*, 48.

Turning to British thinking of the time, writing in the mid-nineteenth century, the renowned constitutional expert Erskine May said: 'Nothing has served so much to raise, in other states, the estimation of British liberty, as the protection which our laws afford to foreigners.'[15] He noted that as well as granting 'inviolable asylum to men of every rank and condition', 'they were equally free from molestation by the municipal laws of England'. Habeas corpus had always been available for the protection of non-citizens in England, the most famous example being the freeing of an American slave held on board a ship in the Thames.[16] The equal protection of the liberty of foreigners within Britain and the tradition of granting political asylum were seen as markers of British civilization.

The period around the French Revolution had challenged this as fear of aliens became rife amongst the British ruling classes, with rumours of spies and saboteurs intent on overthrowing the monarchy. This led to proposed laws to restrict alien entry through executive powers. This would have denied asylum to some without due process. The parliamentary debates on the Bill show conflicting attitudes toward the political status of immigrants in the minds of parliamentarians.[17] Thus, on the one hand, some saw aliens' entry rights as limited during times of emergency:

> An hon. Member has said much about the rights of aliens: no man was more ready to respect them than he was; but his first object was to secure the safety of the state: and that being once out of danger, he would be happy to see aliens in the fullest enjoyment of every right which the law and constitution of England allowed them.[18]

On the other side of the debate were the civil libertarians who viewed the use of powers against aliens as the precursor to a gradual erosion of liberty more generally. As one Member put it:

> The principle of the bill appeared to him of the most dangerous tendency. If once established, he did not well see where it was to stop, or why it might not be extended to British subjects as well as foreigners and lead to a total repeal of the Habeas Corpus Act, upon grounds of danger totally ideal or at least unsupported by any evidence.[19]

15 T. Erskine May, *The Constitutional History of England Since the Accession of George III*, vol. III, Boston: Corsby and Nichols, 1862, Ch. XI, 50.
16 *Sommersett's Case* (1772) 1 State Tr 1 at 20. The law of England, as opposed to the colonies, did not recognize slavery.
17 Debates on the Aliens Bill, Hansard Parliamentary Debates XXX 1792–4 (1817) Hansard: London.
18 *Ibid.*, Lord Fielding.   19 *Ibid.*, M.A. Taylor, 195.

Apart from this danger of sliding towards wider authoritarianism, the proposed law was attacked because 'it violated the rights of aliens. It left them entirely in the power of the king'.[20] Denial of asylum could indeed result in death without any judicial oversight.

Erskine May looking back from the mid-nineteenth century was clear about the aberrant nature of the measures:

> Such restraints upon foreigners were novel, and wholly inconsistent with the free and liberal spirit with which they had been hitherto entertained. Marked with extreme jealousy and rigour, they could only be justified by the extraordinary exigency of the times. They were, indeed, equivalent to a suspension of the Habeas Corpus Act, and demanded proofs of public danger no less conclusive.[21]

Habeas corpus was seen as synonymous with due process. In the migration context, to deny asylum or banish aliens without trial was arguably to deny due process. If not unconstitutional, this was considered politically immoral by many. As we shall see, however, as the aliens power became established such concerns largely diminished. Aliens came to be seen as set apart, a group to be politically and administratively managed, not judicially protected. Exclusion and expulsion were redefined as state security or social policy choices, not punishments or arbitrary inferences with rights of movement.

During these early debates, detention had never been separately considered from the issue of expulsion, despite the habeas corpus context. This failure to unhinge detention from expulsion decisions has, however, proved to be a crucial omission. As alien entry and expulsion became 'bureaucratized', detention pending expulsion became seen as an incident of migration management. This was so despite the fact that imprisonment raised distinct legal and moral concerns. Madison had anticipated the potential for abuse by noting that the logic of excluding a group of persons from constitutional protection knew no limits; detention might then proceed to occupy a central place in alien controls without proper safeguards.

The creation of alienage and establishing the border as a site of political control

The emergence of more modern regulatory nation-states in the later nineteenth century saw the development of centralized power over all

20 *Ibid.*   21 Erskine May, *The Constitutional History of England*, 51–2.

aliens. This entailed the emergence of techniques for identifying and controlling migrants, including through their administrative detention. Torpey charts the evolution in Europe and the United States of centralized immigration laws during the nineteenth and early twentieth centuries and characterizes this as the 'monopolization of the legitimate means of movement'.[22] The new centralized state claimed sole power to determine who could enter and remain though the imposition of laws requiring the presentation of passports and other documents.[23] The border also came to have symbolic importance in enforcing loyalty to the new nation states because '[t]he state tried to homogenise the inside where neighbours are by definition fellow-countrymen; it created a friend/foe division where the enemy is normally to be found outside the territory . . . the borders are frontiers of identity and "otherness", of solidarity and security, of law and order and of military confrontation'.[24] The alien became someone outside this order, subject to the laws of war, if any.

Detention represents another feature of this power. States tended to give wide authority to officials to detain migrants. The emphasis given by Max Weber to rationalization as the basis for many activities of the modern state is clearly apparent here.[25] Executive detention was, from the bureaucratic perspective, a rational means of aiding the new immigration checks. The potential clash with liberty, a moral and jurisprudential question, was less important than pragmatic policy-making.[26] In any event,

---

22 J. Torpey, *The Invention of the Passport*, Cambridge University Press, 2000.

23 This draws upon the studies made by Max Weber at the time which described the modern state:

> The primary formal characteristics of the modern state are as follows: It possesses an administrative order subject to change by legislation, to which the organized activities of the administrative staff, which are also controlled by legislation, are oriented. This system of order claims binding authority not only over the members of the state, the citizens, most of whom have obtained membership by birth, but also to a very large extent over all action taking place in the area of its jurisdiction. It is thus a compulsory organization with a territorial basis. Furthermore, today, the use of force is regarded as legitimate only so far as it is either permitted by the state or prescribed by it . . . The claim of the modern state to monopolize the use of force is as essential to it as its character of compulsory jurisdiction and of continuous operation.

> M. Weber, *Economy and Society*, Berkeley: University of California Press, 1978, 56.

24 M. Anderson and D. Bigo, 'What are EU Frontiers For and What Do They Mean?' in K. Groenendijk, E. Guild and P. Minderhound (eds), *In Search of Europe's Borders*, The Hague: Kluwer Law International, 2003, 8–25.

25 R. Brubaker, *The Limits of Rationality: An Essay on the Social and Moral Thought of Max Weber*, London: Allen and Unwin, 1984.

26 For influential studies of the development of institutions of control and incarceration see those by Foucault relating to prisons. M. Foucault, *Discipline and Punish: the Birth of the*

the emerging idea of a system of sovereign states comprised of national communities whose membership was determined by the government, left little room for aliens to assert rights through courts. Judges tended to defer to the political branches. They viewed control over borders as akin to matters of national security and nation building, issues requiring maximal government discretion. Despite the common law dislike of executive detention, interference with personal liberty was widely assumed to be a necessary part and parcel of immigration control. As such, the government was afforded wide discretion here, too.[27]

We shall explore these developments in the United States and United Kingdom in more detail in this chapter. These countries developed some of the first recognizably modern systems of immigration control and provide important evidence of the interaction of legal theory and political practice in relation to the detention of immigrants. Given both countries' strong historical attachment to habeas corpus, their experiences are particularly significant. During this formative period, the organs of state in the United States and United Kingdom, through these emerging ideological, legal and bureaucratic systems, created aliens as a distinct group set apart from the rest of society with few, if any, safeguards against legislative or executive action remotely linked to controls on movement.[28]

United States of America: the evolution of immigration law and the status of aliens

The history of immigration into the United States is one of the defining stories of the modern world. There is no doubt that the vast migration to the United States was a key factor in that nation's rise to global superpower

---

Prison (trans. A. Sheridan), New York: Vintage, 1979. We can see some overlaps between Foucault's view about these institutions and control over migrants, as both form part of the process of creating deviant groups that became the object of new manifestations of state power.

27 The failure to develop tools of judicial control over the emerging state bureaucracy was also part of a much wider crisis in legal doctrine caused by a shift from judicial to executive adjudication. In a classic commentary Dickinson said: 'That government officials should assume the tradition function of courts of law, and be permitted to determine the rights of individuals, is a development so out of line with the supposed path of our legal growth as to challenge renewed attention to certain underlying principles of our jurisprudence.' J. Dickinson, *Administrative Justice and the Supremacy of Law in the United States*, Cambridge, MA: Harvard University Press, 1927, 1.

28 Detention powers were, however, very much ancillary aspects of this monopolization over the legitimate means of movement compared to other provisions such as head taxes and measures to ensure shipowners did not allow undesirable migrants to embark.

status. Although mass migration did occur, the idea that migration was unrestricted is in fact far from the truth.[29] From the late nineteenth century, federal legislation began a process of selection inspired by anti-Chinese elements on the West coast and concern about pauperism and disease on the East.[30] Throughout this period, however, there was always ambivalence about immigration controls at the political level. Although there were permanent immigration committees in Congress and virtually continuous legislative initiatives, large-scale migration continued with the full encouragement of powerful political interest groups. The major exception was the exclusion of Chinese labourers on the West coast which resulted in wholescale restriction, including lengthy incarceration in some cases.

The first federal powers over the reception and selection of immigrants

Before 1882 there were no significant federal immigration controls of note. Matters were left to the states using police, anti-destitution and public health powers.[31] Throughout the 1870s some sections of public opinion was becoming hostile to some groups of immigrants deemed to be either dangerous, burdensome or not integrating into the community. Federal judicial opinions during this period had, however, reflected a strong preference for open migration.[32] Indeed, in *Henderson* v. *Mayor of*

---

29 Even before federal regulation of immigration took hold, there was extensive state control over migrants through recourse to police powers, disease control and racial laws. See Neuman, *Strangers to the Constitution*, Ch. 1.

30 D. Tichenor, *Dividing Lines: The Politics of Immigration Control in America*, Princeton University Press, 2002, 51. For a detailed consideration of the development of federal controls see Kanstroom, *Deportation Nation*, Ch. 3.

31 Generally see E.P. Hutchinson, *Legislative History of American Immigration Policy 1798–1965*, Philadelphia: University of Pennsylvania Press, 1981. The Immigration Act 1875 created excludable aliens if prostitutes, orientals without their consent or felonious criminals and criminalized bringing them.

32 *Smith* v. *Turner, Health Commissioner of Port of New York* and *Norris* v. *City of Boston* (1849) 48 U.S. 282. 'Twelve States of this Union are without a seaport. The United States have, within and beyond the limits of these States, many millions of acres of vacant lands. It is the cherished policy of the general government to encourage and invite Christian foreigners of our own race to seek asylum within our borders, and to convert these waste lands into productive farms, and thus to add to the wealth, population and power of the Nation. Is it possible that the framers of our Constitution have committed such an oversight, as to leave it to the discretion of some two or three States to thwart the policy of the Union, and dictate the terms upon which foreigners shall be permitted to gain access to the other States?', per Grier J., 458.

New York,[33] the Supreme Court declared unconstitutional the imposition of head taxes upon migrants by the state of New York to fund a migrant asylum and hospital. The courts had noted the need to separate out the desirable from the undesirable migrants, but ruled that the states had no power to do this in ways that impeded the flow of desirable labour. The seaboard states complained bitterly that the *Henderson* decision deprived them of funds from immigrants to pay for the care of the sick and destitute among their number. In an address to the Senate on 6 December 1881, the president said of the Supreme Court decision in *Henderson*:

> Since this decision the expense attending the care and supervision of immigrants has fallen on the States at whose ports they have landed. As a large majority of such immigrants, immediately upon their arrival, proceed to the inland States and Territories to seek permanent homes, it is manifestly unjust to impose upon the States whose shores they first reach the burden which it now bears. For this reason, and because of the national importance of the subject, I recommend legislation regarding the *supervision and transitory care* of immigrants at the ports of debarkation.[34]

A Congressional Committee investigation of the time concluded that federal reception facilities would also be better able to protect immigrants from abuse by fraudsters upon arrival.[35] Furthermore, the improvement of the reception facilities from the perspective of immigrants would increase the attraction of the United States as a destination. On the other hand, the concern about the dumping of destitute immigrants from Europe on America demanded a solution. This also suggested a surveillance and enforcement mechanism for doing so.[36] From the outset the system of reception facilities was thus conceived of in contradictory

---

33 (1875) 92 U.S. 259. 'The man who brings with him important additions to the wealth of the country, and the man who is perfectly free from disease, and brings to aid the industry of the country a stout heart and a strong arm, are as much the subjects of the tax as the diseased pauper who may become the object of the charity of the city the day after he lands from the vessel.'

34 Congressional Record, vol. 13, Part 1, 47th Cong., 1st Sess., 31.

35 Report of 9 Dec. by Committee on Foreign Affairs to accompany bill, House Report (H.R.) 2408: 1934 H.R. 46/1–2, 1879–80 Report, 1.

36 The cases of the time appear to accept that the states retained a concurrent state police power to expel undesirable persons generally, including certain immigrant groups. They were competent 'to provide precautionary measures against the moral pestilence of paupers, vagabonds, and possibly convicts' as well as persons carrying disease. *Mayor of New York* v. *Miln* 36 U.S. (11 Pet.) at 142–3. See the discussion in Neuman, *Strangers to the Constitution*, at 46–9.

terms; as a place of both care and encouragement to inward migration, and of sorting and exclusion.[37,38]

Selection and care: the inspections of immigrants on the East coast in the absence of detention centres

The resulting 1882 Act to Regulate Immigration was important because it created the first general federal system of executive control over entry into the United States. Detention eventually became an important part of that system, but it is striking that this first Act itself did not explicitly mention, much less authorize it. It was simply assumed to be incidental to the other powers conferred by the Act. These imposed a duty on the Secretary of the Treasury to 'examine' passengers and if 'found among such passengers any convict, lunatic, idiot or any person unable to take care of himself or herself without becoming a public charge, . . . such persons shall not be permitted to land'.[39] There was not even a federal agency or official empowered to give effect to the Act. The Treasury contracted with local state officials to carry out the necessary inspections. The latter probably relied upon the state-level police, welfare and public health powers that they had used previously to detain those who were destitute or diseased.[40] Whilst 'arrest' of some sort, usually on ships, was entailed by inspections, longer term incarceration, motivated by both humanitarian and exclusionary impulses appears only to have occurred in cases of illness, insanity or destitution.[41] There were in any event only a small number of beds to hold such persons.

There remained, however, no statutory legal basis for detention at federal level until 1891.[42] The creation of explicit powers was not driven

---

37 Report of 9 Dec. by Committee on Foreign Affairs to accompany bill, H.R. 2408: 1934 H.R. 46/1–2, 1879–80 Report, 5.
38 'It is the service, operations, and experience of this commission . . . that the bill reported herewith seeks to secure by an "immigrant fund" and machinery to be administered by Federal officers, legally and constitutionally organized and responsible for the supervision of this class of foreign commerce.' *Ibid.*, 3.
39 Section 2.
40 For details on the operation of the system by New York state, see Protection of Immigrants, Memorial of the Commissioners of Emigration of the State of New York, urging the necessity of national legislation for the protection of immigrants arriving in this country, the care of the sick etc., 4 March 1878, 45th Cong., 2nd Sess., House Misc. Doc. 22.
41 See Letter from the Acting Secretary of the Treasury, Senate Ex. Doc. No. 32, 51st Cong., 1st Sess. 1890, which gives further details of the inspection and holding of aliens.
42 Unfortunately the very first regulations for operation of the 1882 Act are not available. The Treasury Department issued circulars for giving effect to the law: Checklist of United

by concerns about the legality of such a situation, but rather the failures of the inspection regime to adequately select migrants. Thus in 1889 the Ford Committee[43] had investigated the workings of the 1882 Act and found it wanting:

> The committee visited Castle Garden on several occasions and witnessed the arrival and inspection of immigrants, and it was very obvious to them that it was almost impossible to properly inspect the large number of persons who arrive daily during the immigrant season with the facilities afforded; and the testimony taken puts it beyond doubt that large numbers of persons not lawfully entitled to land in the United States are annually received in this port. In fact, one of the commissioners of immigration himself testified that the local administration of affairs at Castle Garden, by the method and system now followed, was a perfect farce.[44]

There was a call to construct an 'immigrant depot' in New York harbour to enable the authorities to better examine each migrant.[45] The purpose was 'not to restrict immigration, but to sift it, to separate the desirable from the undesirable immigrants and to permit only those to land on our shore who have certain physical and moral qualities'.[46] It noted that only 2,791 immigrants of 300,000–600,000 had been refused landing during a period of annual immigration to the East coast! The Ford Committee said that it was obvious that many were landed in breach of the law but that 'the evidence is so difficult to secure that landings are permitted daily that the officers are convinced should be prohibited'.[47]

The practical problems of inspection of thousands of immigrants per day were overwhelming without detention facilities. In any case of doubt

States Public Documents, 1789–1909, vol. 1, 3rd edn, rev. and enlarged, Washington: Government Printing Office, 1911, at 1082. The federal Immigration Bureau was established by the Act of 1891 and the Superintendent of Immigration was given responsibility for detention. This was passed to a Commissioner-General of Immigration in 1895. The first recorded publication of a set of regulations governing detention is in 1893.

43 Select Committee to Inquire into the Importation of Contract Labourers, Convicts, Paupers, etc., January 1889, 50th Cong., 2nd Sess., H.R. no. 3792 ('the Ford Committee').

44 Ibid., 9.

45 Resolution by the Senate (with the House of Representatives concurring), 12 March 1890. Funding for Ellis Island was confirmed by joint resolution S.R. 46 and became law 11 April 1890 (Public Res. No. 13).

46 These were the words of a further congressional committee of 1891 led by Owen, which confirmed that inspections were still wholly inadequate: 'these examinations were timed on several occasions and were found to average 30 seconds to an immigrant'. Report of the Select Committee on Immigration and Naturalization, 51st Cong., 2nd Sess., H.R. no. 3472, Washington: GPO 1891, II and III.

47 Ibid., IV.

the immigrant had to be either allowed entry or sent back to ship and expelled. Detention might allow more detailed questioning, but also a period for migrants to send for financial or other help from relatives or community groups.[48] More searching enquiries were seen as facilitating both exclusion and entry, although the primary concern appears to have been to ensure wrongful entries were reduced. The bureaucratic logic of the time did not doubt that detention pending final decision was only constrained by a lack of sufficient facilities.

The Immigration Act 1891 and the creation of the detention centre as a legal exception

The Immigration Act 1891 was the first to expressly mention detention, as it made provision for officers to 'inspect all such aliens' or 'to order a temporary removal of such aliens for examination at a designated time and place, and then and there detain them until a thorough inspection is made'. The Act also created the very important provision that came to be known as the 'entry fiction'. According to this, a removal to shore for examination 'shall not be considered a landing during the pendency of such examination'. This was a critical legal (and constitutional) innovation because it meant that those incarcerated must be treated as if they were not there. This was both an attempt to treat the place of detention as if it were simply an extension of being held onboard ship, but also something more serious. The concept of being physically detained within the territorial land-mass of the United States but not being considered legally present was radical. It suggested a kind of limbo – with the detention centre constituting perhaps an extra-legal space – putting immigrants beyond the reach of constitutional norms, pending a final executive decision to land or deport them.[49]

The Act confirmed the dual purpose of detention so that '[d]uring such inspection after temporary removal the superintendent shall cause

---

48 Thus we find that already by 1885 the Contract Labour Act had permitted 'landing for examination'. Art 4: 'Wherever it shall be necessary, for the purpose of making the examination required by said section 8, to remove the immigrant passengers from the vessel to a suitable place provided for the examination, such passengers shall not be regarded as in fact *landed* within the meaning of section 8 so long as they are undergoing the examination and are in charge of the officers whose duty it is to make such examination . . . '

49 This was later taken up by the Supreme Court in its case-law, which confirmed a sharp distinction between those aliens deemed by law never to have entered and those entering both physically and as a matter of law. See the *Mezei* decision discussed below in Ch. 2.

such aliens to be properly housed, fed, and cared for'. However, it made no official provisions for bail or temporary admission as alternatives to detention, although informal practices of bonding migrants had developed. Decisions made by officials relating to the right to land were final, although subject to internal appeal. The ordinary courts were given no role in regulating either expulsion or detention decisions. From the outset, therefore, detention was conceived of as a practical tool to aid rational and efficient administration of the laws. Congress did not appear to consider that there might be a need for separate legal limits upon detention. As we shall see, this was perhaps born of both the extra-constitutional status of excluded migrants resulting from a series of Supreme Court decisions and the relatively brief nature of most detentions.

'A wholesome reform': mandatory detention arrives

In 1892 a further congressional investigation concluded that there was corruption and softness on the part of the federal immigrant inspectors such that unlawful persons were being admitted on executive bond that should have been excluded.[50] There were many cases of charitable societies providing funds to secure the release from detention of alleged paupers.[51] The committee reiterated that there was no such statutory power to bond.[52] Hinting at bribe taking, they noted that '[t]he position of the commissioner of immigration at the port of New York, clothed with the power and responsibility now connected with it, is one which the most incorruptible would shrink from assuming'.[53] The small numbers refused were cited again in pejorative terms. The Committee lamented that Congress might 'fill the statute book with laws; but without faithful, competent, impartial, and intelligent interpretation and administration of them, they are worthless paper'.[54] They also noted the lack of time devoted to inspection so that it was 'of the most superficial character, unreliable and of little value. It is not much more than a listing and enumeration, and does not constitute such an examination as is contemplated by law'.[55]

---

50 House of Representatives Committee on Immigration and Naturalization, Immigration Investigation, 52nd Cong., H.R. no. 2090.

51 *Ibid.*, 12, citing a newspaper headline describing Hebrew charities agreeing to put up their assets as security for bonding persons 'detained as assisted immigrants under the Owen law' totalling over 1,000 persons.

52 The Treasury Department relied upon Attorney General legal advice that they could bond without express authority. *Ibid.*, 11.

53 *Ibid.*, IV.   54 *Ibid.*   55 *Ibid.*, V.

The examinations were 'more of a farce than a reality'. They proposed 'a wholesome reform' such that whenever the inspector was in doubt as to the right of an immigrant to land 'he will detain him for a special inquiry, which shall be conducted by not less than four inspectors'.[56] The new Ellis Island facility and the large force of inspectors 'justified the expectation that the work of inspection done there should be more thoroughly and effectually conducted than that done at the other ports of entry, where it is made on shipboard or upon the wharf'.[57]

This suggestion was taken up in the Immigration Act 1893, which confirmed that 'it shall be the *duty* of every inspector of arriving alien immigrants to detain for a special inquiry ... every person who may not appear to him to be clearly and beyond doubt entitled to admission'.[58] This is a very important moment in the history of detention in immigration cases. It represents the first time that any legislature had dictated that detention *must* be used as a mode of procedure in administering the immigration laws. This purported to remove even the discretion to determine the *necessity* and *suitability* of detention. This reflected the view, confirmed by judicial doctrine of the time, that migrants were essentially beyond constitutional protection until authorized to be admitted.

The limited duration of detention on the East coast

Whilst the result of this amendment appears to be that detentions increased, they were still a minority of cases and generally short. Thus in 1902, it was reported that whilst 80–85 per cent of persons were admitted without problem, the remaining numbers were detained for further inquiry.[59] Regulations provided that '[e]very alien detained for special inquiry ... shall have a speedy hearing, and, upon the conclusion thereof, be either at once landed or ordered deported'.[60] Upon appeal, the case file had to be completed within 36 hours.[61] One observer concludes that, although detentions were often as high as 20 per cent on an annual

---

56 *Ibid.*, IV.   57 *Ibid.*, V.   58 Section 5.

59 Senate Committee on Immigration, Foreign Immigration, 57th Cong., S.R. 3119, 1902 does not give any explanation as to the change in the wording of the law. The Commissioner of Immigration at New York confirmed that '80 or 85 per cent of them pass by the primacy inspection because there is no further reason for holding them. The other 15 per cent are held for what is called a special inquiry' (4).

60 *Immigration Law and Regulations of February 1906*, edn of Oct. 1906, Department of Commerce and Labor, *Bureau of Immigration and Naturalization*, Washington: Government Printing Office 1906, rule 8.

61 *Ibid.*, 9.

basis, over half were detained only temporarily for minor health problems or until funds arrived.[62] Only about 1 per cent were hospitalized, and rarely did detentions pending the hearing of an appeal to the Board of Inquiry exceed 10 per cent. Figures for the key immigrant station at Ellis Island reveal that in 1907, a peak immigration year, there were 195,540 detentions out of 1,123,844 arrivals. Of these, 121,737 were temporarily detained whilst relatives came to prove their financial status, 64,510 were held for specific inquiry and 9,203 were hospitalized.[63] Of those rejected after specific inquiry hearings, 4,376 persons appealed to the Secretary of State. These were likely to be detained the longest, because this was the last stage of the review process.

Of those appealing, a majority were eventually admitted outright or on bond.[64] The total numbers debarred and returned for that year were, in percentage terms very low, at 13,064.[65] We can see that the detention process was linked very clearly to the separation of migrants into admissible and inadmissible categories. Detention was in most cases followed by admission, as can be seen from the fact that up to 1902, less than 1 per cent of arrivals were actually debarred in the end. Even after 1902, in the face of more restrictive legislation, debarments only rose gradually to reach 2 per cent of arrivals by 1914.[66]

Detention powers were sometimes abused by officials for self-enrichment.[67] The department's own reports disclosed common practices by officials at Ellis Island of signing of blank detention cards which were

62 Kraut says that: 'Immigrants who were penniless but claimed to have relatives or friends who would defray their expenses until they found jobs were not immediately admitted. These immigrants, often as many as 10 per cent of annual arrivals, were held briefly until funds from their sponsors were received by letter or telegram.' He also notes that: 'Women and children were those most frequently detained for inadequate funds. They were given a place to sleep in the detention dormitory and were urged to contact by letter those responsible for them. If no one arrived within a week, the detainees could apply to one of the many immigrant aid organizations for assistance or accept deportation.' A.M. Kraut, *The Huddled Masses: the Immigrant in American Society*, Wheeling, Ill: Harlan Davidson Press, 1982, 60.

63 *Ibid.* Original figures found in *1907 Annual Report of Commissioner-General of Immigration*, Washington: Department of Commerce and Labor, 1907, at 81, where the New York commissioner estimates 1,400 detainees per night during that year.

64 *Ibid.*, at Table XVII, 58, shows 1,950 were admitted, 412 bonded and 1,939 debarred.

65 *Ibid.*, at 14. The principal grounds for debarment were pauperism and disease which made up three-quarters of the total. Contract labourers made up the bulk of the rest.

66 See *1913 Annual Report of Commissioner-General of Immigration*, Washington: Government Printing Office, Table XVIIA, 108.

67 See *1902 Annual Report of Commissioner-General of Immigration*, Washington: Government Printing Office, 56.

then given to interpreters or others who 'inspected and detained immigrants at their pleasure'. This also took the form of officials themselves arbitrarily detaining wealthier persons and then demanding bribes 'to avoid long waits in the detention rooms'.[68] Even though this kind of arbitrary detention appears to have been not infrequent, the annual reports of the Commission-General reveal relatively small numbers of habeas corpus applications.[69] This was probably because most migrants and their lawyers directed their energy and moneys to attacking the substantive immigration decision that had led to detention through the statutory right of appeal. There are few indications that detention itself was challenged in habeas corpus on account of its length or reasonableness during the period before World War One. This supports the view that appeal processes were reasonably quick and that, once deportation was confirmed on appeal, aliens were sent back without prolonged detention pending execution.

Avoiding detention: bonding as a flexible alternative

Increasing legislative efforts by Congress to prevent entry by undesired migrants were undermined by the frequent use of discretionary release from detention on bond. This reflected corruption, but also officials' desire for flexibility and pragmatism over the use of detention, even in defiance of Congress. Eventually statutes were amended to include bail provisions to codify what had been a sensible practice. As Hutchinson notes, 'limited numbers of technically inadmissible aliens had been paroled for many years previously by immigration officials and the Board of Immigration Appeals'.[70] Bonds were taken to allow aliens to be released by providing security against them later becoming public charges.[71] This became a way of testing aliens' ability to meet the immigration rules and provided a power to re-detain in the event of them becoming destitute.[72]

---

68 K.H. Claghorn, *The Immigrant's Day in Court*, New York: Arno Press, 1969, 324.
69 For example, the Ellis Island station attracted 62 applications in 1907, only one of which was sustained. See *1907 Annual Report*, 227.
70 E.P. Hutchinson, *Legislative History of American Immigration Policy 1798–1965*, Philadelphia: University of Pennsylvania Press, 1981, 561.
71 House of Representatives Committee on Immigration and Naturalisation, Immigration of Aliens into the United States, 59th Cong., H.R. 3021 at 20. Passed as s. 26 Immigration Act 1907.
72 It is not clear how often, if at all, the authorities did re-detain migrants, or even if there was an effective system for keeping them under surveillance in a vast country.

In conceptual terms, we see here that the border and the interior became interlinked. The alien remained subject to internal controls, even having passed the border. On the other hand, officials did not see the border as sacrosanct; aliens were admitted and given an opportunity to prove themselves. This made sense at a time when the main question was whether migrants would become public charges. There was an important element of pragmatism; there was no sense in which an alien had an absolute obligation to prove entitlement to enter at the border before they could be released.

Chinese exclusion and the racist strand in immigration policy

It is striking that the fundamental doctrines of US immigration law were largely constructed to support an avowedly racist panic over Chinese migrant labourers. From 1882 Congress passed increasingly strict and arbitrary measures to keep out and expel Chinese persons. During a series of landmark cases, the Supreme Court accommodated not only the specific racist policy in relation to Chinese migrants, but also unfettered legislative action in the conduct of immigration control more generally.[73] It was during this time that the first long-term detention of immigrants was observed. Incarceration, on the rare occasions it was considered at all, was seen by the courts as simply another incident of immigration control and therefore entirely at the discretion of government.

The growth of anti-Chinese legislation was driven by the quest for votes from the Western states where agitation against Chinese was the greatest. Riots were commonplace and politicians began to compete in a race to become more restrictionist after 1880. Whilst the rhetoric of the times was openly racist, it also reflected the demands of a wide range of interest groups, including white labourers concerned about job and wage security.[74] It is against this political and cultural background that

---

73 Kanstroom sees racist roots to the jurisprudential and philosophical foundations for the exclusion of Asians through plenary power doctrine in the previous practices towards native American Indians and African-Americans. Both groups were subject to forced legalized removal and denied constitutional protection. There were also detailed discussions within government on plans to deport former slaves to establish black colonies away from mainland United States. See *ibid.*, 63–90.

74 The complex range of, often rival, interest groups arrayed against Chinese workers is discussed by A. Zolberg, *A Nation by Design: Immigration Policy in the Fashioning of America*, Cambridge, MA: Harvard University Press, 2006, 184. A Select Committee on the Causes of the Present Depression of Labour, vol. I, expressed views normal for the times after hearing evidence from witnesses: 'the Chinaman does not come here because

the Chinese exclusion laws were passed from 1882 onwards in a series of increasingly draconian statutes that led to a precipitous decline in the Chinese population in the United States.[75]

Judicial control of detention and exclusion of Chinese on the West coast: the habeas corpus 'mill'

Large-scale exclusion and detention on the West coast began as soon as the first legislation came into force in 1882. As on the East coast in the early years, because no federal detention facilities were created, 'all manner of other solutions were tried, including release on bond, jails, ships, or mission homes' before, eventually, the shipping companies settled upon using insanitary dockside sheds. [76] The reluctance to fund federal facilities was also illustrative of the idea that detention was supposed to be brief, with detainees treated 'as if' still on board the ship that had brought them. Contemporary writers opined that, of all the anti-Chinese practices of the time, 'nothing has created more criticism and ill-feeling, than the place and manner of detention of all classes of applicants for admission'.[77] It was only much later, in 1910, that a dedicated detention centre at Angel Island was constructed.

Although there was no statutory appeal mechanism against exclusion, the Chinese community freely utilized 'one of the few political recourses available for blocking new federal exclusions: legal challenges in the courts'.[78] Despite employing habeas corpus, a remedy originally

he likes our form of government. This he will never acquire. He does not bring with him his family, if he has one; he does not buy a homestead in view of a permanent residence; he avoids taxation; his meat and raiment come from his own country; he sends back to China all the money he earns; he will labour at a price no white man can; he will live upon garbage, and sustain life upon a diet that a civilized white man cannot; and his morals and practice of vice and crime are abhorrent', 1935 H.R. 46/2 No. 572, 6.

75 For a summary of the effects of the Chinese exclusion laws and approving their extension, see House of Representatives Committee on Foreign Affairs, Chinese Immigration, 51st Cong., H.R. 2915, 1890 and also the Senate Committee on Immigration, Chinese Exclusion, 57th Cong., S.R. 776, 1902 which confirmed that the 'sentiment of the American people with regard to the admission of Chinese has been crystallized during the past twenty years into a definite and progressive policy . . . for the exclusion of all classes save those that, in recognition of international comity, should be admitted'.

76 R.E. Barde, *Immigration at the Golden Gate: Passenger Ships, Exclusion and Angel Island*, Westport, CT, London: Praeger, 2008, 57.

77 M.R. Coolidge, *Chinese Immigration*, New York: Henry Holt, 1909. She also notes that they were held in 'a shed' in which the 'odours of sewage and bilge are most offensive; unclear, at times overrun with vermin and often inadequate to the number to be detained', 299.

78 Tichenor, *Dividing Lines*, 109.

designed to challenge detention, legal argument in almost all the cases was about substantive immigration rights. This is not surprising, because ambiguities and gaps in the legislation afforded ample opportunity for the Chinese migrants' claims that they had a right to enter or remain in the United States. Early lower federal court decisions also provided a surprisingly generous approach to challenges to executive decisions adverse to Chinese migrants.

The treaty affirming the right of migration between China and the United States, expressing the cosmopolitan understandings of the era, had recognized 'the inherent and inalienable right of man to change his home and allegiance, and also the mutual advantage of the free migration and emigration of their citizens and subjects respectively from one country to the other'.[79] The Chinese exclusion laws removed these rights for new Chinese migrants and set up a system of return certificates to prove the rights of residence of pre-existing resident Chinese labourers.[80] As well as international law arguments, lawyers for the migrants put forward arguments under the US Constitution, including that the deportation measures constituted 'punishment'. These arguments had considerable force in the face of these racially motivated arrests, detentions and deportations of many long-standing lawful Chinese residents.

On the West coast the federal judges worked tirelessly processing thousands of habeas corpus applications from detained Chinese.[81] They often ordered such persons' released after finding that they had established prior residence in the United States or were part of an exempt class. They were influenced strongly by both the treaty obligations that the United States had signed and the equal protection clause of the constitution,

79 Article 5 Burlingame Treaty 1868.
80 In a further amendment of 1888, these certificates were revoked and those holding return certificates then outside the country could not re-enter. This conflicted with the Sino-American Treaty of 1880, which had guaranteed the right of return to existing resident Chinese (whilst excluding new entrants).
81 For a detailed discussion of the important, if reluctant, role of the courts in securing redress for Chinese immigrants see C.G. Fritz, 'A Nineteenth Century "Habeas Corpus Mill": The Chinese Before the Federal Courts in California' (1988) 32 *Am. J. Legal Hist.* 347. He notes perceptively the difference between executive and judicial conduct in such cases. So that the judges 'unlike the customs house officials who were able and certainly willing to implement a bureaucratic procedure that systematically excluded the Chinese' offered 'too many opportunities for individual expression and argument. While the sheer number and similarity of many of these cases "bureaucratized" the process in some respects . . . they never became automatic decisions with predictable results. Having asserted their right to such hearings, it followed . . . that each Chinese petitioner could present any evidence, testimony, or argument in favour of establishing his liberty', 372.

which arguably gave equal procedural rights to challenge executive exclusion decisions.[82] The important role of detention as founding the courts' jurisdiction was also made clear:

> That any human being claiming to be unlawfully restrained of his liberty has a right to demand a judicial investigation into the lawfulness of his imprisonment is not questioned by any one who knows by what constitutional and legal methods the right of liberty is secured and enforced by at least all English-speaking peoples.[83]

This reassertion flew in the face of the increasingly hostile public mood about such judicially ordained releases and the attempt of Congress to close gaps in the legislation. The District Court continued to assert judicial control despite attempts to deny habeas jurisdiction by the government.[84] The court said that government assertions that its exclusion decisions were final and beyond review were 'wholly without precedent'.[85] Importantly, it concluded that any detention required a full review of the facts giving rise to it so that the merits of the exclusion decision might be considered.[86] This may have been more important, because there was no appeal system for Chinese migrants (as there was for decisions on the East coast under the general Immigration Act). The role of the court was therefore crucial as the only safeguard against arbitrary executive detention and exclusion. Records showed that the vast majority of those bringing habeas cases were released from detention and landed by the courts.[87]

The duration of detention of Chinese migrants: judicially created limitations on the use of the migration power

Whilst there were clearly some Chinese immigrants who were detained for lengthy periods, the overall picture is more balanced. One reason was the striking judicial creation of a two-month time limit upon detention beyond the end of legal proceedings. This applied even after a habeas

---

82 *In re Tung Yeong* 19 F. 184 (D.C.D.Ca. 1884), 190.

83 Per Hoffman J. in *In re Chin Ah Sooey* 21 F. 393 (D.C.D.Ca. 1884).

84 *In re Jung Ah Lung and In re Jung Ah Hon*, 25 F. 141 (D.C.D.Ca. 1885), which was vindicated by the Supreme Court in *United States* v. *Jung Ah Lung* 124 U.S. 621 (1888).

85 *Ibid.*, 143.   86 *Ibid.*, 142.

87 A total of 87% of around 4,000 writs issued over the first five years of the Acts were successful. Fritz, 'A Nineteenth-Century "Habeas Corpus Mill"', 368. Even after the most severe Exclusion Act of 1888, the success rate continued at 86% (*ibid.*, 371). Cited in Joint Select Committee on Immigration and Naturalization, H.R., 4048: 2: 412, 51st Cong., 2nd Sess., 1890–1.

hearing had determined a migrant was illegally present and thus had no right to remain. Effecting deportation proved a problem when the vessels bringing the immigrants had departed. Thereafter they languished in detention. The legislation did not apparently provide for alternative mechanisms of deportation than by the vessel of arrival. The District Court determined that such persons could only be held for a 'reasonable time' and that this should be set at two months in the absence of 'just cause' for further detention.[88] It seems that this was so regardless of whether a detainee could post bond adequate to secure their return for deportation.

This is important because it represents the first time we have record of a court deciding that an immigrant who had been definitively found not entitled to remain could not be kept in detention beyond a reasonable period. The statute was silent on what should happen but the court, enforcing traditional common law presumptions against executive detention, implied a time limit. Aliens did not lose their right to liberty simply because they had no right to enter or remain. The objectives of the Chinese Exclusion Acts, to broadly limit Chinese migration, did not entail indefinite detention of unwanted Chinese migrants. This was a principled solution showing considerable fortitude, given the hostile political environment.

It has long been presumed that the length of detentions on the West coast was longer than for Europeans on the East coast. This seems likely from the anecdotal evidence, and most commentators agree.[89] The fact that lengthy (and often meritorious) legal challenges were entered by Chinese detainees no doubt also prolonged their detention. This is probably

---

88 Hoffman J. in *In re Chow Goo Pooi* 25 F.77, 81–2. The court cited the 'very vague and inexplicit' s. 12 of the Chinese Exclusion Act of 1884. This was eventually resolved by a later decision requiring the vessels bringing them to take them back at the conclusion of habeas proceedings. See *In re Ah Kee* 21 F. 701 (C.C.D.Ca. 1884) when the Circuit Judge Stephen Field (a Supreme Court Justice and well-known opponent of Chinese immigration) returned to California.

89 Lee notes: 'the lengthy inspection processes also increased the detention time for Chinese. Indeed, most immigrants who were selected for further investigation had to endure incarceration on Angel Island for several days, months and even years while awaiting the final decision in their cases. When the station first opened, immigrants waited for their first appearance before immigration officials for months.' E. Lee, *At America's Gates: Chinese Immigration during the Exclusion Era 1882–1943*, Chapel Hill: University of North Carolina Press, 2003, 217. Also, Coolidge, writing at the time before Angel Island was completed in 1910, spoke of Chinese being 'detained for days, sometimes weeks', *Chinese Immigration*, 299.

most obvious during the early Chinese exclusion period before subsequent Supreme Court decisions closed the door to many legal challenges. By contrast, a recent study of a portion of the shipping records for a later period (during World War One) suggests that detention periods declined. Many Chinese were not detained at all (around 25%). For those detained, the mean was around ten days. Interestingly, this average was pulled up by a small number of people detained for very long periods.[90] This sample showed that only 8 per cent were detained longer than a month. The longest detention was, however, 289 days. The mean detention period for those Chinese eventually deported was thirty-four days. By World War One, the combination of restrictive legislation and constitutional exclusion rendered it much harder to launch legal challenges. It is likely, therefore, that detention was shorter as cases were resolved more quickly and Chinese were deported or admitted.[91] Nevertheless, the war also saw the longest recorded period of detention when a Chinese woman claiming to be a merchant's wife was held for twenty months before being admitted, on appeal, after several habeas corpus hearings.[92]

Removing constitutional review of migration control measures: the Supreme Court and plenary power

As noted above, the role of the courts in scrutinizing migration decisions concerning Chinese persons was largely curtailed by a series of Supreme Court decisions. The effect of these was in fact wider, creating broad areas of untrammelled congressional discretion to control migration, known as 'plenary power'. The Court also ruled that detention ancillary to such decisions was an administrative act and not penal. The consequence was that detention practices were largely free from substantive and procedural constraints at the end of this period.

---

90 R. Barde and G.J. Bobonis, 'Detention at Angel Island: First Empirical Evidence' (2006) 30(1) *Social Science History* 103, 113.

91 Barde estimates that the average detention for all detainees in the period before Angel Island was 23 days and the period for those ordered deported or excluded would no doubt have been much higher. See Barde, *Immigration at the Golden Gate*, 67.

92 *Ibid.* Barde describes the detailed case-files concerning one Quok Shee, who claimed to be the wife of a Chinese resident merchant. She was held at Angel Island from September 1916 to May 1918 whilst her lawyers mounted several habeas corpus challenges to the immigration officials' denial of her entry which asserted that she was in fact being brought in for the purpose of prostitution. She was eventually released on bond after the court found that there had been a failure of due process as the decision had relied upon undisclosed informant evidence. See below Ch. 3.

The key case of *Chae Chan Ping* involved a Chinese man who held a certificate entitling him to return to the United States, issued pursuant to the earlier Act of Congress which had now been revoked. He had been detained for over seven months pending the hearing of his case by the Supreme Court. He argued that the Act was unconstitutional because his exclusion entailed a racially discriminatory removal of vested rights, including his right to property. The federal constitution had not given any express power to the government regarding immigration control and thus the Supreme Court first had to imply such a power. It did so in terms powerfully indicative of the new fear of (particularly Chinese) aliens:

> To preserve its independence, and give security against foreign aggression and encroachment, is the highest duty of every nation, and to attain these ends nearly all other considerations are to be subordinated. It matters not in what form such aggression and encroachment come, whether from the foreign nation acting in its national character, or from vast hordes of its people crowding in upon us ... If the government ... considers the presence of foreigners of a different race in the country, who will not assimilate with us, to be dangerous to its peace and security, their exclusion is not to be stayed because at the time there are no actual hostilities with the nation of which the foreigners are subjects.

This is striking language that put international migration on a level with armed conflict: 'the same necessity, in a less pressing degree, may arise when war does not exist, and the same authority which adjudges the necessity in one case must also determine it in the other'.[93] Sovereignty entitled a nation to prevent other countries from 'foisting' their migrants upon them else 'it would be to that extent subject to the control of another power'.[94] The Court concluded that, as an incident of such sovereignty, there could be no legal remedy in the courts to challenge restrictions on immigration by individuals. The only remedy lay in diplomatic negotiations between states.[95]

The implications were stark; from the point of view of domestic law, Congress was largely free from serious judicial control in passing laws on migration.[96] Serious legal constraints were confined to whatever practices

---

93 *Chae Chan Ping* v. *U.S.* 130 U.S. 581, 606.   94 *Ibid.*, 608.   95 *Ibid.*

96 The number of Chinese habeas corpus cases did not disappear, because the Supreme Court also held that the 1884 Act requiring return certificates did not apply retrospectively to all those living in the United States before the 1880 treaty amendments had been effected by the 1882 Act. Those Chinese seeking to return who claimed to have been resident before this date were thus entitled to a hearing on the merits with oral evidence to establish their right of residence. *Chew Heong* v. *United States* 112 U.S. 536 (1884). The Supreme Court

states followed through treaty and customary law. Such regulation was, however, becoming less common because sending and receiving states perceived their interests to be divergent; moving away from cosmopolitanism, states of immigration came to assert maximal discretion over migrant selection, something incompatible with binding commitments to sending nations.

Detention pending admission was first confronted by the Supreme Court in a case concerning the Immigration Act 1891, *Nishimura Ekiu v. United States*.[97] Nishimura was detained upon arrival from Japan after her exclusion on the ground that she was likely to become a public charge. She wished to challenge the facts found against her. Whilst she was considered not to have entered (under the entry fiction) the judgment of the Court, given by Mr Justice Gray, had no doubt that an 'alien immigrant, prevented from landing by such officer claiming authority to do so under an Act of Congress, and thereby restrained of his liberty, is doubtless entitled to a writ of habeas corpus to ascertain whether the restraint is lawful'.[98] This statement of legal formality was then essentially undermined, as the Court ruled that it was not entitled to look into the underlying facts leading to the exclusion decision, the legal precondition for detention, unless authorized to do so by Congress: 'the decisions of the executive or administrative officers acting within the power expressly conferred by Congress, are due process of law'.[99]

The decision in *Nishimura Ekiu* largely denuded habeas corpus of its historic purpose as a safeguard against executive detention. It underlined the emerging judicial view that immigration detention was part and parcel of exclusion. Given that exclusion was a matter for Congress, so was detention. The position of those seeking entry was made even more stark in *United States* v. *Ju Toy* in which Holmes J. said that even a person who claimed to be a US citizen (but was said to be an alien by the government) could have no constitutional due process rights when seeking to enter as '[t]he petitioner, although physically within our boundaries, is to be regarded as if he had been stopped at the limit of our jurisdiction and kept

---

thus overturned Field J.'s decision taken as Circuit Judge in California in *In re Chew Heong* 21 F. 791 (C.C.D.Ca. 1884), in which he noted the 'impatience in the public mind with judicial officers for not announcing the law to be what the community at the time wishes it should be. And nowhere has this feeling been more manifested than in California, and on no subject with more intensity that that which touches the immigration of Chinese labourers' (793).

97 142 U.S. 651.   98 *Ibid.*, 659.   99 *Ibid.*, 660.

there while his right to enter was under debate'.[100] Thus whilst habeas corpus was available, denial of immigration status entailed denial of liberty.

Congress went a step further in the Geary Act of 1892. This Act required lawful long-standing residents of Chinese origin to 'diligently' obtain a certificate to prove their entitlement to reside in the United States. Failing this, they were subject to arrest and deportation at any time or place. They could prove entitlement only by means of a white witness (the irrebutable presumption of the time was that all Chinese were liars) who could attest that they had been present since before the anti-Chinese laws began. As Zolberg notes, this 'rendered all persons of Chinese descent, regardless of status or nationality, vulnerable to police harassment and arbitrary deportation'.[101] In response to these draconian measures, there was an effective campaign of civil disobedience and refusal to comply amongst the Chinese community.

The registration requirement was challenged in *Fong Yue Ting* v. *United States*,[102] where the new Act was upheld as within the wide power of Congress over migration. The petitioners for habeas corpus had all been detained pending deportation for failing to register. It will be recalled that James Madison had called deportation a penal measure, but one hundred years later we find the Court concluding to the contrary that:

> The order of deportation is not a punishment for a crime . . . It is but a method of enforcing the return to his own country of an alien who has not complied with the conditions upon the performance of which the government of the nation, acting within its constitutional authority . . . has determined that his continuing to reside here shall depend.[103]

Mr Justice Brewer delivered a strong dissent arguing that resident aliens at least, rather than aliens seeking admission, should be given constitutional due process protection. He highlighted the risks allowing an unlimited range of legislative action over the immigration power saying '[t]his doctrine of power inherent in sovereignty is one both indefinite and dangerous. Where are the limits to such powers to be found, and by whom are they to be pronounced? Is it within the legislative capacity to declare the limits? If so, then the mere assertion of an inherent power creates it, and despotism exists.'[104] If courts allowed an unduly broad reading of 'immigration powers', this opened aliens up to all kinds of harsh

---

100 198 U.S. 253, 263 (1905).   101 Zolberg, *A Nation By Design*, 191.

102 *Fong Yue Ting* v. *United States et al, Wong Quant* v. *United States et al, Lee Joe* v. *United States et al,* 149 U.S. 698 (1893).

103 *Ibid.,* 730.   104 *Ibid.,* 737–8.

measures whenever the government deemed these to be within the migration power. As Madison might have said, such depredations can as readily be viewed as 'punishment' of aliens as 'protection' for citizens. The Supreme Court came to endorse Brewer J.'s distinction in *Kaoru Yamataya v. Fisher* ruling that resident immigrants, as opposed to those seeking entry, did gain some constitutional due process rights.[105]

Immigration detention: 'not imprisonment in a legal sense'

In what may be viewed as the final rejoinder to Madison as regards detention at least, in *Wong Wing* the Supreme Court held that immigration detention was not really imprisonment but rather a form of 'temporary confinement'.[106] In this case, a Chinese immigrant challenged his conviction and imprisonment for one year with hard labour for illegal residence on the ground that he had not had a jury trial. The Court was faced with a key jurisprudential issue and sought to maintain, as they saw it, a coherent 'theory of our government'.[107] As such, it held that punishment (even of illegally present aliens), required constitutional safeguards in order to respect the separation of powers and the rule of law.[108] Plenary power over immigration did not extend as far as ousting the due process requirement in the punishment of aliens for immigration offences. A right to jury trial was required. This was contrasted with administrative detention, of which the court said:

> We think it clear that detention or temporary confinement *as part of the means necessary to give effect* to the provisions for the exclusion or expulsion of aliens would be valid. Proceedings to exclude or expel would be vain if those accused could not be held in custody pending the inquiry into their true character, and while arrangements were made for their deportation. Detention is a usual feature in every case of arrest on a criminal charge, even when an innocent person is wrongfully accused, but it is *not imprisonment in a legal sense.*[109]

This is an important statement of legal fiction that continues to resonate today. Whilst formal criminal prosecutions must attract judicial safeguards, immigration detention was not treated as imprisonment at all.

---

105 *Kaoru Yamataya* v. *Fisher* 189 U.S. 86 (the *Japanese Immigrant* case).
106 *Wong Wing* v. *United States* 163 U.S. 228 (1896).   107 *Ibid.*, 237.
108 This takes us back to Madison's concerns about the punitive nature of banishment in relation to the Alien Act 1798.
109 *Wong Wing*, 235 (emphasis added).

This vividly recalls Arendt's observation that 'the best criterion by which to decide whether someone has been forced outside the pale of the law is to ask if he would benefit by committing a crime . . . As a criminal, even a stateless person . . . will be treated like everybody else. As long as his trial and his sentence last, he will be safe from that arbitrary police rule against which there are no lawyers and no appeals'.[110] Even an unlawful immigrant must have a fair trial prior to conviction of any sort, regardless of sentence, whilst indefinite incarceration incidental to deportation was a matter of government discretion.

It is important to note, however, that the Court identified immigration detention as a *means towards the end* of expulsion. This suggested perhaps that courts might ensure detention was genuinely linked to ongoing deportation proceedings. To this limited extent, deportees might be brought back within the pale of the law. The Supreme Court, however, did not further explore the limits on administrative detention until one hundred years later.[111] As Kanstroom notes, 'the bright-line distinction drawn' in this case 'masks some complex issues that remain unresolved today'.[112] In particular 'how should courts draw the line between what might be termed regulatory deportation procedures and those punitive deportation procedures that require constitutional protections analogous – if not identical – to those afforded to criminal defendants?'[113] This is an issue that has become increasingly significant in the modern era as extended detentions, motivated by a hostile political climate, have been used to deter irregular migration and to intern aliens convicted of crimes post-sentence.

The Chinese exclusion legislation and the case-law it spawned was an expression of the growing power of the federal state apparatus. The

---

110 H. Arendt, *The Origins of Totalitarianism*, New York: Harcourt, Brace and Jovanovich, 1966, 286. She contrasts the criminal trial of a stateless person with 'the same man who was in jail yesterday because of his mere presence in this world, who had no rights whatever and lived under threat of deportation, or who was despatched without sentence and without trial to some kind of internment because he had tried to work and make a living, may become a full-fledged citizen because of a little theft. Even if he is penniless he can now get a lawyer, complain about his jailers, and he will be listened to respectfully. He is no longer the scum of the earth but important enough to be informed of all the details of the law under which he will be tried. He has become a respectable person' 286–7.

111 See *Zadvydas* v. *Davis* 533 U.S. 678 (2001).

112 Kanstroom, *Deportation Nation*, 122. See G. Neuman, 'Wong Wing v. United States', in D.A. Martin and P.H. Schuck (eds), *Immigration Stories*, New York: Foundation Press, 2005.

113 Kanstroom, *Deportation Nation*, 122.

doctrines it produced have remained in place, largely unchanged, ever since.[114] The courts accommodated and encouraged this because they 'recognized the continental scale of the new economic order and facilitated a concentration of governing authority'.[115] Tichenor notes the broader significance of the period for aliens' state generally: '[i]n just five years, a solid legal groundwork was laid for the exclusion, restriction and expulsion of immigrants. Subsequent judicial rulings reaffirmed the broad, unencumbered power of Congress and its administrative agents to regulate immigration.'[116]

World War One and beyond: internal controls and public security detention

After America entered World War One, there were arrests and detentions of German-Americans and German legal residents during the years 1917–20. They were held without trial under the war powers created by the Enemy Alien statute of 1798.[117] The period after the war, however, saw the new aliens power doctrines put to use as measures of internal security and social control, as opposed to mere exclusion. The borderline

---

114 For a powerful critique of the persistence and anomalous status of the case-law, see L. Henkin, 'The Constitution and United States Sovereignty: a Century of Chinese Exclusion and its Progeny' (1986–7) 100 *Harv. L. Rev.* 853. 'The Chinese Exclusion doctrine and its extensions have permitted, and perhaps encouraged, paranoia, xenophobia, and racism, particularly during periods of international tension', 859. He concludes that '*Chinese Exclusion* – its very name is an embarrassment – must go', 863.

115 S. Skowronek, *Building a New American State: the Expansion of National Administrative Capacities, 1877–1920*, Cambridge University Press, 1992, 41.

116 *Ibid.*, 112. Salyer puts the point about the crucial implication for alien status in general arising from the Chinese cases: 'government officials . . . persuaded Congress and the Supreme Court that the nation's gates could be effectively guarded only if they were allowed full authority and discretion over immigration policy without interference from the federal courts. Ironically, in their efforts to secure the door against Chinese immigration, officials undermined the very principles they accused the Chinese of subverting. The immigration law resulting from this struggle stood at odds with one of the most esteemed Anglo-American legal principles – the rule of law.' L. Salyer, *Laws Harsh as Tigers: Chinese Immigrants and the Shaping of Modern Immigration Law*, Chapel Hill: University of North Carolina Press, 1995, 247–8.

117 See A. Krammer, *Undue Process: the Untold Story of America's German Alien Internees*, London: Rowman and Littlefield, 1997, who notes that of 6,300 arrested, 2,048 were detained for the duration of the war and sometimes beyond until 1920, when the last camps were closed, 14–15.

between immigration law and criminal law became blurred.[118] Detention pursuant to immigration powers in such cases seems to have been used as a means of social control over immigrant elements who could not be easily prosecuted due to lack of evidence or non-commission of a crime.[119]

Fears of Bolshevism following the Russian Revolution were utilized to undermine workers' organizations. Thus, in the immediate post-war period, there was a widespread business-led campaign against organizations and persons said to be Communist or anarchist in orientation.[120] The influence of these sentiments went as far as the Attorney-General's office. Rather than seek criminal prosecutions of such persons, a strategy was developed to use immigration powers, which provided an easier means of undermining such activists. It freed the authorities from the usual procedural safeguards implied by criminal trial such as the rights to counsel, to a public hearing, to challenge witnesses and to separation of prosecution and adjudication through an independent judicial or jury decision.[121] It is estimated that some 6,000 warrants were issued and 4,000 migrants detained, many at Ellis Island which had been transformed from a processing depot into a detention centre for enemy aliens during World War One.[122] Even within the broader powers conferred by immigration law, there was often doubt as to the legality of the Attorney-General's actions.[123]

---

118 See W. Preston Jr., *Aliens and Dissenters: Federal Suppression of Radicals, 1903–1933*, Cambridge, MA: Harvard University Press, 1963.

119 Kanstroom sets out clearly the historical evolution of this by showing the difference between 'extended border control and a post-entry social control law', *Deportation Nation*, 126. He criticizes the way in which both legislators and officials sought to use immigration powers for social control, but also the way that courts bent legal concepts like plenary power to accommodate such practices in areas unrelated to direct immigration control at the port of entry.

120 Kanstroom sets out the history in *ibid.*, Ch. 4.

121 See the discussion of the variable executive practices throughout the period in *ibid.*, 152–3.

122 *Ibid.*, 150.

123 See the account of the contemporary politician and lawyer who campaigned against the measures: L.F. Post, *The Deportations Delirium of the Nineteen-Twenties* (1st pub. 1923), Honolulu: University Press of the Pacific, 2003. There were congressional hearings conducted into the policy: see *Attorney General A. Mitchell Palmer on charges made against Department of Justice by Louis F. Post and others, hearings before the committee on rules*, House of Representatives, Washington, DC (1920). Some of these aliens were detained under alleged immigration powers while further legislation was passed in 1919 to expand the definition of deportable aliens to cover members of organizations who had not been deportable under the old law. These practices were also condemned in a

Claghorn, a contemporary critic, detailed one incident when fifty-four members of the Industrial Workers of the World were shipped by train (the 'Red Special') from the West coast to Ellis Island for deportation after organizing for better pay and conditions. They were said to be deportable under the 1917 legislation on the ground of being anarchists and seeking to destroy property by unlawful means. The executive's actions were challenged in habeas corpus and this revealed the fact that the detentions were often inappropriate:

> In 33 cases, then, for which re-hearings were secured, 21, or just short of two-thirds were either released on parole or discharged outright. And of the men held for deportation, seven were released on bond because of difficulty in arranging for deportation to the home country. In two cases the fact of birth in the country to which it was proposed to send the deportee could not be established, because he had left at so early an age that the country in question refused to receive him.[124]

The power to detain[125] also gave the authorities the ability to control migrants through release on parole under conditions.[126] Claghorn notes that 'as a practical matter, it seems to have been used as a species of probation – a means of testing continued good behaviour'.[127] The conclusion she drew writing at the time was that:

> It would appear, from all the evidence available, that the deportation proceedings of 1919–20 realized many of the possibilities for oppression and lawlessness in the discretionary powers of the immigration officials and in the indefiniteness of the immigration law, and that, in justice to the alien, both law and procedure should be changed to afford the substantial justice that it is the aim of our legal system to secure.[128]

pamphlet signed by the National Popular Government League which included notable lawyer and academics like Roscoe Pound, Zechariah Chafee and Felix Frankfurter (cited in Kanstroom, *Deportation Nation*, 1)

124 Claghorn, *The Immigrant's Day in Court*, 333.
125 Immigration Act 1917 s. 19 listed the classes of deportable persons and stated that such persons 'shall, upon the warrant of the Secretary of Labor, be taken into custody and deported'.
126 Section 20.   127 Claghorn, *The Immigrant's Day in Court*, 353.
128 *Ibid.*, 466. In some prescient remarks she noted the enduring problems faced by migrants because of their vulnerability to arbitrary executive action whenever circumstances dictate: 'It may be said that the special troubles recounted in this chapter were due to an exceptional set of circumstances – to a state of popular excitement following the nerve-racking experiences of a period of warfare, and that under ordinary circumstances such troubles will not arise. But it is not so sure that such events may not be repeated. Times of excitement against the alien may recur, for other reasons than a state of war. It is for that reason especially necessary that the bulwarks of a strictly secured legal procedure

Undeportable aliens during World War One: release and reauthorization

During World War One, execution of exclusion or deportation orders was severely disrupted by the attacks on shipping. The Immigration Act 1917 recognized this, stating that 'all aliens brought to this country in violation of law shall be *immediately* sent back . . . to the country whence they respectively came, on the vessels bringing them, unless in the opinion of the Secretary of Labor immediate deportation is not *practicable or proper*'.[129] This prompted the government to provide further discretionary relief from detention. This was consolidated into the Immigration Rules, which provided that aliens 'whose prompt deportation can not be accomplished because of war or other conditions may, upon permission secured from the department, be released and permitted to accept self-supporting employment under the conditions' set down in the rules.[130] This required employers to set out a scheme of work for the detainee and to pay a portion of their wages to the immigration service as security against absconding.[131] The detainee so released was required to be taken back into custody if the work finished and he had no more or if he violated the conditions of release.[132] He or she could also be re-detained if they 'misbehaved' or 'failed to obey the laws', whether federal or state.[133]

Such an elaborate scheme is striking for many reasons. It presents a first pragmatic solution to indefinite detention, a kind of 'reauthorization' for the 'unauthorized', enabling them to regain a measure of liberty and live in the community. Although deportees, they acquired a unique status to accommodate their *de facto* statelessness. This was, however, not 'full membership' in any sense. They were subject to extraordinary controls and powers of re-arrest not linked to the possibility of deportation or criminal charges. They were 'reauthorized' but remained virtually at the mercy of the executive in ways that would be unconstitutional if applied to lawful residents or citizens. Nevertheless, these 'community release' schemes represent an important early recognition of the limits of the deportation power in cases of *de facto* statelessness.

be firmly established in a time of calm to prevent wholesale injustice against individuals in times of excitement.'
129 Section 18 (emphasis added).
130 Rule 17A(1), Immigration Rules of 1 May 1917, 3rd edn – March, 1919, U.S. Department of Labor, Bureau of Immigration, Washington: Government Printing Office, 1919.
131 See Rule 17A(2) and (3).   132 Rule 17A(3)(e) and (1)(b).   133 Rule 17A(5).

Detention and the emerging problem of statelessness

In the post-war period, rather than transport problems, there was a growing inability of the authorities to secure the admission of detained aliens into another country. This was aggravated by the situation in Europe in which borders had shifted and minorities had been left without citizenship or protection from their former countries of nationality.[134] The statute was silent on what to do, saying merely that persons should be 'taken into custody and deported'.[135] This meant detainees faced indefinite detention. The law reports of the period in the lower courts reveal some examples of the difficulties this presented for judges using the 'old map' of habeas corpus in the new world of alien controls.

In *Re Kosopud*, a group of alleged 'anarchists' who had been ordered deported remained in detention for several months whilst efforts were made to execute the orders. The trial court hearing an application for habeas corpus said:

> Undoubtedly it is a hardship upon persons unable to give bail to keep them confined in jail because of the inability of the Department of Labor to execute more promptly its deportation order. I have given this aspect of the situation much thought, but, whilst fully appreciating the hardship, I am not able to discover any basis . . . upon which a finding can be made that these persons are by reason thereof illegally restrained of their liberty.[136]

This decision, allowing unlimited detention in the absence of bail, contrasts with the earlier federal court Chinese decisions which had confined detention pending removal to two months.

Other cases were resolved in favour of the alien where courts ruled that detention after the final expulsion order of four months[137] or even thirty

---

134 Arendt describes statelessness as 'the newest mass phenomenon in contemporary history . . . [such that] every political event since the end of the first World World inevitably added a new category to those who lived outside the pale of the law, while none of the categories . . . could ever be renormalized'. *The Origins of Totalitarianism*, 277.

135 Immigration Act 1917, s. 19.

136 Cited in Claghorn, *The Immigrant's Day in Court*, 334. The judge cited with approval Lacombe C.J. in *Schlimm v. Howe* (D.C.) 222 Fed. 96, who said, in relation to a German detainee who could not be deported due to transport disruption in wartime: 'His detention was unfortunate, but certainly not illegal. His present condition can be alleviated only by the action of the executive branch of the government. A federal court would not be justified in discharging him.'

137 *United States ex Rel. Ross v. Wallis* 279 F. 401, 403–4 (2d Cir. 1922).

days[138] was outside the power of the statute. In another case,[139] a detainee continued to be held after a deportation order had been upheld on appeal because of lack of diplomatic relations with his country of nationality. There were unsuccessful efforts to remove him to another country which failed due to lack of evidence of citizenship. The court concluded that he should be discharged, but only upon posting bond of $1,000 with sufficient sureties.

Even in the early post-World War One period it was often difficult to find states willing to accept migrants ordered deported. This was the result of several factors: the emergence of much tighter, interlocking systems of immigration control, such that states would not accept persons who could not establish they were citizens; the rise of statelessness amongst Europeans and the increase in national security concerns in relation to migration amongst states. These trends had developed to the point where detention was in practice beginning to become a distinct issue of concern, separate from deportation.

Unlimited detention appeared to flow from the constitutional rulings of the higher courts that minimized the rights of aliens. Whilst it is not true to say that such stateless detainees were always 'outside the pale of the law',[140] their continued status as deportees meant that they were vulnerable to indefinite detention, if too poor to post bond, and to re-arrest, if in breach of bail conditions. The rule of law and the habeas corpus tradition found indefinite executive detention, even of unwanted aliens, offensive, but did not find it easy to shake off the new aliens power doctrinal foundations.

Conclusions on early US detention practices

The detention of migrants pursuant to immigration control was authorized by statute in the United States from 1891. The courts rarely

---

138 *Saksagansky* v. *Weedin* 53 F. 2d 13, 16 (9th Cir.1931).

139 *Ex parte Matthews*, 277 Federal Reporter 858 (1921). He argued his detention was 'unreasonable and unlawful in this; that the government of the United States, . . . has no diplomatic relations with the government of Ukrania and is unable to execute its order or warrant of deportation aforesaid . . . and is making no attempt to do so, and has no intention of so doing, . . . all in violation of your petitioner's right under the Constitution and laws of the United States.'

140 Arendt is referring here to continental European stateless detainees who were held in internment camps under police powers which she suggests were exercised free from judicial review. She notes that the 'the only practical substitute for a nonexistent home-land was an internment camp. Indeed, as early as the thirties this was the only "country" the world had to offer the stateless.' Arendt, *The Origins of Totalitarianism*, 284.

considered it in its own right; rather, it was taken as a tool ancillary to border control. As the latter was largely beyond the jurisdiction of the courts, so was the former. It was not punishment, as it was not considered imprisonment in the legal sense. In the context of European migrants on the East coast, the consequence was less significant because detention was relatively brief. In the main it appears to have been truly ancillary to processing entry candidates, who were mostly admitted.[141] The use of mandatory detention was introduced in early legislation by Congress to counter apparent executive corruption in releasing aliens, but bonding continued to be common. By contrast, Chinese migrants appear to have suffered longer periods of detention. Some of these were eventually released on habeas corpus, if they could not be removed, even after they were ordered deported. Before World War One, lower courts were thus prepared to imply time limits upon the detention power in the case of non-dangerous aliens.

As to the legal status of aliens, those held in detention whilst seeking entry to the territory of the United States were deemed never to have entered and this fiction bolstered the argument for denying them access to constitutional rights.[142] Even those who had been lawfully resident found themselves vulnerable to indefinite detention if their subsequent deportation could not be enforced.[143] During World War One this required special regulations to release detainees into employment on bail. The deportations and harassment of political activists after war led to further extended detention. This was exacerbated by international obstacles to securing removal. The courts still required adequate bail in such cases. The idea that enforcing immigration control 'trumped' other interests (including the common law prohibition on executive detention) had arrived. Jurisprudential logic tended towards seeing detention as normal

---

141 Daniels notes that Angel Island on the West coast, the arrival point for Chinese migrants, was entirely different from Ellis Island in the East. The former 'existed to isolate and to impede the immigration of Chinese and, to a much lesser extent, Japanese and other Asians. Most Chinese applicants for admission were subject to intense cross-examination; physical examinations were relatively thorough for all Chinese and included taking stool samples.' He notes the rejection rate at about 18% compared to 1% at Ellis Island. R. Daniels, *Guarding the Golden Door: American Immigration Policy since 1882*, New York: Hill and Wang, 2004, 24.

142 Neuman argues that the territorial doctrine has since become outdated and overruled. Neuman, *Strangers to the Constitution*, 124. See Ch. 5 below on the position of Guantanamo Bay for further discussion.

143 Although, as Neuman notes, 'aliens were not read out of the Constitution altogether' – the important category of those who had actually entered the United States (whether legally or not) were given the right to some constitutional due process safeguards against deportation. *Ibid.*, 1996, Ch. 1, 14.

in the case of unauthorized migrants. Strikingly, within a few years of World War One, Ellis Island, which had been conceived of as a place of care and the gateway to America, had become a pure detention facility for holding unwanted aliens pending their expulsion.[144]

The emergence of immigration controls in the United Kingdom

In the United Kingdom (UK), whilst temporary Acts authorizing alien detention and deportation on national security grounds were passed similar to the 1793 Act, no general and permanent machinery over immigration control and detention was established until 1905. The later years of the nineteenth century had seen a growing anti-alien trend. As Dummett and Nicol note, the British attitude towards aliens changed during this period for a complex set of reasons.[145] These included fears about anarchists and violent political activists, anti-semitism towards poor Jewish immigrants and economic depression leading to competition for jobs. Conditions in the East End of London, where many Russian Jews were crowded together in poor conditions, allowed local politicians to call for general restrictions on immigration.

A Royal Commission on Alien Immigration[146] took detailed evidence but largely rejected the suggestions that aliens were unclean, spread disease or committed crime. They did nevertheless recommend creating machinery for alien control. It seems this was partly because of a fear that Britain would be left behind. The Commission made a fairly detailed study of European, US and colonial laws regarding immigration. It noted that continental states had few explicit controls: 'the question of the admission and still more of the expulsion of undesirable Aliens is a matter of police regulation; and to be dealt with rather according to the circumstances of each case; than on any general or comprehensive principles'.[147] Echoing the US case-law, it was noted that 'international law recognises the right of any nation to expel foreigners, and it would seem that, unless the action is in contravention of a Treaty, no nation can complain of having its

---

144 Whilst inward migration had been limited by the war, the use of Ellis Island to hold enemy aliens began. Upon the cessation of fighting, migrants were processed again from 1919 to 1924 when the severe restrictions on migration imposed by Congress curtailed this practice. Thereafter and during World War Two the facility was a pure detention centre for deportees or enemy aliens.

145 A. Dummett and A. Nicol, *Subjects, Citizens, Aliens and Others: Nationality and Immigration Law*, London: Weidenfeld and Nicolson, 1990, at 92–100.

146 Parliamentary Papers 1903, Cmd. 1741 ix 1.   147 *Ibid.*, vol. I, 30.

subjects returned to it by a Foreign Government'.[148] They also noted the widespread use of immigration statutes to exclude criminals, the mentally or physically ill and those likely to become a charge in the common law countries.

The Commission recommendations included a suggestion that immigration officers should have power to inspect immigrants and report any suspected of being in a prohibited class to an Immigration Department to be established. Following the tradition of due process, exclusion could only be confirmed after a court hearing, pending which 'the Immigrant may be placed under suitable charge'.[149] This is the first official mention of a system of administrative detention for immigrants in UK law. The reference is oblique and the Commission did not explore the justification for such custody in legal or political terms. Nor was there any attempt to reconcile such administrative detention with traditional concepts of habeas corpus and judicial control. Detention was conceived of as an inevitable part of the mechanism of control rather than a distinct measure.

After various abortive efforts, a Bill was eventually placed before Parliament which aimed at creating a machinery of immigration control. The great English constitutional law scholar and liberal, Dicey, writing in 1905, said of the Bill that it 'assuredly betrays a marked reaction against England's traditional policy of favouring or inviting the immigration of foreigners, and in some of its provisions shows an indifference to that respect for the personal freedom, even of an alien, which may be called the natural individualism of the common law'.[150] Endorsing the view of Erskine May, he said that collectivist bills including 'the Aliens Bill are inroads upon individual liberty as understood by the Liberals say of fifty years ago'.[151] Liberals considered the restrictions to have been passed at the behest of the swelling poor working classes.[152]

---

148 *Ibid.*, vol. I, 31.   149 *Ibid.*, vol. I, 41.

150 A.V. Dicey, *Lectures on the Relation Between Law and Public Opinion in England*, London: Macmillan, 1905, 297–8. Dicey's main criticism is of the trend towards laws which favour collectivism over individual liberty. Trade union agitation for protection against cheap labour from abroad reflected this concern.

151 *Ibid.*, 493.

152 W.F. Craies, 'The Right of Aliens to Enter British Territory' (1890) 6 *LQR* 28, noted that: 'The difference in blood, religion, and habits between such immigrants and the settled population of England or any colony, while considerable, is not so serious in its social and political effects as the immediate economic effect upon the wage-earning classes, who are now the chief depositaries of political power at home and in the self-governing colonies of the Empire.'

The parliamentary debates on the Bill reflect the different attitudes that had developed towards immigrants both in the United Kingdom and in other countries. The Home Secretary, echoing the concern that Britain should be on a par with other nations, said:

> we think it is an anomaly that this country, almost if not quite alone among the civilised countries of the world, should have no power of excluding or expelling any class of alien or aliens, however injurious their presence may be in this country...I venture to think that we shall not get efficient protection from the evils which are so rightly complained of by those who take an interest in this alien question unless we are empowered to take measures against the unrestricted immigration of what is often an evil class.[153]

The transformed understanding as to the state of customary international law in the new world of territorial sovereignty was highlighted by the Attorney-General, who said that: '[t]he hon. Member seemed to think that every alien had a right to land in this country. No such right existed. It rested with every country to say whom it would receive.'[154] This was reflected in contemporary judgments by English courts in Dominion cases such as *Attorney-General for Canada* v. *Cain*, which held that:

> [o]ne of the rights preserved by the supreme power in every State is the right to refuse to permit an alien to enter that State...and to expel or deport from that State, at pleasure, even a friendly alien, especially if it considers his presence in the State opposed to its peace, order, or good government or to its social or material interests.[155]

This right had been increasingly asserted by the Dominions of Canada and Australia to restrict the entry of Chinese and other non-white alien workers in the preceding years.[156,157]

---

153 Akers-Douglas HC, vol. 133, 1147.

154 Sir Robert Finlay, Attorney-General HC, vol. 148, 796.

155 [1906] AC 542, 546 (per Lord Atkinson).

156 See *Musgrove* v. *Chun Teong Toy* [1891] AC 272 in which the Privy Council upheld the power of Australian territories to prohibit the entry of Chinese aliens under international law.

157 Indeed, the Australian High Court held in *Robtelmes* v. *Brenan* [1906] HCA 58 that this power had an extra-territorial element which extended to an alien being forcibly placed on board a ship and taken away under restraint to any other country chosen by the government to effect deportation. One judge thought, perhaps with the right to liberty in mind, that the alien consented to this because one who arrived in a 'sea-girt country...agrees as a term of his admission...that such restraint may be exercised upon him for the purpose of his deportation as may be necessary' (per Griffith C.J.). The Court had relied upon the dicta in *Cain* according to which 'it necessarily follows

Thus, unlike the earlier debates on the 1793 Act, parliamentarians by this time largely conceded the principle that aliens could be subject to detention and expulsion. The critics instead concentrated on narrower issues. For example, there were attempts to impose the burden of proof upon the immigration authorities when seeking to exclude migrants and to require independent courts to decide on expulsion. These comments indicate that there was still a concern that expulsion (and associated detention) was punishment and that this suggested criminal-style protections:

> If a penalty was sought to be imposed on a man it was the duty of the person seeking to impose it to prove the man was in the wrong...A very serious disability was sought to be imposed by this Bill, and surely those seeking to impose it ought to be called upon to prove that the person on whom it was to be imposed came within one of the prohibited categories of immigrants.[158]

The government argued in response that the regulation of immigration was not subject to the usual safeguards. In remarks that identify accurately the emerging paradigm of aliens' diminished constitutional status in the face of bureaucratic border control goals, Winston Churchill derided the government by saying '[t]he Prime Minister had stated that what was wanted was a rough and ready method of dealing with aliens, that it was a matter of administration and not justice'.[159] That aliens might not have a right to 'justice' in matters bearing upon their migration speaks to the disappearing liberal constitutional status of aliens.

The practical problems posed by detention in fact led the government to reject access to the courts to appeal against exclusion, the Attorney-General noting: 'If there was to be a right of appeal there should be a stay of execution; then the immigrant should be kept in the country. But who was to maintain him? Was it the ship-owner? Or was the general taxpayer to find board and lodging for every immigrant who chose to exercise the right this Amendment would confer?... The very essence of the matter was despatch.'[160]

that the State has the power to do those things which must be done in the very act of expulsion, if the act of expulsion is to be exercised effectively at all, notwithstanding the fact that constraint upon the person of the alien outside the boundaries of the State...should thereby result'.
158 Per Gibson Bowles HC, vol. 148, 795.   159 *Ibid.*, 875.
160 Sir Robert Finlay, *ibid.*, 808.

The government clearly envisaged that decisions and expulsions could be taken very quickly as a matter of administration such that the same ship could be used to return undesirable migrants:

> If you deal with the latter [entry] you must deal at once, because if you do not take immediate action the alien will have landed, and the ship will have left, and it will be impossible to deport him in the same ship to the country from which he came. With regard to the other cases, when the alien is already here I think it is quite a question whether efficient steps could not be taken through the medium of a Court of Justice.[161]

It was, however, accepted that despatch could not be achieved in all cases and that some system of detention for further enquiry would have to be set up. Although legal powers to detain were contained in the Bill, no funding or concrete proposals on how this would work were offered. As one critic noted:

> Again, who was to be responsible for the immigrants while they were on shore? Were they going to be surrounded by a regiment of soldiers, or planted in compounds, or put into sheds like cattle, each one in a stall?[162]

Contemporary academic commentators Sibley and Elias expressed concerns about the Bill by reverting to the habeas corpus tradition's dislike of executive imprisonment. Interestingly, they tried to reassert the distinction between expulsion (an administrative act) and detention (something closer to punishment). They thus doubted the purely 'administrative' character of detention pending expulsion:

> While there can be no doubt that the proceedings for the expulsion of an alien is an act of *administration*, it clearly infringes the principles of the Common Law and Magna Carta that a person should be liable to be sent to prison without being charged with committing a crime. But nothing less than this is liable to occur in the case of aliens who are found under the circumstances mentioned in s 3 (1)(b)(i) [they had become destitute after entry] ... till the question of their expulsion is settled by the Secretary of State.[163]

These authors also drew the further distinction between expelling lawful resident aliens and those seeking to enter: 'To create a crime involving banishment is clearly a different thing from prohibiting a class of persons

---

161 Mr Akers-Douglas HC, Vol. 133, 1147.   162 Mr Dalziel HC, Vol. 148, 438.
163 N.W. Sibley and A. Elias, *The Aliens Act and the Right of Asylum*, London: William Clowes and Sons, 1906, 71 (emphasis added).

from entering the country.'[164] Of the detention, bail and deportation of resident aliens, they concluded: 'It is difficult to regard proceedings for expulsion as a purely administrative act.'[165] Sibley and Elias again betray the conceptual difficulty that sometimes beset early immigration law. Possible infringement of the rights of aliens lay in both their physical detention or in the broader concept of banishment as a punishment. These seemed to offend common law ideas of the rule of law. However, this only applied to lawful residents, not those seeking a first landing. This reflected the, then still influential, international law doctrine that resident friendly aliens should not be treated arbitrarily.[166] This period was a transitional one, from the perspective of jurisprudence, from the older cosmopolitan world to the new world of closed sovereign states and wide powers over even friendly aliens.

Inspection and detention under the 1905 Alien Act: due process and despatch

As eventually passed, the Act[167] created a system of inspection for the (generally poorer) steerage passengers, who could be refused leave to land if 'undesirable'.[168] It also permitted expulsion orders for aliens convicted of felonies or those in receipt of parochial relief, without ostensible means or living in overcrowded or unsanitary conditions.[169] To meet the concern about due process, expulsion orders (for those already in Britain) could only be made after a conviction by an independent court.

Whilst awaiting an inspection or appeal or subject to an expulsion order, immigrants were 'liable to be kept in custody in such manner as the Secretary of State directs and, whilst in that custody, shall be deemed to be in legal custody'.[170] This suggested that the government thought that there was no inherent prerogative power to detain aliens pending admission. Conditional disembarkation from ships was permitted where there was 'proper provision' in an approved place 'for the accommodation, maintenance, control, and safe custody of the immigrants so

---

164 *Ibid.*, 68.   165 *Ibid.*, 69.

166 For a deep discussion of the historical position of different international law scholars, see J.A.R. Nafziger, 'The General Admission of Aliens under International Law' (1983) 77 *Am. J. Int. L.* 804.

167 H. Wray, 'The Aliens Act 1905 and the Immigration Dilemma' [2006] 33(2) *J.L. and Soc.* 302–23.

168 There were four classes: those not able to support themselves; lunatics, idiots or those likely to become a charge due to infirmity or disease; certain foreign criminals and those subject to an expulsion order: s. 1(3).

169 Section 3.   170 Section 7(3).

disembarked'.[171] It was the responsibility of the shipowners to hire facilities for the purpose.[172] A person was deemed not to have been landed, even if conditionally disembarked.[173]

By the time the Act came into force, a new government had come to power which, whilst unwilling to repeal it, was not enthusiastic about enforcing it.[174] Civil servants were not encouraged to be too vigorous. This is reflected in the annual reports of HM Inspector under the Aliens Act,[175] which reveal that, in practice, the numbers expelled under the Act were relatively small. Thus in 1906, the first year of operation, 935 persons were refused leave to land and, of these, 796 appealed and 442 appeals were successful. So in the end, 493 people were refused leave out of 27,639 actually inspected. The total number of passengers recorded as arriving in the year was 465,500. Inspection took place onboard ship, but at some busier ports immigrants were conditionally disembarked and inspected in 'receiving houses' paid for by shippers.

There was a high degree of cooperation between the immigration officers and local charities and other immigrant bodies to place migrants with families able to support them.[176] Detention, either on ship or shore, followed a refusal of leave to land pending hearing of an appeal or sailing.[177] The appeal boards operated fairly but quickly.[178] Legal representation and witnesses were allowed.[179] The appeal board was required to sit within

171 The details of the bond system first appeared in the rules of 1905 and the Memorandum sets out the amounts. Regulations etc. 1906, Cd 2879, Rule 7.
172 The legal fiction was created that 'any immigrant who is conditionally disembarked for the purpose of inspection, appeal or otherwise, shall be in the custody of the master of the ship until leave to land has been given, or if leave is withheld, until he finally leaves the United Kingdom.' Order and Directions of the Secretary of State for the Home Department dated 19 December 1905 under the Aliens Act 1905.
173 Rule 10.
174 J. Pellew, 'The Home Office and the Aliens Act 1905' (1989) 32(2) The Historical Journal 369–85. Pellew describes the frustration of the highly-skilled Weberian bureacrats who were stymied in their efforts to implement the Act by their political masters who had turned against it.
175 First Annual Report, 1907; Cd. 3473, vol. 66, 767. Second Annual Report, 1907; Cd. 44102, vol. 87, 941.
176 Fifth Annual Report, 1911; Cd. 5789, vol. 10, 34.
177 Report of the Departmental Committee on the Establishment of a Receiving House for Alien Immigrants at the Port of London. Parliamentary Papers 1911; Cd. 5575, vol. 87, paras 15–17, p. 6.
178 Fifth Annual Report, at 34.
179 See Parliamentary Papers 1911; Cd. 5575, vol. 87 at 34, where there is a detailed discussion about the relative merits of siting the Board at Tilbury with the new receiving house. The difficulty of calling of witnesses from the East End of London are cited amongst other reasons against.

twenty-four hours of receiving the notice of appeal. The most appeals pending in a day was thirty-three, and the most detainees held was seventeen. The average number held was only five to six. In the event of an unsuccessful appeal the alien was 'taken back in custody to his ship and is conveyed in her to his port of embarkation'.[180] There appears to have been little problem with executing the removal of rejected aliens, and so detention could be viewed as truly ancillary to this highly streamlined system.

The demand for a large immigrant receiving house: London's Ellis Island?

There were, however, persistent calls for the construction of more 'receiving houses', especially for the busy London port. Interestingly, these demands came particularly from Jewish groups on welfare grounds. Winston Churchill had campaigned on this issue in an effort to garner Jewish votes before becoming Home Secretary in 1910.[181] There was also bureaucratic support for such facilities. Inspections onboard ships were problematic. Expulsion was the responsibility of the shipper who brought the immigrant. As a parliamentary enquiry found, '[t]he Chief Immigration Officer told us that . . . he was somewhat hampered by the impatience of captains of ships who pestered him and asked him to hurry, and of the pilots who wanted to catch the tide'.[182] The Immigration Board also wished for more time than they had so that officers could get them the necessary information. As a result, some aliens were wrongly allowed in and others wrongly rejected. The system was not effective in meeting the statutory goals. Immigrants were also left in the open air on deck awaiting inspection. Pending appeal they were left on ship and 'this may involve several days detention'.[183]

These factors led this parliamentary committee to endorse the idea of building a large 'receiving house' where aliens could be inspected and detained, if necessary, pending appeal and removal.[184] The ship could then sail without having to wait, reducing expense for the companies and

---

180 Paragraph 16, p. 6.
181 Pellew, 'The Home Office and the Aliens Act 1905', 379–80.
182 Report of the Departmental Committee on the Establishment of a Receiving House for Alien Immigrants at the Port of London. Parliamentary Papers 1911; Cd. 5575, vol. 87, para. 19, p. 7.
183 Paragraph 21, p. 7.
184 Report of the Departmental Committee on the Establishment of a Receiving House for Alien Immigrants at the Port of London. Parliamentary Papers 1911; Cd. 5575, vol. 87.

increasing accuracy in decision-making. This acknowledged what MPs had been saying during the debates on the Bill; any serious enforcement of the Act would require state-run facilities for inspection, care and detention of aliens. However, there was great concern to ensure that there were adequate conditions in the proposed receiving house with lavatories, separate rooms and attendants for men and women, a kitchen able to produce Jewish food and warm bedrooms.[185] This illustrates that, whilst the original Act was motivated by anti-alienism, there were still significant interests seeking to ameliorate its effects on the, mainly Jewish, migrants. The friendly 'alien' was still considered to be worthy of respect, particularly given the large numbers inconvenienced to sift out the small group of undesirables. In the end, no large facility was in fact constructed, due to both declining alien numbers and the refusal of either government or the private sector to fund it. Britain did not, in fact, create specific permanent immigration detention centres until the 1980s, instead continuing to manage detention using prisons and jails.[186]

In conclusion, detention under the Aliens Act was quite rare and, if it occurred, was not prolonged. There were several reasons. First, the numbers of aliens refused admission was small. Second, the appeal process and exclusion appear to have been relatively swift. Third, the lack of facilities for detention meant that the administrators probably had little incentive to use this method excessively. Fourth, the use of conditional disembarkation on bond was common. There are no recorded habeas corpus cases being brought to end detention under the Act. This also suggests that detention was short. We can see that, rather like the early selections at the Ellis Island facility, the system under the 1905 Alien Act was to some extent symbolic. Migration was still largely permitted and only a relatively small number were briefly detained for inspection before being admitted or expelled.

185 Paragraph 25, p. 8.
186 For a discussion of the practice of holding Jewish refugees in the period up to the eve of World War Two, see Association of Jewish Refugees, *Dispersion and Resettlement: the Story of the Jews from Central Europe*, London: De Vere Press, 1955, 18–20, which describes the transit camp at Richborough, Kent, which held some 3,000 Jews pending their onward emigration in 1938–9. They were held behind barbed wire, but permits were issued to make visits outside. Britain had taken in 50,000–80,000 mainly German Jews from 1933, but had become politically unwilling to take more. Upon the commencement of war, many were interned as enemy aliens or aliens. See M. Kochan, *Britain's Internees in the Second World War*, London: Macmillan, 1983. The government initially released most of the 74,000 Germans and Austrians after tribunal hearings cleared them, before reinterning around 22,000 in 1940. Gradually exemptions led to most of these being released again by 1942.

World War One and the first deployment of mass alien internment

The passing of the 1905 Act, although extremely modest in its effects, was clearly a 'landmark in the decline of Liberal England',[187] and as Cesarani notes:

> anti-alienism developed a momentum, dynamic and logic of its own. The existence of the statute and the administrative machinery to enforce it provided the basis for continuity. Politicians and civil servants began to amass experience operating anti-alien measures and laid down precedents for future development... During the years before the First World War the appetite of the anti-alienists increased.[188]

Anti-alien sentiment was driven by a number of factors up to World War One, including anti-semitism, fear of economic rivalry for jobs from labour, hostility towards anarchism or industrial unrest amongst richer people and concern about spying from a threatening Germany such that:

> By the outbreak of the First World War, the notion of tighter controls over aliens was not foreign to public opinion or government. On the contrary, British society had become habituated to immigration restrictions and the identification of foreigners as bearers of disease, criminal proclivities or dangerous ideas. It cannot be maintained any longer that the wartime regulations against aliens came like a bolt of lightning from a clear sky.[189]

Thus the outbreak of war saw the introduction of much more far-reaching legislation – the Aliens Restriction Act 1914 – which straddled alien control and national security goals. The Act created a framework giving the king power 'when a state of war exists . . . or when it appears that an occasion of imminent national danger or great emergency has arisen' to pass Orders in Council to 'impose restrictions on aliens'. These included prohibiting the landing of all or any aliens, or imposing conditions on them; deporting aliens; requiring them to reside in certain places, or prohibiting their entry into others. It permitted the creation of powers 'in respect to arrest, detention, search of premises or persons, and otherwise'.[190] A person bore the onus of proving that he was not an alien where any

---

187 D. Feldman, 'The Importance of Being English', in D. Feldman and G. Stedman Jones (eds), *Metropolis London: Histories and Representations since 1800*, London: Routledge, 1989, at 79.

188 D. Cesarani, 'An Alien Concept? The Continuity of Anti-Alienism in British Society before 1940', in D. Cesarani and T. Kushner (eds), *The Internment of Aliens in Twentieth Century Britain*, London: Frank Cass, 1993.

189 *Ibid.*, 34.   190 Section 1(1)(i).

question arose on such a matter.[191] Most importantly, the Act applied to both friendly and enemy aliens.

The measures were brought into effect by the Aliens Restriction (Consolidation) Order 1914,[192] which required all aliens to register themselves. Enemy aliens could be required to 'reside or continue to reside or cease to reside in any place or district specified'.[193] This power was interpreted by the government to authorize internment.[194] Importantly, however, the Order also gave the government power to deport any alien without giving any reason at all.[195] Deportees could be subjected to indefinite detention until expelled.[196] The combination of these provisions was profound. They enabled a minister to arrest and incarcerate aliens without any grounds being given and with no time-limits. In the event that a person could not be removed, very likely in wartime, detention became internment. There was also no need for the executive to show that the detention or deportation had any connection with the national danger or emergency that the Act was said to be aimed at. In practice, the laws rendered all aliens liable to detention entirely at the discretion of the government.

The initial policy operated by way of selective arrest and internment of Germans and Austrians of military age. This led to the internment of around 19,000 people by May 1915. However, there was ongoing public hostility towards Germans which resulted in riots.[197] After the sinking of the *Lusitania* in May 1915, the government responded by ordering all enemy aliens interned unless exempted by an advisory committee. The new policy also required that all males over military age and women and children be deported to Germany. The deportation of males of military age was no doubt rejected for military reasons. Naturalized aliens were not to be interned unless the advisory body ascertained 'that it would be

---

191 Section 1(4).   192 Sept. 9th Statutory Instruments 1914, Vol. I-6–26.
193 Article 17.
194 The Crown also sometimes relied instead upon the Royal Prerogative as giving power to detain any person, national or alien, in time of war. This common law power was and is of uncertain nature. It is usually suspended when a statute is passed which regulates the same subject matter. However, the 1914 legislation expressly said that it did not suspend the prerogative. Any powers of deportation and detention over aliens under the prerogative therefore remained available to the executive, although such powers were disputed by scholars. See Craies, 'The Right of Aliens to Enter British Territory'.
195 Article 12(1).   196 Article 12(2).
197 P. Panayi, *The Enemy in Our Midst: Germans in Britain during the First World War*, Oxford University Press, 1991.

dangerous if they were allowed to remain free'.[198] The number interned reached 32,440 in November 1915.[199] The final objective became the expulsion of all such persons. The advisory committee did, however, make many thousands of exemption orders relating to both detention and deportation such that 22,000 enemy aliens were still at liberty in summer 1916. About 10,000 older men, women and children were repatriated between May 1915 and June 1916.

How far did the courts respond to protect the liberty of these 'enemy aliens', many of whom clearly presented no security threat whatsoever? The answer is that whilst the courts formally allowed aliens access to habeas corpus, which was not suspended, they failed to investigate the underlying justifications for detention.[200] So long as the alien was found to have links to an enemy nationality, internment was lawful. There was no separate risk assessment undertaken. None of the reported challenges that were brought succeeded. What is more noteworthy is that the courts were often very generous towards the government, even in doubtful cases.

Thus in *ex parte Weber*, the House of Lords refused an application for habeas corpus from an interned person who had *lost* his German nationality by virtue of spending ten years outside Germany. He had lived in the UK for fifteen years and argued that he 'was not an alien enemy; that he was a person in humble amity with His Majesty the King, residing and peaceably trading in his dominions and subject to his protection'.[201] The Court agreed that he was no longer German, but relied upon the (purely hypothetical) facts that he had the right to re-register as German and would be under a duty to perform military service in wartime if residing in Germany. The judgment concluded that he had not 'discharged the burden that is cast upon him of showing that he has so completely divested himself of German nationality that he can be treated, for the purposes

---

198 Asquith announcement to Parliament of 13 May 1915.
199 P. Panayi, 'An Intolerant Act by an Intolerant Society: The Internment of Germans in Britain During the First World War', in Cesarani and Kushner (eds), *The Internment of Aliens in Twentieth Century Britain*, 59.
200 Sharpe notes that some judges and commentators have argued that alien enemies and prisoners of war do not have the capacity to apply for habeas corpus. He disputes this, saying that most of the cases see the courts engage with the jurisdictional question of whether an alien is indeed an enemy or prisoner of war. Having so found, they dismiss the application. 'While the result may be the same in the vast majority of cases . . . the lack-of-capacity rule could have the effect of discouraging an applicant who may be entitled to relief from applying, and in the interests of clarity, it should be abandoned.' R.J. Sharpe, *The Law of Habeas Corpus*, Oxford: Clarendon, 1989, 117.
201 [1916] 1 AC 421, 422.

of this application as though he longer remained a German citizen'.[202] This threw a heavy burden of proof on the alien, contrary to centuries of tradition in habeas corpus. The requirement that tangible proof be offered by the executive that an individual person represented a threat was dispensed with amidst the general mistrust of aliens.

This veneer of judicial protection was again displayed in *R v. Superintendent of Vine Street Police Station ex parte Liebmann*. The applicant had resided without incident in the UK for twenty-five years but was interned under the Royal Prerogative as an enemy alien and prisoner of war. It was accepted that he had lost his German nationality by obtaining a discharge and was not a combatant or spy. He argued that there was no power to detain him, being neither an enemy alien nor combatant.[203] The Crown relied on the prerogative, which it claimed allowed internment of anyone during wartime, including nationals and friendly aliens. The Court rejected that, saying the power was confined to enemy aliens. It also vindicated the formal right of all detained persons, alien or citizen, to seek habeas corpus, saying that:

> these Courts are specially charged to safeguard the liberty of the subject as one of their most sacred duties. The courts owe that duty not only to the subjects of His Majesty, but also to all persons within the realm who are under His Majesty's protection and entitled to resort to these Courts to secure for them any rights which they may have, and this whether they are aliens or alien enemies.[204]

It was, however, concluded that the applicant was a *de facto* enemy alien on the same basis as *Weber*. He was also a prisoner of war, because a 'German' civilian might be a far greater danger in 'promoting unrest, suspicion, doubts of victory, in communicating intelligence, in assisting in the movement of submarines and Zeppelins'. The Court refused to consider whether there was any specific conduct justifying internment of individuals who had no plausible connection with the German war effort. The mistrust of aliens was palpable.

Even in the case of clearly friendly aliens, the same reluctance was obvious. In *R v. Governor of Brixton Prison ex parte Sarno*,[205] an application

---

202 *Ibid.*, per Lord Buckmaster, 425.
203 Interestingly, on this occasion, the Crown had declined to use the statutory powers available under Art. 17 of the Aliens Order to require enemy aliens to reside in certain areas because the minister 'would have to investigate individual cases'. See counsel's submissions for the minister.
204 [1916] 2 KB 742.   205 *Ibid.*, 752.

for habeas corpus was made during the war by a Russian who was detained indefinitely pending execution of a deportation order due to the practical problems of shipping during the conflict.[206] Because this concerned a friendly alien, the government offered a justification for the deportation based upon the fact that 'the applicant had no regular employment, but assists in keeping a house which is the resort of alien thieves and bullies and of prostitutes of various nationalities'. He was suspected of living off immoral earnings and of committing one theft, but had no convictions.

In the face of these modest allegations, the court said that whilst the facts disclosed 'in a time of peace could not be fairly described as a danger to the safety of the realm [but] could fairly be so described in time of war . . . when all the activities of persons engaged in police protection and in bringing criminals to justice must necessarily be restricted because of the demand that has been made upon persons of military age'.[207] The applicant had argued that it was wrong to use the deportation so as to deny him the due process protection of a prosecution through the criminal courts. Whilst the court agreed that 'no action could be taken of the ordinary criminal character because that would require legal evidence equally in the case of the alien and in that of a British subject', deportation of an alien was not a criminal proceeding. Again the judiciary saw indefinite detention of aliens as being merely ancillary to non-punitive deportation under alien powers. This mirrors the earlier American courts that had rejected the argument that deportation was akin to punishment deserving the due process safeguards of criminal law.

From aliens to naturalized citizens: extending the reach of the 'aliens' power

The concern raised by many liberals since the nineteenth century about the harsh treatment of aliens leading to a progressive erosion of the liberty of citizens was eventually realized on a modest scale during World

206 His deportation was made under the Aliens Restriction Act 1914 and the Aliens Restriction (Consolidation) Order 1914, Art. 12(1), which did not require any justification to be offered. The detention power, Art. 12(2), said 'when an alien is ordered to be deported . . . he may, until he can, in the opinion of the Secretary of State, be conveniently conveyed to and placed on board a ship about to leave the United Kingdom . . . be detained in such manner as the Secretary of State directs, and, whilst so detained, shall be deemed to be in legal custody'.

207 The judgment appears to cover regulations that would affect both nationals and aliens and the court refers to the decision in R v. Halliday [1917] AC 260, which had upheld the validity of powers to intern hostile persons of any nationality.

War One. There were many British people of German origin who had naturalized and who, unlike those discussed above, could not be detained under aliens law. However, following the wave of anti-German hostility in the wake of the sinking of the *Lusitania*, the government was able to pass further general internment legislation in the form of Regulation 14B of the Defence of the Realm Regulations.[208] This measure came to be used against both British-born and alien-born citizens. In practice, however, the numbers were small – only 36 detainees by February 1916, of which half were born as aliens. This was truly an innovative and grave restriction on the traditional British citizens. However, perhaps because it was aimed mainly at naturalized aliens: 'in spite of its critics . . . regulation 14B does not seem to have been under any real political threat during the period of hostilities, and remarkably few individual detainees attracted any public comment'.[209]

The legality of this system of internment was challenged in the famous case of *R* v. *Halliday*.[210] Arthur Zadig, a German who had naturalized as British in 1905, was interned indefinitely due to his 'hostile origin or associations' and for 'securing the public safety or for the defence of the realm'. The detainee could make representations to a committee but had no right to legal representation nor to know the evidence relied on by the government.[211] The House of Lords held the regulation within the powers conferred on the government by Parliament in cursory judgments. Of more interest is the single dissent by Lord Shaw of Dunfermline who said of the offending regulation:

> My Lords, I do not think it any mistake to suggest that in substance it repeals the Habeas Corpus Acts . . . The Habeas Corpus Acts are, it is true, procedure Acts. In one sense they confer no rights upon the subject, but they provide a means whereby his fundamental rights shall be vindicated, his freedom from arrest except on justiciable legal process shall be secured, and arbitrary attacks upon liberty and life shall be promptly and effectually foiled by law. Formally in this case the writ of habeas corpus was allowed. It is now being tried. But what has been done by the Courts below is . . . to allow the subjects of the King by law to enter the fortress of their liberties only after that fortress has been by law destroyed.[212]

Lord Shaw argued that the powers were *ultra vires* because they did not provide for proper due process. He therefore argued that habeas corpus

---

208 As amended on 10 June 1915 in Order 551.
209 B. Simpson, *Odious in the Highest Degree: Detention Without Trial in Wartime Britain*, Oxford: Clarendon Press, 1992, 24.
210 [1917] AC 260.   211 Parl. Deb. HC, vol. 88 c. 471.   212 *R.* v. *Halliday*, 294.

went beyond simply requiring government to point to a legal power to detain. He alluded, however, to the ambiguity of the idea underlying habeas corpus. He suggested that it seeks to enforce the principle that there should be no detention without criminal process. On the other hand, it may be directed at preventing 'arbitrary' detention. In either case, the rule of law required that there be individual evidence of danger adduced and scrutinized by a court.[213] He concluded that under these powers 'the Government becomes a Committee of Public Safety. But its powers are far more arbitrary than those of the most famous Committee of Public Safety known to history'.[214]

Later academic critics have also been harsh on the majority. Sharpe notes that *Halliday* 'indicates a marked judicial reluctance in time of crisis to guard the supposedly favoured right to personal liberty when that right must be balanced against claims of public safety'.[215] On a more general level, Simpson states that: 'From 1917 onwards British judges have, with the rarest exceptions, consistently upheld the progressive erosion of British liberty in the name of good government; Zadig's case represents a sort of watershed between the world of Victorian liberalism and the world of the vigilant state.'[216] These words are particularly apposite to the treatment of aliens during the war and it is no surprise that Regulation 14B was designed to deal with naturalized aliens.

Post-Armistice: continued internment pending repatriation

At Armistice there were still 24,255 'enemy' aliens in detention. This fell to 9,831 in February 1919, but even by May 1919 there were still about 5,000 who refused to be repatriated. The government set up a further advisory committee to hear applications for exemption from these people. Of the total who applied, 3,890 were allowed to remain in the UK.[217] The advisory committee report its task was:

> a delicate one, for they very soon found that it was not concerned with the enemy aliens of the actively hostile variety – the spy, the secret agent, the insolent Prussian – that the Committee had to do . . . Those left were,

---

213 Such regulations might be employed against Irish Roman Catholics or East London Jews if the executive felt these groups were dangerous and the 'tolerance of Britain, famous throughout the world may be removed – not because Parliament has expressly said so, but by a stroke of the pen of a Secretary of State'. *Ibid.*, 293.

214 *Ibid.*, 291.   215 Sharpe, *The Law of Habeas Corpus*, 97.

216 Simpson, *Odious in the Highest Degree*, 25.

217 Panayi, 'An Intolerant Act by an Intolerant Society', 62.

broadly speaking, of a different type altogether . . . a considerable number
were old men of prolonged residence, who had been interned for their
own protection or because they were unable during the war to support
themselves outside prohibited areas. Many of these at the time of their
internment had been in same employment for over 20 years, some of them
for over 30 years; most of them had British-born wives, or wives of alien
birth whose residence here had been as long as their own.[218]

It was accepted that the 'great bulk of appeals . . . were those of men of
military age interned during the war, not by way of punishment nor
for any proved, or even suspected, offence, but purely as a measure of
precaution, the *necessity for which disappeared with the conclusion of peace*'
(emphasis added). Many had British-born wives and young British-born
children and knew only English, having retained enemy nationality 'by
an accident'.[219] These were essentially the arguments put during the war,
and rejected by the courts, on behalf of these 'accidental' enemies. All
had refused to be repatriated despite knowing that this would lead to an
'indefinite period of further loss of liberty which after the Armistice had
become an experience increasingly irksome'.

The internment policy thus continued indefinitely after the end of
the war without any individual risk assessment. The mere fact of their
being former enemy (or quasi-enemy) aliens subject to deportation was
considered enough to support incarceration. As the committee put it,
'their first care always was for the State. They were scrupulous to see that
no recommendation of theirs for exemption was calculated to involve
danger to the community even in time of peace'. They never 'allowed
themselves to forget that the *burden lay upon the alien* to justify his
claim to remain here' (emphasis added). Thus, even where the alien faced
internment, he was required to prove his right to be allowed to remain
before he could be released. There was no separate consideration of the
alien's liberty as a distinct issue or contemplation of a less invasive system
of bail and reporting restrictions.

Panayi notes that some of the camps contained aliens up to November
1919 and even February 1920.[220] He concludes that 'the confinement of
adult men within camps and away from their families, for periods of
perhaps four years and more, proved a distressing experience leading, in
some instances, to insanity'.[221] He goes on to say that 'we therefore have

---

218 Parliamentary Papers: Report of Committee Appointed to Consider Application from
      Compulsory Repatriation Submitted by Interned Enemy Aliens (Parl. Papers, 1919, X,
      125) Cmd. 383. The report was completed on 21 October 1919.
219 *Ibid.*, 1.   220 Panayi, 'An Intolerant Act by an Intolerant Society', 66.
221 *Ibid.*, 62.

to question the necessity of subjecting over 30,000 men to prison life merely because of the fact that they were unfortunate enough to reside in a country at war with their own. Much of the blame for this state of affairs lay with public opinion which constantly demanded wholesale internment'.[222] It is difficult to see the justification for this detention in terms of national security, but rather as part of a wider hostility towards aliens. The failure of the political and legal systems to seriously question such mass internment is indicative of the downgrading of the moral and legal status of aliens.

For Gearty and Ewing, speaking of the war, it was 'no exaggeration to say that the way in which the crisis was met has had an enduring impact on the power of the State on the one hand, and the political and personal freedom of the individual on the other'.[223] They are highly critical of the way in which Parliament gave extraordinary wide powers to the executive which the courts failed to control. This is exemplified most clearly in the case of the wartime detention of aliens, both friendly and enemy, pending their deportation or repatriation. The general fear of aliens was clearly apparent in the willingness of the government and the courts to permit the internment of thousands of innocent people. Although this was in principle based upon the state of war, it went far further than could be supported by military necessity. In the eyes of the government, aliens were presumed to be a threat until proven otherwise.

Post-war detention and deportation: the continuation of wartime powers over friendly aliens

The political crisis of anti-alienism continued into the post-war period as the government issued a new Aliens Order in 1919 extending the wartime powers. The courts showed no greater inclination to scrutinize the use of these powers despite the peace. Thus in R v. *Inspector of Leman Street Police Station ex parte Venicoff*,[224] a Russian man was detained for two months pursuant to deportation. He had lived in Britain for over thirty years but was alleged to have forced his wife to be a prostitute before the war.[225] He challenged the facts alleged and said he had not had a fair

---

222 *Ibid.*, 70.
223 C. Gearty and K. Ewing, *The Struggle for Civil Liberties: Political Freedom and the Rule of Law in Britain, 1914–1945*, Oxford University Press, 2000, 90.
224 [1920] 3 KB 72.
225 The relevant law was the Aliens Order 1919, Art. 12(1), made under the Aliens Restriction Act 1914.

hearing. The Court rejected his habeas corpus application in dismissive terms:

> The Legislature in its wisdom took from the Courts *during the war* the power of inquiry into the facts of particular cases where orders were made under the Defence of the Realm Acts or the Aliens Order, and left the matter entirely to the judgment of the Home Secretary . . . in dealing with a regulation such as that with which we are now concerned the value of the order would be considerably impaired if it could be made only after holding an inquiry, because *it might very well be* that the person against whom it was intended to make a deportation order would, the moment he had notice of that intention, take care not to present himself and would take steps to evade apprehension.[226]

The end of the war had not ended aliens' new-found vulnerability to arbitrary detention and deportation. The 'emergency' continued, if not officially, at least in terms of the shift in the attitudes of politicians and judges. Although not expressing themselves in the broad terms shown by the US Supreme Court cases, the effect was the same. Detention was now seen as ancillary to the power to control alien entry and residence over which the government's discretion was maximal. There was no inclination to question detention choices or recognize a distinct liberty interest of immigrants. Any action linked to the aliens power had come to be viewed as a state security power, largely inappropriate for judicial review.

Conclusions

The late nineteenth century saw modern states begin to assert a power to select which movements across borders were legitimate. The history of early US and UK immigration law and practice reveal that, at the outset, detention was seen as an ancillary bureaucratic aspect of this process of classification and selection of migrants. Indeed aliens were initially held onboard ships or at the dockside. As investigations became more searching or prolonged, pressure grew to establish specialist facilities combining elements of care and control. Despite the rhetoric, the vast majority of migrants were admitted and controls remained light. There were few formalities about returning the modest numbers rejected, who were often simply given to the shippers who brought them. Only for Chinese immigrants in the United States did the avowedly exclusionary

226 [1920] 3 KB 72 at 79.

policies lead to arbitrary and extended periods of detention in poor conditions.

During World War One residual cosmopolitan and liberal legal values towards immigration had been substantially undermined. The expansion of state surveillance over all aliens during the war created institutional tools for later use. In the United States, mandatory exclusion by reference to racist or political criteria became widespread. Visa restrictions prevented most of the former migrant groups from arriving. Similarly in the United Kingdom, permanent legislation remained which allowed the government to restrict entry without further reference to Parliament. Political and judicial reasoning endorsed the idea that control on aliens' movements was outside the normal legal order. As Sassen puts it, '[t]he coupling of state sovereignty and nationalism with border control made the "foreigner" an outsider'.[227]

Case-law and practice indicated that both friendly and enemy aliens could be held by executive officers without trial. There was no attempt to equate immigration detention with an exercise of police powers. Thus the state did not have to seek judicial approval or show just cause for detention. Immigration status itself came to be seen as a sufficient reason for detention without due process. In the United States, alien detention became a distinct tool of internal control over aliens, not simply a wartime exigency. The war had seen large-scale executive detention of aliens. Such practices continued afterwards in peacetime through the use of immigration powers against aliens deemed to be anti-social, criminal or subversive. Internal movement of aliens became a security matter which was subsumed under the new aliens power and its agencies.

Courts maintained access to the historical writ of habeas corpus for all aliens, even in wartime. This proved to be a largely rhetorical gesture, at least as regards protecting aliens' liberty. To make effective use of the procedure, aliens had to challenge the refusal to grant entry or residence status. The writ lost its historical constitutional purpose as a guarantee of freedom from executive detention. There was no recognition that detention and deportation were distinct decisions. Instead, 'temporary confinement' came to be seen as an extension of being examined onboard ship, a bureaucratic instrument pending alien authorization or expulsion. Detainees could sometimes seek bail under statute or executive policy, but there was no separate constitutional right to liberty recognized. Liberty

227 S. Sassen, *Guests and Aliens*, New York: New Press, 1999, 78.

was thus fragile, depending upon the vagaries of political and administrative life.

Despite this doctrinal edifice, which freed detention from serious constitutional control, the problem of undeportable aliens would not go away. Sometimes the ships bringing aliens had departed, never to return. The war years had also disrupted transport, making return impossible. After the war, an interlocking system emerged, comprised of nation states, each claiming a monopoly on who might enter. Sometimes no nation would take an alien rendering them *de facto* or *de jure* stateless. Although nations expressed their concern about aliens as instruments of invasion, unlike war, with its conventions for prisoner exchange, migration attracted few international arrangements. In all these cases aliens might be held indefinitely in a legal limbo. The continued presence of these detained aliens was anomalous. Faced with this, government officials devised schemes, and lower courts took pragmatic steps, to release detainees on bond or under supervision.

There thus remained a degree of political and legal pragmatism about the system which recognized that, outside wartime, detention was a means to an end. Although aliens did not have constitutional rights to liberty, there was a reluctance to endorse an absolutist stance which would lead to indefinite detention. This was born of practical considerations, but also an uncomfortable recognition of the dissonance between immigration detention and liberal legal orthodoxy. There was, however, no constitutional resolution of the problem that would protect aliens from long-term detention should future political priorities demand it.

2

Modern immigration detention and the rise of the permanent bureaucratic enterprise

Introduction: the aliens power and the new politics of enforcement

This chapter explores the political and legal evolution of detention since World War Two, particularly over the last thirty years. As we saw, the 'aliens power' had been firmly established in legal doctrine as a, now separate, descendant of the war power. Although extended alien detention had generally been reserved for wars or national security situations, this power had the potential to foster more permanent restrictions. Courts had not found a clear jurisprudential or political reason to apply basic constitutional safeguards to unwanted aliens, non-parties to the social contract. Detention had been glossed over as a 'necessary' part of deportation or as 'temporary confinement'. Detainees were deemed 'not to have entered', despite being incarcerated. The legal foundations were thus firmly in place for employment of mass detention should the political conditions arise.

The immediate decades after World War Two were ones of economic recovery during which migration was often openly encouraged. Barring national security scares, there was no sense of crisis around borders. This had changed decisively by the 1970s when a new and diffuse climate of fear over migration emerged. Those simply entering or arriving without permission, whether seeking asylum or economic opportunity, became seen as a 'security' threat. The period since has witnessed the full flowering of the illiberal potential of the aliens power, with a massive expansion of detention facilities in peacetime. Justification was sought in a range of *bureaucratic instrumental* goals; as a deterrent to irregular migration outside of permitted channels, to secure removal or maintain the 'integrity' of immigration laws and as a form of public or national security precaution. However, the increased hostility toward migration in public debate also meant that expanded detention had *politically symbolic* dimensions. It marked out more clearly the liberal state's capacity for extraordinary measures against 'outsiders' to protect 'insiders'. The permanent emergency had arrived.

We shall examine the record in the United States, United Kingdom and Australia first. These common law jurisdictions all demonstrate similar legal and political trends. There were persistent public crises over permeable borders, with overtones of invasion by the dangerous or deviant, the world's poor or incompatible races and cultures. This underlay moves toward 'group' detention, directed by politicians, not individualized assessment by courts or civil servants. Thus the essentially political 'aliens power' largely prevailed at the expense of the habeas corpus tradition in these countries. Fundamental rights jurisprudence was a limited and residual remedy in the face of the legislative and bureaucratic expansion of detention. By contrast, we also consider modern French political and legal experience. After some uncertainty, detention came to be seen as an exercise of domestic *police* powers.[1] This interpretation necessitated similar safeguards for immigrants as for all criminal suspects. This provides a good counterpoint to developments in the common law world, demonstrating that broad detention powers are perhaps not inevitable in modern states.

The United States of America: the detention paradox

Whilst the immediate aftermath of World War Two saw thousands detained in a Cold War national security scare, when the political crisis of that period receded detention became exceptional, with bail being the norm. Migration policy itself became gradually more expansive with larger numbers admitted even than during the classical heyday in the early twentieth century. Since the 1980s, however, there has been a paradox; in spite of massive legal inward migration, detention policy has become progressively tougher. The explanation is complex. There were several crises in which large flows of poor migrants sought entry by sea from islands in the Caribbean.[2] Undocumented asylum seekers also arrived in considerable numbers from other parts of the world. Large numbers of Latin

---

1 France had, in fact, only passed formal immigration detention powers in 1980 after extra-legal detention was revealed to have been occurring for years. The shock caused by this scandal was another reason that very strict legislative and constitutional controls were imposed.

2 Particularly large numbers occurred during the *Mariel* Cuban episode in 1980–1 when some 130,000 migrants arrived. This was followed by large numbers of Haitians in later years. There has been resort to naval engagements with some of these migrants in the waters off Florida.

American migrants continued illegally crossing the Mexican border. Rising concern about crime was manifested in policies requiring deportation of most foreigners convicted of even relatively minor offences.

These crises saw legislators and officials resort to detention as a political and bureaucratic tool serving a wide range of purposes. Whilst initially aimed at politically identifiable *subgroups*, not *individuals*, it mutated into becoming the default position for most unauthorized persons. The increasing absolutism of these policies required indefinite detention until persons were either deported or granted entry or stay.

Despite a lack of comprehensive evaluation, ever-increasing detention places have nevertheless been funded. By 2008, 378,582 persons had been detained during that year in 33,400 spaces spread over 300 facilities.[3] Detention had become an industry worth some $1.72 billion, mainly paid to a mixture of local, state and private entities. Since the 1980s detention policy has never benefited from liberalization. This may be because, with the most powerful interest groups focused upon arguments over lawful migration quotas, enforcement has been an easy trade-off to make to placate restrictionist elements.[4] Although hugely expensive and chaotically deployed, detention became, along with deportation, orthodox for immigration legislators.

The Cold War cases: preventive detention in 'peacetime' unleashed

Before considering the more recent bureaucratization of detention, we will look at the crucially important Cold War period when the legal foundations permitting this were laid. Fears of Communist subversion between 1948 and 1952 saw 2,000 lawfully resident foreigners held, mostly at Ellis Island, pending expulsion on the basis of secret evidence.[5] Following the earlier plenary power cases and given the panic that gripped the nation at the time, it is not surprising that courts upheld Congress's power to permit the expulsion of Communists.[6] There was, however, no separate

---

3 US Department of Homeland Security, *Office of Immigration Statistics, Immigration Enforcement Actions: 2008*, Washington, DC: Office of Immigration Statistics, 2009, 3.

4 D. Tichenor, *Dividing Lines: the Politics of Immigration Control in America*, Princeton University Press, 2002, Ch. 9, which discusses the debates around the 1996 reforms.

5 D. Cole, *Enemy Aliens: Double Standards and Constitutional Freedoms in the War on Terrorism*, New York: New Press, 2003, Ch. 10.

6 See the important decision in *Harisiades* v. *Shaughnessy* 342 U.S. 580, holding that it is constitutional to deport for past membership of the Communist Party without individual proof of current threat, which simply reaffirmed the Chinese Exclusion cases. The judgment of the Court was given by Mr Justice Jackson, who came to dissent vigorously in *Mezei* when the Court endorsed indefinite detention arising from inability to effect deportation.

state of emergency declared[7] and no powers to intern citizens were taken up. Where deportation proved difficult or proceedings extended, these persons were held indefinitely, potentially for life. These cases presented the first time that the Supreme Court had had to consider detention as a discrete issue distinct from the power to order expulsion. Could the aliens power permit unwanted aliens to be held in detention forever at the discretion of the executive branch of government?

For admission cases, the classic decision in *Mezei*[8] held that this was entirely constitutional. Ignatz Mezei, a returning permanent resident of twenty-five years, had been held for three years on Ellis Island whilst unsuccessful efforts were made to deport him.[9] The government refused to disclose the evidence against him.[10] Lower courts had agreed to bail him to his home town on the pragmatic basis that statutory immigration detention could not continue where deportation itself was patently impossible. The Supreme Court reasserted the orthodoxy that those who had not been 'admitted' were beyond constitutional protection.[11] Only Congress could decide who could be admitted.[12] Turning to the problem of Mezei's indefinite detention, the Court sought various means to show that this was not incarceration in the normal sense. The government was offering Mezei humanitarian consideration by housing him at Ellis Island, his 'temporary haven', rather than keeping him onboard ship. His

The Court had, however, confirmed in *Wong Yang Sung* v. *McGrath* 339 U.S. 33, that procedural fairness obligations under the Administrative Procedure Act 1946 applied in deportation decisions regarding resident aliens.

7 The state of emergency declared by President Roosevelt in 1941 had never been revoked. See *Knauff* v. *Shaughnessy* 338 U.S. 537 (1950), 546.

8 *Shaughnessy* v. *United States ex rel. Mezei* 345 U.S. 206 (1953).

9 He had twice been sent to Europe and returned by Britain and France. Hungary had refused to accept him as a national. He had of his own volition applied to twelve Latin American countries for entry and been refused. Thereafter he declined to search further.

10 The power of alien exclusion pursuant to secret evidence had been created during World War Two, but had never been revoked: 'The special procedure followed in this case was authorized not only during the period of actual hostilities, but during the entire war and the national emergency proclaimed May 27, 1941. The national emergency has never been terminated. Indeed, a state of war still exists. See *Woods* v. *Cloyd W. Miller Co.*, 333 U. S. 138, n. 3.' See *Knauff* v. *Shaughnessy*.

11 The majority decision in *Mezei* has sometimes been viewed as being confined to national emergency situations, but in the much more recent decision in *Zadvydas*, the Supreme Court made clear that, in its view, the case was decided squarely upon the distinction between admission cases and those who have effected an 'entry' in immigration law terms. *Zadvydas* v. *Davis* 533 U.S. 678 (2001), Opinion III A at para. 7.

12 Clark J. delivering the majority judgment at 212 citing *Knauff* v. *Shaughnessy*, 544: Eillen Knauff, a war bride of apparently exemplary character, was detained for over two years before being admitted after a public and Congressional outcry led to her receiving a hearing despite the Supreme Court having ruled against her rights to the same.

'harbourage' was merely a way of keeping him out, rather than locking him in. He was free to go anywhere in the world that would have him. This ignored the reality that contemporary states all asserted control over their borders; there was no more free movement without authorization. As Jackson J. put it in dissent: '[r]ealistically, this man is incarcerated by a combination of forces which keeps him as effectually as a prison, the dominant and proximate of these forces being the United States immigration authority. It overworks legal fiction to say that one is free in law when by the commonest of common sense he is bound.'[13]

The majority also spoke clearly to the outcast status of the alien. To the extent that other nations (of which he might be a citizen) refused to admit him, they should not be able to foist him onto the United States because, in a memorable phrase, 'he is no more ours than theirs'. Mezei was held up as a potential agent of foreign powers seeking to harm or burden the United States. Whilst the fact that refusal to admit him 'plus other nations' inhospitality results in present hardship cannot be ignored ... the times being what they are, *Congress may well have felt* that other countries ought not shift the onus to us'.[14] This is disingenuous, because Congress had evinced no consideration of the novel indefinite detention scenario presented by Mezei. Because he was excluded from *constitutional* protection, the Court did not seek a restrictive view of the statute. He remained in a legal limbo – neither a formal prisoner of war nor a criminal suspect. This revealed the full extent of the aliens power to create essentially 'political' prisoners detained outside the framework of legal rules even during peacetime. Mezei was truly an outlaw, cut off from United States and international law.[15]

The decision was widely condemned in academic circles even at the time.[16] This echoed the powerful dissenting judgment of Jackson and Frankfurter J.J., arguing that Mezei had a right to a procedurally fair

---

13 345 U.S. 206 (1953), Jackson J. (dissenting) 220.
14 Majority Opinion, 216 (emphasis added).
15 He was eventually released on executive parole after four years in detention following executive hearings which apparently concluded that any threat he posed was not, after all, so serious as to justify detention for life.
16 H.M. Hart, 'The Power of Congress to Limit the Jurisdiction of Federal Courts: An Exercise in Dialectic', (1953) 66 *Harv. L. Rev.*, 1362, 1392–6; K.C. Davis, *Administrative Law Treatise* St Paul: West Publishing, 1958, 479–82 ('The holding that a human being may be incarcerated for life without opportunity to be heard on charges he denies is widely considered to be one of the most shocking decisions the Court has ever rendered'). More recently see P. Schuck, 'The Transformation of Immigration Law', (1984) 84 *Colum. L. Rev.* 1, 20 ('among the most deplorable governmental conduct toward both aliens and American citizens ever recorded in the annals of the Supreme Court').

hearing on whether he was truly a threat to national security to ensure that his Due Process right was respected. As they put it 'basic fairness in hearing procedures does not vary with the status of the accused . . . If they would be unfair to citizens, we cannot defend the fairness of them when applied to the more helpless and handicapped alien'.[17] They saw preventive detainees as akin to criminal law suspects, rather than simply unadmitted aliens. Their view was nevertheless a cautious one, conforming to a thin version of the doctrine of the rule of law. It still permitted indefinite detention where the government met its evidential burden to support exclusion. This degree of deference has remained an important element in US jurisprudence. Unadmitted aliens must establish immigration authorization to enter in order to be released. There is no separate constitutional right to be set at liberty by a court in habeas corpus simply because detention is indefinite.[18]

Even in cases involving deportation of lawful residents, as opposed to admission, the Cold War case of *Carlson* v. *Landon*[19] also confirmed a broad, almost unreviewable, discretion in the executive to detain during the proceedings. The alien detainees were accused of being active Communist Party members and denied bail whilst their cases were determined. The relevant Act gave discretion[20] to grant bail, but the government declined to do so in all Communist cases. The Supreme Court majority upheld the policy on the grounds that 'evidence of membership plus personal activity in supporting or extending the Party's philosophy concerning violence gives adequate ground for detention'.[21] This wide view applied even to persons merely accused of being Communists. As in *Mezei*, a less restrictive alternative was rejected because 'detention is necessarily a part of this deportation procedure. Otherwise aliens arrested for deportation would have opportunities to hurt the United States during the pendency of deportation proceedings'.[22] The Court would only interfere if the government's general views about Communists could be said to be unreasonable. Any need for individual risk assessment was rejected, as was release on bail.

Black J.'s powerful and innovative dissent sought to characterize the cases as wholly concerned with criminal due process, not the scope of the

---

17 *Mezei* at 225.
18 See now the United States Court of Appeals for the District of Columbia Circuit decision No. 08–5424, *Kieymba* v. *Obama*, judgment of 18 February 2009 on unremovable Guantanamo detainees.
19 342 U.S. 524 (1952).   20 Internal Security Act 1950, s. 23.
21 *Carlson* v. *Laudon*, per Reed J., 541.   22 *Ibid.*, 537.

aliens power: 'Today the Court holds that law-abiding persons, neither charged with nor convicted of any crime, can be held in jail indefinitely, without bail, if a subordinate Washington bureau agent believes they are members of the Communist Party, and therefore dangerous to the Nation because of the possibility of their "indoctrination of others".'[23] He argued the policy was really a measure of internal security, not migration control. Bail was refused not because it was thought that they would abscond; rather, it was to deny them freedom to associate with others, but '[a] *power to put in jail because dangerous* cannot be derived from a power to deport'.[24] Given that suspected Communists were not all aliens, the logic of the slippery slope beckoned in his view for '[t]he stark fact is that if Congress can authorize imprisonment of "alien Communists" because dangerous, it can authorize imprisonment of citizen "Communists" on the same ground'.[25] This was a crucial insight, a first attempt to separate out 'immigration' uses of a detention power from 'security' or 'social control' uses arbitrarily directed only at aliens.

More importantly for later developments, however, the majority said that the constitutional right to bail only protected criminal suspects, not deportation cases.[26] The dissent rejected this in terms going back to the pre-alienage era: 'the plain purpose of our bail Amendment was to make it impossible for any agency of Government, even the Congress, to authorize keeping people imprisoned a moment longer than was necessary to assure their attendance to answer whatever legal burden or obligation thereafter be validly imposed upon them'.[27] In a more narrow separate dissent based upon statutory interpretation, Frankfurter J. said that Congress had given the executive discretion to grant bail and could not have done so intending that it never be exercised in the case of persons said to be active Communists. They had been the victims of 'an abstract, class determination, not an individualized judgment'[28] which was the hallmark of the common law approach to bail. *Carlson* was an important landmark in allowing the executive (and ultimately Congress) wide discretion to order group or class detention of aliens at the expense of individual risk assessment. Much later, outside a time of national emergency, this

---

23 *Ibid.*, 548. He explains the factual details of the cases to illustrate the slender nature of the threat claimed to exist and the harshness of the decisions.

24 *Ibid.*, 551 (emphasis added).   25 *Ibid.*, 552.

26 'Excessive bail shall not be required nor excessive fines imposed, nor cruel and unusual punishments inflicted.'

27 *Ibid.*, at 557.   28 *Ibid.*, at 564.

precedent facilitated the development of purely bureaucratic mandatory detention of new classes of aliens.[29]

After the Cold War: controlling indefinite detention through statute and discretion

After the end of the heightened national security scare of the late 1940s and early 1950s, detention nearly disappeared. The new Immigration Act 1952 created a range of parole alternatives even after deportation had been ordered.[30] Whilst the law still required detention pending admission, in 1954 the government adopted a presumption of parole save for absconding or national security risks. After this hundreds were released and only twenty-five remained at Ellis Island, which was therefore closed soon after.[31] In 1955, of 200,000 arrivals at the port of New York, astonishingly only sixteen were detained. There were no more reports of *Mezei*-type indefinite detainees.[32]

In relation to deportation post-entry the new law was very liberal. Detention was truly discretionary pending a final deportation order.[33] Even after a final order, there was the possibility of release on bond or conditional parole. Most importantly, there was right to seek habeas corpus if the government failed to show 'reasonable dispatch' during

---

29 Even in the context of the Cold War, scholars of the time criticized these decisions which tended 'to ignore judicial development of the last fifty years. Habeas corpus had been available from the first cases to test the legality of the alien's detention ... The requirement of a fair hearing had been read into immigration laws ...' 'Developments in the Law of Immigration and Nationality' (1952–53) 66 *Harv. L. Rev.* 643, 675.

30 Kanstroom, *ibid.*, argues that contemporary critiques in academic circles also had an influence. L.B. Boudin, 'The Settler Within Our Gates' (pts 1–3) (1951) 26 *N.Y.U. L. Rev.* 266, 451, 634 and see the discussion at M. Dow, *American Gulag: Inside U.S. Immigration Prisons*, Berkeley: University of California Press, 2004, 6–7.

31 The new Administrative Procedure Act 1946 also appeared to require any detention decisions to be made according to common standards of fairness. See *Wong Yang Sung*, but this was subject to statutory exception which was quickly adopted in 1950. A later Supreme Court decision affirmed that this removed immigration decisions from the Administration Procedure Act provisions and that no additional constitutional protections were owed to migrants in deportation cases: *Marcello* v. *Bonds* 349 U.S. 308. For the extended story of the problems experienced by the authorities in deporting Marcello, a leading crime boss, to another country see Kanstroom, 'Developments in the Law of Immigration and Nationality', 178–86.

32 See *Annual Report 1955* of the Commissioner of Immigration and Naturalisation, Washington, DC: Department of Justice, 1955, 6.

33 Section 242(a) 'Pending a determination of deportability ... such alien may, upon warrant of the Attorney General, be arrested and taken into custody.'

deportation proceedings. The ordinary courts were thereby given jurisdiction to 'review or revise any determination . . . concerning detention,
release on bond or parole pending final decision'.[34] This innovative provision recognized the increasing danger and hardship caused by the
extended detention seen in the Cold War cases.

The Act also introduced important time limits on the duration of
detention giving the government six months to effect expulsion after a
final order.[35] This 'removal period' was an express statutory recognition
that a balance needed to be struck between enforcement efforts and
liberty. After this period, the Act required immigrants to be 'subject
to such further supervision and *detention* as is authorized'. The courts,
however, construed the six-month time limit as absolute so that detention
must cease, if not supervision.[36] In practice, until reforms in the 1990s,
detainees were not held longer than six months after a final deportation
order.

Interestingly, the statute did not attempt to fully resolve the 'membership' question of the immigration status of 'deported' aliens released after
six months. The regulations created for the 'supervision' of deportees
required them to appear before immigration officers, submit to examinations, give information about their activities, associations and habits and
conform to reasonable written restrictions on their conduct or activities.[37]
Failure to comply was a criminal offence. These deportees were thus not in
any sense allowed to re-enter society free from constraints. They were in
another legal limbo, subject to state control and without formal residence
rights. Nevertheless, the release provisions showed a sensible pragmatism. Although the courts had allowed it, political controversy around
the indefinite detention of many innocent people during the Cold War
cases had been intense. The 1952 Act was an important first expression
by Congress of the need for alternative arrangements to separate out
detention from deportation issues.

De facto *statelessness and criminalizing non-cooperation with the removal process*

This problem of securing the admission of deportees to other countries
continually vexed the government.[38] Sometimes detainees either had no

34 Section 242(a).   35 Section 242(c).
36 *Lee Ah Youw* v. *Shaughnessy* 102 F. Supp. 799 (S.D.N.Y. 1952).   37 Section 242(d).
38 See dissenting opinion of Black J in *Carlson* v. *Landon* at 549: 'Of necessity, consideration
  of these deportation proceedings by bureaus and courts may last for years . . . Moreover,

nationality, could not prove it, or declined to reveal it. The government could approach countries if the detainee had failed to choose one themselves. However, whichever country was selected, the cooperation of the detainee was required in completing necessary documentation. To compel such cooperation, criminal law was passed penalizing aliens who did not take steps to ensure their departure.[39]

This obligation was considered by an interesting Supreme Court decision which asked whether this statutory crime of wilful failure to apply for travel documents was void due to unconstitutional vagueness.[40] The majority rejected the argument by saying that once the detainee (or government) had selected a country, then he or she would know that they must complete 'such documents as the country in question may require'.[41] The crime was apparently perfected by reference to other countries' bureaucratic requirements, whatever they might be. The better view was the dissent by Black J., who argued that it would be unclear to the detainee what constituted a 'timely' application made in 'good faith' and which documents were 'necessary to his departure' and to whom he should apply.[42] He concluded that the provision 'entangles aliens in a snare of vagueness from which few can escape'.[43] Congress should have indicated when, to whom and what the alien should apply for, else the alien would be convicted for an omission to undertake an uncertain act.

even deportation orders at the end of such proceedings might not end their indeterminate jail sentences since the foreign countries to which they are ordered might refuse to admit them. Such refusals have prevented deportation in thousands of cases.' He cites congressional hearings on the point: 96 Cong. Rec. 10449; H.R. Rep. No. 1192, 81st Cong., 1st Sess., 7, 9, 10.

39 Section 242(e). The crime attracted a sentence of up to ten years and applied in the case of aliens deported on a number of grounds, including those with Communist or anarchists affiliations, who 'wilfully fail or refusal to depart from the United States . . . or shall wilfully fail or refuse to make a timely application in good faith for travel or other documents necessary to his departure, or who shall connive or conspire, or take any other action, designed to prevent or hamper or with the purpose of preventing or hampering his departure'. Implicitly recognizing the harsh nature of the crime, the Act gave courts power to suspend sentence using a broad discretion to take account of the age, health, period of detention already passed, the effect of the alien's release on national security, the likelihood of the alien resuming their activities, the efforts made by him to secure his acceptance in another country and the reason for the government failing to secure a passport or travel documents.

40 *United States* v. *Spector*, 343 U.S. 169 (1952), also see comment at 66 *Harv. L. Rev.* 107–9. The case actually considered the identically worded provision inserted by the Internal Security Act 1950 which was reproduced in the Immigration Act 1952.

41 Per Douglas J. at 172.   42 Per Black J. at 173.   43 Per Black J. at 174.

The problem of establishing what constitutes 'non-cooperation' has persisted until today. Modern immigration statutes and practice have abandoned formal criminal sanctions in favour of extending *administrative* detention for those deemed to have failed to comply.[44] This, however, appears to be far worse, amounting to a punishment dispensed by executive officers to secure what they view as 'compliance' without any due process safeguards. There is virtue in revisiting the 1952 Act's innovative idea of a criminal offence, but one drafted by reference to clearer standards so that detainees would have certainty as to what was required of them and courts could determine both guilt and sentence accordingly. We shall consider this in Chapter 7.

The switch from parole to detention: the Haitian and Cuban flotillas

The liberal parole policy established for admissions cases in 1954 persisted until 1980–1, when Cuban and Haitian persons began to arrive in larger numbers by sea. Previous government policy was to grant asylum to all Cubans arriving in the United States. When the Cuban government deliberately allowed over 125,000 persons, some expelled from prisons and mental institutions, to cross by a 'flotilla' to Florida, this was abandoned. Facing a perception of crisis over the potentially dangerous new arrivals, the government refused entry to many.[45] Pending asylum decisions, a new policy of mandatory detention for all Cubans and Haitians was adopted by the executive without Congressional approval or proper administrative notifications. Given the unprecedented situation, this was an understandable political response. Boats were intercepted and detainees were taken on shore for processing in whatever facilities could be found. The Supreme Court considered the policy change in *Jean* v. *Nelson*,[46] ruling that purely nationality-based discrimination in parole policy derived from *statutory* powers was indeed unlawful. However, it declined to revisit the question

---

44 See Ch. 4 below and the discussion of the EU Returns Directive, which permits detention to be extended by an additional twelve months in cases of non-compliance. The US Immigration and Customs Enforcement procedures on post-removal order detention allow the 180-day 'clock' to be stopped for non-compliance. In all these cases there is no mandatory judicial review of these assessments.

45 R. Daniels, *Guarding the Golden Door: American Immigration Policy since 1882*, New York: Hill and Wang, 2004, 205–7 records that four-fifths of the detainees were quickly released; another 22,000 were held for a longer time but then paroled, leaving 1,800 suspected of crime or mental patients. Most of these were later paroled.

46 472 U.S. 846. Per Rehnquist J., 849.

of the constitutional right to liberty or due process of aliens denied in *Mezei*.

The important dissent by Marshall J. argued for the detainees' right to be considered for parole on *constitutional* grounds. Anticipating emerging new irregular migration flows, he opposed the Cold War-era *Mezei* principle being extended to non-dangerous asylum seekers. The case-law placing unadmitted migrants beyond the protection of the constitution was wrong, because it 'defies *rationality*' (emphasis added) and would, for example, allow the executive to argue that 'legitimate immigration goals justify a decision to stop feeding all detained aliens . . . Surely we would not condone mass starvation'.[47] He argued that the executive should be subject to judicial control and show their detention decisions were supported by evidence. Judicial review should be more searching in non-national security cases. He therefore drew a crucial distinction between substantive rules on *entry*, where Congress was beyond constitutional judicial review and *detention/parole*, where the executive, at least, should be subject to constitutional review. This is the first time that we see a judgment that argued for splitting detention and exclusion decisions. Marshall J. expressed the underlying idea that judicially mandated parole is not the same thing as immigration authorization.

This view of the need for greater judicial control was prescient *vis-à-vis* the Caribbean flotillas. Thus, while the vast majority of the *Marielitos* were eventually paroled under a non-discriminatory policy once the crisis had fallen from public view, 210 were held indefinitely from the 1980s, and others who committed offences while on parole were re-detained on an indefinite basis. Their permanent detention was eventually made mandatory by statute.[48] They were treated as never having entered, and so subject to the *Mezei* principle.[49] A continuing scar on the legal system, the district courts faced sporadic challenges from these 'lifers' whom Cuba had made clear it would not accept back. Faced with the intolerable, lower courts sometimes ruled such detention unconstitutional or contrary to international law, but were overturned by Circuit Courts.[50] Only in 2005

---

47 *Jean* v. *Nelson* 472 U.S. 846. Per Marshall J., 875.
48 See Note, 'The Indefinite Detention of Excluded Aliens: Statutory and Constitutional Justifications and Limitations' (1983) 82 *Mich. L. Rev.* 61.
49 Their detention was in principle rendered unlawful on a narrow point of statutory interpretation in the Supreme Court decision *Clark* v. *Martinez* in 2005.
50 *Barrera-Echavarria* v. *Rison* 21 F.3d 314 (9th Cir. 1994) where an eight-year detention on grounds of dangerousness for an excluded *Mariel* boatlift Cuban was considered 'excessive in relation to its regulatory goal'. *Barrera-Echavarria* v. *Rison* 44 F.3d 1441 (9th Cir. 1995) (en banc) holding that indefinite detention of excludable Cubans was constitutional.

did the Supreme Court rule that the statute used to detain this group was subject to temporary limits, paving the way for the supervised release of the final *Mariel* detainees after some 25 years.[51]

The rise and rise of mandatory detention as a legislative policy

Illegal migration had been a growing source of political tension since the 1980s as the apprehension of undocumented migrants rose to over a million.[52] The executive had signally failed to remove great numbers of both criminal and illegal aliens. A lack of detention space led to a practice of 'catch and release' for many. Given the Cold War precedents ruling out serious constitutional review, Congress began to show increasing interest in detention as an enforcement tool. From 1988, it expanded the range of deportable offences and imposed mandatory detention on such persons pending their final deportation orders.[53] The specified offences triggering deportation and detention became less serious in successive legislation.[54] Matters reached a head in 1996 when the policy was extended to anyone sentenced for one year.[55] Asylum seekers without immigration status were also subject to mandatory detention until and unless they demonstrated a *prima facie* case for asylum.[56] Finally, the traditional rule was maintained that non-citizens 'not clearly and beyond a doubt' admissible at the border were also subject to mandatory detention.[57] This increased federal resort to mandatory detention reflects the complex political balance of the day.[58]

---

51 It is not clear how many were detained from the beginning and how many were re-detained for violation of parole conditions. Therefore the exact duration of these long-term detainees' incarceration is not known.

52 Daniels, *Guarding the Golden Door*, Ch.12, sets out the political backgrounds in more detail and the argument that there was actually continuity in migration.

53 Anti-Drug Abuse Act 1988. For a detailed discussion see P.H. Schuck and J. Williams, 'Removing Criminal Aliens: The Pitfalls of Federalism' (1988) 22 *Harv. J. L. & Pub. Pol.* 367.

54 Immigration Act 1990 and Miscellaneous and Technical Immigration and Naturalization Amendments Act 1991.

55 8 U.S.C. 1182(d)(5)(A) and 8 C.F.R. s. 235.3, which require detention subject only to release in the discretion of the Attorney General in a medical emergency or to meet a legitimate law enforcement objective.

56 INA s. 235(b)(B)(iii)(IV): 'Any alien subject to the procedures under this clause shall be detained pending a final determination of credible fear of persecution and, if found not to have such fear, until removed.'

57 8 U.S.C. 1225(b)(2)(A).

58 Tichenor speaks of the 'popular wave of anti-immigrant policies that seemed to wash over the country between 1994 and 1996', D. Tichenor, *Dividing Lines: the Politics of Immigration Control in America*, Princeton University Press, 2002, 284. This stemmed from a diverse and uncertain set of causes such as large-scale Caribbean irregular migration by

The increasingly tough enforcement measures against irregular migrants were among the concessions offered to restrictionist groups by those seeking to keep migration flowing.[59]

As a result of these trends and legal measures, detention has increased dramatically in scale and duration. The daily population was roughly 2,200 in 1985, 6,600 in 1995, 20,000 in 2001 and 33,400 in 2008.[60] A study on the period 1994–2001 by the Federal Detention Trustee is instructive.[61] The number of aliens ordered detained pursuant to immigration law in 1994 was 72,154. By 2001 this had increased to 188,547. In 1981 the limited detention that there was had averaged a mere four days. By 1994 this had increased to 26.5 days and to 29.5 days in 2001, where it has remained.

This average disguised huge variation depending on status and nationality. Most of those detained were Mexicans crossing the south-western frontier who were swiftly removed, bringing down the average. Non-Mexicans were, however, detained for sixty-three days. For one-quarter of the countries to which aliens were removed detention periods averaged over 120 days. As the report notes, 'for those aliens from countries with strained diplomatic relations with the United States or experiencing socio-political turmoil or economic difficulty, the length of time in detention was the greatest'. Thus, Angolans (316 days), Cubans (294 days), Liberians (232 days), Sierra Leoneans (227 days), former-Yugoslavians (227 days) and Chinese (227 days) experienced the most prolonged detention. The number held for more than 180 days following an order of removal increased from 1,847 in 1994 to 5,266 in 2001.

---

boat, economic uncertainty due to increased competition from legal and illegal Mexican workers and the effects of free trade generated by the North American Free Trade Agreement and cultural concerns about loss of national identity rooted in an English-speaking Western culture.

59 Daniels, *Guarding the Golden Door*, 244. Zolberg says of all the hostility towards immigration 'in the end, the mountain gave birth to . . . more than a mouse, something like a hefty rat, but still considerably smaller offspring than its dramatic travails presaged'. A. Zolberg, *A Nation By Design: Immigration Policy in the Fashioning of America*, Cambridge, MA: Harvard University Press, 2006, 385.

60 See M. Taylor, 'Judicial Deference to Congressional Folly: The Story of *Demore v Kim*', in D.A. Martin and P.H. Schuck (eds), *Immigration Stories*, New York: Foundation Press, 2005, 5.

61 *Detention Needs Assessment and Baseline Report: A Compendium of Federal Detention Statistics*, Washington, DC: Office of the Federal Detention Trustee, United States Department of Justice, 2002. See also Lawyers Committee for Human Rights, Testimony on INS detention, delivered by E. Acer before the US Senate Committee on Judiciary and Immigration Subcommittee, 16 Sept. 1998.

Thus, whilst the statutory provisions required detention during the 'removal period' of ninety days, in many cases it proved impossible to effect deportation in that time. Detention beyond this date continued for long and indeterminate periods at the discretion of the executive. Given the vast numbers of detainees, it was difficult for the administrators to actually review and progress individual cases according to operational standards. Simple tracking and record-keeping were troublesome. Detention continued by default or inertia with minimal diplomatic negotiations unlikely to resolve matters.

The decision in *Zadvydas*: the end of endless immigration detention

In the face of these trends, the power of indefinite detention was eventually challenged in habeas corpus proceedings before the Supreme Court in the landmark case of *Zadvydas* v. *Davis*.[62] In this case two resident non-nationals were detained after having been ordered removed following numerous criminal convictions.[63] In neither case would another country accept them. They had thus remained in detention following the expiry of the statutory ninety-day target 'removal period' for seven years and two years respectively at the date of the hearing.[64] The Attorney General had refused to exercise what he claimed was his absolute discretion to release.[65] The statute precluded bail hearings. The immigration authorities operated their own internal review procedures as to release on parole and these put the burden upon the detainees to disprove their dangerousness.[66] The authorizing statute set no time limit to detention beyond the removal period.

---

62 533 U.S. 678 (2001).

63 The classes of inadmissible and criminal aliens are in fact very wide and do not require any particularly heinous conduct. Thus ordinary visa violators are covered. See 8 U.S.C. 1182.

64 8 U.S.C. 1231(a)(2): 'During the removal period, the Attorney General shall detain the alien. Under no circumstances shall the Attorney General release an alien who has been found inadmissible under section 1182(a)(2) or 1182(a)(3)(B) of this title or deportable under section 1227(a) or 1227 (a)(4)(B) of this title.'

65 8 U.S.C. 1231(a)(6). The Attorney General had a discretion whether to detain for an apparently unlimited period beyond ninety days.

66 The Attorney General had eventually, after large amounts of litigation and just before the Supreme Court case, created an annual review procedure with the burden on detainees to show they did not present a risk to the community or an absconding risk. The review was conducted by executive branch officers, not neutral adjudicators: 8 CFR 241.4(d). The government also disputed that there could be judicial review of the Attorney General's determination of this issue. See Breyer J., III A para. 4.

The Court concluded, by a majority,[67] that the statute, properly interpreted, did not permit indefinite detention, but only for such period as was reasonably necessary to secure removal.[68] In the words of Breyer J., '[a] statute permitting indefinite detention of an alien would raise a serious constitutional problem'.[69] In particular, such an interpretation might lead to infringement of the Fifth Amendment's Due Process clause, which states that no person shall be 'deprived of life, liberty, or property, without due process of law...' Administrative detention of *citizens* had generally only been found to be constitutional where:

> a special justification, such as harm-threatening mental illness, outweighs the 'individual's constitutionally protected interest in avoiding physical restraint'. *Kansas v Hendricks* 521 U.S. 346, 356 (1997). The proceedings at issue are civil, not criminal, and we assume that they are non-punitive in purpose and effect. There is no sufficiently strong special justification here for indefinite civil detention.[70]

In extending this principle to deportee *aliens* the Court clearly asserted their equal right to liberty, save to the extent that detention is necessary to aid removal. If removal is not possible, then detention merely serves to incarcerate *per se*. As to the stronger argument that detention prevents criminal conduct, the Court said 'we have upheld preventive detention based upon dangerousness only when limited to specially dangerous

---

67 Scalia and Kennedy J.J. gave separate dissenting opinions.

68 See the discussion at III. The court used the doctrine of 'constitutional avoidance', which means that where a statute raises a 'serious doubt' as to its constitutionality 'this Court will first ascertain whether a construction of the statute is fairly possible by which the question may be avoided' (*Crowell* v. *Benson* 285 U.S. 22, 62).

69 *Zadvydas* v. *Davis*, III A. para. 1. This comment has attracted attention from scholars who have wondered whether it signifies a retreat from the broad plenary power doctrine of the Chinese Exclusion cases. For a negative assessment see T.A. Aleinikoff, 'Detaining Plenary Power: The Meaning and Impact of *Zadvydas v Davis*' (2002) 16 *Geo. Immig. L.J.* 365 who suggests that Breyer J.'s endorsement of the border/interior distinction and other plenary power cases indicates no fundamental rejection of plenary power.

70 *Zadvydas* v. *Davis*, III A. para.1. The Court here seems to be applying constitutional norms to immigration cases, but on one view *Zadvydas* is a case that turns on statutory interpretation rather than constitutional prohibition. The Court sought to avoid the risk that a statute might infringe the constitution. It did not decide that the constitution did actually protect immigrants directly in detention cases. For a detailed discussion on the interaction between constitutional norms and statutes see H. Motomura, 'Immigration Law After a Century of Plenary Power: Phantom Constitutional Norms and Statutory Interpretation' (1990–1) 100 *Yale L.J.* 545 who shows how courts have increasingly referred indirectly to constitutional standards when interpreting statutes.

individuals and subject to strong procedural safeguards'.[71] The immigration detention power, by contrast, applied to a huge class, including many petty criminals whilst the, purely executive, review was an inadequate safeguard. Plenary power over migration did not extend to enforcement, for Congress had to choose a 'constitutionally permissible means of implementing' the power.

Importantly, following the thinking of Marshall J. in *Jean* v. *Nelson*, they dismissed the argument that the decision amounted to granting the detainees *a general right of residence*; rather, they were being released under supervision on strict conditions: '[t]he question before us is not of "confer[ring] on those admitted the right to remain against the national will" or "sufferance of aliens" who should be removed. Rather, the issue we address is whether aliens that the [Executive] finds itself unable to remove are to be condemned to an indefinite term of imprisonment within the United States'.[72] This was doctrinally important as it left the ultimate question of 'membership' rights to the government. Deportees released under supervision are just that; they acquire no further rights incident to membership as a result of their release.[73]

The Court concluded that, being incidental to deportation, the period of detention must not go beyond that 'reasonably necessary' to secure removal. A presumptively reasonable period was six months (an echo of the earlier 1952 Act scheme). Thereafter, the detainee must be released where they could show that deportation was not reasonably likely within a forseeable period. There were two important limitations upon the *Zadvydas* principle as set out by the majority. First, it only applies to immigrants who have entered the United States. The Court was asked to overrule *Mezei*, but controversially declined to do so, and in fact appeared to reiterate that entry cases were distinct.[74] The second limitation on *Zadvydas*

---

71 *Zadvydas* v. *Davis*, III A. para. 2. Citing *United States* v. *Salerno* 481 U.S. 739 (allowing pre-trial detention only for the most serious crimes and subject to stringent time limits) and *Foucha* v. *Louisiana* 504 U.S. 71 (striking down insanity-related detention that placed the burden on the detainee to prove non-dangerousness).

72 *Zadvydas* at 695.

73 The statute required that some groups of detainees not removed after ninety days be made 'subject to supervision', which included reporting obligations and the obligation to obey 'reasonable written restrictions on . . . conduct or activities' s. 1231(a)(3). This in essence mirrored the old 1952 Act approach with its recognition that where removal had failed, detention should cease and supervised release should take effect.

74 See the earlier litigation conducted on behalf of immigrants detained at Guantanamo Bay in *Cuban American Bar Association, Inc* v. *Christopher* 43 F.3d 1412 (11th Cir. 1995). The balance of judicial and academic opinion indicates that *Mezei* would be upheld if a

related to 'especially dangerous' aliens.[75] The government subsequently took a broad view of this to encompass mentally ill persons who might be dangerous, in order to limit the effect of the judgment.

Kennedy and Rehnquist J.J.[76] by contrast, resisting the idea of a right of release, focused upon procedural protections and proportionality. They concluded that 'both removable and inadmissible aliens are entitled to be free from detention that is arbitrary or capricious . . . it is neither arbitrary nor capricious to detain the aliens when necessary to avoid the risk of flight or danger to the community'.[77] The government's assessment of risk had not been challenged by the detainees.[78] If it had been, the Court could have developed appropriate standards of review. They adverted again to the classical idea of an aliens powers derived from war powers, saying that 'where hostility or tension characterizes the relationship, . . . other countries can use the fact of judicially mandated release to their strategic advantage, refusing the return of their nationals to force dangerous aliens upon us'.[79] Their opinion clearly reiterated the power of the state to intern unwanted aliens for security reasons but extended it beyond the Cold War cases to a time when there was no declared national emergency.

Scalia and Thomas J.J. in their separate dissenting position went further still, effectively bringing *Mezei* into deportation cases. They decided that immigration decisions were all that mattered. Absent immigration authorization, detention was beyond legal control. The majority decision was based upon 'a claimed right of release into this country by an individual who *concededly* has no legal right to be here. There is no such

case arose in which the detainee had never entered as a matter of law. See, for example, Aleinikoff, 'Detaining Plenary Power', who suggests that the Court was wrong to uphold *Mezei* because that undid much of the benefit of the rest of the ruling by retaining plenary power in entry cases. He does acknowledge, however, that this may have been the price for securing a majority.

75 In an *obiter dictum* Breyer J. said that the instant facts did not require the Court to 'consider terrorism or other special circumstances where special arguments might be made for forms of preventive detention and for heightened deference to the judgments of the political branches with respect to national security'.

76 Kennedy J. with whom Rehnquist C.J. joined and Scalia and Thomas J.J. joined in part.

77 Part II para. 7.

78 The dissent specifically and unusually cited international human rights law to support this argument. United Nations Working Group on Arbitrary Detention, UN Doc. E/CN.4/2000/4 (Dec. 28, 1999) and United Nations High Commissioner for Refugees, *Guidelines on Applicable Criteria and Standards Relating to the Detention of Asylum Seekers* (Feb. 10, 1999). Kennedy J. may have misinterpreted these standards as authorizing indefinite detention. We will consider these further in Ch. 3.

79 Part II para. 9.

constitutional right'.[80] Where a person no longer asserted that they had membership/authorization, the courts had no power to prevent their detention. This appeared to be so even if Congress had not spoken definitively about the regulation of detention. Their view went further than plenary power by arguing that *executive* branch policy alone could authorize detention for life. The spectre of the alien as an outlaw subject entirely to political will was clear.

The three opinions provide us with three distinct visions of the aliens power. In a decisive break with the Cold War aliens power case-law, the majority viewed preventive detention as inherently wrong even in relation to unwanted aliens. As a result, similar principles applicable to citizens must apply to aliens. True 'immigration' detention could only last whilst there was a reasonable prospect of deportation. The middle position of Rehnquist and Kennedy J.J. saw nothing wrong, in principle, with the preventive detention of allegedly dangerous aliens; because they are subject to deportation they have fewer liberty rights. The government was free to protect the public by controlling release on parole subject to granting a fair hearing. No emergency was required. The position of Scalia and Thomas J.J. took the aliens power tradition at its highest. Whilst the courts may have a role in deciding on who can be deported, once that has been decided adversely, the matter is one for government. The courts have no role to play because Congress and the executive alone must decide if aliens ordered deported are to be released into the community. What the 'security' of the nation required as regards hardship being imposed upon unwanted aliens was a political question. Unwanted aliens were outside the social contract and therefore beyond constitutional protection. We shall return to these different views when considering the jurisprudence of detention in Chapter 7.

The plenary power doctrine dimmed but not buried: Demore v. Kim

Zadvydas might have suggested a shift away from the broadly unchecked Cold War doctrines in relation to the detention of lawful resident aliens.[81] Perhaps resident aliens might see an emerging constitutional guarantee of liberty pending deportation subject only to detention on the grounds of

---

80 *Ibid.*, para. 1.
81 See P.J. Spiro, 'Explaining the End of Plenary Power' (2002) 16 *Geo. Immig. L.J.* 339 and Aleinikoff, 'Detaining Plenary Power'.

dangerousness or flight risk following a fair hearing.[82] Surprisingly, however, mandatory detention during deportation proceedings was upheld by the Court in *Demore* v. *Kim*.[83] The case concerned the detention of a non-citizen who had been a lawful resident since childhood but who faced possible deportation because of teenage burglary and theft offences. It was accepted that he personally did not present a flight or offending risk, but he was detained under the mandatory provisions created in 1996.[84] The removal proceedings had lasted some six months before a District Court ordered that the mandatory detention provision was unconstitutional and he was released on minimal bond.

The Supreme Court overturned the District Court and distinguished *Zadvydas* in several ways. First, it said that *Kim* was concerned with detention before a final removal order. Detention could be said to be serving a legitimate purpose in ensuring that immigrants were available for deportation. In *Zadvydas*, removal was no longer likely and so detention did not serve the statutory purpose. The Court also relied upon the fact that the evidence showed that in most cases removal proceedings were completed relatively quickly.[85] The Court also said that Congress had looked at evidence on absconding rates for those granted bail and concluded that they were sufficiently high to justify mandatory detention.[86] The Court did not answer the argument that each detainee was entitled to an independent and individualized risk assessment,[87] but simply recited a standard phrase that 'this Court has firmly and repeatedly endorsed the proposition that Congress may make rules as to aliens that would be unacceptable if applied to citizens'.[88]

The judgment in *Kim* was a strange one. On the one hand, the Court conducted a quite detailed review of the evidence that led to the legislation. On the other hand, the Court allowed Congress a wide discretion, saying 'when the Government deals with deportable aliens, the Due Process

---

82 See *Salerno* v. *U.S.* 481 U.S. 739 (1987), which upheld pre-trial detention without bail where a narrow class of particularly serious criminals was concerned, following individualized hearings.

83 123 S. Ct. 1708 (2003).

84 Section 236(c) Immigration and Nationality Act 1952, as amended.

85 At 18, where figures cited by the Court indicated that 85% of cases resulted in a final decision within forty-seven days and the remaining 15%, when appeals were conducted, took four months.

86 The rates in the studies cited by the court and considered by Congress were around 20–25%.

87 Following the *Salerno* decision.

88 Opinion of the Court at 11, citing *Mathews* v. *Diaz* 426 U.S. 67 (1976).

Clause does not require it to employ the least burdensome means to accomplish its goal'.[89] Why not, we may ask? It is difficult to find a *reasoned basis* to allow unnecessary detention, with all its personal and societal costs. *Kim* marked a step back towards the pre-*Zadvydas* era where alienage was again a symbolic marker authorizing political and legislative *unreason* to prevail. Cole said that the 'decision marks the first time outside of a war setting that that the Court has upheld preventive detention of *anyone* without an individualized assessment of the necessity of such detention'.[90] This overlooks the Cold War cases, but his reference to wartime is telling; the gradual slippage, through the aliens power, from the mass detention of war to bureaucratic and political detention in peacetime is obvious.

The effects of Zadvydas and Martinez on the practice of long-term detention generally

One rather accidental effect of the Supreme Court decision in *Zadvydas* was that it had a knock-on effect for excluded immigrants because the same statutory provision applied to them. Thus the later decision in *Clark v. Martinez* largely freed the *Mariel* Cubans who had been held since 1980 or had been re-detained for long periods after breach of parole.[91] The case did not expand the *constitutional* protection given to migrants who have not been admitted. The statutory provision in question was the same one as in *Zadvydas*.[92] The Court felt bound to follow the earlier statutory interpretation rather than 'establish within our jurisprudence, beyond the power of Congress to remedy, the dangerous principle that judges can give the same statutory text different meanings in different cases'.[93]

The ruling did not prevent a statutory amendment. As the Court said, '[t]he Government fears that the security of our borders will be compromised if it must release into the country inadmissible aliens who cannot be removed. If that is so, Congress can attend to it'.[94] There was no constitutional barrier to legislation imposing indefinite detention on unadmitted

---

89 Opinion, 17.

90 D. Cole, *Enemy Aliens: Double Standards and Constitutional Freedoms in the War on Terrorism*, New York: New Press, 2003, 224.

91 543 U.S. 371 (2005).

92 The *Martinez* majority came to this view even though the *Zadvydas* majority had based its reading on the doctrine of *constitutional* avoidance – the ambiguity of the statute should be resolved in a way which did not raise the constitutional concerns presented by indefinite detention of admitted aliens.

93 Opinion of the Court (Scalia J.), 15.   94 *Ibid.*, 14.

aliens.[95] Nevertheless, the Court had clearly seen nothing in the government's evidence about the 'security' threat posed by the detained Cubans to alter its view.

Zadvydas and *Martinez* provide only a legal standard; practical compliance is far from assured. Despite time-limits, the numbers detained have continued to rise, reaching 378,582 in 2008 and straining the administration. A recent survey found much long-term detention, particularly in delayed documentation cases or of persons with mental health problems who become 'lost' in the system. One man was still technically detained in a rest home after 3,244 days.[96] Whilst the initial political prompt for increased detention funding had been criminal deportations of 'serious' criminals, by 2009 the majority of those held (243,900) were non-criminals.[97] Of the 125,583 criminal cases held that year, very few had convictions for serious violent crimes, with most offences being drug, traffic, assault and immigration violations.[98] The costs involved in booking and holding detainees are immense and left little room for reliably applying legal and administrative rules.

As a result, a 2006 study found patchy compliance with the Supreme Court's standards.[99] Systems were lacking to ensure that detainees were

---

95 It noted that following *Zadvydas*, Congress had indeed enacted powers to authorize indefinite detention beyond six months where removable aliens presented national security risks or had been involved in terrorist activities (see s. 412(a) US PATRIOT Act 2001). There is no suggestion that this overrules *Zadvydas*, because the Court appeared to leave open national security detention linked to deportation as possibly constitutional. It does show, however, how the legislature may respond to judicial activity which resolves statutory ambiguity in ways that are deemed unacceptable. The weaknesses of confining judicial protection to that offered by the statutory interpretation method is explained by Motomura, 'Immigration Law After a Century of Plenary Power'. *Martinez* is a further illustration of the point, as a majority in the Court made clear that ultimately Congress has plenary power in immigration detention.

96 D. Kerwin and S.Y. Lin, *Immigration Detention: Can ICE Meet its Legal Imperatives and Case Management Responsibilities?* Washington, DC: Migration Policy Institute, 2009, 19.

97 See D. Schriro, *Immigration Detention Overview and Recommendations*, Washington, DC: Homeland Security, Immigration and Customs Enforcement, 2009. This provides a comprehensive official critique of the current arrangements and proposes much wider use of information systems and community alternatives.

98 Kerwin and Lin, *Immigration Detention*.

99 Office of Inspector General, *ICE's Compliance with Detention Limits for Aliens with a Final Order of Removal from the United States*, Washington, DC: Department of Homeland Security, 2007. The government had introduced guidelines which interpreted the case-law in ways that allowed detention to proceed far beyond the six-month limit in a number of scenarios. The application of these depends upon executive officers' own assessments of when detainees have complied adequately with documentation systems or when removal is likely soon. Discretion remains a key feature. See *Continued Detention of Aliens Subject to Final Orders of Removal*, 66 Federal Register 56967 (November 14, 2001) codified at 8 C.F.R. ss 241.4, 241.13, 241.14 (2005).

not simply held indefinitely past the six-month limit in the hope of obtaining documentation. Over 10 per cent of Chinese, Indians, Pakistanis and Haitians were held for over one year, even though few were assessed as especially dangerous. Some were wrongly said to have failed to comply with documentation procedures. There were weak systems to identify truly dangerous persons and some offices put the burden on the detainee to prove their safety. Once persons were held beyond the *Zadvydas* time limits it was up to them to apply for habeas corpus, and 46 per cent of challenges were successful, indicating widespread illegal detention. In the absence of mandatory judicial review, detention remains arbitrary and unpredictable.[100]

The United Kingdom: executive detention and the revival of the habeas corpus tradition

The United Kingdom has also expanded its detention facilities greatly since the 1980s. It has, however, never adopted legislation requiring mandatory detention. Rather, detention policies have been made by governments acting under statutory powers. This is not to say that there have not been policies of mandatory detention for certain groups. These have not, however, been approved or required by Parliament, which is the supreme law-making body in the United Kingdom. Detention decisions have always been made by executive officers. The absence of judicial approval for detention has led to increasing arbitrariness, particularly as detainee numbers have risen. Courts have played an increasingly important, if residual, role as a retrospective check on executive detention through judicial review, habeas corpus and damages claims brought by detainees.

As we saw, the protection afforded aliens by habeas corpus was extremely limited during the formative period of immigration control in the United Kingdom. Whenever an alien was subject to deportation proceedings, detention was viewed as ancillary to this. There was little acknowledgement by courts of their former role as guardians of individual liberty. This changed dramatically with the increase in migration controls in the 1960s aimed at Commonwealth citizens. This group was considered British subjects and had always previously had the right of abode in the United Kingdom. When British subjects began to be detained pursuant to their deportation, the courts rediscovered habeas corpus. This was mainly

---

100 For a discussion of recent reform ideas see A. Kalhan, 'Rethinking Immigration Detention' (2010) 110 *Colum. L. Rev.* 42.

used as a lever for reviewing the deportation decisions themselves. In the absence of a modern administrative law, courts saw habeas corpus as the jurisdictional basis for challenging these barriers to the free movement of British subjects.

Even after Commonwealth citizens were denuded of legal and political status, the courts continued to use the rediscovered habeas corpus power as a check upon detention of aliens and Commonwealth citizens alike. In the face of rising numbers of administrative detainees, the common law's traditional presumption against detention has been firmly restated as extending to foreigners. This was amplified by the United Kingdom's incorporation of the European Convention on Human Rights with its pro- bation on arbitrary detention. Unlike the former position, detention and deportation/exclusion decisions have been clearly separated in jurispru- dential thinking. These judicially crafted restrictions on executive discre- tion have been possible because, perhaps surprisingly, the legislature has not entered the detention arena, despite the political controversy around immigration being intense during this period. This may be explained by the fact that the courts have continued to allow the executive flexibil- ity over the duration of detention and act mainly as a residual check in extreme or clearly arbitrary cases.

From British subjects to aliens: the detention of Commonwealth citizens

The history of modern immigration control in the United Kingdom is rendered complex because of the influence of the Commonwealth upon immigration status. Whilst aliens were regulated by the post-World War One controls,[101] citizens of colonies and former colonies enjoyed unre- stricted access to the United Kingdom. This group of countries constituted the Commonwealth, an area of free movement of persons based upon a shared citizenship. Such persons were British subjects of the Crown and all equal in terms of immigration status.[102] It was only in 1962 that the first legal restrictions were placed upon entry and residence in the United Kingdom for British subjects who had acquired citizenship of

---

101 Aliens Restriction (Amendment) Act 1919.
102 The British Nationality Act 1948 created the new status of Citizen of United Kingdom and Colonies (CUCK) as the modern statutory name for what had been British subjects. The terminology is confusing, with the status of British subject and Commonwealth citizen also continuing to be used.

independent former colonies.[103] This was driven by racist political ideas that had entered British politics in the 1950s.

Originally said to be temporary restrictions on the movement of British subjects, these were gradually extended. Most Commonwealth citizens were thus excluded from free access to Britain in 1962. However, significant numbers in Africa were still able to come to Britain because they did not acquire the citizenship of their newly independent East African nations. This was either through choice or restrictive nationality law. Increasing discrimination against Asians in Africa led to a movement of Kenyan Asians to Britain. At this point the 1962 restrictions were expanded further in 1968 deliberately to stop this flow. Access for Commonwealth citizens was made conditional upon having a parent or grandparent born in Britain.[104] Although there was still a theoretical common status of British subject for all Commonwealth citizens, it had been denuded of significance. Until then the ideal of the Commonwealth and the equal rights of British subjects were clearly important political values in Britain.[105] This was finally rejected in 1971 when the first single immigration law was passed which explicitly required aliens and most Commonwealth citizens to obtain permission to enter Britain.

Enforcing the new restrictions on Commonwealth citizens led to a whole raft of new detention cases. Separate developments in modern administrative law began to provide a basis for judicial review of immigration decisions.[106] The denial of entry to commonwealth citizens was of 'vital importance to the immigrants since their *whole future* may depend upon it'.[107] However, the detention context still played an important role in how the courts viewed their task. In theory, the burden lay upon the Commonwealth citizen to prove that they were indeed within one of the exempt categories permitted to enter.[108] If they failed to establish this,

103 Commonwealth Immigrants Act 1962. For an excellent history see R. Hansen, *Citizenship and Immigration in Post-war Britain*, Oxford University Press, 2000.
104 Commonwealth Immigrants Act 1968.
105 See Hansen, *Citizenship and Immigration in Post-war Britain*, Chs 1 and 2.
106 *H.K. (an infant)* [1966] 2 QB 617. In this case, the son of a Pakistani man habitually resident in Britain was detained by immigration officers on arrival with his father. It was claimed that he was under sixteen and therefore exempt from controls on his entry under the 1962 Act. The immigration officers did not believe this and he remained in detention for several weeks pending an application for both habeas corpus and judicial review. It was held that he had not been given a fair hearing to prove his age upon arrival.
107 633 D–E (emphasis added).
108 Section 2(2): 'the power to refuse admission . . . shall not be exercised . . . in the case of any person who satisfies the immigration officer that he . . . (b) is the . . . child under 16 years of age, of a Commonwealth citizen who is resident in the United Kingdom'.

then British subjects could thus be imprisoned by executive order pending deportation.

This vulnerability to detention was unacceptable to the court in *R v. Governor of Brixton Prison, ex parte Ahsan and others.*[109] Here a group of Commonwealth migrants had entered the United Kingdom clandestinely and were apprehended.[110] They were alleged to be wet and unkempt. The immigration officer believed that they had just arrived, but they claimed to have been in the United Kingdom for some three days, well beyond the 24-hour period allowed to examine them.[111] The applicants had been detained for two months by the time the application for habeas corpus was heard. The court found that the new laws were a:

> statutory fetter on the freedom of the subject, a fetter necessary for rea-
> sons which concern Parliament but which do not concern this court. The
> consequences may go to the *very liberty of the subject*, as they have done in
> this case. In my view Parliament must not be supposed to have put upon
> the subject the burden of proving freedom from liability to detention in
> prison of a citizen who has done nothing unlawful, unless that burden is
> expressed in the clearest and most unequivocal terms.[112]

The court held that the *executive* must establish beyond doubt that these British subjects met the condition precedent for the exercise of 'immigration' powers.[113] Importantly, the judgment also distinguished earlier wartime case-law applying to British subjects that suggested that the burden was upon the detainee to establish illegality.[114] Those cases were confined to the particular statutory provisions in question. This desire to uphold the liberty of British subjects, even those seeking to evade restrictions imposed by a Parliament desirous of curbing British

---

109 [1969] 2 QB 222.

110 Clandestine entry was not an offence by British subjects as Blain J. notes: 'In the first place there is no law to prevent a British subject arriving by private yacht or some less glamorous vessel at any time of the day or night upon any part of the coast, and no offence is committed if he sails across from Le Touquet or swims from Cap Gris Nez' (at 241C).

111 Schedule 1 Part 1(2).   112 241 D (emphasis added).   113 Lord Parker C.J., 230C.

114 *R v. Secretary of State for Home Affairs ex parte Greene* [1942] 1 KB 87 in the Court of Appeal and [1942] 1 KB 87 in the House of Lords; *Liversidge v. Anderson* [1942] AC 206. These cases related to detention under Reg. 18B of the Defence (General) Regulations 1939 where the minister 'has reasonable cause to believe any person to be of hostile origin or association'. The courts there read the power subjectively such that it was lawfully exercised so long as the minister believed in good faith that the detainee fell into the category concerned. There was no test of objective proof, nor therefore any burden as to that. The condition precedent was merely subjective belief.

Asian immigration is noteworthy. This was so despite the court concluding that:

> This is a thoroughly unmeritorious application. If ever men should be sent back to the country from which they came, it is these men. But to enable that to be done would, in my judgment, mean making bad law.[115]

Only after the passing of the 1971 Act did the courts finally endorse the political reality that Commonwealth citizens were no longer to be given access to the United Kindgom in *Azam*.[116] The Commonwealth citizen applicants were all said to be illegal entrants and detained for some six months pending the conclusion of proceedings. They applied for habeas corpus. They were living in the United Kingdom at the time of the 1971 Act being passed and claimed the benefit of section 1(2) of the Act, which gave indefinite leave to settled persons. To qualify as 'settled' the Act required that they not be in the United Kingdom in 'breach of the immigration laws'.[117] They argued that their original clandestine entry was not a continuing offence. The majority of their Lordships rejected their argument, taking an expansive view of ambiguous statutory words. They were 'present' in breach of the laws so long as their mode of entry was illegal. The court did not adopt a plausible restrictive interpretation which would not have exposed them to detention and expulsion.

This was an important milestone, because it showed the courts rejecting the strong presumption of liberty shown in *Ahsan* for those it perceived to have now become akin to aliens. Only Lord Salmon dissented: 'It is because this subsection affects the liberty of the subject by cutting down his basic constitutional rights, that I consider that it should be confined

---

115 235B. The Chief Justice was happy to note that the loophole that nobody contemplated had been partially closed by the 1968 Act, which increased the time period for examination to twenty-eight days.

116 *Azam* v. *Secretary of State* [1973] 2 All ER 765.

117 Section 33(2). The Act did not define the meaning of 'in breach of the immigration laws'. The majority decided that included British subjects who had entered clandestinely and not presented themselves to an immigration officer within twenty-eight days. This was a summary offence under s. 4A of the 1962 Act (as amended by the 1968 Act). The offence thereunder was not, however, drafted as a continuing offence, and so a person could not be prosecuted after the six-month period of limitations. At this point a British subject should, it was argued, no longer be considered to be present in the United Kingdom in breach of the immigration laws, but rather should be considered there pursuant to their common law right.

to the restricted meaning.'[118] This case was really about the death of the old ideal of the Commonwealth, but it was not clear if it marked a return to the wide 'aliens power' approach to detention too.

The effect of the 1971 Act: the return of the aliens power

The dramatic shift away from the habeas corpus ideal was further confirmed in the decision in *R* v. *Governor of Risley ex parte Hassan*.[119] Here a Pakistani national entered the United Kingdom but was detained one year later on suspicion of having entering illegally in breach of section 33 of the 1971 Act. He claimed to have been given a six-month visitor visa stamped in a passport that he had subsequently lost. He was detained for one month pending an application for habeas corpus. The court said that Ahsan's case 'was based very largely upon the fact that there one was dealing with British subjects, and here one is dealing with an alien who prima facie has no right to be in this country at all'.[120] Therefore the court said that once the government asserted the existence of an immigration power to detain, the burden shifted to the immigrant:

> The gaoler's return is good on the face of it. The gaoler said 'I detain this man by virtue of an order under paragraph 16 of Schedule 2 to the Act of 1971'. Therefore, it seems to me, the onus is upon the applicant to show a prima facie case that his detention is illegal.[121]

The newly downgraded status of Commonwealth citizens under the 1968 Act and their final equalization with aliens in 1971 is apparent. The very

---

118 789e and

> To give section 33(2) an extended meaning would enable the executive, in the future, to seize and imprison a Commonwealth citizen, long resident in this country and leading a blameless life, because of a summary offence which he had committed in the distant past . . . It seems incongruous to describe such a man as being here in breach of the immigration laws. If such a man can properly be so described then he could be kept in prison pending consideration of whether or not he should be deported. He might then have his whole life and that of his family uprooted by being in fact deported. At best, he would be detained in prison for as long as it might take the Home Office to reach a decision. It is not unreasonable to suppose that this might take weeks or even longer. The construction that I favour would make this interference with individual liberty impossible. I certainly do not share the view that there is no harm in construing a statute so widely that it gives the executive such a power because the executive can be relied on not to use it or, if they do, to use it fairly (780h–i).

119 [1976] 1 WLR 971.   120 Per Lord Widgery C.J., 977G.
121 979 A. The court rejected his evidence about the loss of his passport because it contained discrepancies that were sufficiently serious as to undermine the credibility of his story.

limited burden on the executive to justify detention is apparent. Simply asserting 1971 Act powers was sufficient. It is not clear if the court in *Hassan* should be taken literally, for this would mean that anyone, even persons born in the United Kingdom, could be detained. It may be that the court merely meant that where a detainee accepted their alienage (i.e. did not argue that they had the right of abode), then the burden fell on them to prove they had a valid visa.

Courts drew an important distinction between cases like *Hassan* where an immigrant had no document showing permission and other cases where they did. In the latter case, the government sometimes alleged the permit was obtained by deception and detained them as illegal entrants. The courts interpreted the relevant law in a restrictive way and the habeas corpus context influenced them in this.[122] They held that the detention power was dependent on the immigrant actually being an 'illegal entrant', and that the courts must decide this.[123] The courts would not defer to the executive or place a burden on the immigrant who had obtained an apparently valid authorization to be at large.[124] This was an important limit on the aliens power; those holding valid permission should not be liable to summary arrest and expulsion at the discretion of the executive. However this important, if confined, reach for habeas corpus, was reversed by a decision of the House of Lords in *Zamir*.[125] This held that judicial review of illegal entry findings was limited to ensuring that the view taken was one that a reasonable immigration officer could have reached. The Court would not substitute its own view on the question. This decision was consistent with developing ideas of the appropriate role of courts in judicial review. It did, however, leave immigrants who correctly thought they had become members of society vulnerable to arrest, detention and expulsion.

122 *R v. Secretary of State for the Home Department ex parte Hussain* [1978] 2 All ER 423; *R v. Secretary of State for Home Affairs ex parte Badaiki* [1977] *The Times*, 4 May, DC; *R v. Home Secretary ex parte Mangoo Khan* [1980] 1 WLR 569 per Denning M.R., 577B.

123 Section 33 Immigration Act 1971: ' "illegal entrant" means a person unlawfully entering or seeking to enter in breach of a deportation order or of the immigration laws, and includes a person who has so entered.' The immigration law relevant was s. 24, which made it a crime if 'contrary to this Act he knowingly entered the United Kingdom in breach of a deportation order or without leave'.

124 Per Megaw L.J., 431J: 'I do not find it necessary to discuss the suggested question of principle as to burden of proof . . . I have been prepared to consider this appeal on the basis of the court itself assessing the evidence.' He concluded that the applicant must have employed deception to secure entry on the facts.

125 *Zamir v. Secretary of State for the Home Department* [1980] AC 930.

The landmark decision in *Khawaja*: equal liberty for aliens?

In a dramatic and unusual turn, however, the House of Lords overruled its own (then very recent) decision in *Zamir* in a ruling that reasserted judicial control over government actions in respect of aliens.[126] In *Khawaja*, Lord Bridge said:

> My Lords, we should, I submit, regard with extreme jealousy any claim by the executive to imprison a citizen without trial and allow it only if it is clearly justified by the statutory language relied upon. The fact that, in the case we are considering, detention is preliminary and incidental to expulsion from the country in my view strengthens rather weakens the case for a robust exercise of the judicial function in safeguarding the citizens rights.[127]

Lord Bridge seems to make no distinction between 'citizens' and aliens, including the latter amongst the former, even in relation to detention ancillary to expulsion. Similarly, Lord Scarman said, '[h]abeas corpus protection is often expressed as limited to "British Subjects". Is it really limited to British nationals? Suffice it to say that the case law has given an emphatic No to the question. Every person within the jurisdiction enjoys the equal protection of our laws ... This principle has been in the law at least since Lord Mansfield freed "the black" in *Sommersett's Case* (1772) 1 State Tr 1 at 20'. He continued by saying that the fundamental consideration was that the case concerned:

> a power which inevitably infringes the liberty of those subjected to it. This consideration ... outweighs ... any difficulties in the administration of immigration control to which the application of the principle might give rise.[128]

---

126 Something of the remarkable nature of the debate on the bench that day can be gleamed from Lord Templeman's resigned comments on immigration control:

> In an ideal world there would be no restrictions on immigration. In the actual world accidents of history, geography and climate create pressures to emigrate which are not matched by facilities for reception. Hence the imposition of immigration controls designed to produce a logical and just system for admitting those numbers and categories of long-term and short-term applicants for entry who can be absorbed without disastrous economic, administrative or social consequences. If immigration controls are, or are thought to be necessary there must be machinery for the qualification and selection of entrants for the enforcement of the controls.

127 *R v. Secretary of State for the Home Office ex parte Khawaja* [1984] AC 74.
128 *Ibid.*, 780.

For these reasons, the executive bore the burden of proving that an alien was an illegal entrant to the court's satisfaction and to a high degree of probability. Such broad statements of equality between aliens and nationals cannot, however, be considered as unqualified. The facts concerned an immigrant who could show they *had apparently valid authorization*, obtained years before, rather than an alien seeking entry *per se*. Some members of the court highlighted this important distinction.[129] Entry decisions with associated powers of detention and removal could only be challenged where the refusal of entry was itself unfair or perverse.[130]

Khawaja was thus in most respects a case about the power of courts to review immigration decisions. Detention was in a sense an ancillary issue. The courts felt it important to protect immigrants from an arbitrary *revocation* of a prior authorization. First authorizations remained for the government. It seems, however, that the risk of detention incident to expulsion served as historical and jurisprudential inspiration for the court to rediscover the spirit of judicial control embodied in the habeas corpus tradition.[131] The overweening administrative state had attempted to go too far, believing that its powers over aliens were unlikely to be challenged.

The *Khawaja* decision nevertheless turned out to be a crucial case because it boldly declared the equal right of all persons (not just citizens) to enjoy the common law presumption against executive detention. The comments confining its reach to those who have leave to enter have proved

---

129 'The detention and removal of a non-patrial resident in this country, who may or may not be a British subject, who may have been here for many years and who, on the face of it, enjoys the benefit of an express grant of leave to be here, on the ground that he is an illegal entrant seems to me to be dependent on fundamentally different considerations' Lord Bridge, 790.

130 Lord Templeman, 794h:

> Once, however, an applicant has obtained from the immigration officer leave to enter . . . he becomes an entrant entitled as of right to remain . . . during the currency and on the terms of the leave granted to him . . . An entrant threatened with forfeiture of his rights may seek the protection of the court in habeas corpus and judicial review proceedings, asserting that he did not obtain leave to enter by fraud, that he is not an illegal entrant and that therefore the immigration authorities have no power to detain him or to remove him from the United Kingdom. If the court is not satisfied that the entrant obtained leave to enter by fraud, the court will protect the entrant against detention and removal.

131 As we have noted, whilst modern courts have become more involved in authorization decisions, they have used judicial review principles such as unfairness or rationality to guide them, as seen in *Zamir*. This reflects the idea that government discretion over migration should not be replaced by the courts. *Khawaja* is a rare case of the court going further and becoming the decision-maker itself.

less enduring than the broad statements approving the liberty interest of all persons within the jurisdiction. This case came to be seen as a clear affirmation, within the British system of parliamentary sovereignty, of constitutional rights to liberty for aliens against executive action.

The emerging problem of extended detention: searching for the statutory purpose

Whilst detention was a rarity at the time of *Khawaja*, quite soon the reach of its principles was tested as detention periods gradually extended. As noted above, the United Kingdom confers broadly unfettered immigration detention powers upon the executive through primary legislation.[132] These powers have been regulated in practice by general administrative policy adopted by the immigration authorities. The legal framework has remained largely untouched since 1971.[133] There has generally been a right to seek bail from immigration judges.[134] Despite the long-standing existence of powers to detain aliens and (since 1962) Commonwealth citizens, detention was the exception until the 1980s. The statistics from after the 1971 Act came into force, for example, record that only ninety-five persons were detained in 1973, 138 in 1974, 188 in 1975, rising to 1,304 in 1980.[135] The figures were stable thereafter until the mid-1980s when detentions began to rise again as new asylum-seeking groups were held on arrival. In 1987 there were 2,166 detentions and by 1995 the total reached 10,240.

As detention became normalized as a tool, its duration sometimes increased, particularly due to difficulties in securing travel documents. Parliament had never contemplated this scenario. Under the Immigration Act 1971 detention powers are discretionary; permitting, not requiring,

---

132 See Immigration Act 1971.

133 But see Crime, Anti-Terrorism and Security Act 2001, which introduced indefinite detention in national security cases and s. 54 Nationality, Immigration and Asylum Act 2002, which extended bail rights.

134 See Sch. 2 to the 1971 Act, which lays down the rules for the grant of bail by adjudicators (now immigration judges). Certain gaps in this right to apply for bail were filled in the 2002 Act.

135 See Home Office, *Control of Immigration Statistics and Asylum Statistics* and the discussion in M. Malmberg, 'Control and Deterrence: Discourses of Detention of Asylum-seekers' University of Sussex Working Paper no. 20, 2004. The law reports from the period illustrate the increasing length of detention experienced by immigrants during this period. In *Hussain*, detention had lasted some six months by the time the habeas application took place. In *Mangoo Khan*, the Court of Appeal again heard a habeas corpus application from a detainee who had been held for over six months.

detention for an apparently indefinite period pending admission, removal or deportation.[136] In practice, detention eventually came to be administered by executive guidelines.[137] Certain criteria such as use of clandestine entry, deception or false documents, were said to indicate a substantial risk of absconding.[138] Where a person was being deported due to criminal offences, detention was also used as a public security measure. What happened when deportation efforts stalled?

In the first major case to consider indefinite detention due to administrative obstacles, *R v. Governor of Durham Prison ex parte Hardial Singh*,[139] the High Court adopted a very similar approach to that in the *Zadvydas* decision, with Lord Woolf holding that:

> As the power is given in order to enable the machinery of deportation to be carried out, I regard the power of detention as being impliedly limited to a period which is reasonably necessary for that purpose. The period which is reasonable will depend upon the circumstances of the particular case.[140]

This approach was followed in the important decision regarding the long-term detention of Vietnamese asylum seekers held in Hong Kong

136 'a person . . . may be detained . . . pending a decision to give or refuse him leave to enter' (para. 16(1), Sch. 2); 'a person may be detained . . . pending the giving of directions and pending his removal in pursuance of any directions given' (para. 16(2), Sch. 2); and 'Where a deportation order is in force against any person, he may be detained . . . pending his removal or departure' (para. 2(3), Sch. 3).

137 See the guidelines from the Home Office contained in *Immigration Service Instructions to Staff on Detention* dated 31 Dec. 1991 and 20 Sept. 1994. The latest instructions are contained in the *Operation Enforcement Manual*, 21 Dec. 2000. These guidelines state that, in most cases, detention should be a last resort reserved to effect removal or prevent absconding or offending. On the question of bail see *Guidance Notes for Adjudicators from the Chief Adjudicator* (rev. January 2002) (Immigration Appellate Authority).

138 The exercise of this discretion has not been subject to large-scale study, but one important survey found that there was great unpredictability in decision-making despite the guidelines. Although preventing absconding and securing removal were the main goals of detention, officers sometimes took into account objectives such as deterrence or prevention of abuse not listed in the guidelines. There was also great variation in the evidence used to determine absconding risk. The survey is significant in seeking to delve into the 'black-box' of actual decision-making where so little is actually known. It is a beginning in seeking to force executive officers to articulate reasons for detention decisions hitherto left largely up to institutional culture and individual preference. See L. Weber and L. Gelsthorpe, *Deciding to Detain: How Decisions to Detain Asylum Seekers are Made at Ports of Entry*, Institute of Criminology, University of Cambridge, 2000. See also L. Weber and T. Landman, *Deciding to Detain: the Organizational Context for Decisions to Detain Asylum Seekers at UK Ports*, University of Essex, Human Rights Centre, 2002.

139 [1984] WLR 704.   140 At 706.

detention camps by the British governor: *Tan Te Lam* v. *Superintendent of Tai A Chau Detention Centre*.[141] These cases all concerned persons who had arrived by boat and been immediately detained pending expulsion after their asylum cases had been refused.

The Privy Council explained the underlying principle of statutory interpretation as follows:

> the courts should construe strictly any statutory provision purporting to allow the deprivation of individual liberty by administrative detention and should be slow to hold that statutory provisions authorise administrative detention for unreasonable periods or in unreasonable circumstances.[142]

The application of this principle led the court to interpret 'immigration' detention in a narrow manner in order to avoid it becoming punitive or arbitrary.[143] First, the power could only be exercised during the period necessary to effect removal. Second, as soon as it became clear that removal was impossible within a reasonable time, detention must cease. Third, the detaining body must take all reasonable steps to ensure removal within a reasonable time. Finally, drawing on the *Khawaja* idea, the courts themselves, not the government, must decide if these tests were met in individual cases. Whilst Parliament could take this power away, as Lord Browne-Wilkinson put it, 'Where human liberty is at stake, very clear words would be required to produce this result.'[144]

We can see in these cases that the *Khawaja* principle was extended to create a general equal right to liberty for all persons within the jurisdiction of the courts. This was as true for those seeking admission as those being

---

141 [1997] AC 97.   142 At 266a.

143 It is important to note that the legislation in question specifically addressed the reasonableness of the period of detention. Pt. IIIA Immigration Ordinance of Hong Kong stated in s. 13D(1) that a Vietnamese person without a visa '... may ... be detained ... pending his removal from Hong Kong'; s. 13D(1A) then stated: 'The detention of a person under this section shall not be unlawful by reason of the period of detention if that period is reasonable having regard to all the circumstances affecting that person's detention, including – (a) ... (i) the number of persons being detained pending decisions ... (ii) the manpower and financial resources allocated to carry out the work involved in making all such decisions; (b) ... (i) the extent to which it is possible to make arrangements to effect his removal; and (ii) whether or not the person has declined arrangements made or proposed for his removal.'

144 At 268a–b. The *Hardial Singh* principles have, however, caused some difficulty for the immigration authorities in maintaining detention where no state will accept the detainee or where they cannot be removed without breaching human rights obligations. The Hong Kong authorities addressed the problem in Art. 13D(1A) by introducing a range of such factors for courts to assess in determining whether the period of detention was 'reasonable'.

deported after entry. Immigration status did not take away the courts' duty to protect the liberty interest of detainees in habeas corpus.[145] This imposed a duty to read statutory powers as far as possible in a manner compatible with such fundamental rights.[146] Parliament had not specifically contemplated indefinite detention and so there was room for a creative interpretation by the courts. This depended upon a *prior commitment to individual liberty as an overriding interest* capable of ousting immigration control concerns. There was no attempt to disguise detention as temporary harbourage or safekeeping ancillary to expulsion. The UK courts had showed unequivocally that they were prepared to order that detainees without status be set at large as a matter of *constitutional right*. Habeas corpus had rediscovered itself.

The growth of detention: removals, arrivals and crises

Despite this important breakthrough, under government pressure, detention rapidly assumed more prominence in UK immigration practice. The new Labour government of 1997 had not been faced with any immediate sense of crisis. The politically critical number of asylum seekers arriving in Britain had actually fallen. Whilst the absolute numbers and unsuccessful claims were viewed as too high, new policymakers saw the solution in faster processing of claims.[147] Detention was of marginal importance; 'regrettable' although 'necessary to ensure the integrity of our immigration system'.[148] Child detention was said to be particularly regrettable. There was concern that some detainees were responsible for incarceration by using 'every conceivable avenue' to resist removal.

Nevertheless, the cost of detention and its potential for harm led the government in 1999 to pass law to provide routine bail hearings.[149] This

---

145 Regarding the presumption favouring liberty, Lord Browne-Wilkinson (at 268b) said: 'Such an approach is equally applicable to everyone within the jurisdiction of the court, whether or not he is a citizen of the country' (see [1983] 1 All ER 765 at 782, per Lord Scarman).

146 This has been called the 'principle of legality' in recent cases. See *R v. Secretary of State for the Home Department ex parte Pierson* [1998] AC 539; *R v. Secretary of State for the Home Department ex parte Simms and Another* [1999] 3 WLR 328.

147 'Fairer, Faster and Firmer – A Modern Approach to Immigration and Asylum', Home Office, Cm. 4018, July 1998, paras 1.14 and 8.7.

148 *Ibid.*, para. 12.3.

149 Part III Immigration and Asylum Act 1999. This can be seen as part of the first-term liberal package of human rights measures which included the Human Rights Act itself in 1998.

would have entailed two automatic hearings on the eighth day after executive detention and then again after thirty-six days. The Act also created, for the first time, a statutory test for denial of bail. This required there to be substantial grounds for believing a person would abscond, commit imprisonable offences or be a danger to public order.[150] The position of immigration detainees would have moved much closer to that of criminal suspects in being governed by clear rules and judicial processes.

These provisions were never brought into operation and eventually repealed.[151] By 2000, government policy went into reverse as asylum numbers rose again to over 80,000 and political pressure increased. Detention became a key aspect of asylum policy as part of a new model of speedy decision-making in closed centres. Whilst retaining the old policy which reserved detention for removal at the end of cases, the new policy required detention of new asylum seekers if their cases could be decided quickly.[152] The criteria used to select cases were opaque. In June 2001 targets were set to remove 2,500 failed asylum seekers per month. However, delays in producing travel documents continued to hinder actual removal.

By 2002, detention was said to have 'a key role to play in the removal of failed asylum seekers and other immigration offenders'.[153] Detention centres were renamed 'removal centres' to reflect their aim. The government was reacting to persistent pressure over perceptions that there was a loss of control over borders. The Home Secretary felt it necessary to counter 'the claim that people coming through the Channel Tunnel, or crossing in container lorries, constitutes an invasion'.[154] The government sought to pressure other European Union (EU) countries to take action to prevent illegal migrants reaching the United Kingdom at all. In this context routine bail hearings were 'inconsistent with the need to ensure that we can streamline the removals process in particular and immigration and asylum processes more generally'.[155] New dedicated immigration facilities were built with a target of 4,000 places. The aim was to ensure that 'asylum seekers are both supported and tracked through the system in a process of induction, accommodation and reporting and fast-track removal or integration'.[156]

The government began to produce snapshot detention statistics for asylum seekers. At the end of 2001, there were 1,410 asylum detainees of

---

150 Section 46(2).   151 Section 68(6), Nationality, Immigration and Asylum Act 2002.
152 See the Oakington Centre policy of March 2000.
153 *Secure Borders, Safe Haven*, Home Office (2002) Cm. 5387, 66.
154 *Ibid.*, foreword.   155 *Ibid.*, 69.   156 *Ibid.*, 14.

whom 37% had been held for less than a month, 17% for 1–2 months, 17% for 2–4 months and 28% for 4 or more months. The new detention policy was broadly approved of by a parliamentary committee in 2003, save for concerns about the increasing length of detention. It suggested that automatic bail hearings might be appropriate after three months and twelve months in detention.[157] After twelve months, there should be a presumption in favour of release unless there were compelling reasons as to why detention was in the public interest.[158] The recommendations on these issues were not implemented.

The government's move away from individual to group detention was an important philosophical step. The policy of mandatory detention for seven days upon arrival of certain categories of asylum seekers was upheld by the House of Lords in *Secretary of State for the Home Department ex parte Saadi and Others*.[159] The detainee had been specifically found not to be an absconding risk, but the court said that such a risk was not a precondition to the power to detain. This was nevertheless a searching decision that focused upon the danger of detention becoming an arbitrary punishment. To avoid constituting a penalty its use must be restricted to that necessary to process an application to enter or remain.[160] But this was not open-ended, for '[t]he period of detention in order to arrive at a decision must however be reasonable in all the circumstances'.[161] Thus the concept of 'punishment' was an objective one, based on the duration and nature of detention, not the intention of the government. On the facts, the court found that, in the relatively relaxed conditions of the holding centre, seven days was acceptable. The case thus both served as a guide and a warning to the government in relation to future policies of detention on arrival.

A further 2005 policy review said that 80 per cent of asylum claims were being dealt with in two months. Removals had been increasing

---

157 *Asylum Removals*, Fourth Report of Session 2002–3, House of Commons, Home Affairs Committee, HC 654, 84.

158 *Ibid.*, 90.   159 See n. 40 above.

160 Paragraph 16(1), Sch. 2, Immigration Act 1971.

161 Lord Slynn of Hadley at para. 22. His Lordship rejected the argument that any period of detention was unlawful unless it was necessary to prevent absconding, but said: 'This does not mean that the Secretary of State can detain without any limits so long as no examination has taken place or decision been arrived at. The Secretary of State must not act in an arbitrary manner. The immigration officer must act reasonably in fixing the time for examination and for arriving at a decision in the light of the objective of promoting speedy decision-making' (para. 25).

towards a 'tipping point' where more would be removed than made unsuccessful claims.[162] The government went further through the creation of a detained fast-track system for asylum claims. Asylum decisions were taken after three days and appeals after nine. The whole process was concluded within three weeks.[163] However, effecting expulsion remained difficult: 83 per cent of detainees were without documents and most receiving countries required passports.[164] The government said it would make 'redocumentation and return a key feature of our bilateral relations with countries of immigration concern'.[165] It is clear, nevertheless, that long-term detention has not diminished. In 2008 there was a further expansion in the detention estate announced to finally bring detention places up to 3,000. A snapshot taken in 2009 showed that of the 2,885 persons in detention at the time of reporting, 225 had been held for over one year, 295 between six months to a year, with 250 between four to six months. Of 6,975 leaving detention in the quarter, 3,890 were released into the community, not deported.

Administrative overload and damages for unlawful imprisonment in the UK

Increasing detention has meant good administration is increasingly difficult. There has not always been compliance with published guidelines, which of themselves are open to wide interpretation. In responding to particular crises there have also been unofficial policies used to support detention which conflict with those published.[166] This has led to many

---

162 'Controlling our Borders: Making Migration Work for Britain. Five-year strategy for asylum and immigration', Home Office, February 2005. This was part of the New Asylum Model.

163 The scheme was challenged because it was arguably very difficult for some detainees to prepare their asylum cases in the time available. The Court of Appeal upheld the scheme in general, but required the government to more clearly specify what kinds of cases would merit removal from the fast track to avoid unfairness: *R (RLC)* v. *SSHD* [2004] EWCA 1481.

164 'Fair, Effective, Transparent and Trusted: Rebuilding Confidence in Our Immigration System', Home Office, July 2006.

165 12.

166 For an example of a secret policy that was only obtained by accident, see *Nadarajah and Amirthanathan* v. *SSHD* [2003] EWCA Civ 1768. The Court of Appeal ruled that detention pursuant to an unpublished policy of maintaining detention until court proceedings had been issued (rather than upon notification that they would be commenced) was unlawful.

claims for damages for breach of executive detention policy.[167] The courts have held, even where there is a statutory power to detain, failure to follow executive policy may amount to unlawful imprisonment. The Court of Appeal in *ID and others* v. *Home Office*[168] affirmed that the principle of freedom from arbitrary detention applied to all persons and rejected the government's argument that persons who had no permission to enter or remain were in a different position. There was no doctrine of immunity from suit for immigration officials who made bona fide mistakes. This is a significant affirmation of the broader principle that was established in *Khawaja*.

The Court accepted that, whilst unauthorized immigrants were liable to detention, 'English law will remain jealous of their right to liberty and will scrutinise with care the legality of any executive act that deprives them of that liberty.'[169] Although they had to secure entry in order to be free from the discretion to detain for examination, nevertheless:

> so long as detention, which may cause significant suffering, can be directed by executive decision and an order of a court (or court-like body) is not required, the language and the philosophy of human rights law, and the common law's emphatic reassertion in recent years of the importance of constitutional rights, drive inexorably, in my judgment, to the conclusion I have reached.[170]

This stands as a powerful statement of foreigners' constitutional right to liberty, but also as a lament to the relatively unchecked growth of administrative detention that had occurred in Britain in any event.

The foreign prisoners emergency

In 2006, the United Kingdom experienced a further political crisis when it was revealed that there were few proper arrangements to re-detain and deport foreign criminals post-sentence. As a result, many were simply released from prison back into the community. Foreigners were an increasing percentage of the prison population and so the numbers were considerable.[171] The Home Office, under intense pressure, pushed through the UK's first mandatory deportation laws for those sentenced

---

167 See Ch. 38 *Operational Enforcement Manual*, Borders and Immigration Agency, Home Office, which sets out the guidelines for the executive.

168 [2005] EWCA Civ 38.   169 Paragraph 129, per Brooke L.J.   170 *Ibid.*

171 There was a total of 10,097, or 14%, in June 2007 (up by 150% over a decade). The vast majority were held on drug offences, particularly trafficking. Around 1,000 prisoners

to more than one year or convicted of a wide range of crimes.[172] Targets were set for removal of thousands each year from the backlog.

Pending deportation detainees were officially subject to the existing discretionary detention policy, which was not changed by Parliament. However, there was an undisclosed policy change towards a presumption in favour of detention for potential deportees.[173] The new policy was not officially revealed until some two years after it came into effect.[174] Although secret, this is as close as the United Kingdom has ever got to mandatory indefinite detention for a whole group of immigrants. Although likely to attract some public support, the government may have feared that openly introducing something close to mandatory detention would have required parliamentary approval (to amend the discretionary powers set up in 1971). Failure to reveal the policy was certainly contrary to orthodox ideas of the rule of law.

The secrecy surrounding the policy is indicative of the sense of political crisis that engulfed the government. A reasoned enquiry would likely have concluded that mandatory detention, however minor the offence and however low the risk of re-offending, was unwarranted. In the prevailing public climate, however, the UK courts have in any event continued to allow very lengthy detention in cases of convicted criminals whose deportation is delayed. The *Hardial Singh* 'reasonable period' has thus been taken to vary greatly with the type of case. For pure absconding risk cases, with no criminal element, courts have held that sixteen months was too long.[175] This was so, even where the detainee had refused to cooperate with repatriation. On the other hand, it was held that the

---

committing serious offences were not deported between 1999 and 2006. Sources: Home Office and Prison Service.

172 UK Borders Act 2007, s. 32.   173 Section 36.

174 *R (on application) WL (Congo) and KM (Jamaica) and Secretary of State for the Home Department* [2010] EWCA Civ 111. The Court found that the policy deviated from the official published policy and therefore was a breach of legitimate expectation of detainees to be considered under the published policy. Their damages claims failed due to a failure to show they would have been released under the old policy.

175 *R (I)* v. *Secretary of State for the Home Department* [2002] EWCA Civ 888. Dyson L.J. said of the issue of non-cooperation:

> Of course, if the appellant were to leave voluntarily, he would cease to be detained. But in my judgment, the mere fact (without more) that a detained person refuses the offer of voluntary repatriation cannot make reasonable a period of detention which would otherwise be unreasonable. If Mr Robb were right, the refusal of an offer of voluntary repatriation would justify as reasonable any period of detention, no matter however long, provided that the Secretary of State was doing his best to effect the deportation' (para. 51).

government could lawfully detain for thirty-eight months in the case of a somewhat uncooperative convicted detainee.[176] Another man involved in more serious offending, multiple appeals and initial failure to cooperate remained in detention after four years.[177] The latest cases appear to reflect fear of a political backlash as they move close to permitting detention forever where detainees do not provide adequate cooperation. This is so even where the possibility of readmission is speculative.

In conclusion, we can see that detention has expanded greatly over the past thirty years in the United Kingdom. The unwritten constitution's presumption of liberty has been an important residual safeguard, effective because the legislature has never sought to impose mandatory detention. Still, the trend has been to expand the range of groups detained, pursuant to shifts in political priorities, even though the default policy is for individualized decisions. The absence of automatic bail hearings or judicial authorization has allowed detention to grow and this has entailed much that is potentially unlawful, arbitrary or very lengthy.

176 *MH (Somaliland)* [2010] EWCA 1112. The offences were accepted not to be of the most serious sort, but the risk of their repetition was serious. He had not fully cooperated, although had given some information at different times. It was unclear if fuller information would have resulted in removal. Dyson L.J. confirmed that there need be no actual time period specified by the government for execution of deportation:

> Of course, if a finite time can be identified, it is likely to have an important effect on the balancing exercise: a soundly based expectation that removal can be effected within, say, two weeks will weigh heavily in favour of continued detention pending such removal, whereas an expectation that removal will not occur for, say, a further two years will weigh heavily against continued detention. There can, however, be a realistic prospect of removal without it being possible to specify or predict the date by which, or period within which, removal can reasonably be expected to occur and without any certainty that removal will occur at all. Again, the extent of certainty or uncertainty as to whether and when removal can be effected will affect the balancing exercise. There must be a *sufficient* prospect of removal to warrant continued detention when account is taken of all other relevant factors' (para. 65).

177 *R (on application) WL (Congo) and KM (Jamaica) and Secretary of State for the Home Department.* The offences included grievous bodily harm.

> In our judgment, the fact that a Foreign National Prisoner (FNP) is refusing to return voluntarily, or is refusing to cooperate in his return (for example, by refusing to apply for an emergency travel document . . .) is relevant to the assessment of the legality of his continued detention . . . So is the fact that the period of his detention has been increased, and his deportation postponed, by his pursuit of appeals and judicial review proceedings seeking to challenge his deportation order or his application for asylum or leave to remain, particularly if his applications and appeals are obviously unmeritorious. In our judgment, as a matter of principle, a FNP cannot complain of the prolongation of his detention if it is caused by his own conduct (para. 102).

Australia and the aliens power unlimited: taking detention to its logical conclusion?

The Australian policy of mandatory indefinite detention developed since 1989 has been emblematic of many of the trends that we have described so far. The elusive boundary between the aliens power and war powers was almost destroyed as politicians, electors and, ultimately, the courts came to understand 'unauthorized' aliens as akin to a security threat, constituting practically an invasion. A political determination to make border controls 'credible' and to maintain the 'integrity' of the migration system led inexorably to practices that would have been unthinkable at the outset. Thus, whilst initially limited to small numbers of highly visible 'boat arrivals', the policy was extended to all unauthorized persons. This routinely led to non-dangerous asylum seekers, including families and children, being held in harsh prison conditions for years. The courts' interpretation of the Australian Constitution gave an enormous reach to the aliens power sufficient to support alien internment in peacetime. Given her remote island situation and effective visa restrictions, only relatively small numbers of persons were able to access Australian territory by boat or otherwise. Ironically it was thus the very small size of the numbers involved that meant securing the 'visible' border was attainable. Sufficient detention facilities and the necessary political will were the only constraints.

The creation of mandatory detention: the boat arrivals crisis and the non-punitive question

After the abolition of its historical 'White Australia' policy in the 1960s, its relative isolation meant that Australia did not experience the kinds of growing political crises seen in Europe and the United States around asylum and illegal migration. The one persistent exception has related to boat arrivals from Asia. Initially, in the period 1976–81 these had consisted of a few thousand Vietnamese refugees who were fleeing Communism.[178] They were largely welcomed and only held briefly before being resettled. In the late 1980s, thousands of Cambodian refugees were held in camps across South-East Asia. Around this time Australia helped to coordinate a

---

178 See J. Phillips and H. Spinks, 'Boat Arrivals in Australia since 1976', *Parliament of Australia*, 26 May 2010.

regional agreement to resettle them, committing itself to taking considerable numbers from camps in the region.[179] Government policy was that this was the correct channel through which refugees should arrive and called into question the acceptability of 'secondary movements' which were not part of resettlement.

Nevertheless, in late 1989 a boat arrived in Australian waters carrying twenty-six Cambodians. The following years saw a handful of boats each year bringing around 200 refugees annually. The peak year in 1994 saw 900 'boat people' arrive. These new arrivals generated large-scale public and political concern. It was said that professional smugglers were helping refugees 'jump the queue' for settlement and that border security was being compromised.[180] The applicants were kept in unfenced camps for over two years before their claims were refused, but the courts ordered a review of these decisions. It also became clear that Australian law had not been designed for such detention. They had been held pursuant to a provision relating to stowaways and persons seeking to enter illegally (created as an alternative to holding on board ship).[181] The power was only exercisable until the boat bringing the immigrants had left Australia.[182] The government had actually burnt their boats after arrival. Their detention had therefore been illegal for some time.

The realization that the government would have to release the detainees induced a surprisingly large political crisis. Two days before their habeas corpus hearing in May 1992, Parliament retrospectively authorized mandatory detention of those who had arrived between 1989 and 1992 by boat without a visa ('designated persons').[183] A time limit of nine months was, however, placed on their further detention.[184] The Act stated it had been passed 'because Parliament considers that it is in the national interest that each non-citizen who is a designated person should be kept in immigration detention until he or she: (a) leaves Australia; or (b) is given a visa'.[185] This was a very remarkable event because it was the first time in history any statute had mandated a two-outcome solution – either

---

179 A. Millbank, 'The Detention of Boat People', *Parliament of Australia*, 27 February 2001.
180 See K. Betts, 'Boat People and Public Opinion in Australia' (2001) 9 *People and Place* 4.
181 Section 27(1) Migration Act 1958.   182 Section 88, *ibid.*
183 Defined as 'designated persons' in s. 177. The measure was extended to apply to those arriving between 1989 and 1994.
184 Section 182.
185 Division 6, Reason for division. For further explanation of Parliament's rationale see *Asylum, Border Control and Detention*, Report by the Joint Standing Committee on Migration (Parliament of the Commonwealth of Australia, February 1994).

expulsion or authorization – thereby ousting the option of parole. The Act did not explore why the national interest was threatened by paroling a few hundred Cambodian asylum seekers, many of whom were ultimately given refugee status. Nevertheless, the die was cast.

In 1992 the High Court of Australia largely upheld the constitutionality of the Act's mandatory detention power.[186] The Australian Constitution has no higher bill of rights through which statutes may be annulled. For this reason the case was argued by reference to the constitution's separation of powers. It was argued that the Act gave a judicial power, namely that of penal detention, to the executive branch.[187] The Court agreed that the power of involuntary detention was, subject to minor exceptions, part of the judicial power of criminal punishment entrusted exclusively to the courts.[188] The effect of aliens' vulnerability to expulsion was, however, 'significantly to diminish the protection which . . . the Constitution provides, in the case of a citizen, against imprisonment otherwise than pursuant to judicial process'.[189]

The majority relied upon the Commonwealth cases, holding that there was a power to exclude friendly aliens.[190] They also referred to Cold War-era Australian case-law that confirmed that the aliens power included a power to detain for the purpose of deportation.[191] The extended nature of the Cambodian detentions in peacetime was, however, well beyond anything these earlier cases had considered. The High Court said, therefore, that immigration detention could only be an incident of the aliens power if it was '*reasonably capable of being seen as necessary* for the purposes of

---

186 *Chu Kheng Lim and others v. Minister for Immigration, Local Government and Ethnic Affairs and another* [1992] 176 CLR 1 FC 92/051. The Court did, however, rule that the exclusion of judicial review of the limited question of whether a detainee was a 'designated person' was a breach of the constitution.

187 Chapter III of the constitution vests judicial power exclusively in the courts designated therein.

188 Per Brennan, Deane and Dawson J.J. at paras. 22–5, citing Blackstone: 'The confinement of the person . . . is an imprisonment . . . To make imprisonment lawful, it must either be by process from the courts of judicature, or by warrant from some legal officer having authority to commit to prison; which warrant must be in writing, under the hand and seal of the magistrate, and express the causes of the commitment, in order to be examined into (if necessary) upon a habeas corpus' (*Commentaries*, 17th edn (1830), Bk.1, paras 136–7) and Dicey: Every citizen is 'ruled by the law, and the law alone' and 'may with us be punished for a breach of the law, but he can be punished for nothing else' (*Introduction to the Study of the Law of the Constitution*, 10th edn (1959), 202).

189 Per Brennan, Deane and Dawson J.J. at para. 26.

190 *AG for Canada v. Cain* [1906] AC 542.

191 *Koon Wing Lau v. Calwell* [1948] 80 CLR 533, per Webb J. at 64.

deportation or necessary to enable an application for an entry permit to be made and considered'.[192] The Court concluded that the nine-month time limit, the state's duty to act with due diligence in processing their case and the detainees' power to end their detention by requesting removal pointed to these powers being incidental to the aliens power and not punitive.[193] It was clear, however, that the Court adopted an objective test and ignored the legislative purpose. This suggested that at a certain point detention would become a penalty even if designed to control aliens' entry.[194]

The new boat arrivals and the crisis of indefinite detention

Parliament also decided in 1992 to extend mandatory detention from 1994 to cover all non-citizens without a valid visa[195] and to remove the time limits.[196] This included overstayers and others not holding valid visas.[197] Judicial review of detention was excluded by the Act.[198] A parliamentary committee examining the new policy supported it largely by reference to security concerns. It said that '[i]n a world of increasing movement across international borders, Australia must not compromise

---

192 Per Brennan, Deane and Dawson J.J. at para. 32.

193 *Ibid.*, para. 34. See also per McHugh J. at para. 42, who observes that a detainee 'having regard to his or her claim for refugee status, might regard the choice between detention and leaving the country as not a real choice. But for the purposes of the doctrine of the separation of powers, the difference between involuntary detention and detention with the concurrence or acquiescence of the "detainee" is vital. A person is not being punished if, after entering Australia without permission, he or she chooses to be detained in custody pending the determination of an application for entry rather than leave the country during the period of determination.'

194 Per Brennan, Deane and Dawson J.J. at para. 34: 'In the context of that power of a designated person to bring his or her detention in custody under Div. 4B to an end at any time, the time limitations imposed by other provisions of the Division suffice, in our view, to preclude a conclusion that the power of detention which are conferred upon the Executive exceed what is reasonably capable of being seen as necessary the for purposes of deportation or for the making and consideration an entry application.'

195 See s. 178 for designated persons and s. 189 for unlawful non-citizens. Both state explicitly that there is no discretion to release such persons until they have been removed, granted a visa or deported. Such persons 'must be kept in immigration detention. A designated person is to be released ... if, and only if, he or she is (a) removed ... (b) granted a visa' (s. 178) or 'must be kept in immigration detention until (a) removed from Australia ... (b) deported ... (c) granted a visa' (s. 189).

196 'A non-citizen in the migration zone who is not a lawful non-citizen' (s. 14).

197 Overstayers who applied for asylum, however, were entitled to a bridging visa whilst their claims were determined, and so were not detained.

198 Section 474 where a list of 'privative clause' decisions which oust judicial review is set out. See also s. 183.

the principle that those who wish to . . . enter and stay in Australia must be authorised to do so'.[199] Detention was said to ensure that 'the community is not exposed to unknown or undetected health or security risks'.[200] The committee rejected a return to the system of parole because of evidence of limited previous absconding.[201] This would encourage other unauthorized persons to come. The minister had power to grant temporary visas to vulnerable detained people. Finally, it was encouraged by the fact that faster processing was limiting detention to six months. It suggested that after six months' detention, the government should consider parole. Overall, a potential deterrent effect on boat arrivals was seen to outweigh any hardship on individuals who lacked authorization.

The initial impact of the policy was limited because boat arrivals fell away soon afterwards and asylum seekers arriving by air had visas and were not subject to the detention policy.[202] Detention periods were less than a month on average.[203] More serious impacts began from 1998 when a new stream of boat arrivals began. These were brought by smugglers via Indonesia from a wide range of countries, particularly Iran, Iraq or Afghanistan. Numbers arriving rose from 200 in 1998 to 3,721 in 1999 and 2,939 in 2000. There were delays in processing applications and appeals. A growing number of detainees were *de facto* or *de jure* stateless and could not be removed. Detention periods increased so that 18 per cent of detainees in 2000 had been held for over a year.[204] Many hundreds were held for several years with little prospect of release.[205] Families with young children were held under strict conditions. There was considerable pressure to relax the policy on humanitarian and human rights grounds in the face of escapes, hunger strikes and self-harm in centres.[206] The numbers involved were tiny when set against the 3 million visitors annually allowed into Australia or the estimated 53,000 unlawful

---

199 Joint Standing Committee on Migration, 'Asylum, Border Control and Detention', Parliament of Australia, February 1994, para. 4.161.
200 *Ibid.*, para. 4.153.
201 The figures showed that fifty-seven boat arrivals had absconded between 1989 and 1993; eighteen had escaped from detention in 1994. The committee also looked at 8,000 post-entry asylum cases and found some absconding.
202 See Phillips and Spinks, 'Boat Arrivals in Australia since 1976', 10.
203 Millbank, 'The Detention of Boat People', 6.   204 *Ibid.*
205 Amnesty International, 'The Impact of Indefinite Detention: the Case to Change Australia's Mandatory Detention Policy', ASA/12/001/2005, London: Amnesty International, 2005, found 150 detainees who had been held for over three years in May 2005.
206 See Working Group on Arbitrary Detention Visit to Australia, E/CN.4/2003/8/Add.2. New York: United Nations, 2002.

immigrants already there.[207] The politics crystallized around the MV *Tampa*, a ship carrying over 400 asylum seekers. The government sent the navy to repel the ship and began a policy of offshore processing. The immediate election of 2001 saw the government successfully argue for continuing with indefinite detention as a deterrent.

The indefinite detention powers were upheld as constitutional by the Full Federal Court.[208] The applicants were children suffering mental illness and said to be at risk of suicide due to prolonged detention. It was argued that, in these circumstances, detention was not reasonably necessary under the aliens power and was therefore punitive. The Court rejected that, saying that the effect of detention on particular detainees 'does not displace the legislative purpose behind s. 196(1), namely to ensure that detainees are available for deportation or removal from Australia when that is required'.[209] A punitive purpose could only be found if it was contained in the legislative framework itself, not in the consequences of operating the legislation for individual detainees. The objective test for punitive detention set out in *Chu Keng Lim* was abandoned. This was a major philosophical step; so long as the government was detaining with an 'intention' to deport, there was no question of punishment arising.

The segregation of aliens as a statutory purpose: the decision in *Al Kateb*

From 2002 all new boat arrivals were taken to detention centres outside Australian territory, the islands of Nauru and Maunus in New Guinea. Detainees here were physically and legally beyond the reach of the courts altogether. Any rule of law was in abeyance. Meanwhile, indefinite detention on the mainland continued. In the case of stateless persons or those whom no country would accept, this lasted for years. The longest was a Kashmiri man held from 1998 to 2005 before being given a temporary visa after his admission to a mental hospital.[210] Such long-term detainees continued to challenge the statute and one federal court judge, influenced by the common law decisions in *Zadvydas* and *Hardial Singh*, said the

207 Millbank, 'The Detention of Boat People'.
208 *NAMU of 2002 and others* v. *Minister for Immigration and Multicultural and Indigenous Affairs*, New South Wales Registry N726 of 2002, judgment of 9 Dec. 2002, Black C.J., Sundberg and Weinberg J.J.
209 Paragraph 17.
210 Peter Qasim had failed to establish any nationality adequately and had apparently applied to eighty countries for admission.

statutory power was impliedly limited so that detention must cease if removal was no longer reasonably likely.[211]

The government appealed and won the important case of *Al Kateb v. Godwin*.[212] The facts concerned a stateless Palestinian who had been refused asylum. He had requested removal, which triggered a duty to expel him, but the government could find nowhere to send him.[213] He had been detained for over three years before being released on conditions. The government appealed that decision. Looking at statutory construction, the requirement to detain until either a visa was issued or the person was removed was clear.[214] It was argued, however, that Parliament had assumed that removal would be possible within a reasonable time. The majority rejected this because the Act only imposed a duty to remove 'as soon as reasonably practicable'[215] and, whilst not foreseeable, it was not impossible that a country might step forward in the future.[216] Parliament had thereby provided for the issue of time. Possibly lengthy foreign negotiations might be needed to secure readmission and 'detention will continue until that co-operation is provided'.[217] The majority therefore relied on the idea that detention might be an important bargaining tool for the government that courts should stay out of.[218] Al Kateb's statelessness was quietly ignored. The whole approach implied into the statutory framework considerations going well beyond the text. The majority adopted what amounted to a common law presumption in favour of detention in the case of unauthorized aliens reminiscent of Scalia J.'s opinion in *Zadvydas*. McHugh J. summed it up in argument, saying 'it does seem almost a contradiction in terms to say that a person who has no right to be in the country has a right to be released into the country'.[219]

---

211 *Al Masri* v. *Minister for Immigration and Multicultural and Indigenous Affairs* [2003] 126 FCR 54.

212 [2004] 219 CLR 562.   213 Section 198.

214 'must be kept in immigration detention until (a) removed from Australia...(b) deported...(c) granted a visa' (s. 189).

215 Section 198 Migration Act 1958, which applied where a detainee had requested removal.

216 [2004] 219 CLR 562 [231], Hayne J. There was some discussion about the likelihood of a Palestinian state being established!

217 *Ibid.*, [218], Hayne J.

218 The minority relied upon Kennedy J.'s dissenting judgment in *Zadvydas*, where he felt that released detainees would mean the courts interfering with sensitive foreign policy discussions.

219 Transcript [60], McHugh J.

This was the direct opposite of the minority approach which continued to extend the presumption of liberty to all *persons* as the British cases had since *Khawaja*. They therefore were able to rely on the principle of legality that '[c]ourts do not impute to the legislature an intention to abrogate or curtail certain human rights or freedoms (of which personal liberty is the most basic) unless such intention is clearly manifested'.[220] The minority held, therefore, that the statute did contain an implied limit where the legislative assumption that removal was possible proved to be wrong.[221] The mere 'hope' of removal in the future could not triumph over the present experience of failure.

On the constitutional questions, the majority viewed the aliens power as almost without limit. As one put it: 'any law that has aliens as its subject is a law with respect to aliens'.[222] Another said that the power to exclude included aliens' 'segregation from the community by detention'.[223] In argument, the majority judges accepted the need for a 'legitimate purpose relevant to alienage' to support such a power but never found a convincing one. They flitted between peacetime ('so that the person will not melt into the community and be irretrievable from it and will get social service benefits and other benefits'[224] or 'so that they do not work and take jobs from Australian citizens'[225] or 'to detain aliens who are mentally ill or who are a danger to the community'[226]) and wartime ('Why cannot the government, independently of the defence power, lock up enemy aliens for the duration of the war under the aliens power?'[227]). In fact, despite the fears expressed in these views, former detainees had no right to work or benefits, and those that were released relied on charity.

The majority conclusion on the aliens power was therefore hedged uneasily between peace and war. From the perspective of peacetime, their release 'would mean that such persons, by their illegal and unwanted entry, could become *de facto Australian citizens*'[228] without authorization by Parliament. This was a most irrational conclusion given Al Kateb's tenuous legal existence on bail. From the perspective of war, 'Parliament

---

220 *Ibid.*, 577 [19], Gleeson C.J.
221 'the Act envisages that the detention will come an end by the grant of a visa or the removal of the alien' *ibid.* 571 [1], (Gleeson C.J.). The Chief Justice was influenced by the fact that detention did not take account of flight risk, danger to the community or personal circumstances, matters which might have supported extended or indefinite detention in some cases.
222 *Ibid.*, 583 [41] McHugh J.   223 *Ibid.*, 645 [247] Hayne J.
224 Transcript [10] Callinan J.   225 *Ibid.*, [31].
226 *Ibid.*, [32] McHugh J.   227 *Ibid.*, [11].   228 [46] McHugh J.

is entitled to *protect the nation* against unwanted entrants by detaining them in custody.'[229] This new, almost limitless, view of the aliens power led inevitably to the majority conclusion that indefinite detention was not punishment because it achieved a purpose within those covered. It did not seek to incarcerate for breach of an offence, but was 'protective'. *Lim* had confirmed that unauthorized aliens could be detained without judicial order in any event.

The majority's view of the scope of the aliens power was unprecedented. It would permit all kinds of discriminatory and arbitrary action against aliens, both lawfully resident and otherwise. Given their broad under-standing of 'protective' detention, it was no surprise they felt that so long as the detention was 'for the purpose of deportation or preventing aliens from entering Australia or the *Australian community* [emphasis added] the justice or wisdom of the course taken by Parliament is not examinable in this or any other domestic court'.[230] This new concept of denying aliens even bare contact with the 'community' carried the implication of a kind of contagion or that they would thereby have 'won' in their war to gain a foothold in Australia.

The minority views on the constitutional issue were more diverse. They all took as their starting point the common law's concern with liberty which informed the constitution. For Gummow J., the aliens power to detain was not 'at large' but was limited to that connected with an 'alien's entry, investigation, admission or deportation'.[231] Segregation from the community was not one of these purposes. Kirby J. maintained the *Lim* view that all detention was essentially punitive and required judi-cial authorization after a 'comparatively short time'.[232] They would have struck down a statute authorizing alien segregation as a breach of the constitution.

The decision in *Al Kateb* is an exceptional one, going against the grain of the common law case-law implying time limits. It is true that the legisla-tion had gone further in explicitly requiring detention until admission or removal. However, there was still room for interpretation. Parliament had not considered the position of non-removable stateless persons. Indeed, it had previously recognized that speedy processing was essential to reduce detention times and had devoted efforts towards this. The majority opin-ions suggest a political state of crisis and suspicion towards aliens more

---

229 [92] McHugh J.   230 *Ibid.*   231 609 [126] Gummow J.
232 617 [148] Kirby J.

appropriate to the state of war than that befitting a handful of non-dangerous stateless people wishing to be set free in a wealthy nation of 20 million. Their persistent search for 'harms' that release might cause, however symbolic, speculative or trivial, to justify ongoing detention, was striking.

Absent the kind of real risks supporting wartime internment, they had to search further for a new jurisprudential paradigm. They found it in the thoroughly modern idea that only 'authorized' persons had a right to liberty. The power of 'exclusion' included a power of *segregation.* Yet segregation itself imposed 'burdens' on Australia too and gave detainees the 'benefit' of 'life' in remote Australian detention centres. It was certainly far more costly in financial terms than supervised release. It is logically difficult to see why there was any obligation to keep them alive, as their lives were essentially worthless to Australia. Indeed not keeping them alive would promote deterrence.[233] In the end, the majority position only makes political sense if Al Kateb is seen as an enemy engaged in a 'war' with Australian border controls. To release him would mean the court legitimating his 'victory'.

While extreme in its effects, the majority position simply extends much of the modern politics on unauthorized migration and uses it to 'solve' the habeas corpus problem. The nature and degree of threat (whether it be criminal, economic, social or cultural), if any, posed by unauthorized aliens is a matter for the political branch. It is not the courts' role to investigate that assessment nor the means used to tackle it. Both war and aliens powers merge in the face of a *threat,* the nature of which the government need not define, to authorize *measures* that the government need not justify other than by reference to the political and cultural construction of unauthorized migration itself. The circularity of a necessity to detain derived from a threat posed by unauthorized migration was complete.

France: immigration detention under police powers not aliens powers

In France, immigration detention has been conceived in very different terms jurisprudentially and politically. Whilst more detention centres

---

233 As it turned out the government, having established its point of principle, did not re-detain Al Kateb and the others. He was eventually granted full residence status in Australia some seven years after arrival. The powers were retained and, although given further discretionary elements, have still not been repealed in their essence.

have been built recently, the constitutional jurisprudence has never conceived of detention as an adjunct to a broad 'aliens power'. Similarly, the sovereign right to control borders has not formed part of legal reasoning to support detention. Instead, immigration enforcement has been dealt with as a policing matter. Official powers of detention arrived very late in the law and, even then, have remained heavily circumscribed by comparison with other countries.[234] There are a number of historical, political and legal explanations. The historical legacy of previous extra-legal French internment camps left a permanent stain around government abuse of detention powers in general. Politically there have been relatively strong and broad-based immigrant groups who campaign to constrain detention. More recently, however, French governments have followed other countries in expanding detention facilities and powers to meet expulsion targets. The constitutional limits on detention stemming from a constitutional right to liberty to all foreigners regardless of status remain crucial, therefore.

The detention of foreigners: the political scandal of extra-legality

In the absence of specific detention powers, in the past French government controls over foreigners took more improvised forms. Internment camps had developed even before the Vichy era. Thousands of republican Spanish refugees were held in the 1930s.[235] During the war, a large number of camps for Jews and others were established in cooperation with the Nazis.[236] Even during the Algerian War in the 1950s internment was used again.[237] These were populated with persons deemed 'undesirable' who were often foreigners.[238] The legal basis for the camps was doubtful. It was sometimes assumed that a power derived from a vaguely worded section of the Napoleonic 1810 penal code in Article 120 generally allowing detention pursuant to provisional government orders.[239] In fact, in 1933,

---

234 P. Montfort, *La Contentieux de la Retention Administrative des Etrangers en Instance d'eloignment*, Paris: L'Harmattan, 2003.
235 M. Bernadot, *Camps d'etrangers*, Paris: Terra, 2008.
236 M. Bernadot, 'Des Camps en France (1944–1963)' 58 *Plein Droit* Dec. 2003.
237 M. Bernadot, 'Etre interne au Larzac: la politique d'assignation a residence: la guerre d'Algerie, 1958–1962' (2005) *Politix* 1, 39–61.
238 R. Weisberg, *Vichy Law and the Holocaust in France*, Amsterdam: Harwood Academic Publishers, 1996.
239 The original penal code of 1810 was still in force until 1981. This prohibited detention by the police unless, inter alia, there was a 'provisional order of the government'.

a preamble to an immigration law had restricted its use to foreigners.[240] The police detained foreigners given expulsion orders under this penal power.

After World War Two, France took no real measures against illegal immigrants, who were regularized readily.[241] It was only when anti-immigrant sentiment grew in the recessionary 1970s that deportations were commenced. A centre at Arenc in Marseilles was used to detain expelled or excluded migrants, who were held without time limits in poor conditions. When it was discovered, a long campaign by human rights lawyers and immigrant groups began to close what was called a 'secret concentration camp'. In 1975 the French lawyers association took a test case involving a Moroccan detainee. The only law governing immigration, a 1945 *Ordonnance*, contained no express powers of detention. In the face of the legal challenge, the government fell back again on the 1810 penal code and tried to regularize detention by issuing a circular to authorize it. The highest administrative court, the Conseil D'Etat, held that the circular was unlawful.[242] Nevertheless, the general power to detain foreigners under the police powers of Article 120 without judicial approval or time limit was upheld.

After the camp closed, there was strong pressure to create a humane non-penal system on a clear legal basis. The new socialist government in 1980 presented a Bill which delimited detention powers and abolished Article 120. The parliamentary debates of the time revealed great resistance from all quarters to the very idea of detention. In the National Assembly concern was expressed about the lack of judicial control: 'this text distorts several juridical principles, and in particular the essential principle of our law that requires that judicial authority be the guardian of individual liberty'.[243] The idea of internment was also criticized: 'the most serious aspect of this bill is the development of administrative internment in time of peace, which is without historical precedent in our country'.[244] More honestly, with the Algerian War firmly in mind, the Defence Minister, Alain Richard, said: 'Regarding the traditions of our country and the

---

240 Law of 7 February 1933, which restricted the application of Art. 120 to foreigners facing expulsion.
241 For a good summary of the history see C. Richard and N. Fischer, 'A Legal Disgrace? The Retention of Deported Migrants in Contemporary France', (2010) 47(4) *Social Science Information* 581–603.
242 C.E. Ass. 7 July 1978, Syndicats des Avocats de France and Essaka, A.J. 1978.28.
243 National Assembly Debates 29 May 1979, OJ 30 May 1979, p. 4,234 per Bernard Stasi.
244 *Ibid.*, per François Massot.

precedents still present in certain memories of administrative internment and of which none of us can be proud, we are introducing a dangerous instrument in the judicial arsenal.'[245] In the Senate the Bill was amended extensively with cross-party support to ensure that judicial authority for detention was obtained, but in the National Assembly these safeguards were removed again.

Constitutionalizing the liberty of unauthorized foreigners

In reviewing the Bill, the Constitutional Council[246] made the striking decision to extend full constitutional safeguards to the liberty of foreigners.[247] Thus Article 66 of the constitution's requirement that no one be arbitrarily detained applied to both those seeking entry and being expelled.[248] In order to avoid being considered arbitrary, those not immediately expelled could 'if necessary, be maintained in places *not run by the penal authorities*, during the *period strictly necessary* until their departure'.[249] If detention was not necessary to execute the immigration order, however, it would assume the character of a penalty and an arbitrary deprivation of liberty. For those denied pending exclusion, the Bill complied with this standard and contained other guarantees for those held in 'retention' (the very word was developed to set it apart from penal detention): approval by a court within twenty-four hours, access to counsel, doctors and interpreters. This meant that such retention did 'not have the character of arbitrary internment'.

By contrast, for those held in-country pending expulsion the Bill did not require judicial authority until seven days had elapsed. The failure to require prompt judicial approval was fatal to the Bill: 'individual liberty cannot be safeguarded unless the judge intervenes in the shortest delay possible'. The delay proposed was excessive and contrary to the constitution. The law was amended to require judicial approval within twenty-four hours in all cases and allowed a judicially approved extension of

245 *Ibid.*, p. 4,263.
246 The Conseil Constitutionnel is a unique body which is not officially a court but which acts very much like one. Whilst it is composed of political figures, they are given independence to act according to principles of constitutional and internal law. For a discussion see J. Bell, *French Constitutional Law*, Oxford: Clarendon Press, 1992, Ch. 1.
247 Decision no. 79–109 DC of 9 January 1980.
248 'No one shall be arbitrarily detained. The Judicial Authority, guardian of the freedom of the individual, shall ensure compliance with this principle in the conditions laid down by statute.'
249 Article 3 (emphasis added).

six days of detention, making a maximum total of seven days. There was a presumption in favour of assigning migrants to a residence over detention. Extensions could be ordered by the Tribunal du Grande Instance only in cases of absolute necessity during the period strictly necessary before the immigrant's departure.[250]

This first decision on the constitutional status of immigrants by the Constitutional Council has proved to be of great importance. It set the twin tests of strict necessity and judicial control. Whilst there have been statutory extensions in the time periods allowed, these have always been closely analysed as to their necessity and the degree of judicial control. Thus in 1986 the government proposed a law[251] seeking an extension by only three days, to be authorized by a court, where there were 'particular difficulties making an obstacle to securing the departure of the foreigner'. The Council rejected this forcefully, saying:

> Considering that such measures of detention, even if placed under judicial control, *cannot be prolonged, except where there is an absolute emergency and particularly grave threat to public order*, without breaching the individual liberty guaranteed by the Constitution; by extending indistinctly to all foreigners who have been made the object of an expulsion order or a measure of redirection to the frontier [the proposed law] is contrary to the Constitution.[252]

This illustrates important aspects of the French approach to the constitutional status question. Foreigners, even without immigration authorization, have an equal right to liberty. The strict necessity of detention in each type of case must be demonstrated. This 'necessity' is however not considered justification for 'prolonged' detention. This can only be supported where there are declared emergencies or where a person poses a grave threat to public order. Parliament simply could not provide for prolonged administrative detention.

Alongside these judicial safeguards, the political momentum was behind protecting detainees. One of the human rights bodies that had pushed to close the camp at Arenc also successfully lobbied to be funded to monitor the new centres and assist detainees.[253] The new legal status of the centres and the legal limits on detention meant that the human rights

---

250 See Loi Sécurité et liberté of 2 February 1981.
251 Decision no. 86–216 DC of 3 September 1986.
252 Page 5 (emphasis added).
253 See www.cimade.org for the annual monitoring reports, which are astonishingly critical of conditions in the detention centres given that they are funded by government.

bodies could be coopted into making them more humane. Eventually in 2000, a code of rights for 'retained foreigners' was passed which included access to medical and legal advice.

Detention in the legal black hole in the international zone: a prison with three walls?

Despite the law of 1981, there remained a legal lacuna in relation to foreigners at international ports. Pending a decision to exclude, there was no power to detain. Nevertheless 'extra-legal' detention still took place, especially in asylum cases. The government was challenged, but argued that holding newly arrived foreigners at the border was not detention in a strict sense. As we saw in the *Mezei* case, it argued that the foreigner could leave at any time and thus secure their freedom. The 'prison' only had three walls. The administrative court rejected this, saying that 'this holding – by reason of the degree of constraint that it imposes and its duration – which is not set by any text and depends only on the decision of the administration, without the least judicial control, as a consequence affects the individual liberty of the person subject to it'.[254]

Even before the final decision by the Tribunal had been rendered, the government proposed urgent legislation to fill the legal gap.[255] The Bill provided for twenty days' detention in international zones pending a decision and removal.[256] Judicial authority was not required other than to extend this by ten days. The Council said the government's obligation to provide judicial control over detention was not as strict in the case of 'a measure depriving an individual of the right to come and go'.[257] Thus holding in the transit zone 'does not affect liberty of the detainee to the same extent as detention in a detention centre', because they chose to arrive and may choose to leave. Nevertheless, it did interfere with freedom sufficiently to engage Article 66 of the constitution, so that the law must provide 'appropriately for the intervention of judicial authority so that it

---

254 Decision of 25 March 1992.

255 It is notable that the same lack of any legal authority for detention in international zones drew the condemnation of the European Court of Human Rights in *Amuur v. France* (Appn. 19776/92), Judgment of 25 June 1996 [1996] 22 EHRR 533. Here again the argument was put about the nature of passengers in international zones being different to incarceration elsewhere. It was considered that, as in the domestic proceedings, whether an interference with liberty existed would depend on the nature and duration.

256 Decision 92–307 DC of 25 February 1992.   257 Paragraph 13.

can exercise its review responsibility and power'.[258] The absence of judicial authority for twenty days was unconstitutional. Furthermore, even in an international zone case, the detention of duration could not exceed what was reasonable.[259]

Criminal due process in immigration arrests and detention

The constitutional requirement that detention must be validated by criminal judges has led to other striking features of French law. Rather than simply considering bail, the courts developed a strong body of case-law which required the release of detainees where there were irregularities in arrest or detention. In the leading decision *Bechta*,[260] it was held that the courts must ensure immigrants were arrested in compliance with the constitution, the penal code and the immigration code. Where arrests took place to conduct an identity check without the commission of criminal offences or threats to public order, the detention was quashed.[261] Importantly, the court must satisfy itself that continued detention is necessary to secure the departure of the foreigner.[262] The factual elements justifying detention must be provided to the court.[263] The time limits on detention are strictly supervised by the court and they have the power to order the release of a detainee at any time.[264] If there is no challenge to legality of arrest, the reviewing judge must order continued detention unless satisfied that residence is appropriate.[265] Indeed, a detailed review of the case-law of the Cour de Cassation[266] concluded that it imposed obligations on judges to ensure that all 'guarantees conferred on foreigners by the international conventions, the constitution, the laws and regulations

---

258 Paragraph 15.
259 Law of 2 July 1992 now found in Arts L. 221–224 Code de Séjour (the 'Marchand' law) was eventually passed in 1992 and provided for detention for forty-eight hours which could be renewed by the frontier service for a further two days. Thereafter only a court could extend detention. The judge could then decide to extend detention for up to a further eight days. One further such extension was permitted, making a total detention period of twenty days.
260 Civ. 2, 28 June 1995, Bull. no. 221, p. 127, Préfet de la Haute-Garonne c/ M. Bechta.
261 Civ. 2, 13 June 2000, pourvoi no. 99–50.031, Préfet du Val-de-Marne c/ M. Chaibi.
262 Civ. 2, 28 November 1985, Bull. no. 183, p. 121, M. Fentrouci c/ Préfet du Rhône.
263 Article 35 bis, Ordonnance 2 November 1945.
264 Civ. 2, 11 June 1997, Bull. no. 181, p. 107, M. Mohammed c/ Préfet du Pas-de-Calais.
265 Law of 24 August 1993.
266 S. Trassoudaine, 'L'intervention judiciaire dans le maintien des étrangers en retention administrative et en zone d'attente', *Bulletin d'information de la Cour de Cassation.* Accessible at www.courdeCassation.fr/jurisprudence_publications_documentation_2/bulletin.

are effectively respected . . . [which were] threatened by these types of procedure in which the legitimate need for speed and effectiveness cannot
fail to lead to expedient or unacceptable decisions that are contrary to
human rights'.[267]

This system is without doubt a complex and costly one, necessitat-
ing many thousands of hearings every year. In one sense remarkable,
it approximates the due process that ordinary criminal suspects receive
in France. As a result, in around one-third of cases, courts order that
detainees be set free regardless of immigration status or even bail. We can
say this represents detention closely regulated by law and not politics or
bureaucracy.

Extending detention and the emerging deportation targets

Bureaucratic and political demands did, however, begin to express themselves. The short time limits meant detainees were often released because
there was no time to document them. In its decision of 1993 the Council
was asked to reconsider its earlier rulings in the light of the French government's proposed law to add an extra *three days'* detention where immigrants had failed to 'provide travel documents'.[268] The Council restated
its orthodox position.[269] It rejected a three-day extension which was not
absolutely necessary as unconstitutional. Prolongation required an urgent
and serious threat to public order. Merely failing to provide a travel document was not enough. The government passed an amended law to permit
extension where it was 'conducive to obtaining a travel document'.[270]

Detention centres remained a modest feature of French migration law
enforcement throughout the 1980s and 1990s. With the political success
of the National Front in 2002, however, politics shifted to the right. The
new conservative government was committed to tougher enforcement
measures and new detention centres were an important aspect of this.[271]
In 2003 a new law doubled the standard detention period in expulsion

---

267 Paragraphs 287–8.   268 Decision no. 93–325 of 13 August 1993.
269 *Ibid.*, 15–16.
270 Law of 30 December 1993. Where 'the foreigner failed to present a travel document and
    if the facts indicate that a supplementary delay is conducive to allow the obtaining of
    this document'. The travel document extension was increased to five days by the Law
    of 11 May 1998, Aliens (Entry and Residence in France and Right of Asylum) Act. The
    Council did not comment on the extension in its review of this law. Decision no. 98–399
    of 5 May 1998.
271 J. Inda, *Targetting Immigrants: Government, Technology, and Ethics*, Oxford University
    Press, 2006.

cases from seven to fifteen days. It also allowed a further five-day extension where this was necessary to get travel documents, or fifteen days where there was a threat to 'public safety'. The maximum period of detention thus reached thirty-two days. In reviewing the law, the changing political landscape appears to have influenced the Council. It held the new time periods constitutional, relying instead upon the fact that judges still had ultimate control of the process.

The effects of the new deportation system

France has experienced many of the same pan-European political concerns about illegal immigration. There may be 200,000–400,000 such persons in France. It also has had sizeable asylum numbers by European standards. There were for instance around 35,000 applications in 2008. The number of detainees held in France has grown, but the duration is far lower than we have seen in other countries.[272] In 2003, 28,220 persons were held in such institutions, but the average duration of detention was only five days. Following the law of 2003, extending the maximum detention period, the duration jumped but then stabilized. Thus in 2004, 25,849 persons were held for an average of ten days. In 2005, 30,707 were held for on average 10.5 days. In 2007 detentions had increased to 35,008 and the duration was 10.2 days. Although the detention estate increased during the period 2003–8 from 739 beds to 1,724, the numbers and duration did not expand correspondingly.

This remained so even after the government first began to adopt deportation targets in 2003. There were 30,000 deportations in 2008. Many were voluntary repatriations without any detention. There is little doubt that the detention periods available are insufficient to secure documents for many immigrants. Evidence from the official monitor is that 90 per cent of those expelled are removed within the first two weeks.[273] Thereafter further detention is often fruitless and detainees are simply released, their illegal status unresolved. There have been increased tensions in detention centres, which have become far more like prisons than the humane places originally conceived of in 1980.[274] Ex-detainees remain open to

272 See the annual reports produced by the monitoring and assistance organization, *Centres et Locaux de Retention Administrative*, Paris: Cimade, 2004 *et seq*. These figures cover the longer-term centres rather than short-term *zones d'attente* and police stations, where detention is supposed to last only hours or several days.
273 See www.cimade.org, whose annual reports show a consistent pattern.
274 See Richard and Fischer, 'A Legal Disgrace?' 581–603.

re-detention and lack definitive social and economic rights, particularly because France has not pursued regularization often.[275] Release has to that extent been a bare act, divorced from any wider reauthorization by the state. Although not inevitable, this flows from the fact that detention is treated as a completely separate legal decision from that of expulsion. Despite this caveat, it remains significant that, contrary to trends seen elsewhere, a combination of powerful French jurisprudence and political opposition rooted in history has imposed important limits on administrative detention.

Conclusions

For all countries we have reviewed, detention has increased during the last thirty years in both incidence and duration. At a political level, this reflects both long-term fears around migration control and more specific border crises sparking detention responses. The political agenda has moved towards seeing migrants as a threat to be controlled using powerful enforcement tools. As expulsion and prevention became legislative and executive policy, detention increased. It was, however, made more prevalent by the lack of any need for judicial authority, delay during immigration proceedings or appeals, an absence of legislative time limits and finally, administrative problems in securing the expulsion of detainees. Governments found nevertheless that given the political weight attached to maintaining the 'integrity' and 'credibility' of the system, extended detention was preferable to letting unauthorized persons into the community.

There were clear differences in jurisprudential terms, though. In the United States, mandatory detention pursuant to legislative provisions has become well established. Whilst largely eliminated in the 1950s, this policy has mushroomed from the 1980s and has been critical to the huge growth in detention prisons. With no time limits placed upon detention or judicial authorization, the process was determined largely by executive priorities and resources, with detainees held for months and years. When initially practised during the Cold War, the courts endorsed group detention as constitutional. This was then expanded from serious criminals to minor offenders and asylum seekers. The only barrier to such detention is residual – the government should release if six months has passed since the final deportation or expulsion order. Compliance still depends upon

275 C. Eff, 'The Detention Centre Maze' (2006) 37 *Vacarme*.

executive discretion. There is no right to individualized hearings and risk assessments as courts have generally held that enforcement is part of the plenary power of government, regardless of its effects on individuals. We can trace this back to the lineage of the aliens power being located alongside war powers in US constitutional history. Aliens have continued to be seen as a threat the nature of which only the government can evaluate.

The United Kingdom represents a middle position where detention has always been formally discretionary not mandatory. Early Commonwealth cases reinvigorated habeas corpus to challenge executive migration practice. This was extended to aliens and then to unauthorized aliens. The nature of detention as infringing the universal right to personal freedom has always been clearly stated. There has been no attempt to see detention as merely the concomitant to lack of immigration status. These fundamental principles, although not challenged by legislation, have not prevented executive policies from expanding detention. Recurrent political crises have led to wider group detention to show government control over particular problems. In recent years the courts have come to provide residual safeguards against especially lengthy or arbitrary detention. In the absence of mandatory judicial review or any clear time limits, there is little doubt that arbitrariness and excess remain.

Australia's experience shows us how far the 'unauthorized' alien category can become identified with a threat to the security of the nation. The political class having established the principle that aliens must either be authorized or deported, it was difficult to avoid the logic of mandatory indefinite detention. The very fact that tiny numbers of such persons were arriving made the policy possible. The guarantee to the public that the border would thus be secured was very attractive. The absence of any traditional danger to public security was politically irrelevant. That it proved to be legally irrelevant too is more surprising. The Australian courts extended the aliens power concept to authorize wartime internment of non-dangerous aliens in time of peace. Their deference to government choices extended beyond membership rights to enforcement too. A right to be released would defeat the government's decision that a detainee had no membership right. Assessing the consequences of releasing such a person was beyond the courts' powers. 'Exclusion' by detention for life was a preferable outcome to interfering in any way with government control of borders.

In France, by contrast, from the outset there was a constitutional barrier to governments seeking to expand detention. Constitutional and international law perspectives that denied a 'right of release' to unauthorized aliens were ignored. Rather, the equal right to liberty was asserted. Viewing detention as an exercise in police powers has imposed two distinctive features: judicial supervision of arrest and detention and a short duration for the time of incarceration. Only true emergencies and grave public order threats are thought to support prolonged detention within France. The government has not succeeded in arguing that unauthorized immigration presents either.

The effect has been to require the release into the community of many persons with no immigration status, a step which is increasingly unacceptable in many countries. Nevertheless, detention periods, whilst remaining short, have been adequate to allow governments to show they are meeting broad deportation targets. There has also been strong political opposition to expanding detention. The French experience is therefore an important one, rejecting narrow contractarian logic in favour of more basic libertarianism. It strikes a balance between immigration control and liberty that is attuned to the 'normal' relationship between citizens and the state. Detentions of any persons, including aliens, by the state within France have been assessed within the common framework of peacetime.

3

International law and immigration detention: between territorial sovereignty and emerging human rights norms

Introduction: sovereignty and the treatment of aliens

In this chapter we seek to explore the interaction between the development of national detention policies and international law. Until the advent of modern international human rights law, however, there was little international discussion of the issue. Since the ninteenth century, customary international law had given states a right to take action for injury to their nationals abroad, but in practice such protection was largely confined to Western diplomats or business interests.[1] As nineteenth-century liberal cosmopolitanism, with its emphasis on the mutual benefits of free trade in labour, came under pressure, sending and receiving states began to see international obligations differently.[2] In countries wishing to shape or curb mass migration, legal opinion began to discuss immigration control alongside war and invasion as a fundamental aspect of sovereignty. Domestic politics in receiving states gradually eclipsed the idea that there might be serious legal limitations on the treatment of friendly aliens.[3] Diplomatic discussions over migration continued, but trailed way behind the development of border controls and enforcement apparatuses.

1 G. Simpson, *Law, War and Crime*, Cambridge: Polity Press, 2007, 162.
2 For example, the Chinese Exclusion Acts excited heated arguments between the US and Chinese governments. The original Burlingame Treaty had been seen as an important breakthrough for China because it reaffirmed reasonable access to the United States for Chinese migrants. The later Acts appeared to effectively emasculate the treaty.
3 Even after the rise of legal opinion permitting wide power over migration, the law of state responsibility did apparently continue to impose standards for the treatment of non-nationals by other states. See for a general discussion, I. Brownlie, *Principles of Public International Law*, Oxford University Press, 2003. Expulsion should be effected 'with as much forbearance and indulgence as the circumstances and conditions of the case allow and demand, especially when expulsion is decreed against a domiciled alien'. See R. Jennings and A. Watts, *Oppenheim's International Law*, 9th edn, London: Longman, 1992, 945.

That states had an almost arbitrary and unlimited power over migration became an 'accepted maxim', at least in most common law countries.[4] Such expressions have been repeatedly used to support alien detention as simply an inherent aspect of this legal power. James Nafziger argues, however, such broad pronouncements were misleading.[5] Reviewing the opinions of legal scholars of the time, he concludes that the Anglo-American judgments discussed in Chapter 1 practised selective quotation. They were strongly influenced by the positivist view that, in order to be truly 'sovereign', law-makers within a given territory must not be subject to any external power.[6]

In fact, even whilst these judgments were emerging, international law scholars were codifying general rules *requiring* friendly aliens to be admitted subject to, admittedly broad, specific reasons to exclude.[7] State practice since the nineteenth century also shows that no state has attempted anything like absolute exclusion.[8] In fact, migration has continued on a vast scale. Nazfiger concludes that the true norm of international law was (and remains) that 'a state may legitimately exclude aliens only if, individually or collectively, they pose a serious danger to its public safety, security, general welfare or essential institutions'.[9] This formulation is wide, but it does mean that unnecessary detention of aliens might be criticized as a matter of customary international law by countries whose nationals are affected.[10] However, in the absence of diplomatic power to compel this,

---

4 *Nishimura Ekiu* v. *United States* 142 U.S. 662: 'It is an accepted maxim of international law, that every sovereign nation has the power, as inherent in sovereignty, and essential to self-preservation, to forbid the entrance of foreigners within its dominions, or to admit them only in such cases and upon such conditions as it may see fit to prescribe. Vattel, lib. 2, 94, 100; 1 Phillimore (3d ed.) c. 10, 220.'

5 J.A.R. Nafziger, 'The General Admission of Aliens under International Law' (1983) 77 *Am. J. Int. L.* 804.

6 *Chae Chan Ping* v. *United States* 344 U.S. 590, 596; if a sovereign 'could not exclude aliens it would be to that extent subject to the control of another power'. For a critique of this idea see N. MacCormick, *Questioning Sovereignty*, Oxford University Press, 2003.

7 International Regulations on the Admission and Expulsion of Aliens, Institute of International Law (1892), which imposed a general obligation to admit aliens save in cases of serious public interest concerns. Cited in R. Plender, *International Migration Law*, Leyden: Sijthoff, 1972.

8 Nafziger, 'The General Admission of Aliens under International Law' 833–40.

9 *Ibid.*, 846.

10 *Ibid.*, 847. The practical problem for Nafziger's view is that states, whilst never completely barring immigration, have appeared to exercise enormously wide discretion over it. It is true that they have always grounded restrictions in some sort of public policy justification, but the proffered reasons have led to a huge variety of restrictions. The fact that they have never barred all immigration tells us little. States have hitherto not judged that public policy required this. Whilst international political consequences can attend

as we have seen, Western states have generally felt little need to consider it. Enforcement issues like detention practice have been driven almost exclusively by domestic political perceptions. In fact, significant external scrutiny of detention policy has only come about with the arrival of international human rights monitoring bodies.

Detention and the modern migration and human rights puzzle

In the last thirty years, these continued assertions of a broad power to control migration linked to territorial sovereignty have begun to conflict with emerging human rights principles.[11] Whilst in the immediate post-World War Two period there were many international bills of rights drafted, initially their impact upon states' control over migration was rather limited, apart from in relation to the settlement of refugees.[12] Individuals had few mechanisms to challenge migration decisions. Indeed there appeared little need to do so. Given the prevailing peace within developed regions of the world, internment of enemy aliens was not an issue. Economic growth and the associated demand for migrant labour meant that immigration controls were comparatively light and measures like detention were exceptional.[13]

As we saw in Chapter 2, from the 1970s, however, international conditions began to change. Economic stagnation led to restrictions upon migrants seeking work. Detention was increasingly used against those found present without permission. This was accompanied by a growing criminalization of unauthorized migration. There was also increasing use of detention for other undesirable groups, such as those convicted of crimes, driven by domestic political concern.[14] The return of economic growth in the 1990s and the renewed demand for migrant labour did not, however, lead to any relaxation of the detention regimes that that been established in the preceding decades. Refugee applications to developed

---

unnecessarily harsh restrictions, it would appear to be rare for states to any longer argue that immigration controls on their nationals are in breach of customary international law. Restrictions in breach of international migration treaties are, of course, another matter. S. Juss, 'Free Movement and the World Order' (2004) 16 *Int. J. Refugee L.* 289.

11 See for an overview P. Alston, *International Human Rights Law*, Oxford University Press, 2000.

12 In fact, even the Refugee Convention limited its application to refugees created by pre-1951 events until the 1967 Protocol removed this restriction.

13 See S. Castles and M.J. Miller, *The Age of Migration*, 4th edn, London: Macmillan Press, 2009, Ch. 5.

14 See particularly the United States of America in relation to aliens convicted of crimes who are awaiting expulsion.

countries had also increased.[15] Due to visa restrictions, many putative refugees had to be smuggled to reach potential asylum states.[16] Thus, from the perspective of governments, asylum seekers were often unauthorized too.[17] Detention pending refugee status determination became a common and increasing practice amongst states.[18]

Of these groups, the detention of asylum seekers was the first to become a major object of international concern, particularly following the establishment of large-scale detention in camps in, for example, the United States and Hong Kong. Asylum seekers fell within the ambit of the pre-existing 1951 Refugee Convention and, as such, attracted the particular concern of United Nations bodies and non-governmental organizations. Importantly, states parties to this convention had uniquely recognized limits on their immigration powers by conferring rights on asylum seekers.

Beyond asylum seekers, concern has begun to broaden to encompass concern over detention of irregular migrants more generally. During the 1970s the Convention on the Rights of Migrant Workers and their Families had been drafted under United Nations sponsorship. Whilst it only confers a right of free movement within a state[19] upon regular migrants, *both* regular and irregular migrants[20] have a right not to be subject to arbitrary detention.[21] This is an important statement of principle which

---

15 The UNHCR estimates that the global number of refugees reached 27 million in 1995 before declining: *Asylum Levels and Trends in Industrialized Countries, Third Quarter, 2004*, Geneva: UNHCR.

16 The rapid growth of visa requirements for developing and largely, refugee-producing countries, along with the imposition of carriers liability rules meant that it became very difficult to reach Western countries that provided durable asylum without using clandestine means.

17 B. Jordan and F. Duvell, *Irregular Migration: The Dilemmas of Transnational Mobility*, Cheltenham: Edward Elgar, 2002.

18 *Recommendations as Regards Harmonisation of Reception Standards for Asylum Seekers in the EU, Part A: Summary of State Practice*, Geneva: UNHCR, July 2000, 31.

19 Those in a regular situation are entitled to 'liberty of movement in the territory of the State of employment and freedom to choose their residence' (Art. 39).

20 'Migrant worker' is defined as someone who 'is to be engaged, is engaged or has been engaged in a remunerated activity in a State of which he or she is not a national' (Art. 2). This is broad, but it is not clear that it covers persons seeking work who are stopped at the border without a job offer.

21 See Art. 16(1), which grants migrant workers and their families the right to liberty and security of the person. Article 16(4) prohibits their 'arbitrary' arrest and detention, which must be on grounds and in accordance with procedures prescribed by law. Article 16(8) provides that there must be a right to take proceedings to challenge the lawfulness of detention and to be released without delay if it is not lawful. They are also entitled to compensation for unlawful arrest or detention.

confirmed the basic civil law status of unauthorized migrants. The United Nations High Commission for Human Rights considers this convention one of the eight 'core' global human rights instruments. However, the politics of illegal immigration since the 1970s led Western governments to refuse to ratify the Convention.[22] The default position, apart from during regularization programmes, had became such that 'undocumented migrants [were] predominately [*sic.*] treated as criminals rather than as vulnerable people deserving protection'.[23] The Convention was resisted both for constraining enforcement policy and as it conferred legitimacy upon irregular migrants.

This lack of acceptance of international obligations towards irregular migrants means that refugee status has assumed greater importance. Yet, as the Special Rapporteur on the Human Rights of Migrants has put it: 'It is increasingly difficult . . . to make clear distinctions between migrants who leave their countries because of political persecution, conflicts, economic problems, environmental degradation or a combination of these reasons and those who do so in search of conditions of survival or well-being that do not exist in their places of origin.'[24]

The increasing use of detention for rejected asylum seekers, irregular migrants, deportable foreign criminals and national security cases has forced a close examination of the human rights status of unauthorized foreigners. In the absence of effective treaties specifically protecting the different categories of migrants, the international human rights movement has lobbied for an acceptance that *general civil human rights* norms, including the right to liberty, apply regardless of immigration status. This is at odds with a domestic politics that has constructed border controls as a 'security' issue. The modern proliferation of barriers through visas, criminal penalties, databases, detention, deportation and even naval interception, suggests an 'enemy' to be repelled. The political climate and domestic legal tools have created 'irregular' or 'unauthorized'

---

22 There are numerous important standard-setting documents published by the International Labour Organization relating to migrant workers, but these do not touch upon detention. The UN Convention on the Rights of Migrant Workers and their Families is the only multilateral treaty on migrant workers, and it eventually came into force in 2003. There are now forty-one state parties, but the majority are migrant-sending nations rather than host countries. There have been no ratifications by labour destination countries in the EU or other Western nations.

23 P. De Guchteneire and A. Pecoud, 'Introduction: the UN ICRMW' in P. De Guchteneire, A. Pecoud and R. Cholewinski (eds), *Migration and Human Rights: the United Nations Convention on Migrant Workers' Rights*, Cambridge University Press: 2009. 1–44, 22.

24 *Report of the Special Rapporteur on Human Rights of Migrants*, 6 Jan. 2000, E/CN.4/2000/82, para. 30.

migrants – persons who are deemed to be inherently illegitimate.[25] For states to 'respect' the 'rights' of those who are not supposed to be present, would legitimate persons who have been politically de-legitimated.

The cosmopolitan perspective is apt to downplay this domestic political dimension. Border crossings are likely to seem less invasive when viewed 'from above', because migration is recognized as a global phenomenon with mutual impacts. Indeed, a qualified human right to migrate is sometimes mooted.[26] More fundamentally, the international system of human rights aspires ultimately to be a cosmopolitan enterprise, based upon respect for *universal shared personhood*. States are still, however, the fundamental units of international law, and without them there is no human rights system. The increasing tendency of states to invoke the border as a 'security' issue has thus presented a politico-legal challenge for international human rights law. To question either the level of 'threat' posed or the 'illegitimacy' of unauthorized foreigners is to strike at two key political 'givens' within modern Western societies. Some aspects of border control policy therefore challenge the idea that fundamental rights are truly *universal*.

In addressing the relationship between detention and human rights we will focus upon three key sources of law: the Refugee Convention, the European Convention on Human Rights and the International Covenant on Civil and Political Rights, and the activities of their associated monitoring bodies.

World War Two and the refugee problem: camps and authorization for resettlement

Whatever the scope of the classical doctrine of territorial sovereignty, in practice, control over migration had collapsed as a result of World War

---

25 M. Samers, 'An Emerging Geopolitics of "Illegal" Immigration' (2004) 6 *EJML* 27.

26 See for examples the bundle of rights contained in the Universal Declaration of Human Rights 1948, which bear on migration and aliens: Art. 13(1) Everyone has the right to freedom of movement and residence within the borders of each State; (2) Everyone has the right to leave any country, including his own, and to return to his country. Art. 14(1) Everyone has the right to seek and to enjoy in other countries asylum from persecution; (2) This right may not be invoked in the case of prosecutions genuinely arising from non-political crimes or from acts contrary to the purposes and principles of the United Nations. Art. 15(1) Everyone has the right to a nationality; (2) No one shall be arbitrarily deprived of his nationality nor denied the right to change his nationality.

Two and the Cold War division of Europe.[27] Vast numbers of people, perhaps as many as 40 million, found themselves in foreign countries.[28] Some had lost their nationality and others resisted return on political or humanitarian grounds. Some of these persons had been admitted lawfully, others had not. Their basis for staying in their new countries was unclear. Geographical and political borders in Europe had been redrawn. This group of persons, unaccounted for and unstable, presented an international problem of serious proportions.[29] They were held in camps, often for years, whilst the victorious powers negotiated their fate.[30] Millions were repatriated, sometimes by force, to their homelands in the East.[31] As the Cold War took hold, however, political pressure grew to admit many of them to Western nations instead of returning them to Communist countries.[32] This became the central policy and the 1951 Refugee Convention was drafted to define the legal rights of those whom it was agreed could not be sent back to their countries for fear of persecution.

It is important to note that displaced persons were maintained in camps whilst awaiting authorization to resettle in a new state. They were in a legal limbo – it was practically difficult to send them back, but they were not able to choose and access a country of resettlement. To this extent, although not closed, the camps mirror modern detention centres.

---

27 There was clearly a significant refugee issue in the inter-war years in the form of around 2 million Russians who had fled during the period after the revolution. This was addressed with considerable success by Nansen, the first High Commissioner for Refugees, but no binding obligation to resettle was accepted by the majority of states.

28 G. Loescher, *The UNHCR and World Politics*, Oxford University Press, 2001, 34. Sassen says: 'The rising importance of borders and sovereignty over national territories, the increasingly long arm of the state, and the ascendancy of variously conceived constructions of national identities as part of the nation state, all these specify a distinctly novel phase in the history of the European state. They are fertile soil in which the production of mass refugee movements can thrive ... It is in this regard that we can say that the modern refugee is a European product in the same way that the state we see emerging in the twentieth century is a European product.' S. Sassen, *Guests and Aliens*, New York: New Press, 1999, 96.

29 See L. Gordenker, *Refugees in International Politics*, London: Croom Helm, 1987, 30.

30 See T. Judt, *Postwar: a History of Europe since 1945*, London: Penguin, 2007, 27–32 for a discussion of the politics of repatriation.

31 T. Sjoberg, *The Powers and the Persecuted: The Refugee Problem and the Intergovernmental Committee on Refugees, 1938–47*, Lund University Press, 1991. The camp system was operated by the UN Relief and Rehabilitation Administration, established in 1943.

32 The creation of the International Refugee Organization in 1948 crystallized the shift toward asylum and away from repatriation which had hitherto been a key objective of the UN Relief and Rehabilitation Agency. See Gordenker, *Refugees in International Politics*, 28–9.

They were holding bays pending status approval and authorization to be resettled.[33] There was thus from the outset an inherent tension between a right to seek asylum and the right of territorial sovereignty. As Haddad puts it: '[t]he cosmopolitan approach grants the refugee the right to leave the source of persecution, but the right of entry into a state remains the domain of state sovereignty. In other words emigration may be a matter of human rights, but immigration remains a concern of national sovereignty, since nowhere is the right to obtain asylum guaranteed.'[34] We can see this ambiguity most strongly reflected in the modern resort to detention powers to keep out, deter or expel asylum seekers.

The Refugee Convention and detention: an uncertain text

The Refugee Convention was thus written in a very different context. The convention was largely directed at resettlement of displaced persons upon the basis of a common civil, social and economic status. Admitting refugees for resettlement was generally a result of international negotiation, not the exercise of individual choice.[35] The unauthorized arrival of refugees and the use of techniques like detention to prevent this were marginal issues at a time when resettling the thousands in camps was the main focus.

Although its primary focus, the convention did not simply provide rights for *recognized* refugees. It created a hierarchy of rights as refugees achieved greater levels of attachment to the asylum state.[36] Most importantly, mere *physical presence* generated several rights.[37] Further

---

33 See the discussion in M. Klemme, *The Inside Story of the UNRRA: an Experience in Internationalism: a first-hand report on the displaced persons of Europe*, New York: Lifetime, 1949, 270–5. He notes that initially there was no permission for displaced persons to work away from camps as they had to return every night or be classed as 'deserters'. They thereby lost their entitlement to support. For a detailed description of the camps' operation see G. Woodbridge, *UNRRA: The History of the United Nations Relief and Rehabilitation Administration*, vol. II, New York: Columbia University Press, 1950, 496–532.

34 E. Haddad, *The Refugee in International Society: Between Sovereigns*, Cambridge University Press, 2008, 88.

35 As we saw in relation to Australian policy on border control, refugee admission is still sometimes explicitly seen as requiring diplomatic consent by the signatory states rather than a right attaching to any individual who moves to another country and seeks asylum.

36 J.C. Hathaway, *The Rights of Refugees under International Law*, Cambridge University Press, 2005, 156.

37 Most importantly, the Art. 33 non-*refoulement* right applies to all putative refugees, regardless of immigration status, until they are determined not to be refugees, as does Art. 9 on provisional measures.

rights accrued to those 'lawfully present', 'lawfully staying' and 'lawfully resident'.[38] These terms were not separately defined, which presents some difficulty of interpretation.[39] Nevertheless, it is plain that some rights do attach to the modern 'asylum seeker', a concept not mentioned in the convention itself.

It is clear that the convention does permit detention in some cases. The drafting history, with its close proximity to World War Two, reveals that states were keen to retain powers to detain enemy alien refugees during wartime. There also remained concerns about espionage during the Cold War. States' experiences of mass influxes of refugees in the 1930s had also caused problems. The drafters did, however, make a clear distinction between different types of danger. War or times of national security emergency were distinguished from problems arising in peacetime.

Regarding times of conflict, as the Convention on the Protection of Civilian Persons in Time of War 1949[40] had prohibited the blanket detention of enemy aliens during war, so it was agreed that similar rules should apply under the Refugee Convention. However, Article 9 preserved the right of states to take '*provisional measures* in time of war or *other grave and exceptional circumstances*' (emphasis added) pending determination that the person was a refugee and only when essential to national security.[41] This was understood to allow internment to permit states to separate

---

38 Even those 'unlawfully' present are accorded protection under Art. 31 against punishment and detention where they meet the conditions set out therein (see below).

39 The fact that persons who claim asylum may turn out not to qualify for such status presents a dilemma. To fail to confer immediately some of these rights would result in a breach of the convention for those subsequently turning out to be refugees. However those not deemed worthy of refugee status would have wrongfully secured some of the benefits of the convention. At the time of drafting the convention, this did not appear to be a serious concern. In the context of the world war and the East–West politics of the time, many millions of persons were accepted to be refugees. However thirty years later Western states, in the context of South–North migration, came to question this approach by seeking to restrict the rights of the new asylum seekers (as opposed to recognized refugees). 'Asylum seeker', a category not mentioned in the convention, came to assume a distinct and lesser status. As we shall see, the UNHCR rightly considered this to be at odds with the text of the convention. Indeed, the UNHCR sought to argue that all asylum seekers must be assumed to be refugees until their status had been determined. See UNHCR, 'Note on International Protection', UN Doc.A/AC.96/815 (1993), para. 11.

40 Article 44 prohibited internment solely on the basis of enemy alien status for civilians.

41 'Nothing in this Convention shall prevent a Contracting State, in time of war or other grave and exceptional circumstances, from taking provisionally measures which it considers to be essential to the national security in the case of a particular person, pending a determination by the Contracting State that that person is in fact a refugee and that the continuance of such measure is necessary in his case in the interests of national security.'

spies from other refugee enemy aliens.[42] The asylum state should suspend such measures once refugee status was confirmed, unless the individual refugee posed a threat to national security.[43]

Moving away from war to peacetime, the convention drafters drew a distinction between lawfully and unlawfully present refugees. For those lawfully present, Article 26 conferred a right to 'move freely'.[44] This important right of movement was subject only to regulations placed on aliens generally in the same circumstances.[45] By contrast, Article 31 permitted detention of refugees 'unlawfully' present within certain limitations.[46] The meaning of lawful and unlawful is therefore of great importance.

In his detailed discussion of the *travaux préparatoires*, Hathaway suggests that 'lawful presence' arises when a putative refugee has complied with the formalities for lodging an asylum application.[47] He argues convincingly that this should not be entirely determined by national law concepts of 'lawful' stay. To do so would serve to undermine the normative requirements of the convention.[48] Referring to the Ad Hoc Committee's

---

42 N. Robinson, *Convention Relating to the Status of Refugees: Its History, Contents and Interpretation*, New York: Institute of Jewish Affairs, 1953, 95. Hathaway says the US government decision to detain all asylum applicants from over thirty Arab and Muslim countries pending their status determination in 2003 was within Art. 9 only if 'essential' to meet 'an extremely compelling threat to national security'. Hathaway, *The Rights of Refugees under International Law*, 266.

43 Statement of Mr Winter of Canada, UN Doc. E/AC.32/SR.35, Aug. 15, 1950, 10, cited in *ibid.*, 269.

44 'Each Contracting State shall accord to refugees lawfully in its territory the right to choose their place of residence and to move freely within its territory, subject to any regulations applicable to aliens generally in the same circumstances.'

45 This provision was not intended to prevent conditions being imposed prior to admission. *The Refugee Convention, 1951: the Travaux Préparatoires Analysed with a Commentary by the Late Dr Paul Weis*, Cambridge University Press, 1995, 210.

46 'Article 31(1) The Contracting States shall not impose penalties, on account of their illegal entry or presence, on refugees who, coming directly from a territory where their life or freedom was threatened . . . enter or are present in their territory without authorization, provided they present themselves without delay to the authorities and show good cause for their illegal entry or presence. (2) The Contracting States shall not apply to the movements of such refugees restrictions other than those which are necessary and such restrictions shall only be applied until their status in the country is regularized or they obtain admission into another country.'

47 Hathaway, *The Rights of Refugees under International Law*, 170–87.

48 *Ibid.*, 178. He relies upon *Rajendran* v. *Minister for Immigration and Multicultural Affairs* (1998) 166 ALR 619 (Aus. FFC, 4 Sept. 1998). There the court held that the asylum seeker, who had entered as a visitor and was then given a 'bridging visa' pending his refugee status being determined was lawfully present and could thus invoke Art. 32 of the convention. By contrast, the UK courts in *R* v. *Secretary of State for the Home Department*,

view, Hathaway says that the power to detain unlawfully present persons only lasts until they have been admitted to the refugee procedure.[49] Thereafter they have the status of being 'lawfully present' (if not lawfully staying). They cannot be detained on the ground of their irregular entry after this initial stage.[50] They may, however, be made subject to regulations, such as reporting requirements, imposed on aliens generally.

For those unlawfully present, Article 31 sought to restrict punishment and detention, although not eliminate it altogether. It was recognized that refugees sometimes had to breach immigration laws to find refuge. For refugees satisfying three conditions (they must come 'directly' from the country of persecution, present themselves promptly to the authorities and have good cause for illegal entry) there should be no punishment for illegal entry. Similarly, restrictions on freedom of movement of such refugees must not go beyond those 'necessary'.

However, the precise circumstances amounting to 'necessary' detention were not resolved. Most delegates appeared to see situations of mass influx as one instance justifying detention because such situations were a 'real danger, on *both economic and security* grounds'.[51] The French delegate recalled the large numbers of Spanish refugees arriving at the border

ex parte Bugdaycay [1987] AC 514 (UK HL, 19 Feb. 1987) held that a person who applied for asylum at a port of entry and was given 'temporary admission' pending a decision on their claim was not lawfully present. This was based upon the erroneous belief that otherwise a person could never be removed from the United Kingdom unless Art. 32(2) was fulfilled. In fact, if their refugee status was later rejected, then their lawful stay could be terminated and they could be removed. See also *Kaya v. Haringey London Borough Council* [2001] EWCA Civ 677 (Eng. CA, 1 May 2001), where denial of housing to asylum seekers who were deemed not to be lawfully present was upheld as consistent with the convention entitlement to equal access to housing. See also *O v. London Borough of Wandsworth* [2000] EWCA Civ 201 (Eng. CA, 22 June 2000); and *Saadi v. Secretary of State for the Home Department* [2002] UKHL 41 (UK HL, 31 Oct. 2002), where it was said that even a person complying with reporting conditions was not lawfully present: 'until the state has "authorized" entry, the entry is unauthorized'.

49 Statement of Mr Rain of France, UN Doc. E/AC.32/SR.15, 27 Jan. 1950, at 17: '[a]ny person in possession of a residence permit was in a regular position. In fact, the same was true of a person who was not yet in possession of a residence permit but who had applied for it and had the receipt for that application. Only those persons who had not applied, or whose applications had been refused, were in an irregular postion.'

50 Hathaway, *The Rights of Refugees under International Law*, argues this would be contrary to the obvious purpose of Art. 31(2) which is to protect refugees from such detention. He suggests that detention must be 'necessary' even if the asylum seeker is simply being detained under the same law and for the same reason as applies to aliens generally. But this would only cover those asylum seekers meeting the conditions set out in Art. 31(2).

51 Statement of Mr Herment of Belgium, UN Doc. E/AC.32/SR.40, 22 Aug. 1950, 4 (emphasis added).

during the civil war. A second ground seems to have been to investigate the identity, mode of entry and possible threat to security posed by irregular refugees.[52] Perhaps a third ground that assumes some importance in modern times was stated by the president: 'there was general agreement... that every State was fully entitled to investigate the case of each refugee who clandestinely crossed its frontier, and to ascertain whether he met the *necessary entry requirements*'.[53] Although views differed on the reasons for detention, the common assumption appears to have been that it would be of short duration, simply long enough to carry out a bureaucratic process.[54]

Weis, one of the delegates to the conference, speculated some years later regarding Article 31 that 'it results from the history of the provision that refugees should not be kept behind barbed wire. A short period of custody may be necessary in order to investigate the identity of the person. Refugees may also be placed in a camp, particularly in cases of mass influx'.[55] We can see here, however, that there was an important ambiguity over both what kinds of 'camps' were permissible and when they should be employed. Whilst Article 9 saw security detention as confined to wartime or equivalent threats, delegates contemplated irregular border-crossing itself as a potential reason for the creation of camps. The 'security' of the border was seen in broader terms, encompassing a fear of large numbers of irregular persons which shaded into unspecified economic and public order concerns. Although Article 26 created an individual right of free movement, this was undermined by the idea that group detention might be necessary in certain circumstances.

For Western governments in the period up to 1980, the scope of the limitations on detention set out in the Refugee Convention was, however, a largely theoretical issue. Detention was rarely practised. This was a time

---

52 The French delegate spoke of detention 'for a few days, to obtain information on them'. Statement of Mr Rochefort of France, UN Doc. A/CONF.2/SR.35, 25 July 1951, 11. The British delegate said 'provisional detention that might be necessary to investigate the circumstances in which a refugee had entered a country'. Statement of Mr Hoare of the United Kingdom, *ibid.*, 12.

53 Statement of Mr Larsen of Denmark, UN Doc. A/CONF.2/SR.35, 25 July 1951, 13 (emphasis added). This, however, appears to require refugee recognition rather than simply entry into the recognition procedure and so is at odds with the definition of lawful presence put forward by Hathaway.

54 Hathaway, *The Rights of Refugees under International Law*, argues that after this short period, assuming no negative decision on the asylum claim has been made, Art. 26 applies and the putative refugee must be released pending a decision.

55 *Ibid.*, 303.

in which, at least in Europe, the United Nations High Commission for Refugees (UNHCR) had a key role in resettlement of refugees. There were few direct asylum claims made in Europe. Numbers were small and asylum was apparently a largely managed process. In such an environment, European governments accepted the UNHCR's authoritative role in the interpretation of the Convention.[56] A liberal stance on detention did not present any political challenges.

This benign situation is reflected in the first statement on detention by the UNHCR's Executive Committee given in Conclusion No. 7 of 1977 which only felt the need to consider recognized refugees, not asylum seekers. It stated that an expulsion order on public order grounds addressed to a refugee 'should only be combined with custody or detention if absolutely necessary for reasons of national security or public order and that such custody or detention should not be unduly prolonged'. This is a demanding standard, which embodies both strong individual grounds for detention and proportionality of duration. This reflects a high level of protection for what were a small group of persons. The position of irregular asylum seekers was shortly to give the UNHCR much more difficulty in relation to Western governments.

Controlling irregular movements of asylum seekers and the UNHCR's response to increasing detention

The first significant mention of detention of asylum seekers was in 1981 after a Group of Experts had been convened to discuss the growing number of refugees in situations of mass influx. The movements within the Far East from Vietnam, Cambodia and Laos were particularly significant. There were also large numbers of refugees in Central America. The war in Afghanistan generated millions more in Central Asia. Meanwhile in Africa there were post-colonial conflicts and repressive regimes. Many states in the front line were concerned at overwhelming numbers.[57] The need for detention in such situations was clearly one of the concerns the drafters had in mind when drafting Article 31(2). The novelty was that

---

56 C. Avery, 'Refugee Status Decision-making in Ten Countries' (1984) 17 *Stanford Journal of International Law* 183. T.A. Aleinikoff, 'Political Asylum in the Federal Republic of Germany and Republic of France: Lessons for the United States' (1984) 17 *Univ. Mich. J.L. Reform* 183. The *UNHCR Handbook*, Geneva: UNHCR 1979, reflects the high-water mark of the organization's influence and status of the period.

57 See Loescher, *The UNHCR and World Politics*, Ch. 7, who estimates that there were 10 million refugees by the early 1980s.

the countries affected were largely non-Western developing nations. The refugees were often kept in camps for long periods without formal adjudication on their status. The resulting Executive Committee Conclusion 22[58] argued that to respect the principle of non-*refoulement*, such persons must be given temporary refuge in camps providing basic facilities pending more durable solutions. During this period they must not be penalized or exposed to any unfavourable treatment solely on the ground that their presence in the country was considered unlawful and importantly, 'they should not be subject to restrictions on their movements other than those which are necessary in the interest of public health and public order'.[59]

Article 31 of the convention clearly inspired the text, but Conclusion 22 clearly goes beyond this and limits detention by close reference to two narrow public interests.[60] The one significant instance of a Western state being affected by mass influx – the Cuban and Haitian flotillas to the United States from 1980 – resulted in a policy of deterrence through, *inter alia*, mandatory detention of asylum seekers. This clearly did not comply with the text of Conclusion 22. The UNHCR questioned the policy but did not succeed in changing it.[61] Similar deterrence policies, adopted by the United States in relation to Salvadoran refugees entering irregularly, were also criticized by the UNHCR in 1981. The report indicated that the high level set for bail bonds and long detention were among the strategies employed to dissuade Salvadorans from pursuing asylum claims.[62]

The failure to ensure the United States complied with Executive Committee Conclusion 22 was the beginning of a long, and largely fruitless, battle between the UNHCR and Western governments over detention issues. European governments began to use more detention policies as asylum applications rose from 20,000 in 1976 to 158,500 in 1980 and

58 No. 22(XXII) – 1981 Protection of Asylum Seekers in Situations of Large-scale Influx, Report of 32nd Session: UN Doc. A/AC.96/601, para. 57(2).
59 IIA2(a).
60 This is rendered somewhat ambiguous by the later section that states 'the location of asylum seekers should be determined by their safety and well-being as well as by the security needs of the receiving State. Asylum seekers should, as far as possible, be located at a reasonable distance from the frontier of their country of origin' IIA2(g).
61 See Loescher, *The UNHCR and World Politics*, 234–5, where he shows that the criticism was of US interdiction at sea and summary rejection, but also the detention policy itself.
62 Report of the UNHCR Mission to Monitor INS Asylum Processing of Salvadoran Illegal Entrants – 13–18 September 1981, repr. in *Congressional Record*, 11 Feb. 1982, Sections 827–831.

reached over 450,000 by 1990.[63] The total annual recorded asylum applications across Europe, America, Australia and Japan increased from under 100,000 in 1983 to over 891,000 by 1992.[64] This was a shock for the Western asylum and political systems, both in terms of scale and the fact that it occurred outside the traditional refugee processing channels.[65] Governments in Europe reacted with prevention and deterrence strategies which included more immigration detention. An internal UNHCR report, fiercely criticizing the use and conditions of detention in West Germany, set the tone.[66] By the mid-1980s the UNHCR had begun to note publicly the increasing use of detention under ordinary immigration law of asylum seekers.[67] In an allusion to Article 31, it said:

> it frequently occurs that the necessary distinction is not made either in law or in administrative practice between asylum-seekers and ordinary aliens seeking to enter the territory. The absence of such a distinction may, and in many cases does, lead to asylum-seekers being *punished and detained for illegal entry* in the same manner as illegal aliens.[68]

The political situation had markedly changed, as Western countries came to see detention as an aspect of preventing irregular migration. Goodwin-Gill relates that around this time heated debates took place on the scope of detention permitted by Article 31.[69] States were unhappy that the UNHCR did not give weight to their desire to use detention to dissuade employment of fraudulent or damaged documents by asylum seekers, to deter 'irregular movements' and to hold applicants during the adjudication of

---

63 P. Rudge, 'Fortress Europe' in *World Refugee Survey: 1986 in Review Convention Relating to the Status of Refugees: Its History, Contents and Interpretation*, Washington, DC: US Committee for Refugees, 1987, 5–12. See also J. Hughes and F. Liebaut (eds), *Detention of Asylum Seekers in Europe: Analysis and Perspectives*, Amsterdam: Martinus Nijhoff Publishers, 1998.

64 G. Loescher, *Beyond Charity: International Co-operation and the Global Refugee Crisis*, New York: Oxford University Press, 1993.

65 Loescher puts it nicely: 'Apart from the occasional ballet dancer, rocket scientist, or merchant seaman from the Soviet bloc, political asylum had been an exceptional event for the West', *ibid.*, 229.

66 UNHCR internal report, Candida Toscani, *Mission to Federal Republic of Germany, June 6–10, 1983*, Geneva: UNHCR, 1 July 1983.

67 UNHCR 'Notes' on International Protection: UN Docs A/AC.96/660 (1985) paras 26–9; A/AC.96/694 (1987) para. 33 and A/AC.96/713 (1988) paras 16–23.

68 'Note on Accession to International Instruments and the Detention of Refugees and Asylum Seekers', UN Doc. EC/SCP/44, Aug. 19 1986, para. 33 (emphasis addded).

69 This comment formed part of a Note that was considered by a Sub-Committee of the Executive Committee.

claims that were often rejected.[70] Article 31 was in any event only relevant for some refugees fulfilling its conditions of 'coming directly', presenting themselves promptly and providing good cause for their clandestine entry. Outside this, detention appeared to be determined by national law on border control. By contrast, other states viewed detention as *per se* a violation of liberty rights and its use as a deterrent unacceptable. In the face of the new asylum seekers to the West, the UNHCR was no longer given the same authority over the meaning of the Convention by Western governments.

The search for an appropriate international standard on detention of asylum seekers

Ongoing debate between the UNHCR and Western states produced more definitive guidance in Executive Committee Conclusion 44 (Excomm. 44). Going beyond Article 31, this said that, for *all* asylum seekers, detention should be used only when 'necessary'. However, necessary reasons were very broadly defined comprising: 'to verify identity, to determine the elements of the refugee claim, where a person had destroyed their travel documents or used fraudulent documents to mislead the authorities and to protect national security or public order'.[71] It must be said that this was a poorly drafted and ill-considered compromise. It reflected the political concerns of Western states of the time and tended towards a 'security' model of detention. Nevertheless, it remains the only full Executive Committee Conclusion on detention and, as such, an influential statement that has been used as a point of reference by many others bodies, including the Council of Europe and the European Union in drafting rules in this field.

The main difficulty is that the concept of 'necessity' was stretched to include grounds that look to be punitive, going beyond the spirit of Article 31. For example, it is not clear why detention should be 'necessary' where a person has used false documents. The argument might be that such a person cannot be trusted. This might then lead to the further conclusion either that their asylum claim is false and/or that they might abscond if released. However, these further conclusions do not follow inevitably from the use of false documents, a commonplace practice, often essential

---

70 G. Goodwin-Gill, *The Refugee in International Law*, Oxford University Press, 1996, 249.
71 UNHCR Executive Committee Conclusion No. 44 (1986), Detention of Refugees and Asylum Seekers.

for refugees to escape and/or enter another state. This certainly does not support detention.

Using detention to establish identity is also of doubtful utility. A person who has no valid identity documents will not be able to obtain them any more readily by being detained. It may be that the detainee has deliberately lied and that detention will push them into revealing their true identity. However, that begins to look like a punishment without a proper criminal charge. More commonly, asylum seekers carry no documents and identity is simply accepted or doubted depending on the overall credibility of their asylum claim. Detention has very little part to play in the process and certainly cannot be said to be 'necessary' on this account.[72]

Finally, using detention to establish the elements of the claim might be thought to be more readily shown to be 'necessary'. However even here this would be so only for a brief period and only if no other means of obtaining the relevant information are practical. The interview itself should be arranged swiftly so that detention would not result simply from administrative delay. In many cases asylum seekers could be released and an interview arranged later if no flight risk was present.

From the mid-1980s there was continued tension between the UNHCR and European governments, particularly over Tamil asylum seekers whom it considered were refugees, but who were rejected and sometimes detained by governments. Later in 1988, the UNHCR said that little had changed despite the recommendations in Excomm. 44. In fact, it thought state practice may have got worse.[73] The period after the collapse of the Berlin wall was, however, one in which the new High Commissioner, Sadako Ogata, sought to reposition the UNHCR as an agency of humanitarian relief with less focus upon legal protection of refugees.[74] This involved moving towards a greater consensus with European governments to secure support for this work. The measures taken against asylum seekers in Europe were to some extent left unchallenged. Indeed, the UNHCR began to have less influence in any event as European asylum policy began to be coordinated through the European Union.

---

72 L. Takkenberg, 'Detention and Other Restrictions of the Freedom of Movement of Refugees and Asylum-seekers: the European Perspective', in J. Bhabha and G. Noll (eds), *Asylum Law and Practice in Europe and North America*, Washington, DC: Federal Publications Inc., 1992.

73 'On the contrary, detention under harsh conditions, for long periods and without justifiable cause has recently increased.' UNHCR, 'Note on International Protection', UN Doc. A/AC.96/713, Aug. 15, 1988, para. 21.

74 Loescher, *Beyond Charity*, 318.

In conclusion, the guidelines in Excomm. 44 reflected the new politics of asylum. Modest voluntary resettlement programmes were now dwarfed by larger numbers of irregular arrivals. Western states sought to limit their shares of the new asylum seekers by restricting their migration through visas, return to third countries and other measures. For those who managed to arrive, governments denied that there was a right to be released as Article 26 suggested. Instead they used detention to discourage irregular migration in ways that were contrary to the intentions of the drafters of the Convention. The distinction between war- and peacetime measures was blurred as irregular migrants came to be held in closed facilities for long periods during and after consideration of their cases.

The development of proportionality in UNHCR Guidelines and their lack of influence on state practice

It was only later in 1995 that the UNHCR produced its own further guidelines on detention of asylum seekers.[75] They sought to put a more liberal and coherent interpretation on Excomm. 44. Detention practices were said to be 'inherently undesirable', more so in the case of women, children or those with special medical needs. Interestingly, they suggested that detention that is automatic or unduly prolonged would amount to 'punishment' in breach of Article 31.[76] Guideline 3 provided an 'interpretation' of Excomm. 44, but actually tried to limit it. Thus, there was a presumption against detention; other means, including bail or reporting should be used first, unless they would fail. They also stated that 'account should be taken as to whether [detention] is reasonable... and proportional to the objectives...'. This overall proportionality test set out a coherent and sensible view.

However, there was still the problem of the defective criteria set out in Excomm. 44. The UNHCR Guidelines seemed to take these as specific sub-reasons to detain within the overall proportionality framework. They should be limited to cases where identity is *in dispute*, for conducting a *preliminary* interview or where there is *deliberate attempt to mislead* the

---

75 UNHCR's Guidelines on Applicable Criteria and Standards relating to the Detention of Asylum Seekers (rev. Feb. 1999).

76 This was no doubt inspired by the convention drafters' view that detention of unlawfully present refugees, if permitted under Art. 31, would be short.

authorities. Guideline 4 suggested that, pending status determination, alternatives to detention should be considered such as reporting, residency or bail conditions. Guideline 5 called for automatic review of the detention decision by an independent judicial or administrative body, followed by regular reviews of the continuing necessity for detention. The review should take the form of a review of 'all aspects of the case' including the necessity for detention, not simply whether there is a legal power to detain in national law. The guidelines made a valuable attempt to provide an overall defensible and coherent basis for detention that struck a fair balance between refugees and border control.

Following revision of the guidelines in 1999, the UNCHR produced an important discussion paper[77] seeking to 'draw attention to the increasing institutionalization of the practice' of detention and asked the Executive Committee to 'take a strong stand on the issue . . . of arbitrariness'. Drawing upon then-recent Human Rights Committee cases that are discussed below, the paper argued again that detention must be proportionate and that there should be reasonable time frames set by law.[78] The report criticized state practices of mandatory detention for asylum seekers with false or no documents as arbitrary.[79] The report drew an important distinction between 'arbitrary' detention based on standard asylum-seeking practices (such as using false documentation) and 'necessary' detention related to individual risk, particularly of absconding.

The effect of the new UNHCR approach, however, was limited. In 2002, Ruud Lubbers, High Commissioner for Refugees, noted the continued 'general trend towards increased use of detention'.[80] The 'Agenda for Protection' of 2002 again asked for states 'more concertedly to explore appropriate alternatives to the detention of asylum-seekers and refugees, and to abstain, in principle, from detaining children'.[81] Goodwin-Gill, one of the authors of the Agenda, summarizing the UNHCR guidance, said 'detention of refugees and asylum seekers *is an exceptional measure*; as such, it should be applied on an *individual* basis, where it has been determined by the appropriate authority to be necessary in light of the circumstances of the case, on the basis of criteria established by law, in

---

77 Executive Committee of the UNHCR, Standing Committee, 'Detention of Asylum seekers and Refugees: the Framework, the Problem and Recommended Practice' (15th meeting, 4 June 1999, EC/49/SC/CRP13).
78 26(h).   79 14–15.   80 UNHCR, Opening Statement, 30 Sept. 2002.
81 Executive Committee of the UNHCR, 26 June 2002, A/AC.96/965/Add. 1, 9.

accordance with international refugee and human rights law'.[82] As we have seen, this was and remains far removed from state practice, with its group-based approach directed at managing irregular migration.

Conclusions on detention and the Refugee Convention: a protection failure

The conclusion must be that the Refugee Convention has failed to provide practical protection for asylum seekers against arbitrary detention. The reasons are largely political, but the text itself does not help. The Convention drafting is too ambiguous. A right of movement within the territory is given to refugees who are 'lawfully present', but this term has attracted no authoritative interpretation.[83] The relationship between Articles 26 and 31(2) is also unclear. The latter restricts the right of states to detain illegally present asylum seekers unless 'necessary' but only if they fulfil certain pre-conditions. Failure to meet any of these would appear to allow detention that was not 'necessary'. The meaning of 'necessary' has continued to be plagued by disagreements.[84] States argue that until a person has established their refugee status, detention may be 'necessary' to prevent

---

82 G. Goodwin-Gill, 'Article 31 of the 1951 Convention relating to the Status of Refugees: Non-penalization, Detention and Protection', in E. Feller *et al.* (eds), *Refugee Protection in International Law*, Cambridge University Press, 2003, paras 125–31 and 'International Law and the Detention of Refugees' (1986) 20(2) *Int. Migration Rev.* 193.

83 See G. Grahl-Madsen, *The Status of Refugees in International Law*, Leyden: Sijthoff, 1966, 361–2, who suggests that a refugee who is detained pending status determination is not lawfully present. Hathaway concedes that this is a tenable view, see J.C. Hathaway, 'What's in a Label?' (2003) 5 *Eur. J. Migration and L.* 1, 11, n. 41.

84 Only the New Zealand courts appear to have attempted to interpret Art. 31(2). In a national security deportation case the Supreme Court acknowledged that 'Article 31(2) of the Refugee Convention requires Contracting States not to apply to the movement of certain refugees restrictions other than those which are necessary.' See *Zaoui* v. *Attorney-General*, Dec. SC CIV 13/2004 (NZ SC, 25 Nov. 2004), para. 44. Also in *Refugee Council of New Zealand Inc and the Human Rights Foundation of Aotearoa New Zealand Inc and 'D'* v. *The Attorney General (No. 2)* [2002] NZAR 71 (NZ HC, 31 May 2002), 125–31 the trial judge argued for a very narrow set of permissible objectives where detention could be considered 'necessary': (1) to enable the refugee status body to perform its function; (2) to avoid a real risk of criminal offending; and (3) to avoid a real risk of absconding. This was a much tighter and more defensible approach than that adopted by Excomm. 44. However, this was overturned by the Court of Appeal which said, by reference to UNHCR Guideline 3, that the state need only show 'fault' on the part of the immigrant [2003] NZLR 577 (NZ CA, 16 Apr. 2003). This moved decisively back towards the 'anti-abuse' logic of state sovereignty. *E* v. *Attorney-General* had earlier concluded that Art. 31(2) required that 'lesser forms of control would need to be addressed before the more drastic steps of full detention could be justified' [2000] NZAR 354 (NZ HC, 29 Nov. 1999).

illegal entry or abuse of the system or violation of their border controls. Once a person has been denied refugee status, the Refugee Convention has no further application.[85]

No doubt the drafters of the Refugee Convention did not envisage the use of detention outside of wartime or mass-influx situations. Western countries broadly welcomed refugees from Communism and the numbers were relatively small. For Western countries after 1980, irregular migration became the major concern. Asylum seekers were discouraged. Many claims, sometimes even a majority, were held to be unfounded and allegedly based on false testimony.[86] States began to argue that many were in fact economic migrants using the asylum system to get round restrictive immigration laws. They had often broken increasingly strict immigration laws to enter the country of asylum. Quite often initial decisions to reject a claim were reached fairly quickly and detention was extended as a result of the appeals or removal procedure. The executive view in such cases was that the asylum seeker thus refused fell outside the Convention unless and until a court held otherwise.

Excomm. 44 reflects the changed political atmosphere of the time. Whilst humanitarian concerns were offered by some states and organizations, security concerns had come to the fore in the politics of many Western states. As Haddad notes more generally, as states' attitudes in relation to the Refugee Convention came to reflect 'more a communitarian security issue than a cosmopolitan humanitarian concern, it follows that refugees are perceived and controlled more as a matter of national and international security than a matter of human security'.[87] This change is reflected in the increased emphasis on the use of detention as part of the strategy to control borders.

We can conclude that the increased practice of detention in relation to asylum seekers provides a powerful illustration of Haddad's argument that '[t]he issue of asylum and refugees has effectively been "securitised" in western societies. Immigration of any kind is linked to insecurity,

---

85 There may of course be an appeal system, but this is not required by the Refugee Convention. Pending a first merits appeal a person may still benefit from the convention, but it is difficult to credibly say that the presumption that a person is a refugee should remain until all legal avenues have been exhausted. States certainly do not accept this idea.

86 E. Neumayer, 'Asylum Recognition Rates in Western Europe' [2005] 49 *J. of Conflict Res.* 43. This is not the place to consider the merits of the asylum decision-making of the period, which has been subject to great criticism. The point is that executive detention was increasingly intertwined with, and drew support from, poor recognition rates.

87 Haddad, *The Refugee in International Society*, 91.

and where this movement is seemingly out of control the insecurity increases'.[88] The fairly abrupt change in detention practice towards asylum seekers was emblematic of this new desire to be seen to control borders.

General human rights prohibitions and immigration detention

The UNHCR was the first international agency to become involved in scrutinizing immigration detention, but it is not the only one. Bodies overseeing general international human rights law have also been drawn into the debate. It is clear that most norms in international human rights law apply to all those within a state party's jurisdiction, regardless of nationality or immigration status.[89] The extent to which border controls can legitimately curtail these rights has been the subject of very divergent views from monitoring bodies, a reflection of both textual but also political differences. We will focus upon the Council of Europe and the United Nations, whose organs monitor two treaties of particular importance: the European Convention on Human Rights (ECHR) and the International Covenant on Civil and Political Rights.

The European Convention on Human Rights: detention as ancillary to the aliens power

The approach of the Strasbourg Court to immigration detention was from its inception very deferential to state sovereignty. Partly this reflected an initial perception that administrative detention was not widespread. There was thus little sense of a wider political and social dimension. Whilst the Commission had from the 1960s received complaints about detention linked to deportation or extradition, this was generally short and seen as ancillary to expulsion.[90] However, despite the existence of the convention since 1950, the case-law is relatively new and still evolving.[91] In more

---

88 *Ibid.*, 194.
89 There are some obvious examples of norms which are specific in their application. For example, considering the ICCPR, Art. 12 refers to 'Everyone lawfully within the territory of State shall . . . have the right to liberty of movement and freedom to choose his residence.' In addition, Art. 13 states that 'An alien lawfully in the territory of a State Party . . . may be expelled therefrom only in pursuance of a decision reached in accordance with law.' Art. 25 confers the right to vote upon citizens only.
90 Application. 3916/69, *X* v. *Sweden*, Decision of 18 Dec. 1969.
91 The first major decision was *Bozano* v. *France*, Judgment of 18 Dec. 1986, where the Court ruled that there had been a breach of Art. 5(1) because immigration detention

recent years an emerging wider politics critical of immigration detention amongst Council of Europe political institutions has begun to force a revision in the previously deferential approach.

Considering the text, it is notable that there is no general prohibition upon 'arbitrary' detention[92] under Article 5(1), which states that:

> Everyone has the right to liberty and security of person. No one shall be deprived of his liberty save in the following cases and in accordance with a procedure prescribed by law:
>
> . . .
>
> (f) the lawful arrest or detention of a person to prevent his effecting an unauthorized entry into the country or of a person against whom action is being taken with a view to deportation or extradition.

Whilst this express authority for immigration detention in Article 5 is important, more significant has been the broad interpretation of the aliens power adopted by the Court and the Commission.

The first Commission decisions: due diligence and allocating blame

The first ECHR case in which longer-term detention was considered was *Lynas*,[93] where the applicant had been held for three-and-a-half years pending extradition. The Commission recognized that Article 5(1)(f), if applied literally, could be used to justify unlimited detention as extradition proceedings were drawn out either by carelessness or design. The Commission said that:

> only the existence of extradition proceedings justifies deprivation of liberty in such a case. It follows that if, for example, the proceedings are not conducted with the *requisite diligence* or if the detention results from some misuse of authority it ceases to be justifiable under Article 5(1)(f).[94]

and deportation had been an abuse of power engineered to circumvent a national court ruling prohibiting extradition. This case is unique because it involved serious *male fides*, untypical of immigration cases.

92 The drafting history shows there was a clear division between states that favoured a broad prohibition on 'arbitrary' detention (as eventually transpired under the ICCPR) and those, particularly the United Kingdom, who wanted a clear statement of which grounds might justify detention. The crucial text was introduced by the British delegate on 4 February 1950, when the inclusion of five grounds were put as an alternative to a broad prohibition on arbitrary detention. *Travaux Préparatoires*, vol. III, 188–9, Doc. A780.

93 Application no. 7317/75, *Lynas v. Switzerland*, Decision of 6 Oct. 1976.

94 *Ibid.*, 3 (emphasis added).

Thus the bare fact that expulsion action was proceeding was not enough to meet the convention standard.[95] However, it has become clear that this approach provides limited constraints upon detention, depending heavily upon governments' accounts of the state of negotiations with third countries. Legal certainty around the criteria and end-points for such detention is minimal and detainees remain held largely on the basis of diplomatic discussion.

In *X* v. *United Kingdom*,[96] the Commission introduced an apportionment of 'blame' test that further eroded legal certainty. In this case, the authorities detained a Pakistani, pending the issue of a deportation order, on the ground that he might abscond. He had applied for asylum upon arrest and was held for over ten months pending enquiries being made by the authorities. The Commission speculated that 'it is possible that a significant portion of the investigation would have been avoided if he had presented a straightforward asylum case from the beginning'. As the delays were partly caused by the applicant and partly by the complicated nature of the case, there had been no 'clear appearance' of lack of due diligence.

Further undermining the rule of law surrounding detention, the Commission later ruled that there was no need for a separate reason to support it. Thus in *Caprino* v. *United Kingdom*[97] a deportee was held, but no reason was given for detention apart from the existence of a deportation order.[98] The Commission said that whilst '[i]t may be that the applicant's detention was not strictly necessary to implement the envisaged deportation . . . but . . . there was nevertheless an *adequate relationship* between the detention and the deportation proceedings' (emphasis added). The Commission thus rejected the idea that the deportees had a right to liberty

---

95 This is rather like the approach to 'lawfulness', applicable throughout the convention, which requires national law to be of a certain quality and accessibility to meet the international standard. See *Amuur* v. *France* (1996) 22 EHRR 533.

96 Application no. 8081/77, Decision of 12 Dec. 1977.

97 Application no. 6871/75, decision of 3 Mar. 1978 on admissibility of the application.

98 The fact that the deportation order was revoked after it was made did not change the lawful character of the detention. This is an example of the 'fourth instance' doctrine adopted by the Strasbourg Court. This states that the merits of an underlying administrative decision or criminal conviction cannot be reviewed by the international court in order to impugn the compatibility of a detention order with the European Convention: Application 3245/67, *X* v. *Austria*, 4 Feb. 1969, (1969) 12 *Yearbook* 206, 236. The effect of a successful challenge to an immigration decision upon the legality of an underlying detention decision is limited. The European Court of Human Rights, for example, has held that where the deportation order itself is illegal because it violates national or convention law, detention pending execution of that order is, however, not a breach of the right to liberty. See *Chahal* v. *United Kingdom* (1996) 23 EHRR 413.

unless specific reasons for detention were shown. The aliens power was taken to entail detention as an inherent aspect of expulsion and exclusion.

In the same case, however, it drew an interesting parallel with internment in Northern Ireland which had just been criticized by the Court:[99]

> the Commission considers that the detention of an alien in view of his deportation for reasons of national security *can in a certain way be compared to the internment of nationals effected for the same reasons* as both measures aim at removing the person concerned from society mainly because he is considered to constitute a risk to the preservation of peace and maintenance of order in the country.

Where such preventive detention occurred, even during deportation proceedings, the Commission argued that strong procedural safeguards should apply to both citizens and aliens.[100] Distinguishing between expulsion and security aspects of immigration detention was not, however, explored further.

Outside extradition or security deportations, there were in any event few long-term detentions during this time. The major exception was that of the Vietnamese 'boat-people' detainees held in Hong Kong for years.[101] These cases raised important issues of the detention of stateless persons and the limits of Article 5(1)(f) where expulsion proceedings had stalled. However, their application was declared inadmissible, as the United Kingdom had not agreed to Hong Kong falling under the jurisdiction of the convention. The question would have to wait until such practices became more common in Europe itself.

Evolution of the Strasbourg Court case-law: the weakness of the due diligence approach

The Court tended to follow the Commission's approach. The first case-law emerged in the 1990s and related to extradition or national security cases,

---

99 *Ireland* v. *United Kingdom*, Judgment of 18 Jan. 1978, Series A, No. 25, (1979–80) 2 EHRR 25.

100 The Commission agreed that judicial review, as practised in the United Kingdom, of the decision to detain on grounds of national security did not afford adequate judicial control of detention. Whilst the government had an unlimited discretion to detain on public security grounds, the courts limited their review to whether the detention was *ultra vires* or *mala fides*. They did not control 'other aspects of the lawfulness of detention or of the underlying deportation measures'. The Commission also noted that the authorities did not need to disclose the information behind their decision.

101 Application no. 16137/90, *Bui Van Thanh and others* v. *United Kingdom*, 12 Mar. 1990. Thousands of detainees spent many years held in mandatory detention, following denial of refugee status, pending their removal to Vietnam which would not accept them back.

which could last for years. The danger of inactivity by the government was obvious but so, too, was the public security context. These were relatively isolated cases involving individuals. Only in recent years, in the face of increasing use of administrative detention as a policy targeted at groups, has the Court begun to reconsider the broad discretion given to states. A new politics has emerged around the detention of these vulnerable groups, particularly asylum seekers, but also stateless persons. In this area, there has been increasing activity from the political organs of the Council of Europe, which appears to have exerted some influence on the Court.

In the first important case of *Kolompar*,[102] the Court endorsed the Commission's due diligence test.[103] Using a 'blame/causation' test, on the facts it was held that detention of two years and eight months pending extradition did not amount to a violation of Article 5 because it was not attributable to the detaining state. The extradition proceedings had been completed quickly, but the detainee had repeatedly sought to set aside the extradition order. The consequence of adopting a blame-based approach is to render detention a kind of battle of wills, with the danger that this leads to punitive practices. Detainees can be held for longer and longer if they fail to comply or seek to exercise legal rights. This puts detention in a state of grave legal uncertainty, as the attribution of blame is inherently subjective.

Even with its inherent problems as a safeguard, the Court's application of the due diligence test been rightly criticized.[104] For example in *Chahal*, detention for six years in total, including periods of six and seven months waiting for initial and fresh decisions from the immigration authorities, is difficult to reconcile with an exacting due diligence standard. The Court recognized this, but noted the exceptional nature of this factually complex case, which also raised national security issues. The dissenting opinion by Judge De Meyer noted that the serious and weighty nature of the case could explain the length of proceedings but 'they cannot, however, justify the length of the detention, any more than the complexity of criminal

---

102 *Kolompar* v. *Belgium* (1993) 16 EHRR 197.
103 This can be seen as derived from the more general principle of effectiveness which is used by the Court in relation to all articles of the convention. See, for example, *Airey* v. *Ireland* (1979) 2 EHRR 305.
104 See C. Overy and R.C.A. White, *The European Convention on Human Rights* (4th edn), Oxford University Press, 2006, 130.

proceedings is enough to justify the length of pre-trial detention'.[105] Judge Pettiti argued that the United Kingdom should have sought Chahal's admission to a third country rather than detain him. He said that '[a]s implemented by the British authorities, Mr Chahal's detention can be likened to an indefinite sentence'.[106]

By contrast, in another, extradition, case the Court ruled that delays of three and ten months violated Article 5(1)(f).[107] In *Singh* v. *Czech Republic*,[108] immigration detention of two-and-a-half years was criticized because it contained long periods of inactivity by the authorities when faced with practical obstacles to removal. It is therefore difficult to say that any period is too long *per se*; rather, the focus in the case-law has been upon the immigration authorities' action or inaction in attempting to secure removal and the detainee's degree of 'blameworthiness'. The case-law appeared to endorse something close to punitive detention; detainees could be held for longer based upon perceptions of their conduct whilst imprisoned, even though no criminal charge needed be laid against them.

By 2002, the Committee on the Prevention of Torture began to report on the conditions of detention for immigration detainees around this time.[109] The Human Rights Commissioner for the Council of Europe also began to comment adversely in his country reports on the length of immigration detention and the problems caused by an absence of judicial scrutiny.[110] In the same year the Parliamentary Assembly, in a Recommendation on expulsion procedures, expressed concern at deaths in custody and the prevailing climate of hostility towards immigrants.[111]

These developments may have influenced the Court. Faced with greater numbers of *de facto* stateless persons held indefinitely, the Court has recently raised the bar of due diligence. Thus, obstacles to removal may

---

105 See Partly Concurring, Partly Dissenting Opinion at IIA (with whom Judges Golcuklu and Makaryczyk concurred as to Art. 5(1)).
106 Partly Dissenting Opinion, conclusion.
107 *Quinn* v. *France* (1995) 21 EHRR 529.
108 Application no. 60538/00, Judgment of 25 Jan. 2005.
109 Pursuant to its monitoring role under the European Convention on the Prevention of Torture. See the detailed guidance given in *The CPT Standards* (CPT/Inf/E (2002), rev. 2006).
110 See for views on the United Kingdom, Comm DH (2002) 7 and Comm DH (2005) 6 and on France, Comm DH (2006) 2.
111 Recommendation 1547 (2002) Expulsion Procedures in conformity with human rights and enforced with respect for safety and dignity.

require the detaining state to act 'vigorously' to secure travel documents or to negotiate with foreign states to satisfy the test.[112] It is, however, hardly realistic for courts to supervise such negotiations. Even where a state refuses repeatedly to accept a detainee or there is no means of reaching the destination, there is always the theoretical possibility that the position might shift in the light of new evidence or political change. The due diligence test enunciated by the Court has been shown to leave detainees in an uncertain limbo with no clear end-point to detention. It speaks to an era when repatriation was effected quickly or unauthorized migrants were released. The politics of the modern struggle against unauthorized migration have moved on, such that detaining states are willing to incarcerate for long periods now.

European asylum claims: detention at airports and the prison with three walls

The emerging issue of holding asylum applicants at European airports without adequate facilities was more politically sensitive. Unlike other groups of aliens, putative refugees had a clear right under international refugee law to stay in European states until their claims were processed. There was debate about whether airport facilities, as opposed to camps, amounted to detention under Article 5. In 1994 a Committee of Ministers Recommendation called for such claims to be examined 'with all diligence' so as not to prolong holding beyond 'a period strictly necessary for the handling of such a request'.[113] However, there was no consensus at that stage on imposing a maximum period of detention.

---

112 See the decision in Appn. no. 31465/08, *Raza* v. *Bulgaria*, Judgment of 11 Feb. 2010, in which detention of two-and-a-half years was held to be in breach of Art. 5(1) because his deportation was 'blocked solely by the lack of a travel document allowing him to re-enter Pakistan. It is true that the Bulgarian authorities could not compel the issuing of such a document, but there is no indication that they pursued the matter vigorously or endeavoured entering into negotiations with the Pakistani authorities with a view to expediting its delivery... Nor does it appear that any consideration was given to the possibility of sending the applicant to another State willing to accept him' (para. 73). The Court also noted that after his release he was placed under reporting obligations which showed the authorities had other means at their disposal than protracted detention to secure enforcement of the expulsion order (para 74).

113 Recommendation R (94) 5 of the Committee of Ministers on guidelines to inspire practices of the Member States of the Council of Europe concerning the arrival of asylum seekers at European airports, para. 4.

In 1996 in *Amuur* v. *France*,[114] the Court finally considered this newly emerging scenario arising at European airports. The first issue was whether holding pursuant to denial of entry at the border should be treated as a deprivation of liberty at all.[115] In *Amuur*, a group of asylum seekers flew by plane from Syria to France. They were held in the transit zone and a secure hotel. After twenty days they were returned to Syria without their claims for asylum being determined. The French government said this was not detention, as it was merely a method of exclusion.[116] This recalled the legal fictions surrounding those held on ships and at ports of entry in the United States.

The Court equivocated, saying that 'such holding should not be prolonged excessively, otherwise there would be a risk of it turning into a mere restriction on liberty – inevitable with a view to organising the practical details of the aliens' repatriation or where he has requested asylum while his application for leave to enter the territory for that purpose is considered – into a deprivation of liberty'.[117] So in principle, a short period of being held for processing at the border (or in a legally delineated transit zone at the airport) might not amount to 'detention'. On the facts, however, the duration and conditions in the transit zone meant that there was a deprivation of liberty.

The decision also endorsed the idea that migrants who seek entry may be deemed to be giving consent to their continued detention. They could elect to withdraw their application and return to another country. On the facts, however, the Court said that 'this possibility becomes theoretical if no other country offering protection comparable to the protection they expect to find in the country where they are seeking asylum is inclined

---

114 (1996) 22 EHRR 533.
115 As noted above, this had been considered by the Executive Committee of UNHCR in the debates preceding Excomm. 44, after several European nations argued that holding immigrants in international zones was not 'detention' at all. See Goodwill-Gill, *The Refugee in International Law*, 250, where he cites the German and Netherlands delegates to the Working Group on Detention.
116 See *Guzzardi* v. *Italy* (1980) 3 EHRR 333 and *Engel* v. *Netherlands* (1976) 1 EHRR 647, in which the Court distinguished between a deprivation of liberty and a mere restriction on liberty which is now regulated by Art. 2, Protocol No. 4.
117 *Amuur*, para. 43. The Court here seems to have in mind considerations similar to those referred to by the drafters of Art. 31(2) of the Refugee Convention. It is important, however, to note that detention in these cases is permitted because of unlawful presence. The Refugee Convention gives a right of free movement to those lawfully present under Art. 26, which would appear to include those seeking entry once their refugee claims were recorded. See above.

or prepared to take them in'.[118] Syria was not a signatory to the Refugee Convention and therefore there was no legal guarantee that their asylum claims would be considered (much less recognized) there. The difficulty is that this would apply only to asylum seekers. Other categories of migrants held at airports would not be 'detained'. This appeared to endorse the idea that immigrants were held in prisons with only 'three walls', from which they could choose to leave by withdrawing their applications to enter.

Amuur introduced an undesirable lack of clarity into the scope of Article 5(1). Faced with European governments' concerns about rising numbers of asylum claims, the judges appeared to wish to restrict the benefits of Article 5(1) to those who had been held beyond a reasonable processing period. The better view is that immigration detention in locked rooms, or even in closed facilities permitting some degree of movement inside a perimeter, should generally constitute a deprivation of liberty for Article 5(1) purposes.[119] This would avoid all recourse to legal fiction and special zones or periods in which persons were deemed not to be detained. Indeed following *Amuur* in 1997, the Parliamentary Assembly produced recommendations on asylum detention calling for non-custodial measures to be given priority, compliance with Excomm. 44 and a legal maximum period of detention for asylum seekers.[120]

Rejection of a necessity test in the landmark Chahal *case*

Soon after *Amuur*, the Strasbourg Court decided its most important Article 5(1)(f) case. *Chahal* concerned an Indian national who had been a lawful resident of the United Kingdom. A deportation order was made against him on national security grounds related to his alleged sponsorship and participation in political violence in the United Kingdom and India.[121] He remained in detention for three-and-a-half years during the national proceedings because he was said to pose a threat to national

---

118 Paragraph 48.
119 See (Appn. no. 13229/03) *Saadi and Others* v. *United Kingdom*, Judgment of 11 July 2006, where detention in a military barracks which allowed movement within it but not beyond it was held to be caught by Art. 5(1). See also Executive Committee of UNHCR, Standing Committee, 'Detention of Asylum Seekers and Refugees: the Framework, the Problem and Recommended Practice' (15th meeting, 4 June 1999, EC/49/SC/CRP13) which confirms airport transit zones are places of detention.
120 Recommendation 1327 (1997) on the protection and reinforcement of the human rights of refugees and asylum seekers in Europe, adopted 24 April 1997 (14th sitting).
121 This was one of the first cases in which an impact on foreign relations was put forward as damaging national security. It was also a precursor to the internment of suspected international terrorists that emerged later.

security if released. The national courts rejected applications to review his detention without assessing the merits or the full evidence. He had been detained for six years by the date of the Strasbourg Court's judgment. The Court found that Article 3 provided an absolute prohibition on deporting him. The United Kingdom immediately released him because, in the absence of deportation proceedings, there was no other basis for preventive detention.[122]

As regards his detention up until then, the Court held that Article 5:

> does not demand that the detention of a person against whom action is being taken with a view to deportation be reasonably considered necessary, for example to prevent his committing an offence or fleeing.[123]

The Court made clear the contrast with detainees held on remand pending prosecution which required specific public policy reasons, such as a risk of absconding, for continuing detention pursuant to Article 5(3).[124] Similarly, the Court had previously ruled that non-criminal detention of citizens had to be shown to be necessary in the public interest to be allowed under Article 5. Thus, the Court had ruled that mental patients detained under Article 5(1)(e) must present a threat to themselves or others if at large, despite the text imposing no such limitation.[125] A similar approach has been taken to those detained for being under the influence of alcohol.[126] This approach was essentially based upon the same proportionality test that is explicitly articulated in Articles 8–11.

Deportees and unauthorized aliens were therefore clearly marked out as lacking the same basic rights to liberty as citizens in *Chahal*.[127] An absence

---

122 The UK introduced a system of control orders for all persons in 2005, which could have been used to restrict *Chahal* had it been available at the time. See Ch. 5 below.

123 Paragraph 112. This is in contrast to those detained on bail pending criminal charges under Art. 5(1)(c) who must present such a risk of absconding or further offences.

124 See *Scott* v. *Spain* (1997) 24 EHRR 391; *Caballero* v. *United Kingdom* (Appn. no. 32819/96), Judgment of 8 Feb. 2000; *Barfuss* v. *Czech Republic* (2002) 34 EHRR 948.

125 See *Winterwerp* v. *Netherlands*, (1979–80) 2 EHRR 387.

126 See *Wittold Litwa* v. *Poland* (2001) 33 EHRR 1267. For a detailed critique see G. Cornelisse, 'Human Rights for Immigration Detainees in Strasbourg: Limited Sovereignty or a Limited Discourse?' (2004) 6 *Eur. J. Migration and L.* 93.

127 The *Chahal* principles would appear to apply equally to admission and expulsion cases, although the text of Art. 5(1)(f) is drafted differently. Admission might appear to be more demanding of the state because detention must be 'to prevent' an illegal entry. This might imply a necessity test. By contrast, in deportation cases, the only obligation is for the state to show 'action is being taken'. This distinction was rejected by the House of Lords in *Saadi*, and it is suggested that it would be counter-intuitive to allow greater protection for newly arrived migrants as compared with those already established. *Amuur* certainly gives no support for the need to show necessity in order to justify detention in admission cases.

of immigration status or being subject to removal proceedings was *in itself* enough to support detention. The government had no burden of proof. The Court has many times emphasized states' powers to control migration as a fundamental aspect of sovereignty. No doubt the national security context of *Chahal* led the Court to be reluctant to approach the issue of detention. Other rulings have, however, confirmed that the position is the same in cases not touching upon national security.[128] This restrictive approach was inviting to governments wishing to expand administrative detention policy.[129]

In *Chahal*, however, the Court did follow the Commission's approach to judicial review in *Caprino*, seeing the spectre of internment. It therefore held that the domestic courts' failure to rigorously assess whether Chahal's release would really present a security risk was a breach of Article 5(4) – the right to challenge the legality of detention. Where governments specifically detain aliens on security grounds, then courts must adopt heightened procedural due process standards in habeas corpus. This was so even in the context of detention annexed to ongoing deportation proceedings. This prefigured later cases relating to post-9/11 detention of aliens.[130] Whilst laudable, this part of the ruling is, however, hard to reconcile with the *Chahal* principle that detention need not be necessary during deportation to comply with Article 5(1)(f).[131]

*Constraining pure administrative detention post-*Chahal

In recent years, rather than national security detention, many European states have held immigrants for purely administrative reasons. Within European human rights bodies there has been increased concern at the

---

128 Application no. 51564/99, *Conka* v. *Belgium*, 5 Feb. 2002.

129 There is a tendency to put the best interpretation on the case in the Council of Europe's Human Rights File on Aliens which says that detention must be 'necessary in a democratic society'. There must be protection against arbitrariness and 'it follows that a blanket policy of detaining all asylum-seekers on arrival would be incompatible with the ECHR'. It also says that 'so would prolonged detention pending examination of an asylum claim in the absence of a specific reason such as threat to national security'. H. Lambert, *The Position of Aliens in Relation to the European Convention on Human Rights*, Human Rights Files No. 8 (rev.), Strasbourg: Council of Europe Publishing, 2001.

130 See Ch. 5 below.

131 The reasoning of the Court is a little opaque, but it would appear to be based upon the fact that the UK authorities had a discretion to release and refused to do so based on security risks. The result is that, perversely, the executive might adopt mandatory detention or give no reasons to avoid being subject to judicial review under Art. 5(4). They could simply say detention was pursuant to deportation under Art. 5(1)(f) and point to ongoing deportation proceedings.

very lengthy periods of detention and poor conditions affecting these non-dangerous migrants. Thus, without entirely abandoning the established principles, the Court has been searching for new limits upon state discretion.

Some of these concerns were reflected in the first comprehensive Recommendation by the Committee of Ministers on detention of asylum seekers in 2003.[132] It recommended that states follow the guidelines in Excomm. 44, but also urged that alternatives to detention should be considered first. It also emphasized that detention should be 'specific, temporary and non-arbitrary and should be applied for the shortest possible time' and this should only be for the maximum permitted by law or in the absence of a maximum, judicial review should include review of the duration of detention.

The Court appeared to accept some of these ideas in *Saadi*.[133] Whilst still rejecting a test of necessity, it argued for proportionality regarding the duration of detention. The case concerned a challenge by an individual detained pursuant to a UK policy to detain all asylum seekers whose cases were considered simple for seven days, to allow processing of their applications. The oddity was that the policy only applied to migrants *not* considered to be absconding risks.[134] The applicant had in fact been released previously and was not considered a flight risk.

Thus, this was first case considered by the Court involving detention for truly administrative convenience.[135] The Court upheld the government argument that, even where a migrant seeks entry by seeking

132 Recommendation R (2003) 5 of the Committee of Ministers to member states on measures of detention of asylum seekers (adopted by the Committee of Ministers on 16 April 2003 at the 837th meeting of the Ministers' Deputies). By contrast to the more generous approach taken to asylum seekers, the Committee of Ministers gave further guidelines in 2005 relating to the detention of migrants awaiting forced removal. These largely reflect the Court's case-law and do not provide for serious constraints upon lengthy detention during the removal period: Twenty-Guidelines on Forced Returns, Committee of Ministers, Council of Europe (Strasbourg, September 2005).

133 Application no. 13229/03, *Saadi and Others* v. *United Kingdom* (Grand Chamber), Judgment of 29 Jan. 2008. All that is required is that the detention should be a genuine part of the process to determine whether the individual should be granted immigration clearance and/or asylum, and that it should not otherwise be arbitrary, for example on account of its length.

134 This peculiarity arose from the fact that the chosen detention facilities were not secure enough for absconding risks cases.

135 Notably this might be the kind of detention that the drafters of the Refugee Convention had in mind as 'necessary' under Art. 31(2). The Court did not consider the convention, but rejected the idea that Art. 5 contained any inherent right of free movement for asylum seekers (like Art. 26 of the convention). Rather, they could move once the state had had a short period to hold them and process their claim.

asylum through proper channels, the authorization process could entail detention. As an aspect of the aliens power, states could detain aliens at the border or in-country before deciding whether to release them. There was no right of release as such for unauthorized aliens, even if asylum seekers. However:

> [t]o avoid being branded as arbitrary . . . such detention must be carried out in good faith; it must be closely connected to the purpose of preventing unauthorised entry of the person to the country; the place and conditions of detention should be appropriate, bearing in mind that 'the measure is applicable not to those who have committed criminal offences but to aliens who, often fearing for their lives, have fled from their own country' (see *Amuur*, § 43); and the length of the detention should not exceed that *reasonably required for the purpose pursued* (para. 74, emphasis added).

In *Saadi* the Court first held that, at least for asylum seekers applying for authorization, due diligence was not the test. Both the conditions and excessive duration of detention itself might be a sign of arbitrariness.[136] The Grand Chamber, however, accepted that a short period of detention was acceptable as a blanket policy to facilitate processing of large numbers of asylum claims.[137] Thus it pointedly did not directly challenge one of the new techniques developed by European states to tackle what were seen as excessive numbers of asylum claims. Group detention in order to meet processing targets, without individual assessment, was endorsed. The dissenting judgments argued that this amounted to 'criminalizing' refugees because even those fully complying with asylum and immigration law were detained, even when not absconding risks.[138] This goes to

---

136 In the chamber hearing, the concurring opinion of Sir Nicholas Bratza put the matter more clearly when he said that the prohibition on arbitrariness requires both that detention be for no longer than the application takes to process 'and that it be short'. He found that on the facts of that case (seven days' detention to process the application) 'any period of detention significantly in excess of this period would in my view not be compatible with the first limb of Article 5(1)(f)' (Appn. no. 13229/03), *Saadi and Others* v. *United Kingdom*, Judgment of 11 July 2006, Concurring Opinion.

137 It noted 'the difficult administrative problems with which the United Kingdom was confronted during the period in question, with an escalating flow of huge numbers of asylum-seekers' (para. 80). It accepted the government's explanation that the detention centre system was necessary to enable applications to be speedily processed by ensuring detainees were available for interview. This benefited asylum seekers in the queue waiting for decisions. The Court found that there was a close enough connection between the detention and prevention of unlawful entry. The period of detention was short and the conditions were held to be relatively relaxed.

138 The minority opinion was outspoken in its criticism of detention for administrative convenience absent absconding risks, seeing this as supporting arbitrary discrimination

the heart of debate around detention; should it be viewed in aggregate terms as part of effective border control policy, or as a collection of individual deprivations of liberty? The majority struck what can be seen as a *political* balance that controlled asylum detention policy, by focusing upon duration rather than individualized decision-making.

In 1999 the growing difficulty in removing rejected asylum seekers was discussed and produced a Recommendation from the Committee of Ministers.[139] The problem of lengthy detention in such cases, even where the 'due diligence' standard was met, was clearly in issue. The explanatory memorandum says:

> specific measures (such as detention) may be applied by the host country if the rejected asylum seeker deliberately hampers the implementation of return. If detention is resorted to it should not be applied as a sanction but as a specific, temporary and non-arbitrary administrative measure ... in accordance with law and ... relevant international instruments.[140]

The difficulty here is that any detention imposed because of deliberate hampering looks like a sanction; a punishment without a definite crime. Even whilst the Recommendation recognized the problem, it offered no solution. Perhaps rather forlornly, it urged instead that the 'country of origin ... respects its obligations under international law to readmit its own national without formalities, delays or obstacles'.[141] It further urged countries to cooperate to facilitate return by use of readmission agreements.

Facing further cases of indefinite detention, the Court finally moved beyond the due diligence test in the very significant case of *Mikolenko* v. *Estonia*.[142] It favoured the emerging 'realistic prospect of removal' test that we have seen in domestic cases elsewhere. It did so whilst also stepping back from the 'blame' approach. The facts involved a Russian failed asylum seeker who was detained for three-and-a-half years whilst efforts were made to expel him. He had no Russian passport and the Russian

---

against aliens: 'Ultimately, are we now also to accept that Article 5 of the Convention, which has played a major role in ensuring controls of arbitrary detention, should afford a lower level of protection as regards asylum and immigration which, in social and human terms, are the most crucial issues facing us in the years to come? Is it a crime to be a foreigner? We do not think so' (Joint Partly Dissenting Opinion of Judges Rozakis, Ozakis, Tulkens, Kovler, Hajiyev, Spielmann and Hirvela).

139 Recommendation R (99) 12 of Committee of Ministers to member states on the return of rejected asylum seekers (18 May 1999).

140 *Ibid.*, 11.   141 *Ibid.*, 4.   142 Application no. 10664/05, Judgment of 8 Oct. 2009.

authorities said from the outset that they would not accept him back without one. He refused to cooperate with a passport application. At the time, the governments concerned were negotiating a readmission agreement that would allow return without a passport. After three years the agreement was signed. He had been bailed by then. The government argued that these actions were enough to satisfy 'due diligence' and therefore the detention was lawful.

In a new and welcome departure from exclusive reliance upon the old test, the Court said detention was unlawful 'due to the *lack of a realistic prospect* of his expulsion *and* [author's emphasis] the domestic authorities' failure to conduct the proceedings with due diligence'.[143] The Court noted, 'it must have become clear quite soon that [these expulsion] attempts were bound to fail'.[144] His expulsion had become virtually impossible 'as for all practical purposes it required his co-operation, which he was not willing to give'.[145] The decision moved away from accepting that diplomatic negotiations were a legitimate reason to detain. The Court also noted that he had been released on bail eventually without incident and 'thus the authorities had at their disposal measures, other than the applicant's protracted detention in the deportation centre, in the absence of any immediate prospect of his expulsion'.[146] This suggests that the hitherto rejected test of 'necessity' may now be being recognized as part of the assessment under Article 5(1)(f), particularly where detention is prolonged due to bureaucratic obstacles.

Most radically, turning to the 'blame' issue, *Mikolenko* rejected the defence that the detention was 'voluntary' or not caused by the state because of the detainee's choice not to cooperate. This was a controversial step, because it would allow a detainee to 'profit' from their own non-cooperation. Standard immigration practice is to seek to counter this by extending detention in such cases.[147] Such strategies are seen as key tests of state legitimacy in resisting unauthorized migration. Nevertheless the Court's position is defensible and consistent with the Committee of Ministers Recommendation. Detention should never be used as an instrument of executive coercion. To do so puts it into the same moral arena as blackmail or torture. The proper course, if any, in such cases is to apply a

---

143 Paragraph 68.   144 Paragraph 64.   145 Paragraph 65.
146 See also Appn. no. 31465/08, *Raza* v. *Bulgaria*, Judgment of 11 Feb. 2010 for a similar case.
147 The *Zadvydas/Martinez* time limits in the United States do not apply during 'non-cooperation' periods. See now the EU Returns Directive discussed in Ch. 4 below, allowing up to 18 months' detention for non-cooperation.

criminal sanction for non-compliance.[148] It is not yet clear if this decision means that the 'blame/causation' approach has been totally abandoned. The Court accepted, however, that a detainee's blameworthiness could not legitimate unlimited detention. The prison with three walls concept was rejected.

The 2002 Parliamentary Assembly Recommendation[149] on expulsion procedures had suggested limiting detention in transit zones to fifteen days and, elsewhere, to one month. Even within such limits, it urged regular judicial supervision to test the 'strict necessity and proportionality of the use and continuation of detention'.[150] This was important because it went beyond simply asylum seekers, who have always had a special status. This was followed up by an important Recommendation on a Common Policy on Migration and Asylum which advocated 'core rights and procedural safeguards to be enjoyed by all those who are within the jurisdiction of a Council of Europe member state'.[151] The detention principles were a key component and show a move towards a more coherent set of justifications linked to specific evidence. Thus detention should be exceptional and only arise when there is:

> a convincing reason for believing that a person is trying to enter the country illegally, or when there is a legitimate reason specific to the person concerned, such as a person is at high risk of absconding, or when in detention it is necessary to enforce the removal or establish the identity of a person.[152]

Following the French model, it suggested that any detention decision should be confirmed within forty-eight hours by a judge. Finally, detention should not be longer than is reasonably necessary and should not be 'prolonged unduly'. This went well beyond the traditional case-law under Article 5.

The Court has again responded with decisions suggesting, although not deciding definitively, that time limits on detention are required in order to comply with Article 5. In these cases Turkish authorities held illegal immigrants for over one year in detention centres without making the deportation orders which were a pre-condition to a power to detain.[153]

---

148 We saw this in Ch. 2 in relation to the American practice under the 1952 Immigration Act, and this is discussed below in Ch. 7.
149 Recommendation 1547 (2002) Expulsion Procedures in conformity with human rights and enforced with respect for safety and dignity.
150 *Ibid.*, 13.V.(a)–(e).   151 Recommendation 1624 (2003), 4.   152 *Ibid.*, 9.
153 Application no. 46605/07, *Charahili v. Turkey*, Judgment of 13 April 2010. Also Appn. No. 30471/08, *Abdolkhami and Karmia v. Turkey*, Judgment of 22 Sep. 2009, para. 135, where the Court complained that there were 'no clear legal powers for ordering and extending detention with a view to deportation and *setting time limits for such detention*'.

The Court has also hinted that judicial approval may be required. In *Shamsa* v. *Poland*[154] it said, strictly obiter, that 'detention that goes beyond several days which has not been ordered by a court or judge or other person authorised to exercise judicial power cannot be considered "lawful" within the meaning of Article 5(1)'. The Court argued that this was implicit from a review of Article 5 and in particular Article 5(4),[155] (3) and (1)(c). This is a radical decision in the context of immigration with its long periods of incarceration without judicial approval. The *Shamsa* decision is hugely important, but apparently little recognized at present. In the more recent decision of the Grand Chamber in *Saadi*, the Court suggested that administrative detention without judicial authorization would be less acceptable the longer it went on, but did not go as far as to require judicial approval.[156]

Conclusions on Council of Europe case-law and practice

For a long period the ECHR jurisprudence showed the influence of the broad 'maxim' of international law regarding the status of aliens. In *Chahal*, the Court ruled that 'any deprivation of liberty should be in keeping with the purpose of Article 5, namely to protect the individual from arbitrariness'.[157] But it adopted a narrow view of 'arbitrariness' so that detention need not be shown to be necessary, because aliens have no general right to be at large until permitted to be so by national law. This was wholly different to its usual approach to Article 5 in which a fair balance must be struck between the protection of the wider community and any interference with individual rights.[158] The due diligence test, with its emphasis upon blame allocation and diplomatic efforts to

---

154 Applications nos. 45355/99 and 45357/99, Judgment of 27 Nov. 2003.
155 ECHR Art. 5(4) states that: 'Everyone who is deprived of his liberty by arrest or detention shall be entitled to take proceedings by which the lawfulness of his detention shall be decided speedily by a court and his release ordered if the detention is not lawful.'
156 *Saadi*, above n. 133, para. 45.   157 *Chahal*, para. 118.
158 *Soering* v. *United Kingdom* (1989) 11 EHRR 439, para. 89. There is, however, some divergence amongst academics on the question of whether proportionality has a role to play throughout the convention or whether it is largely confined to Arts 8–11. See Overy and White, *European Convention on Human Rights*, 5, where only qualified rights are said to give rise to questions of proportionality. By contrast, see K. Starmer, *European Human Rights Law*, London: Legal Action Group, 1999, 169, who states that 'the principle of proportionality is the defining characteristic of the Strasbourg approach to the protection of human rights'.

secure readmission, saw aliens as disruptive interstate problems, not as individuals.

As the extreme length and prison-like conditions of administrative detention for non-dangerous aliens have become more apparent, there has been a renewed willingness to question the necessity of protracted detention. The political organs and human rights monitors of the Council of Europe have made the Court aware of wider systemic problems. Where it is apparent that removal is no longer likely within a reasonable period, detention must cease. That this is so even if the detainees have themselves refused to assist in their expulsion is an important step, moving away from the previous 'blame' test, with its punitive tendencies. As yet, however, it has been unwilling to impose the stronger rule of law measures, such as mandatory judicial authorization for detention and time limits, urged upon it by the political institutions. Recognizing that European states' practices continue largely unconstrained, the Parliamentary Assembly has recently called again for a comprehensive code to regulate detention, release and conditions in centres. It condemned the fact that detention 'is increasingly used as a first response and also as a deterrent' which 'results in mass and needless detention'.[159]

United Nations activity and the International Covenant on Civil and Political Rights

A number of UN human rights bodies have responsibility to protect the liberty of the person guaranteed by Article 9 of the International Covenant on Civil and Political Rights (ICCPR). The ICCPR has been ratified by a large number of states and commands wide respect as a key source of human rights standards across the world.[160] The Human Rights

159 'The Parliamentary Assembly is concerned by this excessive use of detention and the long list of serious problems which arise as a result and which are regularly highlighted, not only by Council of Europe human rights monitoring bodies such as the European Court of Human Rights, the European Committee for the Prevention of Torture and Inhuman or Degrading Treatment or Punishment (CPT), the Human Rights Commissioner and the Assembly's Committee on Migration, Refugees and Population, but also by other international and national organisations.' Resolution 1707 (2010) *The Detention of Asylum Seekers and Irregular Migrants in Europe.*

160 A total of 148 states have ratified. See I. Brownlie and G. Goodwin-Gill (eds), *Basic Documents on Human Rights*, 4th edn, Oxford University Press, 2002. See S. Joseph, J. Schultz and M. Castan (eds), *The International Covenant on Civil and Political Rights: Cases, Materials and Commentary*, Oxford University Press, 1995; D. McGoldrick, *The Human Rights Committee: its Role in the Development of the International Covenant on Civil and Political Rights*, Oxford: Clarendon Press, 1991.

Committee's[161] opinions have evolved in a very different manner from the Strasbourg Court in relation to immigration detention. This is partly because of the different text of Article 9 compared to Article 5 ECHR. Perhaps more importantly is the historical accident that one of the first cases to come before the Committee was a challenge to the Australian mandatory indefinite detention policy. As we saw, this policy involved unprecedented restrictions upon individual liberty by a liberal democratic country in peacetime. Confronted with this, the Committee was forced to develop proportionality as a central element in its jurisprudence on immigration detention.

Asylum seekers in long-term detention: the growing concern

The Human Rights Committee had been concerned about immigration detention from the mid-1990s, some time prior to giving its first opinion in an individual case. The United Kingdom had been asked to produce detailed reports in relation to the long-term detention of Vietnamese in Hong Kong.[162] Switzerland was criticized for detaining foreigners, including asylum seekers and minors, for three months pending entry and for a further year pending expulsion, which time limits were 'considerably in excess of what is necessary'.[163] The Committee also expressed concern about asylum seekers being detained in Japan for six months and even two years.[164] Its monitoring reports also noted with concern indefinite detention in a range of other countries such as the United States.[165] There was therefore a growing realization that, particularly outside mainland Europe, lengthy detention was occurring and that the importance of necessity and proportionality as limiting principles might have been overlooked.

---

161 This is a quasi-judicial body which can deliver non-binding opinions ('communications') in relation to individual complaints under the covenant where a state has become party to the Optional Protocol to the ICCPR. Far from every state has done so, and thus countries like the UK and the United States do not feature in the case-law.

162 Concluding Comments on the UK (Hong Kong) (1995) UN Doc. CCPR/C/79Add.57 para. 17 expressing concern about the length and conditions of detention. There is no right of individual petition against the UK, as the protocol has not been signed. The Strasbourg Court had no jurisdiction over Hong Kong.

163 Concluding Comments on Switzerland. (1996) UN Doc. CCPR/C/79/Add. 70.

164 (1998) UN Doc. CCPR/C/79/Add. 102, para. 19.

165 Concluding Comments on the USA (1995) UN Doc. CCPR/C/70/Add. 50, paras 283 and 298, expressing concern at the indefinite detention of deportable and excludable immigrants who cannot be removed and the lack of due process for the latter group.

Around the same period, the Working Group on Arbitrary Detention also began looking at immigration detention (again in the context of the Vietnamese in Hong Kong) and in 1997 its terms of reference were expanded to include it.[166] The Working Group's views are really significant in clarifying international lawyers' understandings of 'arbitrary' detention, a term commonly condemned in legal texts and opinions, but not self-defining. In the immigration context it argued that, to prevent arbitrariness, there should be 'a limited period of detention, if not already provided by legislation, and the necessity of applying the restrictive period, where provided for, strictly, to ensure that the detention is not prolonged unreasonably'.[167] It also suggested that simple 'legality' habeas corpus proceedings might be an inadequate safeguard. There should be a compulsory hearing before a tribunal or judge; review procedures should be 'made effective and not a mere formality'.[168]

The role of Article 9 ICCPR: the prohibition on arbitrary detention

The basic provision of the ICCPR relevant for present purposes is Article 9(1), which states:

> Everyone has the right to liberty and security of person. No one shall be subjected to arbitrary arrest or detention. No one shall be deprived of his liberty except on such grounds and in accordance with such procedure as are established by law.

This is supplemented by Article 9(4), which entitles a detained person to bring proceedings in order that a court may decide on the legality of her detention.[169] By contrast with Article 5 of the ECHR, Article 9 does not specify the circumstances in which detention is justified. On one view, Article 9 is concerned purely with the formal legality of detention. The

---

166 Commission on Human Rights, 54th Session, Report of the Working Group on Arbitrary Detention (GENERAL E/CN.4/1998/4419 December 1997), para. 27: 'On several occasions in the past the Working Group considered situations involving detained asylum seekers, including the problem of Vietnamese asylum seekers in Hong Kong and that of Cuban and Puerto Rican asylum seekers in Guantánamo, in addition to certain individual cases which had been brought to the attention of the Group. For reasons peculiar to each of those situations, however, the Group neither adopted a decision nor conducted a mission.'
167 Paragraph 33.   168 Ibid.
169 Article 9(4) states: 'Anyone who is deprived of his liberty by arrest or detention shall be entitled to take proceedings before a court, in order that the court may decide without delay on the lawfulness of his detention and order his release if the detention is not lawful.'

only stipulation is that arrest not be 'arbitrary'.[170] This term is commonly applied in legal contexts relating to detention.[171] However, the majority of the delegates to the drafting committee were of the view that the meaning went beyond mere unlawfulness to encompass injustice, unpredictability, unreasonableness, capriciousness and unproportionality.[172]

This broad approach was adopted by the Human Rights Committee in *Van Alphen* v. *Netherlands*,[173] where it held that '"arbitrariness" is not to be equated with "against the law", but must be interpreted more broadly to include elements of inappropriateness, injustice and lack of predictability'. In that case, detention without considering bail was unreasonable. Around this time, the Committee considered its first immigration detention case in *V.M.R.B.* v. *Canada*[174] in which a Salvadoran was detained for two months pending deportation, on the grounds that he was a danger to the public and likely to abscond. This was confirmed by successive weekly judicial hearings reviewing the merits. He was eventually released when the government rescinded its objections to bail. The Committee, perhaps

---

170 See Art. 32 Vienna Convention on the Law of Treaties, which allows recourse to the preparatory work of the treaty where general rule of interpretation in Art. 31 'leaves the meaning ambiguous or obscure'. Recourse to the *travaux préparatoires* of the ICCPR reveals that the introduction of the word 'arbitrary' into the draft text of Art. 9 by the Australian delegate was certainly controversial. The problem was that an attempt to list all permissible grounds for detention, in a manner like that of the European Convention, had become so long as to be unworkable. The word 'arbitrary' was clearly doing a great deal of work. It was designed to impliedly authorize all kinds of substantive grounds for detention. The British view was the most broad, arguing that any detention based upon national law should not be considered arbitrary. However, most delegates appeared to decide that the word struck a balance between a purely procedural view and a substantive list of grounds for detention.

171 See, for example, the definitions given in *New Shorter English Dictionary*, Oxford: Clarendon Press, 1993: '1. Dependent on will or pleasure; *Law* (now *Hist.*) dependent on the decision of a legally recognised authority; discretionary . . . 2. Based on mere opinion or preference as opp. to the real nature of things; capricious, unpredictable, inconsistent . . . 3. Unrestrained in the exercise of will or authority; despotic, tyrannical . . . ' These are clearly rather different in character and range in their pejorative force. P. Hassan, 'The Word "Arbitrary" as Used in the Universal Declaration of Human Rights: "Illegal or Unjust"?' (1969) 10 *Harv. Int. L.J.* 225.

172 See M.J. Bossuyt, *Guide to the 'Travaux Préparatoires' of the International Covenant on Civil and Political Rights*, Leiden: Martinus Nijhoff Publishers, 1987, 172. Interestingly, an earlier draft of Art. 9 was modelled upon Art. 5 of the European Convention and included a specified set of grounds for detention. This was abandoned when other drafting parties began to add further grounds of their own such that the text became unworkable, with a list a comprising some forty grounds! No consensus could be reached on a concise list and this led to the adoption of the term 'arbitrary' being substituted. See *ibid.*, 164.

173 No. 305/1988.   174 No. 236/1987, UN Doc. Supp. No. 40 (A/43/40), 258 (1988).

unsurprisingly, found no violation of Article 9, as it was not arbitrary to detain given the absconding risk. It therefore accepted that immigration detention was in principle compatible with Article 9, but in the context of a system in Canada that had high due process standards.

The proportionality revolution: the decision in A *v.* Australia

This was the background to the landmark immigration case of *A v. Australia.*[175] We considered the facts earlier in Chapter 2, as it concerned one of the Cambodian asylum seekers who was detained as part of Australia's policy of mandatory detention of all undocumented persons arriving by boat. His asylum application was initially refused after one-and-a-half years, and finally rejected on appeal after three years. He was later released after over four years in immigration detention. Drawing upon its decision in *Van Alphen*, the Committee noted that 'arbitrariness' should not be equated merely with unlawfulness, but must be interpreted more broadly to include inappropriateness and injustice.

Even for asylum seekers, the Committee held that it was not arbitrary *per se* to detain persons requesting asylum, but would be 'if it is *not necessary in all the circumstances* of the case, for example to prevent flight or interference with evidence: the element of proportionality becomes relevant in this context'.[176] A lack of immigration status alone did not mean there was no right to be released. Normative justification for detention must be sought in features other than unauthorized foreigner status.

Turning specifically to illegal entry cases, the Committee said that:

> detention should not continue beyond the period for which the State can provide appropriate justification. For example, the fact of illegal entry may indicate a need for investigation and there may be other factors particular to the individual, such as the likelihood of absconding and lack of cooperation, which may justify detention for a period. Without such factors detention may be considered arbitrary even if entry was illegal. In the instant case, the State party has not advanced any grounds particular to the author's case, which would justify his continued detention for a period of four years.[177]

The Committee therefore concluded that there was a violation of Article 9(1). In addition, it found a violation of Article 9(4), because domestic legislation ensured that there was no power in the domestic

175 No. 560/1993.   176 Paragraph 9.2.   177 Paragraph 9.4.

courts to review the merits of continuing detention and thus to authorize release if found to be 'arbitrary' within the meaning of Article 9(1).

Several years later the Committee also decided another similar complaint in *C* v. *Australia*.[178] The complainant sought asylum after arrival at an Australian port whilst in possession of a valid visa. His mandatory detention lasted for two years before he was released by executive order on the basis of his declining mental health resulting in psychosis. In contrast to the decision in *A*, *C*'s asylum claim had been refused more quickly (after two months) and his review was rejected six weeks later. He was later awarded refugee status after his release.

The government defended the policy on the basis that it maintained the integrity of the immigration system; ensured that only genuine refugees could enter; afforded swift claims processing by ensuring ready access to migrants; facilitated removal of rejected applicants and avoided the difficulties of absconding. The Committee found breaches of Article 9(1) and (4). It implicitly rejected the whole idea of mandatory detention as a tool to process unauthorized persons, at least beyond a short duration. Detention must not be longer than that for which the state could provide appropriate justification.

Whilst on the facts the initial detention might have been acceptable, Australia had not shown that it was necessary 'in the light of the passage of time and intervening circumstances... [nor that] in the light of the author's particular circumstances, there were not less invasive means of achieving the same ends, that is to say, compliance with State party's immigration policies, by, for example, the imposition of reporting obligations, sureties or other conditions which would take account of the author's deteriorating condition'.[179]

The decision in *C* was followed in the later case of *Baban* v. *Australia*.[180] *Baban* was interesting in that the Iraqi complainant had actually escaped after two years in mandatory detention and was in hiding at the time of the decision. His detention was ruled to have been excessive, given the possibility of supervised release. Importantly, it was noted that removal of Iraqis had not been logistically possible during the period, thus rendering the detention's ostensible purpose unattainable. The Committee also appear to have had regard to the harsh effects of detention upon the complainant's son (aged three) as a factor in his case.

Further complaints were brought against Australia's detention policy in the following years but, as we have seen, the policy was not

178 No. 900/1999. Meeting on 28 Oct. 2002.   179 Paragraph 8.2.
180 Communication No. 1014/2001 of 18/09/2003 (CCPR/C/78/D/1014/2001).

changed in its legal essentials. In 2006 the Committee decided in *D and E v. Australia*[181] that detention of over three years in the case of an Iranian family, including two children aged five and one, was a breach of Article 9(1). Their asylum claims and appeals had been rejected within three months of arrival. Although their fears were found credible, it was decided that the feared persecution was not for a convention reason. Thereafter they remained in detention pending consideration of further evidence on their asylum claim that was submitted to the minister. They were eventually released and given humanitarian protection.

In the most extreme case to come before the Committee, *Danyal Safiq v. Australia*,[182] a man of Bangladeshi origin had been held for seven years. His asylum claim had been rejected on appeal after fifteen months, on the ground that he had committed a serious non-political crime.[183] His review before the Federal Court was rejected a year later. Thereafter he remained in detention, but could not be removed, as the Bangladeshi authorities did not accept him as a citizen. He developed a mental illness linked to prolonged detention after six years and was placed in an open mental institution, although still in legal custody. The Committee found a breach of Article 9(1), particularly given his mental state and given that he had not absconded despite being able to do so for a year.[184] Highlighting the gulf separating the government and the Committee, it 'noted that the State party did not accept its views in A. v Australia'.[185] The Minister of Immigration pointedly released Safiq from detention a month *after* the ninety-day deadline set by the Committee for providing it with information on compliance with its views.[186]

United Nations criticism since A v. Australia: *the continued growth of administrative detention*

Whilst it was already moving in that direction, we can see the influence of the proportionality principle enunciated in *A v. Australia* in the subsequent monitoring practice of the Committee and other UN bodies. In 1998, the Working Group on Arbitrary Detention in a report on its visit to the United Kingdom, called for changes in the legal framework to ensure

181 Communication No. 1050/2002, UN Doc. CCPR/C/87/D/1050/2002 (2006) of 9 Aug. 2006.
182 Communication No. 1324/2004, UN Doc. CCPR/C/88/D/132/2004 (2006) of 13 Nov. 2006.
183 Article 1F of the Refugee Convention.   184 7.3.   185 7.4.
186 See ABC News, 'Andrews grants visa to man detained seven years', 23 Mar. 2007.

both proportionality and judicial oversight.[187] Later in 1999 it drafted a set of principles that were incorporated into the guidelines on detention for all prisoners.[188] Compliance is indicative of a lack of arbitrariness in detention. These apply to all immigration detainees and not simply to asylum seekers. They set out procedural rights to information about the grounds for detention and how to challenge it. They require every detainee 'to be brought promptly before a judicial or other authority'.[189] This was a significant proposal which would have required major innovations in state practice. The guidelines also suggest that in respect of detention 'a maximum period should be set by law and the custody may in no case be unlimited or of excessive length'.[190]

In 2001, the United Kingdom was criticized by the Human Rights Committee monitoring report, in a clear reference to the practice upheld by the Strasbourg Court in *Saadi* v. *United Kingdom,* for using detention 'on grounds other than those legitimate under the Covenant, including reasons of administrative convenience'.[191] It was also noted that asylum seekers 'after final refusal . . . may also be held in detention for an extended period when deportation might be impossible for legal or other considerations'. In 2002, the Working Group on Arbitrary Detention, unsurprisingly, severely criticized the Australian detention regime, on a visit aimed at precisely this issue. They called for judicial review as to substance, limits on duration and a move towards a necessity test.[192]

---

187 Report of the Working Group on Arbitrary Detention, Fifty-fifth session. E/CN.4/1999/63/Add.3, 18 Dec. 1998.
188 E/CN.4/2000/4, 28 Dec. 1999, Commission on Human Rights, Fifty-sixth Session, Working Group on Arbitrary Detention, Deliberation No. 5.
189 Principle 3.
190 Principle 7. The one interesting omission in these guidelines is the failure to consider the grounds for detention. This is not surprising given the lack of consensus we have seen on this issue when it has been raised by the UNHCR with states in the past. It appears that consensus around limited duration and judicial review is more readily achieved than on the details of administrative justification for detention. This may reflect inherent limits in any principles of general application as against providing detailed criteria to guide executive discretion in concrete cases.
191 Concluding Observations of the Human Rights Committee: United Kingdom, 06/12/2001. CCPR/CO/73/UK; CCPR/CO/73/UKOT, 16.
192 Report of the Working Group on Arbitrary Detention. Fifty-ninth Session. E/CN.4/2003/8/Add.2, 24 Oct. 2002. Meanwhile the Australian higher courts have continued to question the interpretation of Art. 9 given by the Human Rights Committee. See *Al Kateb* v. *Godwin* per Hayne J., para. 238 of which refers to Art. 9 ICCPR. He implicitly disagrees with the well-known opinions of the Human Rights Committee against Australia on mandatory detention of immigrants. Thus he says there must be 'doubt about whether the mandatory detention of those who do not have permission to enter and remain in

In 2010 the Working Group produced its most comprehensive guidelines whilst noting forlornly the 'tightening restrictions, including deprivation of liberty, applied to asylum seekers, refugees and immigrants in an irregular situation'.[193] It recognized that, under current international law, administrative detention of migrants liable to removal is lawful, but made the radical call for it to be gradually abolished. Detention should be 'a last resort' which is based 'upon the necessity of identification of the migrant in an irregular situation, the risk of absconding, or facilitating the expulsion of an irregular migrant who has been served with a removal order'.[194] Detention should be authorized by a judge and be subject to regular review and there must be a maximum period. In emergency situations, where an exceptionally large number of undocumented migrants enter there must still be judicial review within a set time limit. The Working Group disparaged again the problem of indefinite detention, saying '[w]here the obstacle to the removal of the detained migrants does not lie within their sphere of responsibility' they should be released.[195] To avoid being arbitrary, there must always be a legitimate aim and this 'would not exist if there were no longer a real and tangible prospect of removal'.[196]

Conclusions on the contribution of the International Covenant to the regulation of detention

In retrospect, the decisions in *A* and *C* were a valuable attempt to juridify the process of global migration by balancing sovereignty and individual liberty. The Human Rights Committee accepted the legitimacy of immigration control as an objective of policy. They nevertheless began from the premise that, unless criminally convicted, all *persons* should be at liberty. Strong procedural and substantive due process was owed to all before detention could be supported. Illegal entry or irregular arrival *per se* were not enough to justify detention beyond the short period needed to identify the person or register an application. The presumption must be that, in the absence of specific evidence that a detainee represents a flight or offending risk, supervised release should be granted.

Australia contravenes Article 9'. This is because there is both clear and accessible statutory authority for the detention and access to judicial review. The principle of legality can be developed in more expansive ways, but as regards immigrants there appears to be little consensus on this.

193 Report of the UN Working Group on Arbitrary Detention, 13th Session, A/HRC/13/30, 15 Jan. 2010, para. 55.

194 *Ibid.*, para. 58.   195 *Ibid.*, para. 63.   196 *Ibid.*, para. 64.

Finally, mandatory judicial oversight as to the merits of detention was emphasized. The monitoring reports of the Committee and the contribution of the Working Group on Arbitrary Detention point in the same direction.

If followed, these principles would have required a revolution in the detention practices of, for example, Australia, the United States and most European states. They have not been, and this represents an unusually clear failure of the international human rights system as a tool of legal and political change. This is particularly striking given the fact that the right in question is a fundamental one and the breach is very widespread, obvious and persistent, at least in the view of the UN agencies. It is interesting to consider why this has occurred. The attachment of these states to their detention practices is strong mainly due to domestic political calculations, but also because of normative disagreement with the UN agencies about the scope of the right to liberty.[197]

The Australian response in *C* v. *Australia* is illustrative. To protect sovereignty, it was argued, immigrants must be detained because otherwise *some* of them might enter or remain without permission. There is either no question of proportionality, or such group practices are always proportionate. This is because there is no individual liberty right separate from an immigration right to enter, which is a matter for the state. The Australian higher courts have consistently endorsed this argument in holding indefinite detention constitutional.[198] The US and UK jurisprudence also permits very lengthy detention without judicial approval. Government policy has been to maintain detention for open-ended periods. As some scholars note, this is an interesting illustration of how human rights standards, originally thought to be mainly coercive of non-Western states, are not so readily accepted by Western nations when directed against them.[199]

---

197 For a discussion of the broader question of compliance see H.H. Koh, 'Why do Nations Obey International Law?' (1997) 106 *Yale L.J.* 2599. He notes that 'As governmental and nongovernmental transnational actors repeatedly interact within the transnational legal process, they generate and interpret international norm and then seek to internalize those norms domestically. To the extent that those norms are successfully internalized, they become future determinants of why nations obey' (2651).

198 The key case is *Al Kateb* v. *Godwin* discussed above in Ch. 2.

199 M. Kumm, 'The Legitimacy of International Law: A Constitutionalist Framework of Analysis' (2004) 15 *Eur. J. Int. L.* 907. Kumm describes the period of decolonization and up to the end of the Cold War as one in which 'from the perspective of citizens in comparatively rich Western democracies, international law had serious effects primarily

Beyond asylum: 'criminalization' and detention of irregular migrants

Discussion so far has largely focused upon the position of asylum seekers, who at least have rights of movement under international refugee law. Increasingly serious restrictions, including detention, have also been applied to migrants who are non-documented or in an irregular situation. The process of stripping this group of basic rights has been called 'a counter-offensive ... against human rights as being universal, indivisible and inalienable'.[200] In 2005, the UN Human Rights Commission called on states 'effectively to promote and protect the human rights and fundamental freedoms of all migrants ... regardless of their immigration status'.[201] Similarly, the Global Commission on International Migration established by the United Nations referred to the seven core human rights treaties as applying to migrants.[202] It endorsed the principle that 'entering a country in violation of its immigration laws does not deprive migrants of the fundamental human rights provided by the human rights instruments cited above, nor does it affect the obligation of states to protect migrants in an irregular situation'.

In response to this widespread perception, the UN High Commission on Human Rights created a Special Rapporteur on the Human Rights of Migrants, who was asked to examine ways to 'overcome obstacles existing to the full and effective protection of the human rights of this vulnerable group'.[203] In her first report, she noted the increasingly blurred

for *other* people ... Citizens in Western democracies ... could rely and did rely on the resources of domestic legal systems ... ', 911. Since then, however, they have experienced 'an international legal order that increasingly serves – if not as an iron cage – certainly as a firmly structured normative web that makes an increasingly plausible claim to authority', 912.

200 P. A. Taran, 'Human Rights of Migrants: Challenges of the New Decade' (2000) 38(6) *Int. Migration* 11.

201 Resolution 2005/47.

202 The others were the International Convention on the Elimination of All Forms of Racial Discrimination, International Covenant on Civil and Political Rights, International Covenant on Economic and Social Rights, Convention on the Elimination of All Forms of Discrimination Against Women, Convention Against Torture and Convention on the Rights the Child.

203 Resolution 1999/44 on the Human Rights of Migrants created the Special Rapporteur on the Human Rights of Migrants and reaffirmed that states parties to the ICCPR 'must ensure to all individuals within its territory and subject to its jurisdiction the rights set out therein'.

line between different categories of migrant[204] and defined 'migrants' as persons who are in another country and *inter alia* 'do not enjoy the general legal recognition of rights which is inherent in the granting by the host State of the status of refugee, permanent resident or naturalised person or of similar status'.[205]

Unacceptable detention practices have featured often in these annual reports. In a detailed report on detention the Special Rapporteur argued that the 'criminalization' of irregular migration is 'increasingly being used by Governments to discourage it'.[206] The wide discretion given to immigration officials to detain often led to situations in which migrants have the burden of proof as to the circumstances relating to their documentation, entry or migratory status in order to avoid deprivation of liberty. Such discretion could give rise to 'abuses and to human rights violations . . . de facto discriminatory patterns of arrest and deportation of irregular migrants'.[207] The report also noted that even where judicial review is in theory available, in practice it is very difficult to exercise due to lack of awareness or lack of counsel.[208]

By 2008 the Special Rapporteur argued that 'it is important that irregular migration be seen as an administrative offence'. Detention should be used 'only as a last resort' and in general irregular migrants should not be treated as criminals. The emphasis given here to criminalization is an important one, but must be properly defined. The real complaint is that detention *without criminal law procedures* is occurring at the behest of officials. If this power is used in ways that are unnecessary, capricious or arbitrary, it can be seen as assuming a punitive nature without attendant safeguards. If irregular migrants are politically and culturally stereotyped as deviant, then the danger of officials detaining in such ways is greater still. Most international monitors and standard-setting bodies have therefore called for *criminal-style* procedural safeguards in detention cases. This would inevitably limit the power to detain. Thus, in this important sense immigration detention has not been criminalized enough. The need to tie immigration detention more closely to criminal law is discussed further in Chapter 7.

---

204 Report of the Special Rapporteur on Human Rights of Migrants, 6 Jan. 2000, E/CN.4/2000/82.
205 Paragraph 36.   206 2001 Annual Report, (17) Report 2002, E/CN.4/2003/85.
207 *Ibid.*, paras 21–2.
208 She also highlighted the fact that there are rarely notifications under Art. 36 Vienna Convention on Consular Relations which require their consulate to be informed of their detention upon request by a detainee.

Overall conclusions on international law and detention

The customary international law doctrine of territorial sovereignty does not of itself require broad detention powers, but it has certainly been put forward as a justification for immigration detention. If states were unable to detain those whom they had not accepted for admission or whom they had decided to expel, 'sovereignty' would be undermined. The earliest human rights instruments pertaining to immigrants reflect this. The Refugee Convention authorized detention, but the drafters appear to have accepted this would only be for short periods, perhaps during mass influxes. The same basic position was set out in the ECHR in Article 5(1)(f). Detention to prevent illegal entry or effect deportation was expressly allowed. There was, however, little judicial or other opinion on the scope of these provisions, partly because state practice was limited.

Since the 1980s, state detention practice has increased markedly. It is only during this time that serious consideration of the issue has arisen in international fora. The UNHCR tried to argue for a restrictive approach to detaining asylum seekers, ultimately settling upon a proportionality test. This was, however, rejected by states, who linked asylum seekers closely with irregular migrants as regards detention criteria. The Council of Europe institutions only began to consider the question somewhat later. The Strasbourg Court had generally allowed states to detain so long as they were acting with 'due diligence' to deport. This reflected the strong 'aliens power' tradition. In recent years, lengthy purely administrative detention of non-dangerous migrants and asylum seekers has become very common in Europe. Council of Europe human rights monitors and political organs have also argued for proportionality and definite legal safeguards. More recent Strasbourg cases have responded by controlling the duration of detention in extreme cases and beginning to question the lack of judicial oversight.

The UN monitoring bodies have restated the existence of a universal individual right to liberty which can only be restricted by proportionate measures. Protecting territorial sovereignty is a legitimate goal, but this must not be pursued in ways that disproportionately interfere with individual liberty. Detention of unauthorized aliens requires more than simply immigration status to support it. The open text of Article 9 of the ICCPR was important but so, too, were the extreme practices seen in, first Hong Kong, but later the United States and Australia. Monitoring reports enabled the Human Rights Committee initially to gain an empirical overview of the scale and duration of detention and suggested that arbitrary or punitive practices were at work. Even a proportionality standard is, however, only reactive in responding to the most extreme detention practices. Express time limits, detention criteria and judicial approval remain uncertain areas. More recent guidance from UN monitoring bodies has suggested these criminal-style safeguards are needed.

It is however significant that, despite strong criticism, state practice has remained largely immune to human right bodies' criticism. This represents a fundamental conflict not just over the politics of compliance with international law, but also a dispute about who has fundamental rights. The increasing tendency is for states to treat unauthorized immigration status as denuding persons of an individual right to liberty. Enforcement policy is viewed as proportionate in overall, not individual, terms. It is unusual for such a wide interpretation gap to exist between human rights bodies and liberal democracies over the scope of such a basic right. However, this is suggestive of the broader manner in which governments have come to view irregular migrants, including asylum seekers, and those ordered deported, as in some respects 'outside the applicability and protection of law . . . persons with no legal status, no legal identity, no existence'.[209] Control over access to territory and the state's right and obligation to decide who is authorized continue to trump what international bodies consider are universal legal entitlements.

209 Taran, 'Human Rights of Migrants', 23.

4

Negotiating detention within the European Union: redefining friends and enemies

Introduction: open borders and the meaning of 'security'

The European Union (EU)[1] is the most advanced treaty-based international organization in the world. It has gone furthest along the route towards integration between sovereign states, falling short of actual merger into a federal nation.[2] The principles of direct effect and supremacy of the law evolved by the European Court of Justice (ECJ) have given European law special status going beyond 'ordinary' treaty law.[3] Removing barriers to the free movement of persons within the EU has been a central legal and political project. EU nationals' rights to move have cut into Member State discretion over security and migration. This has arisen largely from their political status as 'friends' ('EU citizens', even) no longer subject to arbitrary prerogative measures, but rather the bearers of migration rights protected by legal reason and principle. Loss of 'sovereignty' over migration is a legal truth for Member States, not just a practical reality.[4]

Administrative detention of foreigners is at first sight anathema in the world's grandest open-borders project. Nevertheless, the same concerns found in national politics over unauthorized migration have been translated up to EU level. The 'security' agenda has been directed outwards to the EU's external borders and inwards towards unauthozised non-EU

1 Throughout this chapter I shall refer to the European Union ('the EU' or 'Union'), which is the current overarching term. I shall avoid reference to the various incarnations ('European Economic Community', 'European Community') that have existed since 1957. This is for clarity of exposition, but hides the fact that at the relevant historical periods, the Union had, and continues to have through the various pillars of the EC treaties under which the different bodies act, multiple identities.
2 F. Rosenstiel, 'Reflections on the Notion of "Supranationality"' (1963) 2(2) *JCMS* 127 for an early account disparaging the idea.
3 See J.P. Weiler, 'The Community System: the Dual Character of Supra-nationalism' (1981) 1 *YEL* 267.
4 For debates on the meaning of 'sovereignty' see N. MacCormick, *Questioning Sovereignty*, Oxford University Press, 2003.

nationals detected internally. Whilst unthinkable for EU citizens, broad detention powers over asylum seekers and unauthorized migrants have been endorsed. Through undermining internal border controls, the EU has both created new 'friends' and constructed new 'enemies' against whom controls have been enhanced.[5]

As we shall see, the premise of EU free movement law is that internal border restrictions on migration by EU citizens are both illegal and undesirable. Private choice should be determinative of mobility. All migration by EU citizens is presumed 'authorized' by operation of law. EU law has thus gradually eliminated most 'immigration' control altogether for EU citizens.[6] States can only use coercive measures to exclude where 'core' security threats of a serious criminal nature arise. There is little discretion to protect broader notions of economic, cultural or psychological 'security' through border control. Security as it relates to borders has been confined and codified. Law has largely replaced the political.

Given this deep commitment to unrestricted migration as essentially desirable, it appears contradictory to see unauthorized migration by *non-EU* citizens as an *unqualified* security threat. Only by reverting to the broader notion of 'security', one which is inapplicable to EU citizens' migration, can unauthorised migration in itself be considered a 'threat'. The more recent troubled parameters of European immigration politics have largely determined the nature of border enforcement measures thus far. Nevertheless, the very cosmopolitan, open-borders premise of the EU provides an important challenge to the construction of the 'outsider' as a threat.

Immigration controls in the Union: EU and non-EU citizens

Free movement rights were present in textual form in the European Economic Community Treaty, which created the framework for a common market. As the Union has endured and progressed, a combination of case-law and secondary legislation has removed much of the Member States' power over immigration control for nationals of the Member States. Indeed, it is striking that powers of detention have never expressly been included in any of the many measures passed in the field

---

5 W. Wallace, 'Rescue or Retreat? The Nation State in Western Europe, 1945–1993' (1994) XLII *Political Studies* 52–76 and R. Cooper, *The Breaking of Nations*, London: Profile, 2004.
6 R.C.A. White, 'Free Movement, Equal Treatment, and Citizenship of the Union' (2005) 54(5) *ICLQ* 885–905.

of EU citizens' migration. The creation of an EU citizenship, alongside that of Member States nationality, has further deepened the nature of EU supra-nationalism.[7] The move away from unilateral sovereign control over migration, towards the free movement model of the EU, has inexorably eroded immigration detention powers. This was a result of case-law on fundamental rights, particularly proportionality and non-discrimination. The right of free movement bestowed on EU citizens has defied unwarranted interference by Member States.[8] Moving from the national to the supra-national level has undermined the legitimacy of detention. The nationals of other Member States have been elevated by a process of law/jurisprudence and moral/political evolution to a new status.[9] They are not quite equal to nationals, but they are far from being aliens. *Prima facie* they have rights to enter and reside in other Member States free from control. It is much more difficult to deport them because of this higher status.[10] With this change, detention of such persons has therefore become difficult and rare.

Turning to non-EU citizens, however, we find a more complex and uncertain picture. The pre-existing practice of immigration detention of non-EU citizens by Member States was extensive. Although official figures are not collected at EU level, detentions in the Union are probably 100–200,000 persons per year.[11] The EU was therefore inheriting a substantial detention practice. Having acquired powers over migration of non-EU citizens only relatively recently, EU policies have expressed

---

7 N. Reich, 'A European Constitution for Citizens: Reflections on the Rethinking of Union and Community Law' (1997) 3 *ELJ* 131–64; S. O'Leary, *The Evolving Concept of Community Citizenship: From the Free Movement of Persons to Union Citizenship*, The Hague: Kluwer Law International, 1996.

8 R. Koslowski, 'Intra-EU Migration, Citizenship and Political Union' (1994) 32 *JCMS* 367–402.

9 H.S. Feldstein, 'A Study of Transactions and Political Integration: Transnational Labour Flows within the European Economic Community' (1967) 6 *JCMS* 24–55.

10 C. Vincenzi, 'Deportation in Disarray: The Case of EC Nationals' (1994) *Crim. L. Rev.* 163–75.

11 See *Detention in Europe: Administrative Detention of Asylum-seekers and Irregular Migrants* (Jesuit Refugee Service, Brussels, 2004) which estimated that the Member States at that date conducted around 100,000 detentions annually. The ten new Member States had some 4,900 places in 2007, and around 3,500 of these were filled on a daily basis. They estimated around 35,000 detentions in these new states. The figures are only estimates, because no official data is published. This yields a figure of 135,000, but working from the data on removals shows that 200,149 were removed from the EU-27 states in 2004. These are generally detained before removal, so the total could be closer to 200,000. See A. Kalmthout, F. Hofstee-van der Meulen and F. Dunkel (eds), *Foreigners in European Prisons, vol. 1*, Nijmegen: Wolf Legal Publishers, 2007.

both liberalizing and exclusionary tendencies. For authorized migrants, particularly long-term residents, the language of inclusion and equality is apparent. By contrast, unauthorized migration has been re-negotiated as a pan-EU security threat justifying extraordinary powers, with detention being enlarged beyond previous state practice. The EU has inscribed into its new laws on unlawful aliens an obligation to detain and expel such persons from Europe as a common security goal of the Member States. In principle, freeing such persons without expelling them is a breach of this reciprocal obligation of expulsion.

The liberty of EU citizens: the evolution of the right to free movement and the abolition of immigration control

The original 1957 treaty provisions gave free movement rights to economically active nationals of other Member States.[12] Despite this, Member States were still permitted to prevent or deny free movement for unspecified reasons of public policy, public health or public security. Furthermore, the Treaty did not spell out the formalities surrounding exercise of the free movement rights either. States thus retained a discretion to detain and expel those foreigners not qualified to enter or remain. In an era of relatively full employment, however, border controls were politically unimportant. In fact, consensus was reached at European level to pass three extensive pieces of legislation that removed large chunks of border control.[13] Directive 68/360 stripped away detailed examination at the border; Directive 64/221 placed onerous restrictions on the power of Member States to deport nationals of Member States and their families; Regulation 1612/68 gave migrant workers and their families enhanced rights against discrimination. It also gave non-EU citizen families rights to enter the Union to join EU migrant workers.[14] These provisions were

---

12 See Arts 39 and 43 EEC Treaty, which refer to Member State discretion in relation to 'public policy, public security and public health'. Also Art. 49 was eventually interpreted by the ECJ to encompass a right to move to receive services.

13 See also the precursors Reg. 15/61, OJ No. 57, 26.8.1961, 1073/61 and OJ No. 80, 13.12.1961, 1513/61 on workers, and OJ No. 56, 4.4.1964, pp. 845/64 on establishment and services. The former still retained the right to discriminate in favour of nationals in access to employment during a transitional period. We look at the later legislation because it is more comprehensive and represents the realized free moment project.

14 This section will not consider the equivalent provisions in relation to cross-border service providers and self-employed persons, but it should be noted that border restrictions were removed for these groups too.

important political statements about both the status of migrants and the erosion of the border as a place of control. Given the supremacy of EU law, they were real inroads into traditional territorial sovereignty doctrines.[15]

Whilst constituting a complete code governing migration, detention was not mentioned in these instruments.[16] At the outset, the Directive on entry and residence at Article 1 required Member States to 'abolish restrictions on the movement and residence of nationals of the said States and of members of their families'. The right of entry must be given 'simply on production of a valid identity card or passport'. Thus, no visa could be demanded from EU citizens.[17] There was no detention power to examine documentation or eligibility pending a decision at the border. The Directive on deportation regulated all 'measures' concerning entry or expulsion from taken on grounds of public policy, public security or public health.[18] Detention was not authorized, but may have been assumed to be a 'measure' implicit in the deportation power. This would accord with international law recognized at the time.[19] If so, it could only be based upon tangible security grounds relating to the 'personal conduct' of the individual.[20] Furthermore, criminal convictions could not in themselves justify such measures.[21] This ruled out the kind of mandatory detention that we have seen elsewhere in this book. Thus, detention of EU citizens has never been explicitly authorized by European legislation, despite the sizeable body of laws on free

---

15 T. Staubhaar, 'International Labour Migration within a Common Market: Some Aspects of EC Experience' (1999) 27 *JCMS* 45. W. Streeck and P.C. Schmitter, 'From National Corporatism to Transnational Pluralism: Organized Interests in the Single European Market' (1991) 19 *Politics and Society* 133–64.

16 It is important to state, however, that during this time lengthy detention does not appear to have been practised by Member States. This may have reflected the continental preference for issuing expulsion orders giving a person time to make their own arrangements for leaving a country rather than using direct coercion.

17 Article 3, but this does go on to say that is so 'save from members of the family who are not nationals of a Member States. Member States shall accord to such persons every facility for obtaining any necessary visas'. Here we can see an early example of the different approach taken to the migration of non-EU citizens. They do not have the same status as EU citizens in that they can be subject to some pre-entry control in the form of a visa. This preserves, at least formally, the privileged status of EU citizens. However, given that the visa must be provided readily to non-EU citizens who are family members, the constraint is largely symbolic.

18 Article 2.   19 See Ch. 3 above.   20 Article 3(1).   21 Article 3(2).

movement.[22] It would not doubt have proved hugely difficult to agree on the scope of such powers, and very damaging to the emerging idea of a borderless Europe.[23]

In the next phase during the 1970s, in response to increasingly anti-immigrant policies, the ECJ embarked upon a series of decisions that brought EU migrants a new constitutional status within the EU legal order.[24] This drew inspiration from the original Treaty provisions as the constitutional framework governing the free movement rights of nationals of the Member States. In relation to deportation, the Court raised the bar so that expulsion was only allowed if 'there was a genuine and sufficiently serious threat affecting one of the fundamental interests of society'.[25] The deportee must engage in 'personal conduct constituting a present threat to the requirements of public policy' suggesting that a propensity to re-offend was required.[26] Deportation to make an example of someone or to deter others was illegal.[27] Only non-discriminatory criminal penalties could be employed for such purposes. Henceforth, EU migrants were firmly placed under the protection of judicial reason, not left to political discretion.

Migration rights were fundamental constitutional entitlements that could only be taken away in exceptional cases. Furthermore, as with deportation, detention fell away. A good early example was the *Caprino* case, in which an Italian national was held in detention pending deportation under national law but released upon UK accession to the European Economic Community because deportation was no longer lawful.[28] Thus the difficulty deporting EU citizens made detention a relatively rare

---

22 The recasting of the free movement rights into Directive 2004/38 on the rights of free movement and residence for EU citizens and their families does not change these rules.

23 Another factor may be that, in EU law, the identity of the law-making and law-execution bodies is different. Execution is traditionally a matter for Member States and detention is an execution issue *par excellence*. See E.C. Page, 'Europeanization and the Persistence of Administrative Systems', in J. Hayward and A. Menon (eds), *Governing Europe*, Oxford University Press, 2003.

24 C-41/74 *Van Duyn* v. *Home Office* [1974] ECR 1337; C-67/74 *Bonsignore* [1975] ECR 297. See F. Wooldridge, 'Free Movement of EEC Nationals: the Limitations Based on Public Policy and Public Security' (1977) 2 *E.L. Rev.* 190 and G.F. Mancini, 'The Free Movement of Workers in the Case-Law of the Court of Justice', in D. Curtin and D. O'Keefe (eds), *Constitutional Adjudication in EC and National Law: Essays in Honour of Justice T.F. O'Higgins*, Dublin: Butterworths, 1992.

25 C-30/77 *Bouchereau* [1977] ECR 1999, para. 35.

26 Paragraphs 28–9.   27 C-67/74 *Bonsignore*.

28 *Caprino* v. *United Kingdom*, Appn. no. 6871/75, Decision of 3 Mar. 1978 on admissibility of the application.

event linked to serious criminal offenders.[29] Similarly, the ECJ took an expansive view of the actual Treaty rights themselves, so that migrants did not face a high hurdle to establish rights of entry or residence.[30] This further eroded the power to detain, because fewer and fewer EU citizens fell below the threshold of free movement rights.

EU citizens who fell outside EU free movement law, particularly those not economically active, could still be expelled.[31] The Court, however, began to hold that border surveillance measures which excessively deterred or interfered with migration were in breach of EC law. In *Casati*, the ECJ said more generally of migration control rules that:

> The administrative measures or penalties must not go beyond what is strictly necessary, the control measures must not be conceived in such a way as to restrict the freedom required by the Treaty and they must not be accompanied by a penalty which is so disproportionate to the gravity of the infringement that it becomes an obstacle to the exercise of that freedom.[32]

This meant that citizens of the EU had 'constitutional' rights under the Treaty to move and reside and that these could not be undermined simply for states to monitor migration. The introduction of EU citizenship as a complementary status alongside national citizenship in the Maastricht Treaty in 1992 gave further impetus to the special status of citizens and their free movement rights.[33] Eventually, in *Baumbast*, the Court ruled that there was a fundamental right of residence in other Member States simply by virtue of EU citizenship. This burgeoning case-law set the stage for a final, perhaps logical, elimination of Member States' power to detain for border-control purposes in the important *Oulane* decision.

In *Oulane*,[34] a French national was arrested in Holland twice and detained for one week on each occasion. He had no identity papers and no fixed address. His North African origins probably drew in the immigration authorities, who held him pending proof of his nationality. On his first

---

29 See now the Citizens Directive 2004/38, which sets out much of the case-law but also creates higher public policy thresholds for permanent residents and those having resided for ten years or more in a Member State.

30 See C-292/89 *R v. Immigration Appeal Tribunal ex parte Antonissen* [1991] ECR I-745; C-66/85 *Lawrie-Blum* [1986] ECR 2121.

31 The obvious example would be non-economically active persons who were still resident beyond any period that could fall within a 'visit' under Art. 49 EC Treaty. The right of residence was reserved for workers or the self-employed and their families.

32 C-203/80 *Casati* [1981] ECR 2595, para. 27.

33 Arts 17 and 18 Treaty on European Union.

34 C-215/03 *Oulane*, Judgment of 17 Feb. 2005.

arrest he was eventually released when he provided a French identity card. On the second occasion he was deported to France before proof was available. His second detention was said by the government to be justified because of a fear that he would abscond before expulsion.[35] On both occasions his status had been effectively that of an EU citizen with a temporary right of residence as a 'tourist'.[36] The ECJ, building on the earlier case-law on free movement, held that whilst Member States could impose a penalty for failure to hold an identity document:

> [D]etention and deportation based solely on the failure of the person concerned to comply with legal formalities concerning the monitoring of aliens *impair the very substance* of the right of residence conferred directly by Community law and are manifestly disproportionate to the seriousness of the infringement.[37]

The Court said the failure to comply with such rules did not constitute a threat to public policy or security.[38] The Court thereby rejected the argument that ensuring that a person was indeed an EU citizen with entitlement to be in Holland was a security issue permitting detention. There had to be a core security justification for detention, such as that the migrant would commit criminal acts.[39] Detention orders, like deportation, could be justified, but only based on the express deportation grounds of public policy, security or health.[40] Administrative reasons relating to immigration control were not enough.[41]

---

35 EU law does allow Member States a discretion to order expulsion of EU citizens who stay beyond three months without becoming economically active and who are not self-sufficient. Such persons are entitled, however, to individual consideration and should not be expelled simply because they have had recourse to social assistance.

36 Specifically, at the relevant time he had a right to stay up to three months in order to receive services under Art. 49 of the EC Treaty, as it then was, in addition to any rights derived from EU citizenship. The modalities of exercising this right, including the right to enter based upon presentation of an identity card or passport, were set out in Directive 73/148/EC on the removal of restrictions on the movement and stay of nationals of the Member States in relation to the establishment and receiving services.

37 *Ibid.*, para. 40 (emphasis added).   38 *Ibid.*, para. 41.

39 *Ibid.*, paras 9 and 11 state the facts in terms which indicate that a fear of absconding was the ground for detention, but the referring court did not put its questions on that basis. The Court says 'the questions referred are, however, based on the assumption that there was no genuine and serious threat to public policy' (para. 42). Any preventive detention would have to relate to crime serious enough to justify deportation under EU law.

40 Paragraph 41.

41 It is not clear what the Court would have decided had the Dutch authorities correctly ordered Oulane to leave because he in fact had no legal entitlement to remain in Holland under EU or national law (but was not a public security threat). It is arguable that the

Conclusions: EU citizens, narrowing 'security' and abolishing executive detention

The *Oulane* decision is a milestone in international law on migration. It reverses the inexorable trend towards the common use of administrative detention as a means of examining and expelling migrants. The nations of the Union are now unique in no longer being able to lawfully detain a group of persons (the nationals of other Member States) in order to establish their entitlement to be present. This was last seen in the classical era of *laissez-faire* migration that prevailed during much of the nineteenth century. The movement of EU citizens is not considered to be inherently a security issue. For many years the ECJ sought justification for its free movement case-law by reference to the removal of obstacles to trade. We can now, however, see the Court going further by narrowing the Member States' concepts of border 'security'. The whole idea of 'unauthorized' migration has disappeared for EU citizens. They are entitled to move across borders. They cannot be considered a 'security' threat, justifying incarceration, by their presence alone. The removal of this coercive power for one group challenges, in both practical and philosophical terms, its extensive use to establish immigration status in general.[42]

Non-EU citizens and the emergence of EU powers over asylum and immigration

Non-EU citizens are relatively new as objects of mainstream European law. They did not feature in the original EEC Treaty and still do not have general treaty-based rights to migrate into the EU.[43] Indeed, for many years, there were no ordinary powers to legislate in relation to

Court might have said again that imposing a fine was appropriate, but not detention. It is not clear, however, that EU law would regulate such a case involving a person, because he would be without a right to be in another Member State. The broader view is that every EU citizen in another Member State is entitled to protection qua EU citizen arising from the fundamental right of residence derived from the Maastricht Treaty.

42 As a practical matter, if immigration or police officials mistakenly detain an EU citizen, the authorities could be liable in damages. This may require them to rethink the kinds of practices that they use to establish nationality and immigration status. Without a good reason to doubt a migrant's EU citizenship, detention will become more risky.

43 As set out above, there had been measures like Reg. 1612/68 to allow family members to join EU citizens working in other Member States. There were also certain migration rights under agreements between the Union and particular third countries such as the EC–Turkey Agreement and Decision 1/80 of the EC–Turkey Association Council.

immigration and asylum of non-EU citizens.[44] Immigration powers over such persons, a significant bastion of sovereignty, were essentially reserved to Member States.[45] It was, however, recognized amongst some Member States that joint action relating to migration could facilitate the removal of internal border controls and create better surveillance and policing of the EU external border. The resulting Schengen Treaty of 1985 created such a framework outside the EU system for most continental Member States to collaborate on migration issues.[46] A key aspect of the Schengen arrangements was the development of a powerful security and policing apparatus directed at non-EU citizens. This was employed to police the external border of the participating states through establishing both a common database of persons who should be excluded on security grounds and common stricter border controls.[47] Security was therefore a key feature of European supra-national policy on migration even before the Union itself acquired powers in this field.[48]

The Union finally secured legislative power in this area in 1999.[49] Because of the removal of internal EU borders, each Member State's

44 There had been considerable intergovernmental negotiation on migration issues, but this was outside the traditional framework and was not subject to parliamentary or judicial scrutiny. See K. Hailbronner, *Immigration and Asylum Law and Policy of the European Union*, Amsterdam: Kluwer, 2000, which sets out Union policy as it evolved under the so-called Third Pillar.

45 There were, however, several special regimes governing particular types of non-EU citizens that had been established by the Union. Most prominent among these were the rights of family members of EU citizens and the rights of Turkish nationals.

46 The creation of a common short-stay visa scheme for non-EU migrants to Schengen countries was one important way that border controls could be removed. The Schengen system was eventually brought within the EU legal architecture through a protocol to the Amsterdam Treaty. See P.J. Kuijper, 'Some Legal Problems Associated with the Communitarization of Policy on Visas, Asylum and Immigration under the Amsterdam Treaty and Incorporation of the Schengen Acquis' (2000) 37 *C.M.L. Rev.* 345; E.B. Haas, *The Uniting of Europe: Political, Social and Economic Forces 1950–1957*, Stanford University Press, 1958, argued that functionalism would lead to growing integration in a wider range of fields.

47 See Schengen Information System set up under Arts 92–119 Schengen Implementing Agreement. D. O'Keefe, 'The Schengen Convention: A Suitable Model for European Integration?' (1992) 12 *YEL* 185.

48 M. Anderson, *Policing the European Union*, Oxford: Clarendon Press, 1995, 164–5, states 'the third pillar of TEU may be seen as the culmination of the integration between international law enforcement concerns and concerns about migratory movement and asylum seekers'.

49 The Parliament was only given a consultation role which was subject to the Council deciding to move towards the co-decision procedure (see Art. 67 EC Treaty) which would give a shared role to the European Parliament. A decision to partially do so was taken by Council Decision 2004/927/EC. The Draft Reform Treaty now provides for this (see Art. 69) entirely.

migration policy affected the others. Migration across Europe is easy once a foothold has been obtained in any Member State. The treaty text made clear the connection between internal freedom and external constraint as measures were required 'aimed at ensuring the free movement of persons' which required 'directly related flanking measures with respect to border controls, asylum and immigration'.[50] The Union's primary legal texts do not create the same radical political goals and associated rights in respect of non-EU citizens as they did for Union citizens.[51] Migration policy was always intended to reflect Member States' existing national priorities rather than dramatically alter them.

The Tampere European Council meeting of 1999 fleshed out more fully the Union's objectives in the field of migration control; common policies on asylum in line with the 1951 Refugee Convention, strong action against irregular migration across the Union's external border and a clear commitment to better integration of long-term residents based upon approximation of their status to that of EU citizens.[52] The period since has, however, continued to be one in which the political climate has been intensely hostile to immigration and asylum.[53] It was also one marked by fears of links between aliens and terrorism following the attacks in the United States and then Madrid and London.[54]

Security has therefore remained a key feature of the Union agenda on migration.[55] There are, however, contrary tendencies: humanitarianism has jostled with economic self-interest and cultural integration. In places, EU policy seeks to confer directly effective rights on non-EU citizens, in others it seeks to maintain Member State control and, in others still, it

---

50 Article 61 EC Treaty.
51 B. Tholen, 'The Europeanisation of Migration Policy – The Normative Issues' (2004) 4 *Eur. J. Migration and L.* 323, sets out the range of competing policies dynamics within the EU and provides an agenda for future research.
52 See Tampere European Council Conclusions, 15 and 16 Oct. 1999. See also A. Geddes, *Immigration and European Integration: Towards Fortress Europe?*, Manchester University Press, 2000.
53 A.E. Kessler and G.P. Freeman, 'Public Opinion on Immigration from Outside the Community' (2005) 43(4) *JCMS* 825.
54 S. Lavenex and W. Wallace, 'Justice and Home Affairs, Towards a "European Public Order"?', in H. Wallace, W. Wallace and N. Pollack (eds), *Policy Making in the European Union*, 5th edn, Oxford University Press, 2005, 460–1.
55 See EU Council: The Hague Programme: Strengthening Freedom Security and Justice in the European Union, Council Doc. 16054/04. This states that the security of the Union requires 'a more effective, joint approach to cross-border problems such as terrorism, organized crime, irregular migratory flows and smuggling of human beings as well as the prevention thereof. Notably in the field of security, the co-ordination and coherence between the internal and the external dimension has been growing in importance and needs to continue to be vigorously pursued'.

seeks to exclude unwanted persons.[56] The prominence of security concerns, however, is significant from the perspective of detention powers.[57] The Union is increasingly shaping and directing executive action in policing and migration issues.[58] Hitherto the Union worked by setting legislative frameworks, leaving execution to the Member States. In migration control we are starting to see increased executive and enforcement action by the Union.[59] Although 'EU' detention centres have not yet arrived, Member States have been facilitated in their new role as agents of the Union in detaining non-EU citizens.

The selective arrival of EU detention powers

Detention powers in the legislative programme rolled out since Tampere tell us much about the new friends and enemies.[60] We can detect a clear distinction between immigration laws and those governing asylum and illegal migration; only the latter are subject to express 'security'-type measures. The EU has transplanted upwards the Member States' concern about securing external borders against unauthorized persons. Detention powers are a key expression of this. The EU border is becoming more heavily policed by explicit authority of EU law both to expel and prevent entry of unauthorized persons.[61] Authorized persons such as long-term residents, family members and students have not become explicitly subject to these powers. In this respect we see the restrictive and liberalizing tendencies of supra-nationalism coalescing around authorization of migration.

'Friendly' aliens and detention powers: a policy of silence

The previous long-standing EU rules on immigration relating to family members of EU migrant workers, EEA citizens,[62] Turkish workers

56 J. Huysmans, *The Politics of Insecurity: Fear, Migration and Asylum in the EU*, London: Routledge, 2005.

57 J. Huysmans, 'The European Union and the Securitization of Migration' (2000) 38 *JCMS* 751.

58 See N. Walker, 'In Search of the Area of Freedom, Security and Justice: A Constitutional Odyssey', in N. Walker (ed.), *Europe's Area of Freedom, Security and Justice*, Oxford University Press, 2004.

59 See as one example the creation of Frontex, the European border agency.

60 For a detailed review of EU policy in this area, see 'Special Issue: Migrants and Minorities in Europe' (2005) 43(4) *JCMS*.

61 C. Boswell, 'Migration Control in Europe after 9/11' (2007) 45 *JCMS* 589, argues that these controls have not been driven by security concerns in recent years.

62 The European Economic Area comprises the EU states plus Norway and Iceland.

admitted under the EC–Turkey Association Agreement and Eastern European self-employed persons were all silent as regards detention.[63] The new
immigration measures follow this pattern. The EU legislature was content
to leave implementation matters, such as detention, to the Member States.
The failure to affirm detention as a legitimate tool of control for these
groups suggests that political concerns over the security of the Union's
borders were less serious here. The measures concern families and persons
who have established a legal right to reside in at least one Member State
already. This does not involve the 'irregular' EU external border crossing
which has become the focus of enforcement efforts. The Union has thus
not *mandated* detention powers over these migrants.[64]

The Directive on Long-term Residents is the key measure in this field.[65]
It provides permanent residence and free movement rights for those who
have stayed for a qualifying period in a Member State. Whilst it confers
powers of expulsion and/or withdrawal of residence permits on narrow
public policy grounds, there is no mention of detention.[66] There is only
an oblique reference, in that each Member States expelling a non-EU
citizen 'shall take all the appropriate measure to effectively implement
it'.[67] Similar considerations apply to the Family Reunification Directive.[68]
This gives rights to non-EU citizens to join and reside with their non-
EU resident families in the Union.[69] There are public policy exclusion
and expulsion powers,[70] but again there is no requirement to implement

---

63 For a detailed description of the measures passed and treaties signed by the Union before
   it acquired general powers over migration see H. Staples, *The Legal Status of Third Country
   Nationals Resident in the European Union,* The Hague: Kluwer 1999.
64 The Directive on temporary protection required Member States to give temporary permits
   to persons from countries deemed to be in a situation of armed conflict or endemic
   violence such that they could not return for the time being. Once the situation in
   the country of origin had ended, expulsion followed national law and procedure. The
   Directive was silent on the mechanics for returning such persons. There was, however, a
   hint of concern in that Member States 'shall take the measures necessary to ensure that
   the enforced return ... is conducted with due respect for human dignity' (Art. 22(1)).
   See Council Directive 2001/55/EC of 20 July 2001 on minimum standards for giving
   temporary protection in the event of a mass influx of displaced persons.
65 2003/109/EC of 25 Nov. 2003 concerning the status of third-country nationals who are
   long-term residents.
66 Articles 6, 12, 17 and 22 set out substantive and procedural protection against expulsion
   or deportation that mirrors some of the concepts found in relation to EU citizens. For
   a detailed analysis see S. Peers, 'Implementing Equality? The Directive on Long Term
   Resident Third Country Nationals' (2004) 29(4) *E.L. Rev.* 437.
67 Article 22(3).   68 2003/86 22 Sept. 2003, L251 12.   69 Article 6.
70 Recital 14 speaks of 'public policy may cover a conviction for committing a serious crime'
   also public security and policy include someone who 'belongs to an association that
   supports terrorism, supports such an association or has extremist aspirations'.

these orders by arrest and detention.[71] Following the *Oulane* approach in relation to these Directives would rule out detention merely to check immigration status. This is consistent with the Tampere objective of providing 'nearly' equal rights for lawful foreigners, especially those who are highly integrated.

More equivocal is the common code[72] on border movements, which sets out the rules governing non-EU citizens seeking to enter the Union at the border of any Member State.[73] Persons not fulfilling the requirements for entry 'shall be refused entry to the territories of the Member States'.[74] Here we see the first sign of force expressed in relation to immigration as 'border guards *shall ensure* that a third-country national refused entry does not enter the territory of the Member State concerned'.[75] This must imply some form of physical restraint in cases of resistance. However 'any measures taken in the performance of [border guards'] duties shall be proportionate to the objectives pursued by such measures'.[76] Guards must also not discriminate on specified grounds and must 'fully respect human dignity'.[77] These principles suggest a degree of ambivalence about the moral and legal status of those barred entry at the EU border. Whilst these persons *must* be excluded as a matter of common EU border enforcement, detention is not expressly authorized. As we shall see, it is only when a person has been subject to a *removal order* that detention has become closer to being an obligation on Member States.

In summary, no *immigration* measures have required Member States to detain non-EU citizens. Movements of lawful resident non-EU citizens and their families *per se* has not been considered a danger to EU security. For these groups, 'security' is narrowly interpreted to cover only public order threats. However the *requirement* that border guards prevent entry into the EU using force against *all non-EU citizens refused entry*, regardless

---

71 We can also mention the Students Directive, which provides common standards for admission of students from outside the Union but no express discussion of detention powers in the Directive. Council Directive 2004/114/EC of 13 Dec. 2004, OJ L 375/12, 23.12.2004 on the conditions of admission of third-country nationals for the purposes of studies, pupil exchange, unremunerated training or voluntary service.

72 Regulation 562/2006 of the European Parliament and of the Council of 15 Mar. 2006 establishing a community Code on the rules governing the movement of persons across borders (Schengen Borders Code).

73 The exceptions are refugees, asylum seekers and those non-EU citizens benefiting from third-country agreements (Art. 3).

74 Article 13(1).   75 Article 13(4) (emphasis added).

76 Article 6(1).   77 Article 6(1)(2).

of any individual threat to public order, suggests a broader EU security dimension around sealing the external border.

'Hostile' aliens: detention powers over unauthorized migration in the EU

By contrast, for non-EU citizens there has been an equation between unauthorized border-crossing and threats to EU security requiring strong coercive measures. There are now three Directives which clearly authorize detention under EU law – the Reception Conditions Directive, the Asylum Procedures Directive and the Returns Directive.[78] They represent the first time that an express power of detention over anyone has been confirmed in any EU legislation.[79] This is indicative of the Union adopting further the attributes of a modern state seeking to assert legal control over its territorial borders.[80] For asylum seekers, however, legislating to incarcerate for administrative purposes generated strong controversy and little consensus. Humanitarian considerations collided with the Union's political rhetoric of strong borders. The majority of asylum applicants enter the Union without permission. In relation to asylum, the final texts thus speak of a confusing set of compromises. By contrast, in relation to the expulsion of unauthorized migrants, there was a surprisingly great readiness to adopt extended detention. It was accepted that this group constituted a more unequivocal threat which was not mitigated by humanitarian obligations.

Asylum seekers: provisional authorization and tenuous liberty

First we can look at the Reception Conditions Directive. This created a kind of provisional authorization for all those who seek asylum regardless of their immigration status or lack thereof. It is important in giving

---

78 Also see Council Regulation (EC) 343/2001 of 18 Feb. 2003 establishing the criteria and mechanisms for determining the Member States responsible for examining an asylum application lodged in one Member State by a third-country national in which Art. 16 lays down an urgent procedure for requesting take-back where in detention.

79 See now the Framework Decision on the European Arrest Warrant – E. Guild (ed.), *Constitutional Challenges to the European Arrest Warrant*, Nijmegen: Wolf Legal Publishers, 2006.

80 For a review of the Union's policies in this field see K. Hailbronner, 'Asylum Law in the Context of a European Migration Policy', in Walker (ed.), *Europe's Area of Freedom, Security and Justice*, and also H. Battjes, *European Asylum Law and International Law*, Leiden: Martinus Nijhoff, 2006.

a temporary status and entitlements that would otherwise be lacking for irregular migrants. Thus it requires asylum seekers to be given housing, educational, medical and material support during the assessment of their cases. After one year, asylum seekers must be allowed access to work if their cases are unresolved. The Directive therefore attempts to recreate a status for those who, because they cross an international frontier without permission, would otherwise be without basic socio-economic rights.

The Directive also regulates the civil liberties of such putative refugees.[81] Article 7 (entitled 'Residence and Freedom of Movement') suggests an entitlement to liberty as 'asylum seekers may move freely within the territory of the host Member State or *within an area assigned to them*' (emphasis added). However, Member States may 'when it proves necessary, for example for legal reasons or reasons of public order . . . *confine an applicant to a particular place* in accordance with their national law'.[82] We can see that the grounds to detain are very opaque: 'legal reasons' are not specified. They could include a fear that a person might abscond. 'Public order' is more exact and there is a body of ECJ case-law on the scope of this type of derogation.[83] The reference to 'national law' seems to permit wide variations of an uncertain nature. There is also no requirement for judicial authorization of detention, nor a right to bail.

Despite all these strong reservations, we can see that Article 7 creates a basic right of free movement for asylum seekers which is subject to derogation only when necessary.[84] This was an important step which rejected the emerging idea that illegal modes of entry or lack of authorization should denude asylum seekers of a bundle of rights, including liberty.

---

81 In fact, detailed detention provisions were originally put in the Asylum Procedures Directive, but these failed to be agreed. The Reception Condition Directive merely cross-referenced to these. When agreement proved impossible, some crude provision were put into the Reception Conditions Directive as an alternative to a detailed code. The text reflects this contorted parentage and birth.

82 Emphasis added. The Union legislature was clearly still uncomfortable using the term 'detention' and it only appears in the definitions section, where 'detention' is referred to as including confinement to a particular place, Art. 2(k) Directive 2003/9. 'Detention' is thus a label applied to 'confinement to a particular place' rather than, more logically, the other way around.

83 See above Case 67/74 *Bonsignore* v. *Oberstadtdirektor of the City of Cologne* [1975] ECR 297.

84 See S. Peers and N. Rogers (eds), *EU Immigration and Asylum Law*, Leiden: Martinus Nijhoff, 2006, 302.

The exceptions, however, spoke of Member States' continued security concerns over irregular migration. As we saw in relation to the Refugee Convention itself in Chapter 3, the basis for restrictions on the movement of asylum seekers is not clearly delineated.[85] Whilst mandatory detention might appear incompatible with the Directive, the lack of precision in the exceptions allows for considerable latitude here. Thus, for example, the United Kingdom has continued to use fast-track *mandatory* detention for many asylum seekers. It is not clear what the justification for this policy would be in terms of the criteria set out in the Directive, but the language is vague. The Directive appears to have largely accommodated existing state practice and continues to afford a large degree of discretion in controlling movements of persons who are still considered unauthorized until awarded refugee status.

The negotiation of asylum detention: a failure to agree on legal limits

The emaciated and vague detention measures left in the Reception Conditions Directive were never intended to be complete.[86] In fact, detention of asylum seekers was pushed between the Commission, Council and European Parliament over a five-year period during the drafting of the Asylum Procedures Directive. The great divergence between apparently 'similar' liberal European states in their interpretation of the right of personal liberty of non-citizens was enormous.[87] There was real reluctance by Member States with more extensive detention powers to accept limitations on these. However, there was also strong opposition from the more liberal EU Parliament to providing EU 'legitimacy' to an open-ended detention regime. The Commission was caught in the middle; its text referred to certain international standards which were too weak for the Parliament and too onerous for the Council.

---

85 Article 31(2) speaks of restrictions which are 'necessary' in the case of illegally present refugees. Article 26 gives a right of movement to those lawfully present. It is the space between these that is not clear.

86 See Peers and Rogers, *EU Immigration and Asylum Law*, 370–9, for the history of this Directive.

87 For more generally on this see G. Gilbert, 'Is Europe Living Up to its Obligations to Refugees?' (2004) 14(5) *Eur. J. Int. L.* 963, who argues that 'harmonization . . . inevitably leads to equalizing down at the expense of the refugee when it is attempted to attune those independent approaches'.

The Commission's first draft Directive[88] was modelled upon UNHCR Executive Committee Conclusion No. 44.[89] Although, as was noted in Chapter 3, this is an imperfect text, the Commission was at least applying one international standard.[90] The Parliament modified the text to move towards a right to liberty subject to due process safeguards modelled on the French system.[91] The grounds for detention were limited to threats to public order or national security and to ensure removal following a failed asylum claim. Detention should be 'only for as long as is necessary' and should subject to mandatory judicial reviews of detention at regular intervals to scrutinize both the grounds and legality of detention. The detainee should also be given legal assistance.[92] This suggested that asylum seekers were not a security threat to be held under discretionary detention, but had a basic right to cross the EU external borders.

The Commission rejected most of the Parliament's suggestions in its amended draft, but introduced some interesting new limitations on detention. Detention was only justified when 'objectively necessary' to make an efficient examination of the claim or when there was a 'strong likelihood' of absconding. Purely administrative detention to process applications

---

88 Draft Article 11 reads as follows:

  1. Member States shall not hold an applicant for asylum in detention for the sole reason that his application for asylum needs to be examined. However, Member States may hold an applicant for asylum in detention for the purpose of taking a decision in the following cases, in accordance with a procedure prescribed by national law and only for as long as is necessary:
      (a) to ascertain or verify his identity or nationality;
      (b) to determine his identity or nationality when he has destroyed or disposed of his travel and/or identity documents or used fraudulent documents upon arrival in the Member State in order to mislead the authorities;
      (c) to determine the elements on which his application for asylum is based which in other circumstances could be lost;
      (d) in the context of a procedure, to decide on his right to enter the territory.
  2. Member States shall provide by law for the possibility of an initial review and subsequent regular reviews of the order for detention of applicants for asylum detained pursuant to paragraph 1.

89 See discussion above in Ch. 3.
90 E. Guild, 'Seeking Asylum: Storm Clouds between International Commitments and Legislative Measures' (2004) 29 *E.L. Rev.* 198, 214, notes that the original proposal was much more powerfully protective of asylum seekers.
91 European Parliamentary Committee on Citizens' Freedoms and Rights, Justice and Home Affairs.
92 This was allegedly to comply with Arts 5 and 6 ECHR, but this is not yet the position of the Strasbourg Court.

was allowed, but limited to two weeks. The UK had pressed for this to allow her to use closed 'fast-track' centres.[93] There was also a power to detain up to one month in order to send asylum seekers to other EU states which they had passed through.[94]

The Home Affairs and Interior Ministries in the Council rejected even these safeguards. Their final text required only that no one should be detained for the 'sole reason' of having made an asylum claim. Of course, immigration authorities tend to justify detention by reference to mode of entry, lack of ties, false documents, deception and other grounds, not simply having claimed asylum. The procedural guarantee in Article 18(2) was merely the minimalist one requiring the 'possibility of rapid judicial review' for persons in detention. There was no mandatory court oversight of detention required and no requirement that judicial review be on the merits rather than simply confined to errors of law.

This skeletal text leaves regulation of detention of asylum seekers in a dangerous limbo of uncertainty. The 'right' to freedom of movement in the Reception Conditions Directive is equivocal. Of course, Member States are required to adhere to ECHR case-law as members of the Council of Europe.[95] This case-law is, however, very open-ended and does not impose clear criteria for detention, due process, nor fixed time limits. As EU law *authorizes* detention, it would have been better, from both the perspective of clarity and effective supervision, for a comprehensive code of rules *controlling* it to also derive from EU law.[96] It is clear that the Member States wished to maintain maximal political discretion over a highly prized tool of border control. We shall discuss shortly the potential role of the ECJ in providing limitations upon these powers.

---

93 See *Saadi* v. *Secretary of State for the Home Department* [2002] UKHL 41.
94 Pursuant to what used to be regulated by the Dublin Convention 1990 and is now governed by Commission Regulation (EC) No. 343/2003 of 18 Feb. 20003 establishing the criteria and mechanisms for determining the Member State responsible for examining an asylum application lodged in one of the Member States by a third-country national.
95 In the event of conflict between either the ECHR or the Refugee Convention and EU law, the former treaties must prevail. See Art. 309 EC Treaty and Battjes, *European Asylum Law and International Law*, Ch. 10, for an explanation.
96 Overlapping legal regimes also create serious problems for legal certainty from the perspective of Art. 5 ECHR. The final Council text in Art. 18 does not meet the requirements of being a 'procedure prescribed by law' given that it contains no proper rules to regulate detention. Whilst national laws might provide such detail, the fact of two regimes of detention serves to create a lack of certainty, for both those subject to detention and those employing it, as to the correct rules.

Irregular migrants as an enemy: extended detention of the non-dangerous in the Returns Directive

Irregular migration has been identified over the past twenty years in mainstream European politics as a threat justifying increasingly strong coercive measures.[97] The EU Returns Directive embodies this most clearly with its wide and largely unaccountable detention powers. Whilst some EU social and employment policies serve to prevent exploitation of irregular migrants, broad 'security' rationales have become uppermost as grounds for controlling irregular migrations. An EU border and immigration politics that, whilst not preventing unauthorized entry and stay, maintains that 'unauthorized' persons are illegitimate has adopted strong measures against them.[98]

The Returns Directive[99] on returning migrants found to be staying illegally within the EU represents something much closer to a code regulating each aspect of detention and is in that sense to be welcomed. The European Parliament embraced detention of this group of migrants

---

97 For a detailed review of EU policy in the area see R. Cholewinski, 'European Union Policy on Irregular Migration', in B. Bogusz, R. Cholewinski, A. Cygan and E. Syszczak (eds), *Irregular Migration and Human Rights: Theoretical, European and International Perspectives*, Leiden: Martinus Nijhoff Publishers, 2004; M. Samers, 'An Emerging Geopolitics of "Illegal" Immigration in the European Union' (2004) 6 *Eur. J. Migration L.* 27.

98 An early example is the Note on Joint Flights aimed at removing non-EU citizens subject to expulsion orders. This provides detailed Common Guidelines which permit 'coercive measures' to be used on those who 'refuse or resist' removal, which respect the individual's rights and are proportional. This includes 'immobilization' by restraints that 'will not endanger their dignity or physical integrity'. The exact nature of permitted restraints is to be agreed by the authorities engaged in each flight. Sedation is permitted to ensure flight security. Council Decision 2004/573/EC of 29 Apr. 2004 on the organisation of joint flights for removals from the territory of two or more Member States, of third country nationals who are subjects of individual removal orders', OJ L 261, 6.8.2004, 28.

99 Directive 2008/115/EC of the European Parliament and of the Council of 16 Dec. 2008 on common standards and procedures in Member States for returning illegally staying third-country nationals (OJ 2008 L 348, 98). It is important to note that Member States were given a right to disapply most of the Directive in cases of migrants refused entry at ports or intercepted at sea: see Art. 2(2). There were, however, minimal guarantees in Art. 4(4) that could not be disapplied in any case: otherwise national law governs detention procedures in such cases. This suggests that, as we saw in the United States case-law, persons who have actually crossed a border are treated as worthy of more legal protection than others.

without the scruples it showed over asylum seekers.[100] There was a clear political consensus amongst EU institutions that illegally present immigrants merited such measures.[101] This was indicative of a Union coming to assume the values and methods of interior ministries in relation to border control.[102] The perceived mutual interest in preventing unauthorized persons from remaining within the Union became inscribed in the law as a duty to effect expulsion.[103]

Consensus on the detention issue was nevertheless hard to achieve because of the diversity of national laws. One survey[104] showed that most states had an upper time limit on detention but some, such as the United Kingdom, Ireland, the Netherlands and Malta did not. Those with time limits ranged from thirty-two days in France to eighteen months in Germany. Some states required judicial authorization, but many did not. The grounds for detention were conceived of significantly differently across Member States. There was no willingness for compromise by strong detention regime countries in the Council. Furthermore, the Parliament, often seen as more 'liberal' than other institutions, made only modest changes to the text.[105] The final version of the Directive thus removed

---

100 See the previous critical position expressed by the Committee on Citizens' Freedom and Rights, Justice and Home Affairs, *Report on the Situation as regards Fundamental Rights in the EU* (2003), 22/3/04 no. 27, where it said it was 'concerned at the plight of foreigners being deprived of their freedom in holding centres, despite the fact that they have been charged with no crime or offence and calls for holding centres . . . to meet human rights standards'.

101 Only a minority opinion in the parliamentary committee voiced opposition in principle saying that 'third-country nationals, as communitarian citizens, shouldn't undergo this privation of their personal freedom or prison punishment because of an administrative breach' and that 'a prolonged detention of people in terrible conditions . . . should never been [sic] authorized by our EU legislation'. Report on the Proposal for a Directive of the European Parliament and of the Council on common standards and procedures in Member States for returning illegally staying third-country nationals. Committee on Civil Liberties, Justice and Home Affairs, 20.9.2007, Final, A6–0339/2007 Guisto Catania, 29.

102 G. Lahav and A.M. Messina, 'The Limits of a European Immigration Policy: Elite Opinion and Agendas within the European Parliament' (2005) 43(4) *JCMS* 851–75, who find that whilst concern amongst European parliamentarians has risen, their preference is still for national governments to regulate migration.

103 Article 6(1). There are provisions for exceptions to be made but the basic duty is clear.

104 See *Detention in Europe: Administrative Detention of Asylum-seekers and Irregular Migrants* (Jesuit Refugee Service – Brussels, 2004) and also B. Nascimbene (ed.), *Expulsion and Detention of Aliens in EU Countries*, Milan: Guiffre, 2001.

105 See D. Acosta, 'The Good, the Bad and the Ugly in EU Migration Law: Is the European Parliament becoming Bad and Ugly? (The Adoption of Directive 2008/115: the Returns Directive)' (2009) 11 *Eur. J. Migration and L.* 19–39.

most of the important limits on detention set by the Commission text.[106] At one stage, the Council had introduced mandatory detention where the relevant conditions were met.[107] The final text, however, leaves detention as a discretionary power rather than a duty.

Key elements of judicial and legal control were, however, removed from the final version. Whilst the previous text said detention should only occur as a last resort after consideration of alternatives,[108] the final text reverses that presumption, saying that '*unless* other sufficient but less coercive measures can be applied' detention may be used.[109] Whilst not a presumption in favour of detention, this is an important indication that the 'right' of liberty is still contested in the final text. Similarly, a previous draft had required judicial approval to support detention apart from in urgent cases.[110] There was also a requirement for judicial review once a month.[111] These were dropped from the final text. This only required approval for detention by 'administrative *or* judicial authorities'.[112] Member States were allowed to leave it to detainees to commence proceedings to challenge the 'lawfulness' of detention.[113]

The requirement for regular further judicial authorization was also removed in favour of detention being 'reviewed at reasonable intervals of time' at the behest of the detainee *or* the administration.[114] Only cases of 'prolonged detention' must be subject to 'the supervision of a judicial authority'. The provisions therefore leave executive immigration

---

106 See the more liberal original draft by the Commission, COM (2005) 391 final, 2005/0167 (COD) Proposal for a Directive of the European Parliament and the Council on common standards and procedures in Member States for returning illegally staying third-country nationals.

107 Member States 'shall keep under temporary custody a third-country national, who is or will be subject of a removal order or return decision' (Art. 14(1)). Report on the Proposal for a Directive of the European Parliament and of the Council on common standards and procedures in Member States for returning illegally staying third-country nationals. Committee on Civil Liberties, Justice and Home Affairs, 20.9.2007, Final, A6–0339/2007. This has now been removed from the text.

108 'Where it would not be sufficient to apply less coercive measures, such as regular reports to the authorities etc . . . Member States shall keep under temporary custody persons subject to removal order' Art. 14(1). Committee on Civil Liberties, Justice and Home Affairs, 20.9.2007, Final, A6–0339/2007.

109 Article 15(1). Only unaccompanied minors and families with minors benefit from a more generous approach so that detention must be a 'measure of last resort and for the shortest appropriate period of time' Art. 17(1).

110 See draft Directive, M. 106 above, Art. 14(2). In urgent cases the order must be confirmed by judicial authorities within seventy-two hours.

111 *Ibid.*, Art. 14(3).   112 *Ibid.*, Art. 15(2).   113 *Ibid.*   114 *Ibid.*, Art. 15(3).

officials largely free from judicial control in relation to day-to-day detention decision-making. Whilst maintaining basic principles of the rule of law such as access to the courts, they denude them of effectiveness because they rely upon detainees taking action for themselves. Often this is impractical due to lack of access to information or legal assistance. Detention remains largely administrative under the Directive.

Importantly, however, there are only two grounds for detention in the Directive. First, in the presence of 'the existence of reasons in an individual case which are based on objective criteria defined by law to believe that [a foreigner] may abscond'.[115] This sets a low standard of proof but does require justifications which are objectively reasoned. The second ground is when the foreigner 'avoids or hampers the preparation of return or the removal process'.[116] This is a novel basis for detention which was a response to the problems of documentation and *de facto* statelessness that have become so prevalent. One who is judged as 'hampering' is surely likely to abscond if released in any event. There was thus no need for the second ground for detention. To this extent, the 'obstruction' ground seems to serve largely to provide authorities with a coercive tool with uncertain parameters. Assessments of when someone is 'hampering' are conducted by executive officers, affording them an extremely large, almost arbitrary, discretion given the lack of definition to the concept.

The duration of detention under the Returns Directive and the decision in Kadzoev

The fixing of the maximum permitted periods of detention was, however, the most controversial issue in the Directive.[117] There was a clear levelling down towards Member States with longer maximum periods. The original Commission draft Directive set a legal maximum of three months on detention.[118] The European Parliament amended this to eighteen months in cases where, despite all reasonable efforts, removal would take longer due to a lack of cooperation by the detainee, documentation delays by third countries or if the detainee posed a proven threat to national

115 *Ibid.*, Art. 3(g).   116 *Ibid.*, Art. 15(1).
117 That the Directive set such a maximum was a milestone in international law which has, as we saw in Ch. 3, generally adopted a case-by-case approach.
118 Article 14(4).

security, public policy or public security.[119] The Council draft did not have any fixed time limit, but detention had to cease when removal become 'impossible'.[120] In the end, those Member States with unlimited detention gave ground in the Council and time limits were fixed.[121]

The final text says that detention must be 'for as short a period as possible' but allows an initial period of six months. However, this can be extended to eighteen months in cases where, despite the reasonable efforts of the authorities, removal is delayed due to, first, a 'lack of cooperation' by the detainee or where there are 'delays in obtaining necessary documentation from third countries'.[122] Public security was removed as a ground.[123] Under Article 15(4), detention must cease in any event when 'it appears that a reasonable prospect of removal no longer exists for legal or other considerations' because it is then no longer justified. This reflects the growing recent consensus that we have noticed in both the United Kingdom, United States and European Court of Human Rights that sees detention as conditional upon removal being possible in a reasonable time frame.

We have already noted the problem of defining and controlling the 'lack of co-operation' ground for extended detention. The second ground for extended detention is even more objectionable from the perspective of the rule of law. If a detainee is from a slow or non-compliant state, their ongoing detention is entirely in the hands of decisions or indecisions of such foreign powers and officials. Detention would appear to serve only as a bargaining counter to try and encourage diplomats to act. Liberal

---

119 Report on the Proposal for a Directive of the European Parliament and of the Council on common standards and procedures in Member States for returning illegally staying third-country nationals. Committee on Civil Liberties, Justice and Home Affairs, 20.9.2007, Final, A6–0339/2007, 22. This was an extension from twelve months proposed initially by the Committee. See Provisional 2005/0167 (COD), 13.6.2006.

120 Outcome of Proceedings Strategic Committee on Immigration, Frontiers, Asylum and Mixed Committee (EU–Iceland/Norway and Switzerland), 7 Dec. 2002, 42.

121 In fact, some Member States, like the United Kingdom, have an opt-out from all of these measures and exercised it in order to retain indefinite detention among other powers.

122 Article 15(6). The previous draft referred to public security grounds for prolonged detention. This has been removed because the Returns Directive is only concerned with administrative expulsion, not public security deportation measures. Member States no doubt still have a power to

123 The removal of the public order ground for detention is sensible, given that a public order risk would give rise to a fear of absconding in any event. The removal is significant in that it keeps the focus of the Directive on immigration enforcement, rather than policing powers. This avoids the blurring of the two issues that can lead to very extended detention amounting to internment in, particularly, terrorism cases. See Ch. 5 below.

democracies should not delegate the power of incarceration in such an uncertain and arbitrary manner which is beyond the control of courts, the detainee and the detaining state.

Where the time limits have expired or Article 15(4) applies, a detainee must be released immediately regardless of other circumstances. This was confirmed by the ECJ in *Kadzoev*,[124] where a Chechen Russian who had illegally entered Bulgaria had been held in detention for three years. He had claimed asylum several times, but each claim was rejected. He was ordered to be deported. He had supplied the government with two different names. The Russian authorities did not accept he was Russian and no other country appeared likely to take him back. He had no address to be bailed to in Bulgaria and no means of support. He was said to have shown 'aggressive' conduct, although this was disputed. It was obviously going to be difficult for the government to keep in contact with him if bailed. The Court confirmed that nevertheless he had to be released because the Directive did not permit detention beyond eighteen months on any grounds. This followed from a strict textual interpretation of the Directive alone. This is striking, as it ruled out any extended public security detention annexed to deportation by Member States.[125] The ECJ therefore also rejected any idea that there was an inherent EU prerogative (devolved to Member States) to protect public safety by using immigration detention powers.

The Court, however, carefully avoided reference to any 'fundamental rights' of non-EU citizens.[126] It certainly made no attempt to raise such objections to the Returns Directive itself. In this we immediately see a contrast with the free movement rights of EU citizens discussed earlier. In fact, by contrast, there were two features of its decision that reduced the protection the Directive affords. First, the requirement in Article 15(4) that there 'no longer' exists a reasonable prospect of removal had to be assessed in light of the eighteen-month period allowed under the Directive. This would permit detention even where the authorities know at the outset that securing documentation may take some time, so long as it *might* not exceed eighteen months. This invites authorities

---

124 C-357/09 PPU *Said Shamilovich Kadzoev (Huchbarov)*, Judgment of Grand Chamber, 30 Nov. 2009.

125 It is possible that 'emergency' powers by a Member State could be taken, but these would have to be non-discriminatory internment provisions, not deportation powers.

126 Advocate General Mazak did, however, speak of the detainees' 'fundamental right to freedom, any exceptions being subject to strict conditions...' C-357/09 PPU *Said Shamilovich Kadzoev (Huchbarov)*, Opinion, 10 Nov. 2009 (para. 65).

to view eighteen months as a standard reasonable period of negotiations. The Court appears to have endorsed the EU legislative's assessment of the balance to be struck between liberty and border control here without even considering that there might be a fundamental rights 'problem'.

Second, the Court ruled that detention during periods where an asylum claim was being considered 'stopped the clock' under the Returns Directive. 'Asylum' detention must be considered and justified separately under the Reception Conditions Directive. Detention periods under the two Directives are therefore cumulative and could go well beyond eighteen months. Importantly, however, the Court held that legal challenges to deportation not linked to asylum claims did not stop the clock. Thus, eighteen months was the total period allowed to secure removal.

The Returns Directive: the rule of law avoided

In summary, the Returns Directive did create some legal certainty with long-stop end-points to detention. It did so, however, by adopting following the very longest fixed periods of detention employed in Member States. In striking a balance between individual liberty and enforcement measures against unauthorized migration, it clearly favoured the latter. The absence of mandatory judicial review and the broad grounds for detention mean that the Directive affords wide discretion to officials. There are possibly punitive elements present as regards the obligation on detainees to cooperate. These should be the subject of defined criminal offences with judicial trials, not administrative discretion. Much detention will persist due to the vagaries of international negotiations. A potential eighteen months appears a disproportionate period of administrative detention for non-dangerous persons.

As we saw in Chapter 3, international law under both the ICCPR and ECHR has sought to circumscribe purely administrative detention. Nevertheless, these standards are not a code, but embody broad standards of reasonableness and proportionality. Whilst the Directive has been widely condemned as hostile to human rights standards, it is not certain that it infringes them.[127] European states have for many years had systems of

---

127 See A. Baldaccini, 'The European Directive on Returns: Principles and Protests' (2010) 28(4) *Refugee Survey Quarterly* 114–38. In a novel move many Latin-American 'sending' countries have attacked the Directive because of its effects on their national migrant workers, who make up large numbers of the EU migrant population. Spain alone has some 2 million workers. D. Acosta, 'Latin-American Reactions to the Adoption of the EU Returns Directive', CEPS Working Paper, Nov. 2009.

indefinite administrative detention that were not generally struck down by the Strasbourg Court. The Directive, with its easy political transplantation of national practices up to EU level, whilst preventing the most extreme cases, largely reflects the normalization of lengthy executive detention of unauthorized persons.

Importantly, the Directive provides no 'regularization' mechanism for those released.[128] They remain in a legal limbo, outsiders without any clear set of civil, social or economic entitlements, even though EU law considers that their basic liberty should be restored as enforcement efforts have failed.[129] There is thus no 'reauthorization', which remains a matter entirely for the political discretion of governments. This omission, when combined with the time limits, creates a group of people who will remain 'outlaws' in terms of EU law. Thus, despite having been through the full EU prescribed removal procedure, once released they have no legal status and are subject to the, now standard, national prohibitions on rights to work and other socio-economic rights. Whilst future removal may be possible in such cases, it was incumbent on the EU institutions to provide for the legal status of these persons in the interim. Whilst being pragmatic, humane and complying with universal human rights norms, such a step would have required a political decision seen as legitimating irregular migrants. This was beyond European migration politics at the time.

The possibility of an EU constitutional right to liberty

The EU has hitherto not often had to confront serious issues concerning civil liberties. Cases involving deportation and detention of foreigners will be significant in defining the approach to such fundamental rights in the Union. There is no separate bill of rights within the EU Treaties. The ECJ has, however, gradually granted itself a power to review EU legislation to ensure that it complies with fundamental rights, including those derived from the ECHR and the ICCPR. This was part of a broader development of 'general principles' of EU law by the Court. These included

---

128 See E. Mincheva, 'Case Report on *Kadzoev*, 30 November 2009' (2010) 12 *Eur. J. Migration and L.* 361–71, who discusses the legal vacuum left by the Directive and the Commission's review of this issue in the Member States.

129 Article 9(3) contemplates the 'postponement' of removal on various grounds, including where removal proves impossible due to practical obstacles, but provides only that states may impose bail conditions on such persons. It does re-regulate the status of such persons to cover work, social security or education, for example.

the requirement that EU legislation be proportionate and that it be non-discriminatory. More recently, the Charter of Fundamental Rights has been adopted by the Union. This package of principles and the Charter may provide additional protection against administrative detention going beyond national and international human rights law.

There is no exclusively contractarian logic tied to citizenship of the Member States in EU human rights protection.[130] The Preamble to the EU Charter of Fundamental Rights expresses this duality, saying that the Union 'places the individual at the heart of its activities, by establishing the citizenship of the Union *and* by creating an area of freedom, security and justice'. Guild argues that, unlike national constitutions, the Charter follows international human rights instruments so that '[t]he individual who is protected is, as regards the large majority of rights, the human being rather than the citizen'.[131] The key question is; does this 'individual' include unauthorized foreigners?

More importantly, Article 6 states that: 'Everyone has the right to liberty and security of the person.' The is no specific exception for migration control equivalent to Article 5(1)(f). This would be implied within the more general derogating provision at Article 52 which requires interference with such rights to be necessary and proportionate.[132] This is important because it goes further than the ECHR jurisprudence that we considered in Chapter 3, where the Strasbourg Court held in *Chahal* that these limitations were not applicable to immigration detention.[133]

---

130 For a discussion of the different types of 'right' within the EU legal order see C. Hilson, 'What's in a Right? The Relationship between Community, Fundamental and Citizenship Rights in EU Law' (2004) 29 *E.L. Rev.* 636.

131 E. Guild, 'The Variable Subject of the EU Constitution, Civil Liberties and Human Rights' (2004) 6 *Eur. J. Migration and L.* 381–94, 394.

132 Article 52(1). 'Any limitation on the exercise of the rights and freedoms recognised by this Charter must be provided for by law and respect the essence of those rights and freedoms. Subject to the principle of proportionality, limitations may be made only if they are necessary and genuinely meet objectives of general interest recognised by the Union or the need to protect the rights and freedoms of others.'

133 The Charter also prohibits in Arts 20 and 21 discrimination by reference to a range of criteria. Having said this, the Charter also draws a distinction between EU citizens and others in relation to a right of freedom of residence and movement between and within the territory of the Member States. Article 45 gives this right to EU citizens and says that it 'may be granted, in accordance with the Treaties', to lawful resident non-EU citizens. The implication of this may be that non-EU citizens other than lawful residents are not entitled to freedom of residence and movement, although their right to liberty must be preserved. This might suggest a power to specify a place of residence for such groups.

In principle, detention provisions within the EU can be ruled invalid if incompatible with these above-described fundamental rights recognized by the Union.[134] The Court could require them to be interpreted and applied in a manner compatible with fundamental rights.[135] In a recent case, the Court approached the matter in this way, reading down the Directive on family reunion for lawfully resident migrants in a manner compatible with Article 8 ECHR.[136] The ECJ has never been afraid to overturn Member State actions that challenge fundamental rights recognized by Union law.[137] If the ECJ is becoming a guarantor of fundamental rights within the EU, it will have to decide how much 'liberty' is due to unauthorized non-EU citizens. As we have seen, international human rights law has found it difficult to decide on where the boundary lies between border control and individual liberty. Whether the Court follows a more cosmopolitan view will be an important factor in controlling detention.[138]

The constitutional status of unauthorized third-country nationals in the EU

What is the constitutional status of unauthorized non-EU citizens under the law of the Union? In broad terms, EU legislation has created important equality rights. In relation to detention, however, the legislature has

---

134 See T. Tridimas, *General Principles of EC Law*, Oxford University Press, 1999, Ch. 1.

135 See Tridimas, *ibid.* and cases such as C-392/93 *The Queen* v. *HM Treasury ex parte British Telecommunications plc* [1996] ECR I-1631, para. 28.

136 Directive 2003/86 on the right to family reunification [2003] OJ L 251/12. C-540/03 *European Parliament* v. *Council*, Judgment of 27 June 2006. The Court said that the Directive gave a limited discretion to Member States to derogate from the Directive's basic right of family reunion, but this did not itself mandate or authorize breaches of Art. 8 ECHR. The Court noted both the reasonableness of the Directive's derogations.

137 There are numerous cases. See D. Chalmers and A. Tomkins, *European Public Law*, Cambridge University Press, 2007, Ch. 6. Judicial review is, however, complicated by the ambiguity surrounding the purpose of EU policy in this area. The Treaty states that migration measures shall be taken '[i]n order to establish progressively an area of freedom, security and justice . . .', Title IV EC Treaty. The policies adopted thus far seek to combat illegal migration, but also to protect refugees. There are clearly potential conflicts between these goals. Is EU policy to secure the border (implying greater use of detention) or is it to admit refugees and offer humanitarian protection (less detention)? The ECJ will have to decide difficult questions about the role to which a judicial body should seek to interfere with such choices.

138 The ECJ in *Akrich* showed that it is capable of great ambivalence on this question. There it held that a deported third-country national could not claim the benefit of Regulation 1612/68 protection, as he had no legal foothold in the EU.

already begun to mark out unauthorized foreigners as distinct.[139] The extent to which judicial review may act as a more demanding constraint on detention where authorized by legislation must be assessed by reference to the Court's view of the status of non-EU migrants. How far should we view the Union's 'constitutional bargain' as including all foreigners regardless of immigration status?[140]

At a general level, a review of the personal status of third-country nationals suggests that most aspects of the internal market rights conferred by EC law apply to them in the same way as to nationals. As Guild and Peers put it: 'It is clear that the EC Treaty was designed and worded with the intention that its provisions would in principle apply to all persons within its scope and jurisdictions, including third country nationals.'[141] However, in the specific area of migration rights, the

---

139 Note also the legislature's equal treatment Directive expressly excludes nationality discrimination and third-country national immigration control from its reach, thus permitting inferior treatment on the basis of nationality. Article 3(2) Directive 2000/43 of 29 June 2000 implementing the principle of equal treatment between persons irrespective of racial or ethnic origin (OJ 2000, L180/22).

140 D. Curtin, *Postnational Democracy: The European Union in Search of a Political Philosophy*, The Hague: Kluwer, 1997; D. Kostakopoulou, 'European Citizenship and Immigration after Amsterdam: Silences, Openings and Paradoxes' (1998) 24 *J. Ethnic and Migration Studies* 639; R. Bellamy and D. Castiglione, 'The Communitarian Ghost in the Cosmopolitan Machine: Constitutionalism, Democracy and the Reconfiguration of Politics in the New Europe' in R. Bellamy and D. Castiglione (eds), *Constitutionalism, Democracy and Sovereignty: American and European Perspectives*, Aldershot: Avebury, 1996. See A. Clapham, 'A Human Rights Policy for the European Community' (1990) YEL 309–66, 311, 'rights have an important role to play in the process of European integration, but it must be said that they may well operate as a double-edged sword. Not only are they a cohesive force but they may well be divisive.'

141 E. Guild and S. Peers, 'Out of the Ghetto? The Personal Scope of EU Law', in Peers and Rogers (eds), *EU Immigration and Asylum Law*, 113. Their review of the provisions of free movement of goods and capital, along with consumer, social and environmental policies suggested a 'presumed inclusion' of third-country nationals. Only in relation to free movement of persons did the law and case-law point away from this. See C-230/97 *Awoyemi* [1998] ECR I-6781 where the court ruled that the transport policy on mutual recognition of driving licences did apply to resident third-country nationals, but that free movement of workers under Art. 39 did not. The general prohibition on discrimination on the basis of nationality is silent as to whether it includes third-country nationals, but the recent case-law suggests that it is limited to EU citizens. See C-95/99 to C-98/99 *Khalil and others* and C-180/99 *Adou* [2001] ECR I-7413 where the Court said the provision 'prohibits discrimination against Community nationals on grounds of nationality' (para. 40). C-360/00 *Ricordi* [2002] ECR I-5089, para. 31 also makes the same point.

case-law so far indicates that the Court has not laid down any general rule on the constitutional status of non-EU citizens.[142]

The Court's early rulings held that persons who did not have substantive migration rights derived from EU law fell outside the scope of the Court's jurisdiction in respect of fundamental rights.[143] This was on the basis that their immigration status fell within the exclusive competence of Member States. The Court has, however, recently taken some more steps towards protecting the fundamental human rights of non-EU citizens within its jurisdiction. In *Akrich*, the Court held that the deportation of the non-EU spouse of a migrant EU citizen must respect their right to family life.[144] The decision in *Carpenter* held that where the deportation of a non-EU spouse would interfere with her EU spouse's ability to provide cross-border services, it had jurisdiction to rule on its compatibility with fundamental rights.[145] These cases both concerned spouses of migrant EU citizens, so they may be seen as relying upon the ancillary nature of the non-EU citizens rights. A more powerful example is the decision by the Court holding that family reunification legislation, which gives rights for resident non-EU citizens to be joined by their families, must be applied in a manner compliant with fundamental rights.[146]

None of these cases, however, concerned unauthorized entry by a person who had no lawfully resident family member in the EU. It remains to be seen the extent to which the Court will find that unauthorized migrants without more have a fundamental right to liberty of the person. Certainly the *Kadzoev* decision can be read as a purely legislative interpretation, although the result did in the end protect the detainee's liberty. The Court did not announce any fundamental right to liberty for unauthorized non-EU citizens arising from EU law. As we have seen already, courts have found it difficult to reconcile border controls with a right of release for persons who have not been authorized to cross the border.

---

142 See P. Oliver, 'Non-community Nationals and the Treaty of Rome' (1985) *YEL* 57 for a discussion of the early case-law. There was a reluctance to interfere with Member State immigration control whilst the Union still had no general power over migration of non-EU citizens.

143 See *Demirel* [1987] ECR 3719; *Diatta* [1985] ECR 567.

144 Case C-109/01 *Akrich* [2003] ECR I-9607.

145 Case C-60/00 *Carpenter* [2002] ECR I-6279.

146 Directive 2003/86 on the right to family reunification [2003] OJ L 251/12. C-540/03 *European Parliament* v. *Council*, Judgment of 27 June 2006. The Court did not need to annul the Directive because it directed Member States to apply it in a manner that complied with Art. 8 ECHR.

Common EU border security politics

More broadly, we can ask how far Member States continue to hold discretion over detention policy, given the common EU interest in securing the external frontier and preventing illegal movements internally.[147] With the goal of the creation of an area of freedom, security and justice, it appears that access to that common EU space is now controlled by EU institutions according to EU principles of law. Indeed, as we saw in *Kadzoev*, Member States have lost the ability to extend detention on grounds of public security. The days of purely 'national' security immigration detention appear limited in the interconnected space of the EU. This suggests that all non-EU citizens present in the Union now fall within the scope of EU immigration detention law. It is arguable, therefore, that if this coercive force is to apply to them so, too, should fundamental rights protection. As Weiler put it: 'Once an individual, for whatever reason and on whatever basis, comes within the field of application of Community law, his or her fundamental human rights must be guaranteed.'[148]

This point is made more pressing by the increasing tendency of the EU to cooperate with transit countries to combat irregular migration. As a result, detention is occurring in more remote places which provide fewer safeguards and less public scrutiny. This has emerged as part of the response to migration flows into Europe from Africa across the Mediterranean. Migrants have been landed by smugglers or taken by naval patrols to territories such as the Canary Islands which, although part of Spain, offer less legal and practical help.[149] An emerging issue for the future will be detention which is carried out, not within the Union at all, but in states on the borders with the Union. This is because the Union is increasingly seeking to promote border controls in North African and Central Asian countries to prevent entry into Southern Europe. This has been and remains a key pillar of the Union's strategy on reducing irregular

---

147 See the Presidency Conclusions of the Tampere European Council, 15 and 16 October 1999, para. 3: 'This in turn requires the Union to develop common policies on asylum and immigration, while taking into account the need for a consistent control of external borders to stop illegal immigration and to combat those who organise and commit related international crimes.'

148 J.H.H. Weiler, 'Thou Shalt Not Oppress a Stranger: On the Judicial Protection of the Human Rights of Non-EC Nationals – A Critique' (1992) 3 *EJIL* 65–91, 90.

149 Although these are real practical problems, in principle, ECHR and EU fundamental rights protection should apply to such locations. Malta has also experienced relatively large numbers of irregular migrants and has adopted rather strict detention measures as part of its response.

immigration through blocking significant migration routes into Europe. The Union has thus entered partnership agreements with developing countries. In order to secure concessions in economic affairs, these states have agreed to better border controls.[150]

The creation of the EU border agency has accelerated this process.[151] In 2003, the United Kingdom proposed the establishment of regional and transit processing centres outside the EU for asylum seekers.[152] This plan was not adopted, but instead it seems that neighbouring states are to be provided with increased logistical and financial support but will be in charge of detention facilities.[153] This offshore detention of irregular migrants, if funded and encouraged by policies of the Union, raises some challenging legal and political questions relating to jurisdiction and state responsibility in international law.[154] There are certainly few legal remedies and guarantees as to the conditions for detainees.[155] The EU may here be moving towards the kind of 'extra-legal' detention that we have seen in relation to offshore processing at Guantanamo or the islands around Australia. This will require a greater willingness by the legal system of the

150 Samers argues that there has been a 're-scaling of control to third countries, a spatial expansion of control far from the EU's existing borders'. He argues for a 'virtualism' – such that it is 'far easier to construct a security agenda abroad far from the watchful eye of Brussels-based NGOs and human rights campaigners, than it is to legitimate it in the EU and its Member States'. M. Samers, 'An Emerging Geopolitics of "Illegal" Immigration in the European Union' (2004) 6 *Eur. J. Migration and L.* 27, 43.

151 Council Regulation 2007/2004 establishing a European Agency for the Management of Operational Cooperation at the External Borders of the Member States of the European Union.

152 A. Geddes, 'Europe's Border Relationships and International Migration Relations' (2005) 43(4) *JCMS* 787–806, who sets out the wider notion of EU borders going beyond the territorial towards relations with neighbouring states. G. Noll, 'Visions of the Exceptional: Legal and Theoretical Issues Raised by Transit Processing Centres and Protection Zones' (2003) 5 *Eur. J. Migration and L.* 303–41, 338.

153 For example, a report by the Union's border agency on its visit to help Libya secure its southern border noted that there were 60,000 immigration detainees held there. See Frontex-led EU Illegal Immigration Technical Mission to Libya, 28 May–5 June 2007, 10. The report relates that the Libyan authorities apprehended some 32,000 immigrants and repatriated some 53,000. It is clear that repatriation is not straightforward and that extended detention is the result.

154 For a detailed analysis of the issues, particularly over non-*refoulement*, see R. Weinzierl, *The Demands of Human and EU Fundamental Rights for the Protection of the European Union's External Borders*, German Institute for Human Rights, 2007.

155 The UNHCR Special Rapporteur on the Human Rights of Migrants notes the 'externalization of migration control policies and criminalization of labour migration....' whereby 'neighbouring and transit states receive funds to build detention centres, interception and expulsion ... these have been treated as criminal without proper safeguards', 2008 Annual Report, 25 Feb. 2008, Bustamante A/HRC/7/12.

EU to bring such unauthorized persons within the constitutional embrace of fundamental rights protection.

Conclusions

As we have seen, the immigration detention of migrant EU citizens has become very rare. It is now subject to exacting legal standards. Generally only those convicted of serious crimes who present a genuine threat to public security may be detained for a period to effect their deportation after their criminal sentence. 'Pure' administrative detention is virtually impossible. This is further evidence that migration by EU citizens has been essentially depoliticized and that law has replaced the political. Migration is no longer a 'security' issue for prerogative political action.[156] Deportation is a narrow tool focused upon individuals who have been shown to be dangerous through an exacting forensic process.

In relation to non-EU citizens, however, the Union has assumed the attributes and practices of a sovereign state seeking to assert control over its borders through, *inter alia*, detention. Whilst detention had to be legislated for as part of the comprehensive EU package on asylum and immigration, Member States were reluctant to concede explicit limits over a sensitive area of border control. For asylum seekers, the Parliament was reluctant to accept that this group must be treated as a 'security' rather than 'humanitarian' issue. The ambiguous Directives on detention of asylum seekers reflect this lack of consensus. However, the Returns Directive reflects more obviously the broad 'security' agenda around irregular migration. It thus provides Member States with clear and broad authority to detain for long periods without reliable safeguards. In fact, for those refused entry or intercepted at sea, even fewer constraints apply. Whilst placing a time limit on detention modestly increased legal certainty, the balance struck strongly favoured Member State discretion over any idea of fundamental liberty rights.

The decision in *Kadzoev* merely states that the time limits in the Returns Directive cannot be exceeded. It does not go further in exploring the *constitutional* constraints, if any, on EU migration powers. There is thus as yet no constitutional ruling holding that unauthorized migrants have

---

156 This legal perspective was, however, first seriously called into question by French government action against EU citizens of Roma origin from Romania taken in summer 2010, which apparently violated EU law through forcible mass arrests and deportation.

a basic right to liberty. This will be an important test of what kind of 'contract' the EU treaties are; will their reach go beyond EU citizens and the favoured group of lawful long-term resident third country nationals? Whilst removing border controls promoted the migration rights of EU citizens, it appears arbitrary to exclude non-EU citizens from fundamental rights protection, given the extensive EU regulation of their movement now. As Weiler notes, 'one of the moral assets of European integration – its downplaying of nationality as a principal referent in trans-national intercourse' is threatened by such distinctions.[157] Such a distinction is most obviously, but not exclusively, suspect in the case of long-term resident non-EU citizens.[158] It is hard to see why immigration detention, other than for serious public security grounds, would be an appropriate measure for this group.

The more difficult case is that of migrants seeking entry to the Union for the first time, or those being expelled following a short or irregular stay. Asylum seekers also fall into this group. The legislature has recently authorized detention for these people for potentially lengthy periods. The extent to which non-EU citizens are deemed to acquire fundamental rights where EU law regulates their migration is a critical one. We have seen how in nations like the United States and Australia, exclusion from fundamental rights protection has led to arbitrary and unlimited detention. The imposition, as a matter of EU law, of significant limits on the detention of non-EU nationals would be indicative of an outward-looking internationalist body, not one simply seeking replicating traditional ideas about territorial sovereignty and security in relation to the Union's borders. The EU conceives of itself as policing a common border and therefore the EU Constitution should regulate this policing effort. Thus, although

---

157 Weiler, 'Thou Shalt Not Oppress a Stranger', 68. He notes that 'in the very concept of citizenship a distinction is created between the insider and outsider that tugs at their common humanity' but also accepts that a deepening of European integration for EU citizens means that 'there is a delicate path to tread' between a sense of European identity and increased xenophobia to outsiders.

158 Groenendijk puts it well: 'The gradual extension of the rights attached to the status of Union citizen and the principle of equal treatment of Union citizens with nationals of the Member State in which they reside, has the unintended but nefarious effect of stressing the differences between EU nationals and third country nationals. Since most of the latter category are non-European and non-white, the distinction . . . tends to legitimate racial discrimination.' K. Groenendijk, 'The Growing Relevance of Article 39 (ex 48) EC Treaty for Third Country Immigrants', in *Thirty Years of Free Movement of Workers in Europe*, Luxembourg: European Communities, 2000, 222–3.

administrative detention must be used in some cases involving first entry to or expulsion from the Union, non-EU citizens should still benefit from the fundamental right to liberty that applies to EU citizens and lawful residents. This is explored further in Chapter 7 but, in outline, it should include judicial authorization and ongoing scrutiny to ensure that detention is humane, absolutely necessary and not unduly lengthy.

5

Security and immigration detention: the problem of internment in peacetime

The aliens power: the permanent emergency power?

As we have seen, the most commonly stated rationale for immigration detention has been an instrumental one; to ensure expulsion is successful. Not infrequently, however, 'immigration' powers have been used to detain foreigners to achieve non-immigration objectives.[1] Moral panics in relation to crime have coalesced around aliens and supported the use of preventive detention without trial pending deportation. The fear of anarchists in Edwardian England through to the American Red Scares in the 1920s and the Cold War all show the same pattern of incarceration aimed at the suppression of political activity by foreigners deemed subversive by the state.[2] Whilst this has been ostensibly linked to deportation, citizens have been left free to engage in such action without internment. In more recent years, the risk posed by international terrorism has led governments to use 'immigration' powers to preventively detain unwanted foreigners. Detention of foreigners has proved a flexible political tool to meet many situations beyond merely expulsion goals. Governments have been able to employ what would normally be considered 'emergency' powers to preventively detain without generalizing the powers to all.[3]

In this chapter we examine the contention that lack of immigration status serves as a justification for dispensing with orthodox notions of the rule of law and due process. There is, of course, no doubt that permanent

---

1 It is important to note at the outset that in many instances security-related detention can be perfectly consistent with achieving purely immigration control objectives. Persons who are correctly found to be likely to commit offences are perhaps also likely to abscond and thus evade immigration control. The greater threat is likely to include the lesser in most cases.
2 See D. Kanstroom, *Deportation Nation*, Cambridge, MA: Harvard University Press, 2007 and R. Winder, *Bloody Foreigners: the Story of Immigration to Britain*, London: Abacus, 2004, Ch. 16.
3 Cole speaks of the need to 'break the seemingly endless cycle of overreaction and apology'. D. Cole, *Enemy Aliens*, New York: New Press, 2003, 233.

incarceration will limit the risk of aliens committing harmful or unacceptable acts. Save for in exceptional circumstances, preventive detention of *citizens* is either unconstitutional or politically unacceptable.[4] In the case of migrants, by contrast, far from being exceptional, preventive detention has become quite normal. This is very clear in the growth of mandatory detention for those convicted of even relatively minor criminal offences, but goes further to include persons merely suspected of posing a threat. Most importantly, in cases involving allegedly dangerous aliens, detention periods have been especially prolonged by executive agencies and legislators. In such cases, detention can drag on for years whilst diplomatic negotiations take place between countries, with only speculative chances of successful expulsion.

It will be argued that it has become increasingly hard to view such detention as a legally circumscribed measure to secure expulsion. Such prolonged preventive detentions have come to assume their own unique character which is determined not by law, but by a *political assessment* about the respective costs and benefits of releasing such detainees, whether at home or abroad. There is no doubt that such cases present huge challenges for liberal governments caught, as they are, between their obligation not to kill detainees or send them to where they may be killed or tortured and their political vulnerability if such persons were to harm the public upon being released. We may say this scenario tests the limits of liberal politics; states may be too liberal to dispatch such persons to their deaths, but are not liberal enough to allow them full criminal due process protection and free them if they are not convicted.

Authorization of aliens and fundamental rights

As we shall see, the legal and moral justification for this is said to be that aliens' right to liberty is more restricted than citizens' where they have (or may turn out to have) no authorization to be present. This answer suggests again that a lack of a *membership* right on the part of an alien excludes them from fundamental rights protection. We have already noted, however, that adjudicating on membership claims is not the only role for courts in immigration law. Whilst establishing membership is of great importance, the protection of the rule of law and the control of state violence is also a fundamental issue for liberal legal systems. To

---

4 Even in the case of patients with mental illness or disorder who are dangerous, the modern approach has been to limit the use of closed asylums, practising detention in only very rare circumstances with attendant due process safeguards.

conclude that non-members have no rights is to put the regulation of their detention beyond the rule of law into the realm of political arbitrariness. They thereby become outlaws, largely at the mercy of their captors whether through individual decision, executive order or legislative power.[5]

These arguments go right back to the criticism made by James Madison in 1798 of executive deportation without criminal trial safeguards.[6] Whilst it is now accepted that deportation is not 'punishment', here by contrast we are talking about public safety detention, which is hard to distinguish from incarceration pursuant to criminal conviction and punishment. As we saw in Chapter 2, the US Supreme Court decision in *Zadvydas* explored these issues in the context of non-terrorist criminal aliens and concluded that there was no adequate justification for treating deportable aliens differently once the immigration removal process had failed. Detention beyond this point, even to protect the public, was a denial of a general right to liberty held by all persons. They must either be charged or released. Recent anti-terrorism measures that have employed 'immigration' powers have forced deeper consideration of these issues to which we now turn.

Exploring the legal status of foreign detainees in national security cases: modern outlaws?

As we have seen, the aliens power has never left behind its war power ancestry and has proved a flexible weapon in the hands of governments facing security challenges. Thus the *immigration* law envelope has been stretched as far as possible to authorize preventive detention. Unauthorized or deportee status is said to 'diminish' or even extinguish the right to liberty. Thus extended security detention has been achieved without requiring the passage of emergency powers that would be applicable to all, citizen and alien alike. As we shall see, there are close parallels between this and the placing of aliens in 'extra-legal' locations like Guantanamo Bay, or in offshore processing centres. In both instances aliens have been placed in legal categories that are said to put them (and only them) beyond fundamental rights protection contained in either domestic constitutions or international treaties. By relying on 'immigration' powers these other, more demanding, legal principles can be avoided.

---

5 Labelling a particular detention as 'immigration'-related affords the government the opportunity to evade safeguards available to criminal suspects. Any immigrant could be arrested and held pending expulsion, in lieu of charging them. Thus the executive would have a choice about how to proceed. To argue that this is permissible because deportable foreigners are different is simply circular reasoning. The nature of this difference must be specified without reference to immigration status.

6 See Ch. 1 above.

As we noted, *criminal law* applies generally without regard to nationality. It begins with arrest that is based upon reasonable suspicion of commission of an offence. There must be a clearly defined charge formulated swiftly (within a set period) and eventually, within a reasonable period, a trial. Pending trial a person must be entitled to be brought before a court to see if bail is appropriate. Detention ends with acquittal or is prolonged by conviction and sentencing by a court. This model represents the liberal bench-mark and is expressed in both national constitutions and international conventions.[7] Habeas corpus was developed as a tool for ensuring that these conditions were met. These procedural safeguards have long been held to apply equally to aliens charged with crimes.[8]

Defence powers may be applied to enemy aliens during wartime, but are regulated by international humanitarian law. Enemy aliens captured on the battlefield should be held under the conditions laid down for prisoners of war until repatriation at the war's end.[9] By contrast, non-combatant enemy alien civilians present in the territory of a state at war with their own were previously in a perilous legal position.[10] As we saw in Chapter 1, mass internment without any individual assessment of risk was not unknown.[11] This has been criticized in retrospect as excessive, arbitrary and politically motivated.[12] Since the Fourth Geneva Convention 1949, the position for this group has, as one commentator notes, 'changed

---

7 See the due process clause of the US Constitution and Arts 5 and 6 of the ECHR for just two examples.

8 *Wong Wing* v. *United States* 163 U.S. 228 (1896).

9 Prisoners of war who escape must not be punished in respect thereof (Arts 91–3 Third Geneva Convention). The only exception is where violence against life or limb is used during an escape. All prisoners must be released and repatriated 'without delay after the cessation of active hostilities' (Art. 118). There is an exception in cases where a prisoner has committed an indictable offence (Art. 119). Conditions of captivity are marked out in Arts 21–34 giving rights to hygiene, clothing, food, religious observance. See D. Fleck (ed.), *The Handbook of International Humanitarian Law*, Oxford University Press, 2008, 368–417.

10 The position of persons not caught in the uniform of a warring state is the subject of considerable debate. The US government coined the phrase 'unlawful combatant' for this group and decided that they fell outside the protection of the Geneva Conventions altogether.

11 P. Gillman and L. Gillman, '*Collar the Lot*': *How Britain Interned its Wartime Refugees*, London, New York: Quartet Books, 1982, and J.C. Bird, *The Control of Enemy Alien Citizens in Great Britain 1914–18*, New York and London: Garland Publishers, 1986. A. Krammer, *Undue Process: the Untold Story of America's German Alien Internees*, London: Rowman and Littlefield, 1997.

12 See, for example, Lord Brown of Eaton-under-Heywood in *R (on the application of Al-Jedda)* v. *Secretary of State for Defence* [2007] UKHL, 'the internment condemned in wartime Britain was mostly of enemy aliens, many of them refugees from Nazi Germany, posing at most the scantiest of risks to the community' (para. 138).

greatly from enslavement to the securing of human rights through modern humanitarian law'.[13] Thus detention is now only lawful in such cases where 'absolutely necessary' or where it is otherwise not possible to control enemy aliens sufficiently. Detention must still be subject to review by a quasi-judicial body[14] and should in any event cease when the war ends. Thus we can see that the laws of war provide precise legal standards for the protection of non-combatant enemy aliens.

Emergency powers laws have been used in wartime or during civil unrest to modify the standard due process model, permitting detention without bail, charge or trial.[15] Such internment of citizens is rare in stable democracies.[16] Even then, there has been strong criticism of the impact on civil liberties. For example during World War Two, we can cite the displacement and internment of American citizens of Japanese and German origin and the incarceration by the United Kingdom of citizens suspected of Nazi sympathies.[17,18]

13 Fleck (ed), *The Handbook of International Humanitarian Law*, 280.

14 Fourth Geneva Convention 1949, Arts 41 and 42.

15 For modern human rights law and the approach to internment of citizens see *Lawless v. Ireland* (1979–80) 1 EHRR 1 and C. Overy and R.C.A. White, *The European Convention on Human Rights*, 4th edn, Oxford University Press, 2006, Ch. 21.

16 In the UK there was extended pre-charge detention under successive Prevention of Terrorism Acts designed to tackle terrorism in, and related to, Northern Ireland. Internment was also tried for a period but abandoned. See R.J. Spjut, 'Internment and Detention without Trial in Northern Ireland 1971–75: Ministerial Policy and Practice' (1986) 49 *MLR* 712.

17 *Korematsu* v. *U.S.* 323 U.S. 214; it is important to note that the majority decision directed itself only to the constitutionality of the criminal conviction of Korematsu for failure to leave his home. The minority opinions, by contrast, argued that the war powers scheme that required him to leave to go and be detained in an internment camp for Japanese-Americans were indivisible. The minority do not, however, explore the alien/citizen distinction other than Murphy J.'s comment: 'It seems incredible that . . . it would have been impossible to hold loyalty hearings for the mere 112,000 persons involved – or at least for the 70,000 American citizens' (242) and Jackson J. noting that German or Italian enemy aliens would not have been guilty of any offence by being in the area concerned (243). In *Ex Parte Endo* 323 U.S. 283, the majority decided that the war powers as drafted gave no power to detain a Japanese-American who was accepted as loyal pending returning them safely to the community after a period of internment on suspicion of espionage. *Liversidge* v. *Anderson*, aliens were to be detained under the Royal Prerogative if an enemy alien and under Reg. 18B Defence (General) Regulations. The initial reluctance to detain aliens gave way in May 1940. In the end some 28,000 aliens and 2,000 British citizens (most of whom were of alien origin) were detained. A.W.B. Simpson, *In the Highest Degree Odious*, Oxford: Clarendon Press, 1992, 163. Also see Krammer, *Undue Process*.

18 Simpson criticizes internment of British citizens during World War Two in the following terms: 'Law is just in the business of drawing firm lines of demarcation – between mine and thine, guilt and innocence, between citizens and non-citizens. Respect for the rule of law entails respect for these boundaries . . . ' Simpson, *In the Highest Degree Odious*, 14.

Given that criminal laws apply equally to foreigners, in principle, emergency laws derogating from criminal due process should also apply to them to the *same extent as citizens*, but no more. As we saw, however, during World War One in Britain, the new-found *aliens power* was asserted as a basis for internment of friendly aliens. This was a crucial step, because it revealed a political and legal shift away from internment of *enemy* aliens towards a more general power over all aliens. The fact of a war or emergency was enough to direct measures at friendly aliens. This shift was profound. Whilst, at least initially, politically conditional upon a 'state of emergency' being declared, the extraordinary powers continued after the war. The alien had politically and legally mutated into something of a permanent 'enemy' regardless of the state of war or the existence of an officially declared emergency. The Cold War immigration cases in the United States mirrored this pattern, with a shift towards peacetime quasi-internment. It became accepted that the aliens power was wide enough to be used even in the absence of *de jure* states of emergency.

As we have seen, in a historical era now remote from the world wars, extended alien detention has been normalized. In peacetime, the doctrinal, as opposed to the political, basis for these practices has coalesced around the idea that detention is ancillary to the sovereign power to control borders and therefore not truly internment. The challenge, which sits at the apex of law and politics, has always been to decide what transforms 'deportation' or 'exclusion' measures into arbitrary internment. This requires the legal system to make a profound choice about how far government security choices can exclude foreigners from fundamental rights protection. If foreigners have been declared political 'enemies', are they beyond the law's embrace?

The modern era of counter-terrorism

The threat of international terrorism had been apparent for many years before the attacks on the World Trade Center and the Pentagon in the United States. The criminal justice system had not been the only tool used against persons thought to be involved in such activities. Immigration powers to deport foreigners were also becoming important.[19] This was nothing new and the courts continued to give the executive wide discretion

19 The United States in response to the Oklahoma bombings (by US citizens) had passed mandatory indefinite detention powers for deportable aliens suspected of terrorism. See Anti-terrorism and Effective Death Penalty Act 1996. During the First Gulf War in 1991 the UK used deportation and associated detention in relation to 176 Iraqis. See *R v. Secretary of State for the Home Department, ex parte Cheblak* [1991] 2 All ER 319,

in such cases, as they had during wartime and in the Cold War. Detention, although sometimes lengthy, appeared to have some link to ongoing immigration action. The new situation arising after 11 September 2001 saw such detention of foreigners become more widespread. Unsurprisingly, it became difficult to expel persons who had been labelled terrorists to other countries, even their own. Alienage became an important legal and political tool to support extraordinary measures against such persons.

The employment by the United States of quasi-military, rather than immigration powers to effect incarceration at Guantanamo Bay raised similar broad issues of principle regarding the status of aliens in relation to constitutional and international law. There were clear parallels with the immigration context. First, because of the US courts' traditional view that aliens had no constitutional rights until they had physically and legally entered the United States.[20] Second, because of the selection of an offshore facility previously used to detain immigrants. The use of long-term detention without trial on the basis of suspicion and undisclosed evidence forced the courts in the United Kingdom and United States to really reconsider the status of aliens in a profound manner. These cases are thus landmarks in our evolving understanding of the equal rights of aliens and the extent to which immigration status or alienage denudes individuals of fundamental rights.

The United Kingdom: the problem of undeportable foreigners

The UK government had apparently already identified a number of lawfully resident foreigners who might be linked to Muslim terrorist organizations before 11 September 2001.[21] The obvious option of prosecution in the ordinary courts had been ruled out, partly because the authorities did not wish to disclose secret intelligence sources during any trial. It was accepted that their right to a fair trial would have been compromised by a failure to disclose this evidence. Nevertheless, the government would

---

where there was no detailed consideration of the detention issue as a distinct feature. For a detailed review of this period see D. Bonner and R. Cholewinski, 'The Response of the United Kingdom's Legal and Constitutional Orders to the 1991 Gulf War and the Post-9/11 "War" on Terrorism', in A. Baldaccini and E. Guild (eds), *Terrorism and the Foreigner*, Amsterdam: Martinus Nijhoff, 2005. The use of deportation in terrorism cases was first considered in detail in *Rehman* v. *Secretary of State for the Home Department* [2001] UKHL 47.

20 See the US Supreme Court decision in *Mezei*, and the entry fiction case-law discussed in Ch. 2, above.

21 *A and Ors* v. *Secretary of State for the Home Department* [2003] UKSIAC 1/2002 (29 Oct. 2003).

normally have sought to use the wide deportation discretion to expel them. However, it was thought that this would be likely to result in their being tortured in the only countries to which they could be sent.[22] This was prohibited under Article 3 of the ECHR.[23] The final piece in the jigsaw related to detention pending deportation. Could the deportees be held in detention whilst efforts were made to deport them? This might involve inducing a safe country to accept them, or obtaining guarantees from their own country not to torture them.

The legal advice given to the government was that domestic law, as interpreted by the courts, only permitted detention for the period reasonably necessary to effect deportation.[24] Once deportation was no longer reasonably foreseeable, detention must cease. Advice also indicated that the effect of the Strasbourg Court's decision in *Chahal* was that detention could not proceed where a person faced torture upon return. This was on the basis that deportation proceedings could no longer be said to be ongoing in such circumstances. For this reason, no action was taken against them, but no doubt they were placed under surveillance. To complete the factual picture, it was accepted that there was also a substantial threat from British citizens active in the same or similar terrorist groups.

It is important to state at this point that this legal advice may have been wrong. There was no clear Strasbourg authority on the point, because the *Chahal* decision found that his detention was not in breach of Article 5(1)(f) to the date of judgment. It said nothing about future detention post-judgment, as indeed it could not.[25] The government appeared to

---

22 Unusually in asylum cases, the government accepted the existence of the risk of torture faced by the men concerned without challenge. This was never considered on appeal and was indeed a prerequisite for the long-term detention of such persons under the legislation.

23 See *Chahal* v. *United Kingdom* [1997] 23 EHRLR 413.

24 *Hardial Singh* v. *Secretary of State for the Home Department* [1984] WLR 704.

25 Indeed, the Court itself bizarrely accepted that ongoing detention caused by the agreement of the UK government not to deport Chahal after the end of the domestic proceedings (1994–6) meant that this period of detention was completely outside the scope of its Art. 5(1)(f) review: 'Although he has remained in custody until the present day, this latter period must be distinguished because during this time the Government have refrained from deporting him in compliance with the request made by the Commission under Rule 36 of its Rules of Procedure' (114). This suggests that where a state has completed deportation proceedings diligently but failed to expel the alien due to a legal or practical obstacle, then ongoing detention is automatically a lawful choice as the lesser of two evils – imprisonment over possible torture. It is suggested that this must be wrong: the state must have an on-going duty to consider whether prolonged detention pending hearing at Strasbourg is appropriate.

assume that they had to release him. This may be because they had run out of fresh ideas on where or how to deport him. However, as Finnis points out, the lawfulness of continuing detention under Article 5(1)(f) might be viewed as depending on 'what duration is reasonable in all the circumstances'.[26] It was certainly not beyond argument to say that, where a state is trying conscientiously to send a seriously dangerous alien to a third country or secure promises from his or her own state not to ill-treat them, this satisfies the due diligence requirement. In other words, in the special case of those suspected of terrorist offences who present a threat to life and limb at home, perhaps Article 5(1)(f) might have permitted lengthy detention whilst serious diplomatic and other negotiations took place.[27]

The solution: the indefinite detention of foreigners as an immigration measure under the Anti-terrorism, Crime and Security Act 2001

There is no doubt that this situation presented real political and security difficulties. The legal position was also unclear, but the balance of opinion was that nothing more could be done under the law as it was. However, matters no doubt became more acute for the government because of the risk that persons known to be dangerous might commit atrocities without having been deported. The aftermath of 11 September led the government to propose a wide range of measures to increase police powers to prevent terrorism.[28] These included extended detention powers in

---

26 J. Finnis, 'Nationality, Alienage and Constitutional Principle' (2007) 123 *LQR*, 418–55, 435. He argues that it is 'reasonable to allow the executive, properly supervised, more time to secure removal, perhaps a long or even "indefinitely" extended time' in the case of persons reasonably suspected to be terrorists, where the 'authorities are definitely taking action . . . to secure his removal to another state where he will not be at real risk of ill-treatment'. This view is controversial, but not beyond argument, because Strasbourg has never been faced with such a situation before.

27 The UK did in fact eventually begin such negotiations to secure commitments from governments not to ill-treat deportees, but only well after they had detained the foreigners. See *Abu Qatada* v. *Home Secretary* [2007] UKSIAC 15/2005 (26 Feb. 2007) [171–7] and Annex 1A (Memorandum of Understanding between the United Kingdom and Jordan). In this case SIAC was convinced that there was no real risk of torture for the applicant in Jordan. By contrast, in *DD* v. *Home Secretary* [2007] UKSIAC 42/2005 there was a real risk of torture in Libya despite assurances from the government.

28 For a detailed overview of the legal position facing the government see Bonner and Cholewinski, 'The Response of the United Kingdom's Legal and Constitutional Orders to the 1991 Gulf War and the Post-9/11 "War" on Terrorism' in Baldaccini and Guild (eds), *Terrorism and the Foreigner*.

respect of certain foreigners. Examination of the drafting of the Bill is instructive. The detention powers were explained by the government in terms which sought to keep them firmly within the rubric of immigration control:

> This Part contains measures concerned with the capacity of the UK's immigration and asylum procedures to deal with people whose presence in the UK is not conducive to the public good.[29]

The newly created powers would 'allow the detention of those the Secretary of State has certified as threats to national security and who are suspected of being international terrorists where *their removal is not possible at the present time*'.[30] This required an amendment to domestic law to permit ongoing detention beyond the 'reasonable' period for removal. More problematically, however, the government still had to overcome the objection that such measures would breach Article 5 of the ECHR. Although, as noted above, it is not certain this was required, as a precaution, they decided to derogate from Article 5 on the basis that there was a state of emergency under Article 15. They thus filed a notice to that effect with the Council of Europe and placed a derogation order[31] before Parliament.

The Bill was scrutinized by the Joint Committee on Human Rights, the parliamentary body charged with scrutinizing legislation, which made a key observation that pinpointed one of the key contradictions inherent in seeking to protect national security by using immigration powers:

> we note that ... the Bill does not in itself make clear that the purpose of detaining the suspect is solely to find a safe country to which to remove him or her. A suspect might be very willing to go to a country which supports, or at any rate, does not oppose terrorism. The question would then arise as to whether the government would be prepared to remove a suspected international terrorist to a place where he or she would be free to resume terrorist activity. If it was not prepared to do so, the proposed arrangements look more like *a form of indefinite internment* than detention pending removal. This would make it more likely that the detention would be held to violate Article 5(1)(f).[32]

---

29 Paragraph 70.
30 Paragraph 11, *Explanatory Notes* to Anti-terrorism, Crime and Security Act 2001 (ACSA).
31 Human Rights Act 1998 (Designated Derogation) Order 2001 (SI 2001/3644). We shall not discuss the actual merits of the government position that there was a state of emergency, because it is not crucial to the analysis that follows. The acceptability of acting upon that derogation order by using extended detention powers over immigrants is the key question.
32 Paragraph 23 (emphasis in original), Joint Committee on Human Rights, Second Report on Anti-terrorism, Crime and Security Bill, 16 Nov. 2001

In order to maintain the 'immigration' nature of the measure, the government had to assure Parliament that the detainees would be released to *any* country that would accept them. This however merely confirmed the apparent contradiction in allowing very dangerous people to be loose in countries (perhaps supportive of them) where they could continue their activities against the United Kingdom and its allies. This was arguably a security measure that did not achieve security and/or an immigration measure that did not control migration.

At this stage the Joint Committee somewhat tentatively felt that the detention powers might breach the European Convention:

> by relying on immigration legislation to provide for the detention of suspected international terrorist, the Bill risks discriminating, in the authorization of detention without charge, between those suspected international terrorists who are subject to immigration control and those who have an unconditional right to remain in the United Kingdom. We are concerned that this might lead to discrimination in the enjoyment of the right to liberty on the ground of nationality. *If that could not be shown* to have an objective, rational and proportionate justification, *it might lead to actions* which would be incompatible with Article 5 of the ECHR either taken alone or in combination with . . . Article 14.[33]

Their rather hesitant tone, speaking in terms of 'risks', may have arisen from the fact that there was no clear Strasbourg case-law on the issue, because no state had ever derogated from Article 5 only in respect of non-nationals. Importantly the Committee seemed to share the, with hindsight, unlikely assumption that *some* safe country could be found to take in persons who had been accused by the UK government of being international terrorists.

Parliament also insisted upon a measure of procedural due process within the Act; there had to be reasonable grounds for suspecting the detainee was a terrorist. The detention power was made subject to a sunset clause, requiring Parliament to review it again. These steps and the historically broad uses of aliens powers persuaded the minister (and his legal advisers) that is was possible to certify that the Bill complied with the ECHR.[34] The certification, however, could not have been a very confident one, given the views expressed by the Joint Committee.[35]

---

33 *Ibid.*, paragraph 38 (emphasis added).   34 As required by the Human Rights Act 1998.
35 See J.L. Hiebert, 'Parliamentary Review of Terrorism Measures' (2005) 68(4) *MLR* 676 for consideration of the role of the Joint Committee on Human Rights in the process up to and after the House of Lords judgment.

There were clearly difficult issues and the judgement made by the government was not seriously questioned at the time. As one leading academic human rights commentator approvingly put it: '[t]his UK action seems a justifiable exercise in the lesser evil. The government did not act in secret. It engaged in public justification. Faced with two ways of jeopardizing the human rights of *suspects*, it chose the lesser form. Such a policy seeks to preserve the idea of pre-commitment, by focusing on preserving terrorist suspects from torture and by insisting on accountability and public review.'[36] As we shall see, the 'suspects' detained were all, and could only be, foreigners. In the context of what were avowedly emergency powers, this turned out to be crucial.

Indefinite 'immigration' detention: the enduring doubts and the litigation

Although the difficulties expressed by the Joint Committee were not enough to prevent the detention provisions being passed, doubts continued to be expressed about the Act's compatibility with human rights.[37] With the benefit of hindsight, it is clear that had Parliament been aware that the detentions would continue for years without an end in sight, they might have viewed the matter differently. However at the beginning, in the highly charged climate of the time, this was not so obvious. The Act as finally passed in Part IV (headed 'Immigration and Asylum') authorized the minister to issue a certificate in respect of a person where he:

> reasonably – (a) believes that the person's presence in the United Kingdom is a risk to national security, and (b) he suspects that the person is a terrorist.[38]

'Terrorist' was defined widely to mean a person who was or had been concerned in acts of international terrorism, a member of such a group or a person who had links to such a group.[39]

The Act authorized 'deportation' or other removal action against such a person 'despite the fact that (whether temporarily or indefinitely) the action cannot result in his removal from the United Kingdom' because of international law or practical constraints. This covered both Article 3 ECHR constraints and cases where a detainee could not be sent back

---

36 M. Ignatieff, *The Lesser Evil: Political Ethics in an Age of Terror*, Edinburgh University Press, 2005, 50 (emphasis added).

37 See A. Tomkins, 'Legislating Against Terror' (2002) *PL* 205.

38 Section 21(1) ACSA.   39 *Ibid.*, s. 21(2).

because of statelessness or lack of travel documents. It is important to note however that, under general immigration law, a deportee would still be liable to criminal prosecution for failing to leave in breach of such an order.[40] Such a person would be criminalized for doing something that was impossible to avoid. The power to 'deport' someone who was acknowledged to be undeportable was quite clearly creating a unique legal limbo without precedent. The statute made no attempt to 'regularize' their status during the indefinite period pending deportation. The final link in the chain was the power contained in section 23, which authorized but did not require detention when a person could not be deported due to legal or practical obstacles.

The first detentions took place in December 2001 and the litigation commenced. This sought to challenge in general the compatibility of the detention provisions of the Act with the European Convention. There were also judicial review actions brought to test the specific decisions to certify and detain under the machinery set up for that purpose by the Act. The Special Immigration Appeals Commission ('SIAC') held that the legislation was discriminatory, but this was overturned by the Court of Appeal. The key difference between these two decisions goes to the heart of the ambiguity that runs throughout the issue of preventive detention.

SIAC had rejected the key government argument which was to the effect that: 'aliens have no general right to be here – at large among the population – even when they face persecution abroad'. It said in response:

> That seems to us to be an over-simplification. The effect of the decision in *Chahal*, as we understand it, is that if the alien cannot be deported he must be allowed to remain . . . A person who is irremovable cannot be detained or kept in detention simply because he lacks British nationality. In order to detain him there must be some other justification, such as that he may have committed a criminal offence.[41]

As noted above, this last step was not one that *Chahal* itself had decided, but it seemed to follow from the principle that Article 3 ECHR prevented removal. SIAC found that there must in principle be a right of release in such cases. This was consistent with the line of cases ever since *Khawaja* endorsing the basic right to liberty of foreigners regardless of immigration status. SIAC also therefore concluded that detention only of foreigners would be discriminatory unless 'the threat stems exclusively or almost exclusively from that alien section' of the population. Because the agreed evidence was that perhaps 1,000 British citizens had also

---

40 See Immigration Act 1971.   41 See note 21. Paragraph 94.

undergone training in terrorist camps, it was impossible to say the threat was so confined.

By contrast, the Court of Appeal rejected that argument very succinctly, where Lord Woolf simply said:

> I say those comparators were not in an analogous situation because the nationals have a right of abode in this jurisdiction but the aliens only have a *right not to be removed*.[42]

This is a striking image, evoking the Australian case-law on mandatory detention. This suggested a power existed to seclude aliens suspected of terrorist activities from the wider community indefinitely. This would effectively terminate their capacity to lead autonomous lives, but would stop short of sending them to their deaths. It is immediately difficult to understand why a liberal state would endorse such contradictory reasoning, but it was nevertheless not clearly excluded by any previous authority.

Brooke L.J. approached the issue by referring to a broad range of international treaties which permitted detention of non-nationals during times of emergency. He said that although detention must be directed at a legitimate aim and be proportionate:

> On the other hand, both customary international law and the international treaties by which this country is bound expressly reserve the power of a state in time of war or similar public emergency to detain aliens on grounds of national security when it would not necessarily detain its own nationals on those grounds.[43]

In fact, the international humanitarian law treaties he referred to did not purport to say anything about the treatment of citizens at all. As regards aliens, they only regulated matters during times of war or armed conflict. By contrast, the case turned upon the European Convention which applies to all those within the jurisdiction, even during emergencies. The reference to earlier rules regarding warfare is understandable, but shows the slippage in legal thinking as *enemy* aliens logic was extended to aliens generally.

After the Court of Appeal judgment, the Act was considered again by Parliament, which was required to renew the detention measures. By this time, the detainees had been held for some fifteen months. The Joint

---

42 *A and others* v. *Secretary of State for the Home Department* [2002] EWCA Civ 1502, para. 56 (emphasis added).
43 Paragraph 131.

Committee again considered the issues and this time, no doubt influenced by the outcome of the litigation, more readily accepted that the measures related to immigration and not security:

> If the person voluntarily agrees to be deported to a specified country, he or she must be released and removed to that place. While a person is detained, the Secretary of State has an implied duty to search diligently for a place to which the person could be safely and practicably removed, and detain the person only as long as necessary to find a safe place and make arrangement for removal. The Home Secretary has informed us that, so far, fifteen foreign nationals have been detained, of whom two subsequently left the country voluntarily and thirteen remain in detention.[44]

They noted, however, that the Act did not expressly limit detention to this purpose and in these circumstances. It was not clear, therefore, that it was an immigration and not a security power, although they accepted it was being operated in that way. In the light of the Court of Appeal judgment, the measures were continued.[45]

At the end of 2003, a high-level panel of parliamentarians, the Newton Committee, recommended abolishing the detention provisions because they allowed indefinite detention without adequate ongoing assessment of the need for it.[46] It also noted that no other Council of Europe government had taken such steps and doubted the efficacy of the measures given the threat from British citizens. The government refused by continuing to refer to the lesser liberty interest of foreigners:

> The Government believes it is defensible to distinguish between foreign nationals and our own citizens and reflects their different rights and responsibilities. Immigration powers and the possibility of deportation could not apply to British citizens. While it would be possible to seek other powers to detain British citizens who may be involved in international terrorism it would be a very grave step. The Government believes that such draconian powers would be difficult to justify.[47]

---

44 Paragraph 10, Joint Committee on Human Rights, Fifth Report on Continuance in Force of Sections 21 to 23 of the Anti-terrorism, Crime and Security Act 2001.

45 Lord Carlile of Berriew QC was appointed as an independent monitor by the government of all the detention decisions and the general operation of Part IV provisions.

46 Newton Committee: Privy Counsellor Review Committee, *Anti-terrorism, Crime and Security Act 2001 Review* (2003–4 HC 100, Dec. 2003), paras 186–201. See discussion in T.R. Hickman, 'Between Human Rights and the Rule of Law: Indefinite Detention and the Derogation Model of Constitutionalism' (2005) 68(4) *MLR* 654–80 at 666–7 on the role of the Newton Committee.

47 Counter-Terrorism Powers: Reconciling Security and Liberty in an Open Society (Home Office, Cmd 6147, February 2004), 36.

The government also made clear that the emergency showed no sign of abating. The creeping realization that what had been passed as an immigration measure was in fact resulting in indefinite internment, caused the Joint Committee to argue that renewal of the legislation should only be for six months with a commitment to find another anti-terrorism policy. The passage of time was beginning to influence decision-makers, but they had still failed to fully articulate an argument of principle against the policy. The debates before and after the Act was passed illustrate the confusion in Parliament and the courts surrounding the status of aliens. It would be fair to say that the government had not demonstrably acted in violation of fundamental rights, even though the policy was harsh in its effects, because the situation of aliens was widely thought to be distinct. The stage was set for a resolution of these doubts. This eventually came in the House of Lords judgment in December 2004.

The *Belmarsh* decision in *A* v. *Secretary of State for the Home Department*: the equal liberty of aliens

The decision of the House of Lords to declare the detention regime under the Anti-terrorism, Crime and Security Act 2001 (ACSA) incompatible with Articles 5 and 14 ECHR (and also Articles 9 and 26 ICCPR) was a landmark in many ways. For our purposes, the case may represent a decisive rejection of long-held, but perhaps poorly justified, beliefs about the scope of the power over aliens. The decision rejected an orthodoxy that had emerged from a century which had included two world wars; the belief that the liberty right of aliens was generally less extensive than that of citizens. Although much commentary has focused upon the judicial review aspects, such as the proportionality test applied, the crucial issue was the status of aliens.[48] The government had convinced the Court of Appeal and Parliament that the detention powers should be seen as ancillary to immigration control in respect of a group of persons who had

---

48 See D. Bonner, 'Checking the Executive? Detention without Trial, Control Orders, Due Process and Human Rights' (2006) 12(1) *EPL* 45. C. Gearty, 'Human Rights in an Age of Counter-terrorism: Injurious, Irrelevant or Indispensable?' (2005) 1 *EHRLR* 25. The government succeeded in persuading a majority of the House that there was a threat to the life of the nation, but not that the means employed to meet the threat were compliant with Arts 5 and 14.

no right to be within the jurisdiction anyway. The House of Lords viewed the issues in a radically different way.[49]

A security measure not an immigration measure

In assessing the issues of proportionality and discrimination, the court declined to engage in a separate assessment of the detention policy by reference to its link to deporting aliens. They took the view that the policy had to be considered as a response to a security threat facing the country from all sections of the community, thus removing its 'immigration control' cloak. Otherwise one would have:

> to accept the correctness of the Secretary of State's choice of immigration control as a means to address the Al-Qaeda security problem, when the correctness of that choice is the issue to be resolved ... Suspected international terrorists who are UK nationals are in a situation analogous with the appellants because, in the present context, they share the most relevant characteristics of the appellants.[50]

Lord Hope of Craighead made it plain that:

> it would be a serious error, in my opinion, to regard this case as about the right to control immigration. This is because the issue which the Derogation Order was designed to address was not at its heart an immigration issue at all. It was an *issue about the aliens' right to liberty*.[51]

The characterization of the measures was made clear again in relation to the issue of the justification for the difference in treatment. Lord Bingham accepted that Article 5(1)(f) permitted detention pending deportation: 'and that is a position in which a national could never find himself. The question is whether and to what extent states may differentiate *outside the immigration context*' (emphasis added).[52]

This approach has general implications for the protection of the human rights of immigrants. This is because the methodology of the court was to establish the *objective* nature of the measure taken against aliens. To the extent that the measure was not truly one of immigration control, it

---

49 *A v. Secretary of State for the Home Department* [2004] UKHL 56. See B. Dickson, 'Law Versus Terrorism: Can Law Win?' [2005] 1 *EHRLR* 11–28; 'A. v Secretary of State for the Home Departement' [2005] 68(4) *MLR* 654–80 for broader discussion of the case.
50 Paragraph 53. 51 Paragraph 103 (emphasis added). 52 Paragraph 56.

fell to be assessed according to standard non-discrimination and human rights principles.

The new cosmopolitan view: fundamental rights over immigration authorization

Thus the crucial heart of the judgment is an attempt to move away from the traditional view that the sovereignty of nations must entail a broad and ill-defined power over aliens, in favour of a universalism based upon more recent international human rights practice. In many ways, of course, universalism has always been at the core of human rights philosophy; the judgment in *A and others* simply rejected the last, anomalous, exception for aliens.

Lord Bingham conducted a detailed review of recent standards emanating from the United Nations and Council of Europe regarding anti-terrorism and non-discrimination. In this context, it is instructive that he relied heavily upon the contemporaneous material from the Committee established to monitor the implementation of the International Convention on the Elimination of All Forms of Racial Discrimination 1966. This convention had been drafted in a manner which attempted to preserve a power to discriminate against aliens for certain purposes. Thus Article 1(2) stated: 'This Convention shall not apply to distinctions, exclusions, restrictions or preferences made by a State Party to this Convention between citizens and non-citizens.' It was only in 1993 that the Committee had clarified the meaning of Article 1(2) in a General Recommendation.[53] They made plain that this power should 'not be interpreted to detract in any way from the rights and freedoms recognized and enunciated in other instruments, especially the Universal Declaration of Human Rights, the International Covenant on Economic, Social and Cultural Rights and the International Covenant on Civil and Political Rights'.[54] Thus the fundamental rights of non-citizens must be protected without discrimination.

The Committee had reaffirmed in 2002 that states must 'ensure that measures taken in the struggle against terrorism do not discriminate in purpose or effect on grounds of race, colour, descent or national

---

53 'This Convention shall not apply to distinctions, exclusions, restrictions or preferences made by a State Party to this Convention between citizens and non-citizens.'
54 General Recommendation XI 1993 at para. 3.

or ethnic origin'.[55] Importantly the Committee had, in a report on the United Kingdom, said that it was 'deeply concerned about provisions of the Anti-terrorism Crime and Security Act which provide for indefinite detention without charge or trial, pending deportation, of non-nationals of the United Kingdom suspected of terrorism-related activities'. It said these appeared to discriminate without any objective basis.[56] Finally, the Committee had specifically mentioned detention in a 2004 General Recommendation, where it said states should '[e]nsure that non-citizens detained or arrested in the fight against terrorism are properly protected by domestic law that complies with international human rights, refugee and humanitarian law'.[57] Lord Bingham concluded: 'these materials are inimical to the submission that a state may lawfully discriminate against foreign nationals by detaining them but not nationals presenting the same threat in a time of emergency'.[58]

Having built the positive case for universalism, Lord Bingham then rejected the traditional view that aliens had a lesser status derived from customary international law and many treaties[59] allowing states to discriminate against non-nationals by detaining them. His rejection of this view was simple because the case was based upon the subsequent European Convention and the International Covenant and so the position in relation to other documents was not relevant.[60] It is clear that Lord Bingham favoured the more recent international material that was specifically addressed to balancing non-discrimination, human rights and anti-terrorist measures. The older treaties reflected the era of their drafting, the influence of the world wars and the traditional view that there were inherent arbitrary powers over aliens.

---

55 Statement of 8 Mar. 2002. See also General Recommendation No. 30, 'Discrimination against non-citizens'. For a detailed summary of the UN response see E.J. Flynn, 'Counter Terrorism and Human Rights: the View from the United Nations' (2005) 1 *EHRLR* 29.

56 Concluding Observations on the United Kingdom (10 December 2003, CERD/C/63/CO/11), para. 17.

57 See also General Recommendation No. 30, 'Discrimination against non-citizens', para. 20. See also Compilation of General Comments and General Recommendations Adopted by Human Rights Treaty Bodies, UN Doc. HRI/GEN/1/Rev.6 (2003), 140 (General Comment No. 15, 'The Positition of Aliens Under the Covenant', adopted 1986).

58 Paragraph 63.

59 These materials included the Geneva Convention Relative to the Protection of Civilian Persons in Time of War 1949, the Geneva Convention Relating to the Status of Refugees 1951 and the Convention on the Status of Stateless Persons 1954.

60 Paragraph 70.

For Lord Nicholls of Birkenhead the confusion over the status of aliens meant that 'the government may have regarded the human rights of non-nationals in this field as less weighty than the corresponding rights of nationals . . . Unwanted aliens who cannot be deported, as much as nationals, are not to be detained indefinitely without charge or trial save in wholly exceptional circumstances'.[61] Lord Hope was in one sense stating the legally obvious when he said: 'I would therefore take as my starting point the proposition that the article 5 right to liberty is a fundamental right which belongs to everyone *who happens to be in this country*, irrespective of his or her nationality or citizenship.'[62] However, this was a clear rejection of the orthodoxy that had pervaded legal thinking for many years: that unauthorized aliens start off from a position of inferiority.

Baroness Hale went furthest in making the link with modern equality law when she said of the argument that aliens had a lesser status:

> The unsurprising answer is that some differences in treatment are indeed allowed. Foreigners do not have to be given the same rights to participate in the politics and government of the country as citizens . . . Nor do they have to be given the same rights to come or to stay here . . . *But while they are here they have the same rights as everyone else . . .* [this] also includes not being locked up except in the circumstances allowed under article 5.[63]

This is perhaps the boldest statement of the principle of universal human rights that has emerged from any immigration case. It rejects the idea that 'authorization' is a prerequisite to the enjoyment of equal 'rights'. This goes further than simply confirming that the right to liberty is preserved. It speaks to an undefined cosmopolitan bundle of rights that travel with migrants, regardless of status – a 'membership' of the human race. Whilst in some ways a logical conclusion of the history of the post-war human rights movement, this is nevertheless not without difficulties. Most obviously, modern immigration law explicitly imposes many prohibitions on foreigners by reference to lawful status or residence. Basic rights to social security, education, work, healthcare or marriage are denied on the basis of immigration status. For lawful migrants, they are conditions on entry. For unlawful migrants, they represent deterrents and disincentives to stay. The extent to which such restrictions are legitimate under international human rights law will be considered further in Chapter 7.

---

61 Paragraph 84.   62 Paragraph 106.   63 Paragraph 229 (emphasis added).

The 'prison with three walls' revisited

The House also rejected the government's *Mezei* arguments that aliens and citizens were not in a similar situation because the former could end their incarceration by returning to their country; their prison only had 'three walls'. Their detention was thus 'consensual'. Even if not consensual, where other countries were the reason for non-removal, the United Kingdom was 'blameless'. This was *Mezei* logic, too – other nations should not be able to foist unwanted foreigners on Britain. None of this could be said to apply in the case of internment of nationals according to the government. The argument was rightly rejected on pragmatic grounds because 'this freedom is more theoretical than real... They prefer to stay in prison rather than face the prospect of ill treatment in any country willing to admit them'.[64] Lord Hope said 'it would be more accurate to say that the detainees who remain here are in a cul-de-sac from which, as they have no safe country to go to, there is no escape'.[65] Lord Roger said 'the reality is that... they have nowhere to go and so face remaining in detention, indefinitely, for years on end'.[66]

Only Lord Walker was convinced by the argument, using it as Lord Woolf had, to argue that citizens and deportable aliens were not comparable:

> It is *fundamental*. British citizens have a right of abode... They cannot be deported, whatever crimes they have committed or may be thought likely to commit.... Suspected terrorists who are British citizens could be detained only in 'a prison with four walls' – that is, to use the normal phrase, they would have to be interned. Their internment would be... a grave invasion of their individual human rights...[67]

Rather than being 'fundamental' because derived from reasoned legal argument, Lord Walker's view amounts to a political 'axiom' widely held since World War One by officials, judges and legislators. Detention pursuant to deportation is not really detention at all, but a form of exclusion from the community. Because such aliens have no right to be present, they have no right to be released. They can leave, if they can find somewhere to go, or choose to remain in segregation. The state of emergency has no independent role to play in this view which is solely based upon unauthorized status.

64 Paragraph 81.   65 Paragraph 123.   66 Paragraph 188.
67 Paragraph 212 (emphasis added).

Conclusions: asserting judicial control over political detention

The majority judgments in *A* are unsettling in their quiet and painstaking examination and ultimate rejection of this deeply-held belief.[68] One critic argues that the judgments 'failed to advert to the principle that the nation does not have to accept from foreigners the same degree of risk as it accepts from its nationals (who by reason of their nationality are un-deportable) and may obviate the risk from foreigners by their deportation and detention *ancillary* to deportation'.[69] Of course, the House of Lords did not ignore this at all. It is well established that public security can support extended detention whilst deportation is a realistic prospect. Viewed narrowly, the House simply decided that where deportation is not likely, detention must be seen as a security measure.

Finnis argues that the decision was a repudiation of 'the core con-stitutional distinction between nationals and aliens'.[70] This is, however, misleading. As we have seen, in relation to habeas corpus, aliens' equal right to liberty has enjoyed a renewed status in modern British jurispru-dence. The *Belmarsh* case reflects a recognition that unlike wars, which finish, the ongoing struggle against non-state armed groups or indeed illegal immigration itself may prove a constant feature. In such circum-stances, a permanent 'state of emergency' (whether legally declared or not) may prevail and immigrants are more likely to be the target of oppressive executive and legislative security measures.[71] If aliens' fundamental rights were compromised based on immigration status, it would invite abuse of power and undermine the rule of law.

More boldly, however, the decision must be seen as a *political challenge* to the government's *monopoly of choice* over defining the 'enemies' of the

---

68 As Finnis critically puts it – the judgment 'ignores the constitutional principle on which Parliament, well aware of the risk of home-grown terrorism, was proceeding: when non-nationals present a significant risk to the public good they, unlike nationals, can entirely properly be required to leave the country', J. Finnis, 'Nationality, Alienage and Constitutional Principle' (2007) 123 *LQR* 418–55, 441.

69 *Ibid.*, 438.   70 *Ibid.*, 441.

71 See the debate in C. Warbrick, 'The European Response to Terrorism in an Age of Human Rights' (2004) 15 *EJIL* 989 and G. Neuman, 'Comment, Counter-terrorist Operations and the Rule of Law' (2004) 15 *EJIL* 1019. Warbrick argues that, at least in the modern conflict with international terrorism, human rights law should always apply, perhaps alongside international humanitarian law. See E. Guild, 'Citizens, Immigrants, Terrorists and Others', in A. Ward and S. Peers (eds), *The EU Charter of Fundamental Rights: Politics, Law and Policy*, Oxford: Hart, 2004, 236–40, for a discussion of anti-terrorism in the EU context.

state.[72] The House forced the government to articulate justifications for its choice of enemy based upon *reason*, not simply political factors feeding upon arguments of inherent alien inferiority. Finding those justifications wanting, it forced the government to re-examine its methods of fighting the security threat. If there were also equally dangerous citizen 'enemies', politicians must use identical methods to address that threat. In this manner the court rejected 'political' detention in favour of legal controls, even during a security emergency.

As Goss argues, 'the dialectic of "us-Them"' serves to direct people's anger to a group held responsible, to create consensus and to confer powers on government because 'the costs of actions seem to be borne by a distinct, smaller, and ostensibly well-defined group of people'.[73] The public are more ready to support measures that they, often rightly, believe will not be turned against them.[74] Assessment of risks becomes distorted 'in times of crisis, when panic, fear, hatred, and similar emotions prevail, rational discourse and analysis are pushed aside in formulating the nation's response'.[75] The *Belmarsh* decision was a hugely significant example of the way that constitutional courts are capable of performing the role of reasoned interlocutor in such times.

There is also a less expansive and dramatic reading of the case. The court was clearly heavily influenced by the fact that the agreed evidence was that UK nationals presented a significant threat, as well as aliens.[76] If there had been no or little such evidence, would the result have been the same? It is suggested that it would have. Their Lordships would still have reached the same conclusion that these were security measures as deportation was impossible. The condemnation of *de jure* discrimination would have had

---

72 Lord Hoffman in fact held that there was no 'threat to the life of the nation' at all and recalled: 'There have been times of great national emergency in which habeas corpus has been suspended and powers to detain on suspicion conferred on the government. It happened during the Napoleonic Wars and during both World Wars in the twentieth century. These powers were conferred with great misgiving and, in the light of sober retrospect after the emergency had passed, were often found to have been cruelly and unnecessarily exercised' (para. 89).

73 O. Gross, 'Chaos and Rules: Should Responses to Violent Crises Always be Constitutional?' (2003) 112 *Yale L.J.* 1011, 1037. See also C. Sunstein, *Laws of Fear*, Oxford University Press, 2007, Ch. 9, who makes similar points about risk perception being distorted when only aliens will be subject to harsh measures.

74 Gross, 'Chaos and Rules', 1083.   75 *Ibid.*

76 See C. Forsyth, 'Showing the Fly the Way Out of the Flybottle: the Value of Formalism and Conceptual Reasoning in Administrative Law' (2007) *CLJ* 325, who argues that the decision was essentially a narrow one based upon 'logic' rather than 'substantive' moral thinking (345).

the same force. This was not wartime and the detainees were not 'enemy aliens'. There was no justification to draft legal powers only aimed at deportable aliens. General emergency powers were appropriate. The core reason for the decision was the assumption by the executive of powers of arbitrary detention over persons, not the fact that there happened to be British terrorists too.[77]

The confirmation of the Belmarsh decision by Strasbourg

It must be recalled that this was a decision by a national court inter-preting the meaning of the European Convention. Importantly, however, it was confirmed by the Strasbourg Court itself when it was asked to review the House of Lords decision in the context of the application by the detainees for damages for their unlawful detention.[78] Because of the unusual nature of this request, the Strasbourg Court did not go into great detail in developing its own reasoning. It said that only if the national court had misinterpreted the Convention or its case-law, or the decision was 'manifestly unreasonable' would it overrule a national court deci-sion. On the issue of proportionality and discrimination in relation to the derogation, the Court agreed with Lord Bingham's approach. This is significant because of the heavy reliance he placed upon material from outside the ECHR. This shows a willingness to be pluralist in reasoning under the ECHR by reference to a wide range of international human rights sources in relation to anti-terrorism. The conclusion reached was that this was essentially national security detention (rather than immi-gration control) and that this must be practised in non-discriminatory ways. The British legislation and the derogation order did not achieve this obligation and were thus in breach of Article 14 taken with Article 5(1).

As regards Article 5, the British government raised a new argument, not put before the House of Lords, to the effect that they had complied with Article 5(1)(f) on the facts of the applicants' cases. They argued that their serious attempts to find safe countries and/or secure promises not to torture the detainees met the 'due diligence' test. Here the Strasbourg Court agreed in principle that such measures could support detention under Article 5(1)(f). But in an important and surprising ruling, the

---

77 As Lord Nicholls of Birkenhead put it: 'Indefinite imprisonment without charge or trial is anathema in any country which observes the rule of law. It deprives the detained person of the protection a criminal trial is intended to afford. Wholly exceptional circumstances must exist before this extreme step can be taken' (para. 74).

78 Application No. 3455/05, A and others v. UK, judgment of 16 Feb. 2009.

Court held that the due diligence test did not vary with the national security risk posed. The standard remained the same with no less diligence permitted in terrorism cases. On the facts, the British government had done very little during the period 2001–3 and thus had not met the due diligence test apart from two detainees who had been returned in three days and three months, respectively. The Strasbourg Court thus confirmed an important bracket around the aliens power. 'Immigration' detention, properly understood, relates only to those powers objectively shown to be linked to practicable deportation. The courts have an obligation to properly police the boundary between security and immigration powers to ensure that the latter does not subsume the former.

Authorization to be released under the control order regime: a prison without walls?

Important though it was, the judgment in *A and others* has to be seen in light of the fact that, under the UK Constitution, Parliament remained supreme. The judgment did not invalidate the legislation, but merely declared to Parliament that it was non-compliant with human rights standards.[79] The detainees remained in detention pending the design and passage of a new legislative scheme of non-discriminatory 'control orders' to replace discriminatory detention.[80] New legislation conferred powers to limit the movements of persons, require them to reside in certain places, limit their contacts and communications, call the police or report throughout the day or night, wear electronic tags and restrain their travel. In short, this regime allowed for the most extensive limits upon a person, short of actual detention. Those remaining detainees were all put under intensive forms of this regime.[81] This was exceptionally invasive and in practice meant their capacity to lead autonomous lives, with goals, ambitions or social and cultural ties to the wider community was virtually over. Although their right of release had been respected,

---

79 See s. 4 Human Rights Act 1998, which allows a court to make a declaration of incompatibility with rights under the European Convention on Human Rights. Under s. 10 the government then has a power to introduce remedial legislation, but is not obliged to do so.

80 L. Hanlon, 'UK Anti-terrorism Legislation: Still Disproportionate?' (2007) 11(4) *IJHR* 481; A. Tomkins, 'Readings of *A v Secretary of State for the Home Department*' (2005) 3 *PL* 259; and K.D. Ewing, 'The Futility of the Human Rights Act' (2004) *PL* 829.

81 Prevention of Terrorism Act 2005.

the conditions under which they where 'authorized' to be at large were extremely draconian.

There was a power to challenge the orders before an independent court, but the government had a low burden of proof of dangerousness and also restricted the controlees' access to the evidence supporting the order. The courts did review individual orders and tried to subject them to 'intense scrutiny', but they were limited in their ability to assess the degree of risk posed and granted a 'degree of deference' in such assessments to the government.[82] In many cases, secret evidence was relied upon, seen only by the controlee's special advocate. As a result, there was a challenge to this scheme's fairness under Article 6 of the ECHR, which requires a fair hearing in respect of civil rights and obligations. The House of Lords ruled that suspects must be given access to the basic case against them so that they could challenge it, even if this was only through special advocates.[83]

The ongoing problems of the system led the Joint Committee on Human Rights to say they 'amount to internal exile, banishing an individual, and effectively, his family from his and their community'. They referred to them as 'historically despotic executive orders' which would contribute to the 'folklore of injustice'.[84] Even with the safeguard of knowing the 'gist' of the case against, the Committee thought 'in the light of five years experience of the operation of the system . . . that the current regime is not capable of ensuring the substantial measure of procedural justice that is required'.[85] Thus, although the powers are non-discriminatory in design, they have operated *de facto* as severe restrictions on deportable foreigners. It is very hard to know how far British citizens have been considered suitable for control orders by the government. Whilst the courts forced the law to be drafted in a non-discriminatory manner, the political choice as to who to apply it to remains in the end with the government.

We can see here that even release and 'reauthorization' after the *Belmarsh* decision has not led to a meaningful resolution of the political and legal difficulties posed by undeportable deportees. In fact, most of those under such orders actually absconded, but no crimes were found to have been committed by them after this. In the end, only criminal

---

82 *Secretary of State for the Home Department* v. *MB* [2006] EWCA Civ 1140.

83 *R (on appn. AF)* v. *Secretary of State for the Home Department* [2009] UKHL 28. See D. Bonner, 'Checking the Executive? Detention without Trial, Control Orders, Due Process and Human Rights' (2006) 12 *EPL* 45.

84 Ninth Report of the Joint Committee on Human Rights, Session 2009–10 HL Papers 64, HC 395, para. 45.

85 Paragraph 88.

prosecution followed by either acquittal and regularization or conviction and imprisonment, will provide a stable situation in such cases.

The United States response to September 11, 2001 and the use of immigration powers

We have seen that shortly before the attacks on the World Trade Center and the Pentagon, the Supreme Court had decided in *Zadvydas* that, broadly speaking, detention was permitted to secure removal, but should be limited to six months following the end of the ninety-day removal period set by Congress.[86] That case was, however, one involving an ordinary criminal alien. The Court had left open the possibility that national security cases might be treated differently. *Zadvydas* also only applied once a final removal order had been made, so that detention during lengthy removal proceedings was still constitutional.[87] The immigration authorities therefore had quite wide, possibly indefinite, powers to detain whilst seeking the removal of aliens where some evidence suggested they were security threats.

This was the legal framework facing the immigration authorities following the attacks of 11 September 2001. The fact that the perpetrators were foreign and that there was little prior intelligence to suggest that American citizens had provided support for terrorism led, naturally enough, to a focus upon foreigners in the ensuing investigation. However, despite the extraordinary emergency facing the country, new legal powers were only passed later in the US PATRIOT Act.[88] Thus, immediately following the attacks, immigration law powers to detain overstayers were quickly alighted upon as a means of pursuing the criminal investigation.

In the aftermath of the attacks, a huge police investigation ('PENTTBOM') was led by the Federal Bureau of Investigation (FBI). This resulted in a core group of persons thought to have links to the actual perpetrators being drawn up. Soon after, numerous other leads and reports from the public were gathered and a long list was compiled. Many of these persons were foreign Muslims of Arab or Pakistani origin. We do not know the relative balance of foreigners and US citizens. It would be surprising if no US citizens were named. The FBI set about arresting

---

86 See Ch. 2 above.   87 See Ch. 2, *Kim* v. *Demore.*
88 Section 412 of the Act did, however, provide for mandatory indefinite detention of suspected foreign terrorists. Even then, however, the measure required a positive certification that such a person was someone in respect of whom there were reasonable grounds to believe he was a terrorist (although the latter term was very widely defined).

these foreigners and any others that they encountered in seeking them. In most cases, there was insufficient evidence to arrest them on terrorist charges, so the FBI sought to enlist the Immigration and Naturalization Service ('INS') in holding these persons under immigration powers whilst enquiries were made about them. The Attorney General set out the new policy:

> Let the terrorists among us be warned: If you overstay your visa – even by one day – we will arrest you. If you violate a local law, you will be put in jail and kept in custody as long as possible . . . In the war on terror, this Department of Justice will arrest and detain any suspected terrorist who has violated the law. Our single objective is to prevent terrorist attacks by taking suspected terrorists off the street. If suspects are found not to have links to terrorism or not to have violated the law, they are released. But terrorists who are in violation of the law will be convicted, in some cases deported, and in all cases prevented from doing further harm to Americans.[89]

This passage was a *de facto* 'declaration of war' on suspected irregular immigrants under the guise of a national security measure. It deemed all such persons to be potential terrorists, at least until proven otherwise.[90] Immigration law violations, if any, would provide a formal legal basis for their incarceration, but thereafter they were to be held until cleared of links to terrorism. There was no rational reason or evidence to equate all, or indeed any, immigration violators with terrorism. Nevertheless, in so doing, the immigration laws came to assume great prominence during the investigation in the months after 11 September 2001.

Under the new policy, those immigrants arrested were to be held until cleared by the FBI, and refused bail. Even when immigration judges granted bail, the policy was to appeal and ask for a stay of execution. As a result perhaps 1,000–1,500 aliens were arrested in the initial sweep.[91] Subsequently another 3,500 were held. Of the 5,000 detained it appears that only three were ever charged and one convicted of terrorist offences. Even the sole conviction was for providing support for possible future terrorist activity.[92] Many were detained for extended periods in excess of the

---

89 John Ashcroft speech to US Conference of Mayors, 25 Oct. 2001.
90 D. Cole, 'In Aid of Removal: Due Process Limits on Immigration Detention' (2002) 51 *Emory L.J.* 1003.
91 The exact figures are uncertain because the records are not accurate. See *ibid.* Also D. Cole, *Enemy Aliens: Double Standards and Constitutional Freedoms in the War on Terrorism,* New York: New Press, 2003, 24–5.
92 D. Cole, 'The Priority of Morality' (2004) 113 *Yale L.J.* 1753, 1754.

ninety-day removal period set by the immigration laws. Even detainees who wished to return voluntarily to their countries were held pending investigation. There were huge delays, as the FBI was overwhelmed and could not issue clearance reports swiftly in time for bail hearings. The policy also included holding the detainees in maximum security facilities under harsh conditions. Some detainees were subjected to abuse.[93] Eventually, following legal advice that the detainees could not be held for criminal investigation purposes, they were deported or bailed.[94] The period spent in detention ranged, but significant numbers were held for six months or more.

The data and factual background were considered exhaustively in a critical review conducted by the Office of the Inspector General ('OIG'), Department of Justice.[95] The review suggested that the basis for arrest in the first place was inadequate, relying as it did upon tip-offs from the public, but also chance encounters with immigration violators.[96] The OIG also said of the prolonged detention of such persons:

93 See also Supplemental Report on September 11 Detainees' Allegations of Abuse at the Metropolitan Detention Center in Brooklyn, New York (Office of the Inspector General, December 2003) which concluded that 'staff members did abuse some of the detainees. We did not find that the detainees were brutally beaten, but we found evidence that some officers slammed detainees against the wall, twisted their arms and hands in painful ways, stepped on their leg restraint chains and punished them by keeping them restrained for long periods of time' (48).

94 'The INS has the authority to detain an alien with a final order of removal during the 90-day removal period as long as the INS is acting with reasonable dispatch to arrange the removal of the alien from the United States. This authority may be called into question if the INS cannot establish that it diligently pursued the steps necessary to remove the alien. Section 241(a)(2) of the Immigration and Nationality Act (INA) states that the INS had the authority to detain an alien with a final order of removal for up to 90 days, the length of the removal period. However, case law provides that detention must be related to removal and cannot be solely for the purpose of pursuing criminal prosecution. While there is no bar to the government's continuing a criminal investigation during the removal period for possible prosecution of the alien, the INS must also be proceeding with reasonable dispatch to arrange for removal and the investigation for criminal prosecution cannot be the primary or exclusive purpose of detention' (INS legal opinion of Jan. 2002).

95 *The September 11 Detainees: A Review of the Treatment of Aliens Held on Immigration Charges in Connection with the Investigation of the September 11 Attacks*, Office of the Inspector General, US Department of Justice, April 2003. Statistics at 104.

96 'PENTTBOM leads that resulted in the arrest of a September 11 detainee often were quite general in nature, such as a landlord reporting suspicious activity by an Arab tenant. For example, several Middle Eastern men were arrested and treated as connected to the September 11 investigation when local law enforcement authorities discovered "suspicious items," such as pictures of the World Trade Center and other famous buildings, during traffic stops.'

We do not criticize the decision to require FBI clearance of aliens to ensure they had no connection to the September 11 attacks or terrorism in general. However, we criticize the indiscriminate and haphazard manner in which the labels of 'high interest', 'of interest', or 'of undetermined interest' were applied to many aliens who had no connection to terrorism. Even in the hectic aftermath of the September 11 attacks, we believe the FBI should have taken more care to distinguish between aliens who it actually suspected of having a connection to terrorism as opposed to aliens who, while possibly guilty of violating federal immigration law, had no connection to terrorism but simply were encountered in connection with a PENTTBOM lead.[97]

The policy set by the Attorney General to detain all suspected terrorist immigration violators had in practice been 'applied much more broadly to many detainees for whom there was no affirmative evidence of a connection to terrorism'.[98] The OIG review therefore concluded that there had been significant administrative failures that arose from a hasty and ill-thought-out policy of detention of all immigration violators by reference to national origin and immigration status. In another important submission to the National Commission enquiring into the September 11 attacks, David Martin,[99] former General Counsel to INS, said: 'immigration arrest and detention constitute a serious intrusion on liberty and so must be subject to prompt review and justification'.[100] He thus concluded that any such measures must 'be kept to a minimum justified by the facts of the specific case . . . the government's use of detention after September 11 often fell short of this standard'.[101] Thus he emphasized that the government, 'although initially justified in its use of detention, did not follow through with needed measures to file charges in a timely fashion, to keep detention to a minimum or to release or deport promptly those for whom continued detention should not have been seen as justifiable'.[102]

Damages claims were settled with the government for these detentions and the treatment the detainees received. The American Civil Liberties Union also filed a complaint with the United Nations Working Group on Arbitrary Detention ('WGAD').[103] The WGAD opinion of 2004 only considered the last of the detainees mentioned in the complaint, who

---

97 OIG Report, n. 95 above, 69.   98 *Ibid.*

99 D. Martin, 'Preventive Detention: Immigration Law Lessons for the Enemy Combatant Debate. Testimony Before the National Commission on Terrorists Attacks upon the Untied States, December 8 2003' (2003–4) 18 *Geo. Immigrat. L.J.* 303, 309.

100 *Ibid.*, 311.   101 *Ibid.*, 310.   102 *Ibid.*, 310–11.

103 See *America's Disappeared: Seeking International Justice for Immigrants Detained After September 11*, New York: ACLU, 2004.

remained in detention three years after his arrest. The WGAD found his detention conditions amounted to torture and the duration of incarceration and absence of judicial control was in breach of Article 9 ICCPR.[104] He was eventually released in July 2006, when the Canadian government agreed to take him in to consider his asylum claim.[105] He had by that time been detained for almost five years largely under immigration powers with only a brief and abortive prosecution on minor criminal charges.[106]

The available evidence reconfirms the view that immigration powers of detention are a tool that can be used for purposes and in ways that are not subject to proper judicial or legislative control. Most of these detentions can be viewed as arbitrary in the sense that the detainees were held for extended periods with no objective evidence to justify this in immigration or law enforcement terms.[107]

---

104 Opinions adopted by WGAD, Sixty-first Session, E/CN.4/2005/5/Add.1 (19 Nov. 2004). Benamar Benatta, an Algerian military official legally visiting the United States, had been detained on 25 Sept. 2001 after being returned to the US after seeking asylum in Canada. He continued to be held even though cleared on 15 Nov. 2001 of links to terrorism. He had been charged with use of false documents then this was dropped. He had been held incommunicado for seven months at the outset. He was unable to post bail of $25,000, so remained in immigration detention pending ongoing proceedings in which he sought asylum.

105 See *Washington Post*, 'Domestic Detainee from 9/11 Released', 21 July 2006.

106 There were damages actions brought for unlawful detention to investigate terrorism offences based upon the use of minor immigration offences. See *Turkmen and others* v. *Ashcroft and others* (Case 1:02-cv-0237-JG-SMG 14/6/2006). Gleeson J. justified his rejecting the claims conclusion by analogy: 'An officer who wants to search a suspect's car for a handgun can pull him over (a Fourth Amendment "seizure") for changing lanes without using his blinker (a traffic violation), even if the officer has no interest in enforcing the law requiring drivers to signal a lane change. *United States* v. *Scopo* 19 F 3d 777 (2d Cir. 1994). Similarly the government may use its authority to detain illegal aliens pending deportation even if its real interest is building criminal cases against them' (4–5).

107 In another case arising from the round-up of aliens, the Court of Appeals held that, in relation to the harsh conditions of detention, the September 11 situation was not enough to generate a special privilege in the government: 'The strength of our system of constitutional rights derives from the steadfast protection of those rights in both normal and unusual times. With some rights, for example, the right to be free from unreasonable searches, the existence of exigent circumstances might justify governmental action that would not otherwise be permitted . . . But, . . . the exigent circumstances of the post-9/11 context do not diminish the Plaintiff's right not to be needlessly harassed and mistreated in the confines of a prison cell by repeated strip and body-cavity searches. This and other rights, such as the right to be free from use of excessive force and not to be subjected to ethnic or religious discrimination, were all clearly established prior to 9/11, and they remained clearly established even in the aftermath of that horrific event.'

The mandatory indefinite detention of removable 'terrorist' aliens: a theoretical power

The above-noted limits of the *Zadvydas* decision meant that indefinite detention narrowly tailored to cover suspected terrorists might be held constitutional.[108] Perhaps to remove any doubt, however, Congress passed the US PATRIOT Act 2001, which contained specific statutory powers to provide for indefinite detention. Section 412 of the Act amended the basic Immigration and Nationality Act so that an alien certified shall be taken into custody and held until removed from the United States. Certification may take place where the Attorney General has reasonable grounds to believe that an alien is deportable on the basis of the alleged conduct of a wide variety. Such alleged actions are enough to justify certification as a 'terrorist', but there are many non-terrorist crimes and even lawful activities brought within the definition.[109] The label 'terrorist' may apply to ordinary violent crime in some cases.

Congress, perhaps mindful of the *Zadvydas* decision, imposed further safeguards, including a requirement that detention cease if an alien 'is finally determined not to be removable'.[110] The detainee must be placed in removal proceedings or charged with a criminal offence not later than seven days after arrest or otherwise released.[111] Where a detainee's removal is 'unlikely in the reasonably foreseeable future' then they may be detained for 'additional periods of up to six months only if the release of the alien will threaten national security of the United States or the safety of the community or any person'.[112] The certification must be reviewed every six months by the Attorney General and the alien can submit evidence to him to rebut the certificate. There also must be filed with Congress every six months reports on the number of persons held and what has happened to them.[113]

---

108 See R.H. Fallon and D.J. Meltzer, 'Habeas Corpus Jurisdiction, Substantive Rights, and the War on Terror' (2007) 120 *Harv. L.R.* 2029, 2087, who argue that, so long as the procedure for determination of 'terrorist' status was adequate, then indefinite detention would be constitutional.

109 See *How the USA-PATRIOT Act Permits Indefinite Detention of Immigrants Who Are Not Terrorists*, New York: ACLU, 2001. Also J. Zelman, 'Recent Developments in International Law: Anti-terrorism Legislation – Part Two: the Impact and Consequences (2002) 11 *J. Transnat. L. and Pol.* 421, 424–5. See also Cole, 'In Aid of Removal', who states that merely innocently providing humanitarian funding to an organization considered terrorist or brandishing a kitchen knife in a domestic dispute would fall within the definition of terrorist (at 1027–8).

110 Section 236A(a)(2).   111 Section 236A(a)(5).   112 Section 236A(a)(6).

113 Section, 236A(c).

Despite these safeguards, they have no trial and no procedural safe-guards. There is no criminal conviction required. There is no need to show that detainees pose a danger to the community or a flight risk. Once certified, they will remain in detention indefinitely. This could last throughout the 'removal proceedings', which can take several years, and on into the post-removal order period. The only end point date is when they are finally determined by the executive not to be removable. Once certified, the detainee would effectively have a burden to disprove the certification and/or that they were dangerous to secure release.[114] Even if removal is not reasonably foreseeable, they can still be held in detention.

These powers are very clearly not about enforcing immigration con-trol. They are not even demonstrably about protecting the public from terrorism, because there is no clear link between certification and propen-sity to terrorism. Interestingly, these enhanced powers of detention have not been employed to date. This appears to be largely because the ordi-nary immigration powers are adequate.[115] The length of detention dur-ing removal proceedings is such that – perhaps particularly during less extraordinary periods than the aftermath to September 11 – investiga-tions may be carried out without resort to the additional powers of section 412.[116] As Cole puts it, 'the Attorney General was able to effec-tuate a mass preventive detention campaign'[117] by relying upon existing immigration detention powers.

Guantanamo Bay: the immigration roots of the offshore policy

The use of the facilities at Guantanamo Bay in Cuba to detain foreign prisoners captured around the world as part of the post-September 11 hostilities has been the subject of widespread coverage.[118] The status of the prisoners in international law has revolved around their claim to

---

114 Zelman, 'Recent Developments in International Law', 438–9.
115 Martin, 'Preventive Detention', 314. Cole, 'The Priority of Morality', 1777, who notes that the Attorney General was able to 'subject over 5000 foreign nationals to preventive detention ... by instead using pre-existing immigration and criminal law authorities'.
116 In addition, there appears to be no reason why aliens cannot be taken to Guantanamo Bay and held there under military powers, freed from any constraints imposed by the US PATRIOT Act or Immigration Act 1952. The United States has indeed used military powers to detain US citizens found on the US mainland alleged to have links to terrorism. See *Rumsfeld* v. *Padilla* 124 S. Ct. 2711 (2004).
117 Cole, 'The Priority of Morality', 1778.
118 Lord Steyn, 'Guantanamo Bay: the Legal Black Hole' (2004) 53 *ICLQ* 1; M.J.G. Mansilla, 'The United States Supreme Court and the Guantanamo Bay Prisoners' (2006) 80 *Australian L.J.* 232; G. Guillaume, 'Terrorism and International Law' (2004) 52 *ICLQ* 537; J.R. Pariseault, 'Applying the Rule of Law in the War on Terror: an Examination of

protection under the Geneva Conventions.[119] It is not so widely known, however, that the use of the base was first employed in relation to immigration cases. The fact that the practice of holding aliens on this base for considerable periods without legal rights such as access to lawyers, due process, judicial review or habeas corpus had become well established was a significant factor in the choice of Guantanamo Bay to house post-September 11 prisoners. The base was taken on a perpetual[120] lease from Cuba in 1903 under which 'ultimate sovereignty' was retained by Cuba, but the United States exercises 'complete jurisdiction and control'.[121]

The initial use of Guantanamo Bay for immigration purposes appears to have begun in 1991 when, following a coup, large numbers of Haitians fled by boat to the United States.[122] The US president authorized a policy of interception and detention at Guantanamo in order to stem the numbers. By 1992, 12,500 persons were held there whilst they were screened to see if they had *prima facie* asylum claims. When the base was full, the president authorized forced repatriation without consideration of asylum claims for those intercepted at sea. This policy was challenged as being in breach of domestic and international asylum law. One Court of Appeal circuit held quite firmly that statutory and constitutional rights need not be respected for aliens detained at Guantanamo. This was both because the base was not US territory and because the constitution and statute did not have extra-territorial effect.[123] Another Circuit[124] tentatively held, in a preliminary injunction hearing, that 'It does not appear to us to be incongruous or overreaching to conclude that the United States Constitution limits the

---

Guantanamo Bay through the Lens of the US Constitution and the Geneva Conventions' (2005) 28(3) *Hastings Int'l and Comp. L. Rev.* 481.

119 The government claimed they were not prisoners of war or civilians but rather 'unlawful combatants' because they were not regular soldiers in the uniform of a state.

120 The perpetuity was created by Treaty Defining Relations with Cuba, May 29, 1934, T.S. No. 866.

121 Lease of Lands for Coaling and Naval Stations, Feb. 23, 1903, U.S.–Cuba, Art. III, T.S. No. 418.

122 See S.H. Legomsky, 'The USA and the Caribbean Interdiction Program' [2006] 18 *Int. J. Refugee L.* 677 for an overview of the practice in the region.

123 *Haitian Refugee Center Inc* v. *Baker* 953 F.2d 1498 (11th Cir. 1992), 1513.

124 *Haitian Centers Council Inc* v. *McNary* 969 F.2d 1326 (2d Cir. 1992), 1343. This was vacated as moot and eventually settled, so never proceeded to a final detailed determination. Mahoney J. dissented, relying upon the long line of alien authority: 'The Bill of Rights is a futile authority for the alien seeking admission for the first time to these shores', *Kwong Hai Chew* v. *Coldring* 344 U.S. 590, 596 n. 5; 'an alien seeking admission . . . requests a privilege and has no constitutional rights regarding his application', *Landon* v. *Plasencia* 459 U.S. 21, 32.

conduct of United States personnel with respect to officially authorized interactions with aliens brought to and detained by such personnel on a land mass exclusively controlled by the United States.'

When the cases came to the Supreme Court in *Sale* v. *Haitian Centers Council* v. *US*,[125] the status of Guantanamo was not decided. Instead the Court ruled that asylum law did not apply to aliens outside the United States, relying upon the presumption against extra-territoriality: 'that presumption has special force when we are construing treaty and statutory provisions which may involve foreign and military affairs for which the President has unique responsibility'.[126] This implied, combined with traditional teaching about the lack of constitutional rights for unadmitted aliens, that Guantanamo detainees would not attract legal rights.

There was further use of Guantanamo Bay as an immigration detention centre in 1994 when, following the collapse of the Soviet Union, the Cuban government experienced increased outward migration. Much of this was irregular (by boat to Florida) and the Castro government did not seek to prevent it. As numbers increased, in August 1994 President Clinton reversed the long-standing policy of granting refugee status to all Cubans arriving. He feared a new *Mariel* exodus. Instead, boats were intercepted and Cubans seeking asylum taken back to Cuba, but this time held in Guantanamo Bay detention facilities. The asylum seekers were held there indefinitely whilst negotiations for Cuba to take them back were conducted. There was concern about the conditions under which they were held[127] and a failure to accord them rights under US domestic law to access asylum procedures and under the 1951 Refugee Convention.[128]

A challenge was brought to seek to apply the provisions of domestic and international law to around 20,000 Cubans and Haitians then held in the case *Cuban American Bar Association and others* v. *Christopher.*[129]

---

125 509 U.S. 155 (1993).   126 Opinion of Stevens J., 187.

127 Riots and treacherous escape attempts had resulted from poor medical, nutritional or housing facilities. See S. Mikolic-Torreira, 'The Cuba Migration Agreement: Implications of the Clinton–Castro Immigration Policy' (1994) 8 *Geo. Immigr. L.J.* 667.

128 J. Wachs, 'The Need to Define the International Legal Status of Cubans Detained at Guantanamo' (1996) 11 *Am. U. J. Int'l. L. and Pol.* 79–99, at 80–6. He concludes in terms that have continued to resonate: 'By allowing the United States to circumvent or deny the application of international instruments to the aforementioned issues, and to the larger Guantanamo crisis, the world community has thus far allowed the United States to invent it's own, ad-hoc legal standards for the treatment of asylum-seekers detained on "foreign" land' (99).

129 43 F.3d 1412 (11th Cir.), 1424–5.

The Circuit Court held first that Guantanamo Bay could not be considered US territory, nor that 'leased military bases abroad which continue under the sovereignty of foreign nations ... are 'functionally equivalent' to being land borders or ports of entry of the United States'.[130] They also rejected the extra-territorial application of the US Constitution or statutes to persons held there. They relied upon their earlier authorities relating to unadmitted aliens held in mainland US detention facilities: 'The individual[s] ... here, who are outside the borders of the United States, can have no greater rights than aliens in *Jean I* who were physically present in the United States.'[131] This conclusion was supported by the Supreme Court's own previous case-law declining to apply extra-territorially the Fifth Amendment to enemy aliens held overseas.[132]

We can see therefore that by 2001 there had been extensive use of Guantanamo Bay as a holding centre for immigrants.[133] During this period, the balance of judicial authority had held both (a) that Guantanamo Bay was not US territory, so courts had no jurisdiction derived from geographical sovereignty, and (b) that no relevant US constitutional or statutory law had extra-territorial effect for aliens held there. This apparently unfettered power over aliens held at the base influenced the government in utilizing the base for anti-terrorism purposes. The Department of Justice assessed the 'litigation risk as minimal'.[134] Detention in a quasi-military, rather than immigration context, would appear to be even less likely to invite the courts' intervention. This assessment turned out to be wrong. The post-September 11 detentions caused the Supreme Court to reassess the status of Guantanamo Bay for aliens detained there. This may, ironically, in time come to cause a reassessment of the rights of aliens held in

---

130 A.1(a).
131 See the litigation in *Jean* v. *Nelson* 727 F.2d 957 (11th Cir. 1984) (en banc), which was affirmed by the Supreme Court, although on a more narrow basis.
132 *Johnson* v. *Eisentrager* 339 U.S. 763 (1950), discussed below.
133 G.L. Neuman, 'Anomalous Zones' [1996] 48 *Stan. L.R.* 1197 who, commenting on the refugee litigation, said: 'Guantanamo may then be seen as an example of what I call an "anomalous zone", a geographical area in which certain legal rules, otherwise regarded as embodying fundamental policies of the larger legal system, are locally suspended' (1201). T.D. Jones, 'A Human Rights Tragedy: The Cuban and Haitian Refugee Crises Revisited' [1995] 9(3) *Georgetown Immig. L.J.* 479.
134 See the unclassified paper written for a seminar on National Security Strategy Process at the National War College – D.F. McCallum, 'Why GTMO?' (available at www.ndu. edu/nwc/writing/AY03/5603/5603G.pdf) cited in G.L. Neuman, 'Closing the Guantanamo Loophole' [2004] 50 *Loyola L. Rev.* 1–66 at 4.

immigration detention, both there, but also at the US border, another of what Neuman calls 'anomalous zones', which he argues 'unleash a subversive potential that extends beyond their designated boundaries and their original purposes'.[135]

The Supreme Court revisits Guantanamo Bay in the context of anti-terrorism policy

The US government detained and brought many hundreds of aliens to Guantanamo following the invasion of Afghanistan. They were held without charge or trial for an indefinite period whilst they were subjected to harsh treatment designed to extract information from them. They challenged their detention and treatment in the federal courts. In *Rasul* v. *Bush*,[136] the Supreme Court decided that federal courts had jurisdiction under the Habeas Corpus statute[137] to hear petitions from alien detainees at the base. The decision distinguished the holding in *Johnson* v. *Eisentrager*[138] that denied a right to seek habeas corpus to Germans held in German prisons by occupying forces, following conviction for war crimes by military tribunals. The Court noted the differences between the cases: that the instant detainees were not enemy aliens (as their countries were not at war with the United States); they denied their involvement in any aggression; had not been tried or even charged; and were held in a place where the United States exercised exclusive jurisdiction and control. These features moved the detention centre at Guantanamo decisively away from an exercise of 'war powers' towards another model. But which? Were unadmitted aliens entitled to criminal due process or was this a special case of holding under emergency alien powers?[139]

Writing for the majority Stevens J. said: 'Considering that the statute draws no distinction between Americans and aliens held in federal custody, there is little reason to think that Congress intended the geographical coverage of the statue to vary depending on the detainee's citizenship. Aliens held at the base, no less than American citizens, are entitled to

---

135 Neuman, 'Anomalous Zones'.   136 542 U.S. 466 (28 June 2004).
137 28 U.S.C. 2241.   138 339 U.S. 763 (1950).
139 Scalia J. in his dissent characterized the situation squarely in terms of war powers: 'Today, the Court springs a trap on the Executive, subjecting Guantanamo Bay to the oversight of the federal courts even though it has never before been thought to be within their jurisdiction – and thus making it a foolish place to have housed alien wartime detainees' *Rasul* v. *Bush*, 506.

invoke the federal courts' authority under S2241.'[140] This dim echo is as close as we get to a recognition of any broader non-discrimination norms recognized by international human rights law.[141] At this stage the Court was proceeding step by step.

The irrelevance of alienage to the whole question of executive detention became apparent in the later case of *Hamdi* v. *Rumsfeld*.[142] By contrast with *Rasul*, this concerned a US citizen who was detained in Afghanistan and transferred to Guantanamo Bay. After two months, his true citizenship was discovered and he was transferred to detention in South Carolina.[143] The government, in an unusual show of non-discrimination, nevertheless maintained that he was an enemy combatant, too, and subject to detention without criminal trial, just as aliens were. The Supreme Court plurality agreed that preventive detention even of citizens was permitted in the security situation.[144] They said that a citizen, like an alien, 'if released, would pose the same threat of returning to the front during the ongoing conflict'.[145]

---

140 Stevens J., 481–2. He cited a long line of English common law cases that allowed courts to exercise habeas jurisdiction over aliens within sovereign territory, but also persons in areas where the sovereign exercised practical control. Scalia J. in his dissent, however, argues that the latter cases only apply to citizens held in such places, not aliens.

141 He concluded that, based upon a somewhat ingenious view of more recent authority, all that federal courts required to be seized of jurisdiction was the presence of the custodian, not that of the detainee. See D. Golove, 'United States: the Bush Administration's "War on Terrorism" in the Supreme Court' (2005) 3 *I.J. Const. L* 128 at 133. He notes that the Court was confused about whether the case concerned extra-territorial jurisdiction to adjudicate or extra-territorial jurisdiction to prescribe laws. Given that the custodian was within the United States, jurisdiction to adjudicate was clear. In theory the degree of control over Guantanamo was irrelevant save to the extent that no local Cuban courts could provide a remedy. However, he explains why the court also sought to discuss the nature of Guantanamo itself so as to prepare the ground for the issue of extra-territorial application of the US law and the constitution in later cases. An assertion of jurisdiction without any law to adjudicate would be an empty exercise.

142 542 U.S. 507.

143 It is not clear why the transfer took place, but the suggestion is that the Cuban base was reserved for aliens.

144 This was a timid opinion which rather generously held that Congress had, in the general words of the Authorization for Use of Military Force ('AUMF'), given the executive power to detain even citizens during the emergency presented by September 11. This was a prerequisite to detention, because an earlier Act of Congress had required that congressional authority must be obtained to detain citizens (see 28 U.S.C. s. 2241). This was passed partly in recognition of the serious wrong committed against Japanese-Americans during World War Two (see *Korematsu* v. *U.S.*).

145 *Hamdi* v. *Rumsfeld*, 519.

This was reflected in the plurality's final step in deciding on what due process was appropriate in such cases. Although the Court spoke of 'the privilege that is American citizenship'[146] it decided that 'the full protections that accompany challenges to detentions in other settings may prove unworkable and inappropriate in the enemy-combatant setting'. Thus, even citizen-detainees like Hamdi could be subjected to special non-criminal procedures.[147] As Golove puts it, the plurality 'seems here to be relegating the citizen to precisely the same position as the enemy alien under the laws of war'.[148] Of course, 'relegation' of citizens can be viewed as an 'elevation' of aliens if the consequence is that both are entitled to some form of due process when held as enemy combatants, because both pose the same risk.[149] This kind of reasoning echoes that of the House of Lords in A, which required the government to fully accept the political consequences of extending emergency powers to citizens.

By contrast, the opinion of Scalia J., who had vehemently defended executive detention of aliens in Rasul, attacked such practices in his strong affirmation of a liberalism firmly tied to citizenship status. He was emphatic that any preventive detention was unconstitutional in terms powerfully defensive of the right to liberty: 'The very core of liberty secured by our Anglo-Saxon system of separated powers has been freedom from indefinite imprisonment at the will of the Executive.'[150] Thus when 'the government accuses a citizen of waging war against it, our constitutional tradition has been to prosecute him in federal court for treason or some other crime'.[151] He reiterated his 'war powers' view of Guantanamo in drawing a sharp distinction between citizens and aliens, saying that 'captured enemy combatants... have traditionally been detained until the cessation of hostilities and then released... That is probably an accurate description of wartime practice with respect to enemy aliens. The

---

146 Ibid., 532. Slip Opinion, 25.
147 The plurality suggests that citizen-detainees should know the factual basis of their classification and have a fair opportunity to rebut this. However, they allowed the use of hearsay evidence and a presumption in favour of the government's evidence. They also suggested that a military tribunal compliant with Art. 5 Geneva Convention might be adequate.
148 Golove, 'United States', 143.
149 Golove notes of aliens, in tones both desperate and naïve, that '[s]urely, they are not entitled to more than U.S. citizens, and it seems unlikely that they could be entitled to less than the tribunal provided for in Article 5 of the Geneva Convention and the long-standing military regulations' ibid.
150 Hamdi v. Rumsfeld, 554, Scalia J. (partly concurring, partly dissenting) Introduction.
151 Ibid.

tradition with respect to American citizens, however, has been quite different. Citizens aiding the enemy have been treated as traitors subject to the criminal process'.[152] On this basis, Scalia J. would have ordered the release of Hamdi, as he was detained without statutory authority.

In the next Supreme Court in the series, *Hamdan* v. *Rumsfeld*,[153] this time concerning habeas corpus brought by a foreign detainee at Guantanamo Bay, Scalia J. swapped sides again and dissented. The majority decision was significant because the Court held that it retained jurisdiction despite Congress having passed legislation following *Rasul* that apparently sought to undo this ruling. This stated that 'no court... shall have jurisdiction to hear or consider... an application for... habeas corpus filed by... an alien detained... at Guantanamo Bay'.[154] That there was an attempt to exclude habeas corpus for aliens only is significant given that the *Hamdi* decision upheld the principle of preventive detention of citizens too. Congress apparently did not wish or feel able to take away the rights of citizens to challenge detention, only aliens. Despite the legislative text, the Court ruled that the statute did not have retrospective effect so that detainees who already had challenges pending were entitled to proceed with them.[155] The effect of this ruling was dramatic.[156] As Scalia J. put it: 'The Court's interpretation transforms a provision abolishing jurisdiction over all Guantanamo-related habeas petitions into a provision that retains jurisdiction over cases sufficiently numerous to keep the courts busy for years to come.'[157] That the Court should take such a step in defence of aliens detained outside the mainland during a national security situation of this kind is an important indicator of their new-found status.

The most recent decision in *Boumediene*[158] confirms and extends the earlier cases in its recognition of the constitutional status of aliens brought to and held in *de facto* US territory. It is significant because the Court held that the *constitutional* right to habeas corpus (not simply the statutory right referred to in *Rasul*) applied to aliens held at Guantanamo. These

---

152 II.559.   153 542 U.S. 507.

154 Section 1005(e)(1) Detainee Treatment Act 2005.

155 Stevens J. delivering the majority decision at 5. He examined the legislative history and text, concluding that Congress had deliberately eschewed limited habeas corpus in pending cases. See T.M. Franck, 'Case Comment: United States: *Hamdan v Rumsfeld* – Presidential Power in Wartime' (2007) 5 *I.J. Const. L.* 380–8.

156 Apparently every detainee then held at Guantanamo Bay had filed habeas corpus either individually or as part of a class action.

157 Dissent at ID.   158 *Boumediene et al.* v. *Bush* 553 U.S. (2008).

aliens thus benefited from the Suspension Clause of the constitution.[159] Save for where a valid suspension had been effected, Congress could not therefore interfere with their right to challenge the legality of their detention in accordance with judicial standards appropriate in habeas corpus proceedings. This meant that legislation passed by Congress, in response to *Rasul* and *Hamdan*, retrospectively removing aliens' habeas corpus rights and replacing them with a system of military tribunals to determine their status as 'enemy combatants', was unconstitutional.[160] The statutory framework permitted only very limited review of the tribunal determinations by the ordinary courts. This was not equivalent to normal habeas corpus review in its ability to cure erroneous factual determinations.[161] This put detainees at risk of wrongly being declared enemy combatants which, 'given the consequence of error may be detention of persons for the duration of hostilities that may last a generation or more, is a risk too significant to ignore'.[162] The case did not, however, lay down what due process standards were appropriate in such cases, leaving that to further cases. Furthermore and importantly, the Supreme Court did not suggest that indefinite detention of aliens declared 'enemy combatants' after procedurally fair hearings would be unconstitutional.[163]

On one level, these cases are about narrow questions of the interpretation of US domestic law. The majority opinions generally avoid any discussion of international human rights law or broader questions over

159 Article I(9) cl.2: 'The Privilege of the Writ of Habeas Corpus shall not be suspended, unless when in Cases of Invasion or Rebellion the Public Safety may require it.' It appears to be assumed throughout that whatever threat was posed by Al Qaeda and the other groups targeted in the war on terrorism, they did not amount to an 'invasion or rebellion' upon which suspension of habeas corpus could be justified. The court reached the conclusion that the presence of an alien upon US sovereign territory was not a pre-condition for the exercise of constitutional habeas corpus rights. Rather, this arose by virtue of a functional and prudential analysis of degree of control exercised and the practical implications of asserting jurisdiction (Opinion, 15–34 and 64–8).

160 The first piece of legislation setting out the Combat Status Review Tribunal (CSRT) procedures was the Detainee Treatment Act 2005. The legislation purporting to remove the power to seek habeas corpus review for Guantanamo detainees was the Military Commissions Act 2006.

161 The closed and restricted nature of the Combat Status Review Tribunals (CSRT) meant there was a significant risk of erroneous findings and the limited powers of the review by the DC Court of Appeals to overturn the CSRT decisions or admit fresh evidence meant this was not removed (Opinion of the Court, 58–64).

162 *Ibid.*, 56–7.

163 'We do not address whether the President has authority to detain these petitioners nor do we hold that the writ must issue. These and other questions regarding the legality of the detention are to be resolved in the first instance by the District Court' (Opinion, 2).

the status of aliens in general.[164] This is in stark contrast to the House of Lords approach in its decision on internment in *A* and reflects both US legal traditions and a desire to rule on a narrow basis.[165] However, as Fletcher[166] pertinently observes, when reviewing these Supreme Court cases, the differing opinions illustrate differing conceptions of the status of aliens as against citizens. In words echoing the opinion of Lord Bingham in the *A v. Secretary of State* case, he summarizes the modern conception emerging from human rights law as:

> The central idea in international as well as domestic constitutional law has become the person, the human being abstracted from membership in a political community. Citizenship in one state or another no longer determines legal standing.[167]

By contrast, the more traditional view, rooted in the law of war (and immigration law, we might add), sees 'nationality and citizenship to be critical markers for the distinction between friends and enemies at war'.[168] This was exemplified by the switch in the opinions of Scalia J. Fletcher says, however, '[e]mphasizing citizenship as the relevant variable flouts the general tendency in modern legal thinking away from citizenship and toward personhood as the condition for bearing rights'.[169] The rational reason for this is derived from the fact that 'in the realm of criminal justice and of detention on the basis of predicted dangerousness there is no apparent difference between citizens and aliens'. To draw such distinctions between resident aliens and citizens within the United States would breach the equal protection clause of the constitution. With this in mind, Fletcher concludes that the Supreme Court in *Rasul*, *Hamdi* and *Hamdan* (and now *Boumediene*) found a way 'of affirming the trend in contemporary jurisprudence away from the rights of citizens and toward the rights of persons'.[170] Similarly Dworkin, endorsing the case-law, argued that

---

164 The major exception is *Hamdan*, where the majority invoke Common Article 3 to the Geneva Conventions, as well as domestic military justice codes. This is, however, in the context of conventions which inherently distinguish between aliens and nationals. The ICCPR does not appear in any of the judgments.

165 See W.M. Reisman, '*Rasul v Bush*: a Failure to Apply International Law' (2004) 2(4) *J. Int. Crim. Just.* 973–80. More broadly see C. Booth and M. Du Plessis, 'Home Alone? The US Supreme Court and International and Transnational Judicial Learning' (2005) 2 *EHRLR* 127.

166 G.P. Fletcher, 'Guantanamo Disentangled? The US Supreme Court Steps In: Citizenship and Personhood in the Jurisprudence of War: Hamdi, Padilla and the Detainees in Guantanamo Bay' (2004) 2(4) *J. Int. Crim. Just.* 953–66.

167 *Ibid.*, 954.   168 *Ibid.*   169 *Ibid.*, 960.   170 *Ibid.*, 965.

'America owes its duty to respect fundamental human rights, including the right not to be imprisoned unjustly, to all people who come under its authority; and there can be no moral justification for discriminating against foreigners'.[171]

The extent to which this equality of status is borne out will depend upon the ultimate nature of the substantive rights to be accorded to aliens to challenge their detention. These remain unresolved to date, although *Boumediene* suggested some elements of due process that cannot be taken away by legislation.[172] On this issue, other commentators have sought to argue for the continuation of a clear distinction between citizen and alien. Thus Fallon and Meltzer argue, in one sense uncontroversially, that 'the Constitution is a continuing compact among the American people, established and accepted principally for the benefit of Americans'.[173] They thus favour high levels of due process for citizens akin to criminal safeguards, whilst aliens held on *de facto* US territory should only benefit from 'fundamental' constitutional rights.[174] This apparently plausible distinction turns out to be unsustainable. Why should the risk of an erroneous decision, leading to potentially life imprisonment, be any more acceptable in the case of an alien?

Conclusions on US security detention

It is important not to overstate the significance of the decisions from *Rasul* to *Boumediene*. The constitutional standards appropriate to test legality of detention have yet to be finally determined.[175] Detainees who have been released secured this as a result of political engagement resulting in diplomatic agreement from other nations to accept them, not by

---

171 R. Dworkin, 'Why It Was a Great Victory' (2008) 55(13) *New York Review of Books*, 5.
172 See Opinion of the Court, 58–64. The Court suggests that the review body must be able to consider new evidence not put before the tribunal, and that it should not be confined to reviewing whether the CSRT acted in accordance with the relevant military procedure regulations.
173 R.H. Fallon and D.J. Meltzer, 'Habeas Corpus Jurisdiction, Substantive Rights, and the War on Terror', (2007) 120 *Harv. L.R.* 2029, 2083.
174 *Ibid.*, 2094–5.
175 The adequacy of the CSRT was rejected in *Boumediene*. Even when 'enemy combatant' status is established, the question of indefinite detention will arise to be determined again. On the trial procedures for detainees actually prosecuted see C. Bradley, 'The Military Commissions Act, Habeas Corpus and the Geneva Conventions' (2007) *Duke Law School Working Paper Series* 96, who argues that there are aspects of the review hearings (the admission of coerced evidence and denial of classified information) that may breach due process standards.

court order.[176] Nevertheless, from the perspective of aliens, whether held under immigration or military powers, the implications may prove to be important. Actions taken in the 'war on terrorism' have caused the courts to begin to revisit the historically low legal status given to unadmitted aliens. It is significant that the Supreme Court has tried quite hard to cautiously fill gaps in the jurisdictional reach of habeas corpus, even in a time of national crisis. The Supreme Court decision in *Boumediene* goes further because it rejects the view, first laid down in the immigration indefinite detention case of *Mezei*, that the only due process available to unadmitted aliens is that given by Congress. It may prove inconsistent to continue to reject constitutional due process in immigration cases after *Boumediene*.[177]

This said, substantive, as opposed to procedural, protection is still some way off. None of the cases suggest that indefinite detention is unconstitutional in principle. Certainly, as the years go by, indefinite preventive detention without trial for aliens is a continuing source of embarrassment to US law. This looks anomalous, given the persistent theme within the majority decisions that, in the context of the struggle against terrorism at least, aliens and citizens may not present wholly different legal categories. It is important to recall that unadmitted Cubans were detained for over twenty years in US detention facilities without trial following the *Mariel* flotilla. Indefinite detention is neither new nor constitutionally heterodox and it seems unlikely that aliens properly found to be enemy combatants will be ordered released by any federal court.[178]

What about those detainees who are eventually cleared of terrorist links but cannot be repatriated or sent to third countries due to practical or legal constraints? So far the courts have stuck to the *Mezei* principle and refused them any constitutional right of release into US territory.[179] Only

---

176 See C. Stafford-Smith, 'Getting Your Friends in Trouble' (2006) 3(1) *Muslim World J. of Human Rts* 6.

177 Neuman, 'Closing the Guantanamo Loophole', who argues that US law should apply in order to avoid a lawless enclave.

178 Scalia J. in his dissent in *Boumediene* claims that thirty aliens declared non-combatants and released by the military from Guantanamo Bay had gone back to recommence military action on behalf of radical Islamic groups (Scalia J. joined by Roberts C.J., Thomas and Alito J.J., 3–4).

179 See now the US Court of Appeals for the District of Columbia Circuit decision in No. 08–5424 *Kieymba* v. *Obama*, judgment of 18 Feb. 2009, in which it held that Chinese Uighur detainees taken and held at Guantanamo Bay detention centre could not be released by court order into the United States *even where the government refused to file habeas returns and accepted that it had no power to detain the persons concerned*. The Court accepted

the Supreme Court can resolve the issue, but highly visible indefinite detention in facilities on the mainland United States or at Guantanamo Bay for non-dangerous aliens looks increasingly untenable. This will ultimately raise the question of granting aliens some form of status after admission to the United States as an alternative to detaining them. Judge-led review of the status of aliens arising from the anti-terrorism cases may have served to increase political pressure upon the government to seek alternative solutions but it does not dictate the form these will take, if any.

Overall conclusions

The recent use of detention as an anti-terrorism and security measure in the United Kingdom and United States has very largely been targeted at aliens. This has forced some deep questions to the surface regarding the relevance of alienage. The new situation has produced, as we have seen, practices supporting ever longer periods of preventive detention of aliens. This was novel as it occurred outside of a declared war. Detention of aliens (rather than citizens) presents governments with a more favourable political calculus when attempting to show strength in the face of security threats.[180] By contrast, it is clear that severe political problems may be presented for governments who allow aliens adjudged to be dangerous to remain at large – even in liberal democracies ostensibly committed to civil liberties. The risk of an alien, most of all one not entitled to be in the country, committing a violent crime is extremely worrying to those engaged in modern political life. The US and UK governments have sought to rely on formal 'immigration' powers to detain on an indefinite basis where there was no real prospect of expulsion.[181] Detainees become political pawns as governments try to use diplomatic means to pressure

that the government could refuse to admit them to the United States whilst it negotiated for other countries to take them. They were not 'enemy combatants' and therefore there was no lawful basis to continue their detention under statutory or prerogative power. The government said nevertheless that they were potentially dangerous, without adducing evidence adequate to support this. Having been abducted they had, of course, not applied for entry into the United States under immigration law and the government said they would be refused entry if they did. The Court agreed, by a majority, that *Mezei* was controlling even in this scenario.

180 J.H. Marks, '9/11 + 3/11 +\7/7=? What Counts in Counterterrorism' [2006] 37 *Colum. H.R.L. Rev.* 103 and Gross, 'Chaos and Rules:' discuss the psychological factors present amongst the public that sustain such policies.

181 As Simpson puts it in relation to terrorists, 'a figure ... who sits outside these two categories: not quite an enemy entitled, after all, to certain protections under the Geneva Conventions and Protocols, nor quite a criminal entitled to due process and

countries into taking such persons. This becomes increasingly untenable, however, particularly in the case of terrorists, because the problem has been defined as a global one. Deportation does not remove the alleged threat, it merely moves it, freeing it to re-emerge.

The human rights bodies and courts faced with this new practice had a choice; they could either embrace this 'war-time' or 'immigration' argument to support alien detention or they could reject it. They have largely chosen the latter course, influenced both by basic due process arguments but also, in the context of aliens, emerging non-discrimination principles. The reality that the struggle against international terrorism does not resemble conventional war and could last for a generation, was no doubt, a key factor. The basic human rights framework was well understood, but there had to be a period of reflection in light of the post-2001 security situation. However since then, most human rights bodies and opinion has stressed the continued relevance of the established framework.[182] Thus, for example, the Working Group on Arbitrary Detention spoke without distinction between citizens and aliens when it said:

> The use of 'administrative detention' under public security legislation, migration laws or other related administrative law, resulting in a deprivation of liberty for unlimited time or for very long periods without effective judicial oversight, as a means to detain persons suspected of involvement in terrorism or other crimes, is not compatible with international human rights law. The Working Group therefore recommends that all States review their legislation and practice so as to ensure that persons suspected of criminal activity or any other activities giving rise under domestic law to deprivation of liberty are in fact afforded the guarantees applicable in criminal proceedings.[183]

civil rights . . . If a criminal is at war with a particular society, and an enemy is at war with a particular state, then we might suggest that this new (or revivified) character is at war with everyone or with international society or the international community', Law, War and Crime, 171. He overlooks, however, the immigration category as an alternative box within which to place a detainee. This is now a category with certain legal limits to it imposed by the cases discussed.

182 P. Hoffman, 'Human Rights and Terrorism' (2004) 26 H.R.Q. 932. Many commentators have argued that the use of arbitrary detention is in fact counter-productive in the fight against terrorism: D.P. Forsythe, 'United States Policy toward Enemy Detainees in the "War on Terrorism"' [2006] 28 H.R.Q. 465; D. Kerwin, 'The Use and Misuse of "National Security" Rationale in Crafting U.S. Refugee and Immigration Policies' (2005) 17 Int. J. Refugee L. 749.

183 Commission on Human Rights, Sixty-first Session, Report of WGAD, Developments concerning deprivation of liberty as a measure in countering terrorism, E/CN.4/2005/6 1 December 2004, 77.

As Dworkin put it in more broad philosophical terms in a paper critical of anti-terrorism measures taken post-11 September 2001:

> Amongst the most fundamental of all moral principles is the principle of shared humanity: that every human life has a distinct and equal inherent value. This principle is the indispensable premise of the idea of human rights, that is, the rights people have just in virtue of being human, and it is therefore an indispensable premise of an international moral order. Various international covenants like the Universal Declaration of Human Rights of the United Nations and the Geneva Conventions are statutory attempts to codify that basic moral principle into particular rules that can be made binding as a matter of domestic and international law.[184]

The decision in *A* v. *Secretary of State for the Home Department* represents a real milestone in apparently endorsing the equal rights of aliens to be free from executive detention, even during periods of emergency. This approach reflects and was intended to embrace the basic international human rights norms reconfirmed even in the face of the struggle against terrorism. It also confirms Dworkin's appeal to the fundamental equal value of every person, including aliens, regardless of immigration or other status.[185] We can also see that the enduring power of the rule of law has provided a very powerful rejoinder to governments. As Dauvergne notes: 'The desire of states to move away from rule of law principles proves a test of their resilience . . . [t]he attention to indefinite detention is dragging migration law to the center of the legal stage. It is indisputable that these are the key cases of our times: they define "us" as "civilized" nations and peoples.'[186]

Given the constitutional history of aliens in the United States, it is not surprising that the position there is less clear. There has been no clear

---

184 See R. Dworkin, 'Terror and the Attack on Civil Liberties' (2003) 50(17) *New York Review of Books.*

185 Of course, aliens are treated differently than citizens for many purposes. Their entry and residence can be made conditional upon working or residing in certain places and not claiming social security. They can be deported if they fail to observe these conditions. These powers are those of immigration control because they seek to regulate the terms upon which migration takes place, if at all. They are backed by migration measures in the form of expulsion. But where this consequence does not take place because of the failure or inability of the authorities, migrants are left in an odd position. They are not wanted and yet they remain within the jurisdiction. Should they suffer loss of fundamental rights simply because they are unwanted aliens? Executive detention is simply one such harsh measure; others might include denial of the right to work and to welfare, possibly resulting in destitution. We shall explore this issue more in Ch. 6 below.

186 C. Dauvergne, *Making People Illegal: Migration Laws for Global Times* Cambridge University Press, 2008, 117.

statement that aliens have an equal liberty right reflecting international law. Immigration detention can be very lengthy and may be indefinite in national security cases by virtue of statutory power and lack of constitutional rights.[187] The decisions of the Supreme Court on the Guantanamo cases gave a right to due process review of preventive detention. It is not certain that they will be any more successful in asserting rights to be released than aliens previously held outside the United States or at its borders.[188] The international human rights monitoring bodies consider the detentions to be clear breaches of numerous human rights obligations, but this cannot prevail over domestic US law.[189]

Recent events may be moving towards an approach which considers the objective nature of government action rather than attempting to rely upon the nebulous concept of aliens' lesser constitutional status. Such arguments about status lead ultimately to arbitrary power being exercised over aliens based upon circular reasoning lacking any firm foundations. They more readily reflect political calculations which suggest that 'policies that impose burdens on others – and therefore appear less costly financially and politically – usually involve interference with civil liberties, in particular the rights and liberties of non-citizens'.[190] Alien detention is

---

187 See the *Zadvydas* qualification which held that, although ordinary criminals who had entered the United States could not be held in preventive detention indefinitely, national security cases might be different. See also s. 402 US PATRIOT Act 2001. In relation to unadmitted aliens, see the *Mezei* decision and its progeny effectively putting all aliens, whether national security cases or not, outside the constitution.

188 It is, of course, arguable that immigration control detention secures the goal of preventing detainees from entering the country. This is a different goal from the holding at Guantanamo, which relates to national security.

189 See Commission on Human Rights, *Situation of Detainees at Guantanamo Bay*, E/CN.4/2006/120, 27 February 2006 in which Special Rapporteurs for each of the Commission's mandates provided a damning assessment. See paras 17–33, where the Special Rapporteurs conclude that detention without trial breaches Art. 9 and Art. 14 ICCPR. They concluded that detainees captured in the war against the Taliban might have been lawfully held under the Geneva Conventions for a period during hostilities that had passed. Detainees found elsewhere were entitled to full protection under ICCPR Arts 9 and 14. As a matter of fact, he concludes their detention is to secure information rather than prevention of further terrorist attacks. Thus he does not address a critical point about the legitimacy of preventive detention squarely. Preventive detention was something that we have seen was endorsed in the context of immigration proceedings in *A v. Australia*. Jackson poignantly recalls that in the 1950s and 1960s a large number of scholars, judges and others in the United States fell behind proposals to create a United Nations writ of habeas corpus. This was in the context of the detention of dissidents in Eastern Europe who were beyond domestic legal assistance: V.C. Jackson, 'World Habeas Corpus' (2006) 91 *Cornell L. Rev.*, 303.

190 Marks, '9/11 + 3/11 + 7/7=?'.

of great symbolic value. Governments can be seen to be taking execu-tive action against a threat without waiting for the slow and uncertain workings of the criminal justice system.[191] They can also take such action without facing the legal constraints and *political* damage that imposing internment and other emergency measures on citizens would bring.

In summary, we can see that in relation to detention of aliens pursuant to anti-terrorism, there may be an emerging view held amongst both courts and human rights bodies, that the executive must follow well-established practices under criminal law or humanitarian law. Persons detained must either be prosecuted fairly and speedily or designated as prisoners of war. In these models executive detention must end, at some definable time independent of the executive will, with conviction, acquittal or peace. The immigration model (or the 'enemy combatant' model) should not become a third way when, in practice, it results in aliens being subject to lengthy or indefinite detention without trial.[192]

The link to immigration control begins to look weak in such cases when the alien is *de facto* or *de jure* undeportable. In these circumstances, incar-ceration may be viewed as punishment without trial. Ongoing detention achieves security objectives, not immigration goals. The obvious point, sometimes overlooked, is that keeping aliens *within* a state by means of detention cannot be viewed as a measure of immigration regulation. Put simply, the control of immigrants does not necessarily amount to immigration control. Only measures that secure the physical expulsion of aliens (as opposed to their seclusion from the community) are truly immigration measures.

---

191 See C. Sunstein, *Laws of Fear*, Oxford University Press, 2007, Ch. 9; D. Moeckli, *Human Rights and Non-discrimination in the 'War on Terror'*, Oxford University Press, 2008, Ch. 4.

192 'Rights would be worthless – and the idea of a right incomprehensible – unless respecting rights meant taking some risks. We can and must try to limit those risks, but some risk will remain. It may be that we would be marginally more secure if we decided to care nothing for the human rights of anyone else' Dworkin, 'Terror and the Attack on Civil Liberties'.

6

Global migration and the politics of immigration detention

Introduction: the new detention as politics or as law?

The last thirty years have revealed a distinct politics of immigration detention which was not apparent in earlier periods of migration control. As we
have seen, although restrictions on migration have been long standing,
the scale and duration of detention was previously limited. Apart from
during wartime or national security scares, in practice, detainees were
not held for long periods and there was little impetus to construct large
permanent detention spaces. Whilst deportation and exclusion policy
were debated, detention rarely attracted serious concerns. This has now
all changed. Modern practices tell us much about the politics of migration in contemporary societies. Detention reveals itself to be of a highly
political nature, having arisen largely outside the realm of precise moral
and legal reasoning. This politicization of detention has been expressed
in arbitrary practices that cut across liberal principles of the rule of law,
equality and respect for individual liberty.

This will lead us to assess the intimate and dialectical relationship
between law and politics. The treatment of migrants is an important
test of the extent to which political actors within modern democracies
have been willing and able to consistently pursue non-liberal methods.
It has long been clear that contemporary immigration politics inhabits
an uncertain and shifting space between liberal and non-liberal ideas.
The liberal tradition finds expression in the *legal* values of respect for
individual autonomy and reason. Expression of such ideas would see
detainees being treated according to precise legal standards, for example,
as criminal suspects or prisoners of war. Such standards reflect well-
established legal and moral principles over pure political calculation.
By contrast, where mainly *political* factors determine how persons are
detained there are few legal standards on view. We may consider such
immigrants as 'emergency detainees' or 'unwanted persons'. The same

may be said where detainees are held in special zones, deliberately created by the political branch to exist outside the reach of the law.

We have seen that the modern detention network has grown and developed largely under the impetus of political action, not legal logic. Courts have generally legitimated these developments by following a narrow, non-intrusive version of the rule of law. Nevertheless, a more critical politics of resistance to the illiberal dimension of the new detention has been long standing from within civil society and increasingly so at international level.[1] More recently, as the contradiction between the ideal of a liberal legal order and the arbitrary and politicized nature of immigration detention has become more obvious, we have seen more courts themselves beginning to question the system. Mass administrative detention, created for instrumental and political ends, put migrants almost beyond the reach of the legal order and thus created a crisis for the ideal of the rule of law. That this took place within the citadel of legal liberalism, respect for individual liberty, is all the more striking.

Liberalism, justice and the problem of migrants

The starting point of this chapter is to consider why it is that the modern politics of migration has produced some very illiberal outcomes in relation to detention. One answer will look to the political process itself. This is considered below in more detail. This section, however, argues that endemic problems within liberal political theory about how to conceptualize migration have also contributed to the malaise. As a result, whilst driven by political pragmatism, the new detention has found its path largely free of obstacles from within the liberal political tradition.

As we have seen, this was not always so. To modern readers, early writers on political theory in the classical period often displayed surprisingly strong cosmopolitan tendencies. Drawing no clear distinctions between constitutional law, international law and morality, free migration came to be viewed during this period as a public good, if not an absolute right.[2] The emerging belief in the mutual benefits of international trade also

---

1 See now, for example, the creation of the organization the Global Detention Project, which aims to measure the growth and development of immigration detention practices globally, promote scholarship in the field and to encourage accountability and transparency in the treatment of detainees. Details at www.globaldetentionproject.org.

2 D. Galloway, 'Liberalism, Globalism, and Immigration' (1993) 18 *Queen's L.J.* 266 discusses the early classical writers in some detail.

contributed to economic migrants' status.[3,4] The distinction between 'aliens' and 'citizens' appeared to be diminishing outside wartime. However, by the late nineteenth century, legal and political ideas toward migration had changed with the rise of 'sovereignty' as the bedrock principle. On the international plane, the sovereign equality of states was the basic 'rule' of international society rather than any higher set of natural rights or norms of international justice. In international law it was accepted that self-interest would govern the interactions between states. In political terms, aliens and migration had come to be viewed as just another source of tension between nations. Regulation of borders became an essential aspect of modern statehood – an expression of this new sovereignty over the internal legal space of a nation. The twin concepts of sovereignty/alienage largely erased discussions of justice across borders.

Political ideas have only relatively recently re-emerged from behind the barricade of sovereignty. Before that, modern theorists often simply assumed that borders were closed.[5] The complex modern politics of migration has more recently led to a deeper examination of the nature of

---

3 This resulted in increasing guarantees for aliens who sought to trade with other nations – a kind of constitutionalism across borders. Schmitt puts it thus: 'In the idea of a free global economy law not only the overcoming of state-political borders, but also, as an essential precondition, a standard for the internal constitutions of individual member states of this order of international law; it presupposed that every member state would establish a minimum of constitutional order. This minimum standard consisted of the freedom – the separation – of the state-public sphere from the private sphere, above all, from the non-state sphere of property, trade, and economy.' C. Schmitt, *The Nomos of the Earth in the International Law of the Jus Publicum Europaeum*, New York: Telos Press, 2006, 209.

4 'The dualistic separation of international law and constitutional law is here, as in other cases, only a matter of façade. In reality, a common constitutional standard overcame the division between internal and external that appeared to be so sharp throughout the nineteenth century and up until the Great War (1914–1918)' Schmitt, *ibid*. He is referring here in particular to the fact that an occupying power in a European land war accepted that they did not become sovereign and undertook to allow the institutions of private property to continue without attempting to confiscate them or incorporate them into the attacking state's economy. The Hague Conventions on the laws of war were a natural result.

5 Despite its modern origins in the eighteenth-century revolutionary period, political theory has only come of age since the publication of John Rawls' work *A Theory of Justice* in 1971: J. Rawls, *A Theory of Justice*, Cambridge, MA: Harvard University Press, 1971. Rawls himself did not address cross-border migration issues in his work in any detail. In a later short work he considered international law and justice, concluding against principles of international redistributive justice: J. Rawls, *The Law of Peoples*, Cambridge, MA: Harvard University Press, 1999.

states' obligations to foreigners.[6,7] Within this debate it is useful to distinguish between 'impartialists' and 'partialists', as these terms are used by Gibney.[8] By impartialists we mean those political theorists that do not make a sharp distinction between citizens and aliens in relation to theories of justice or ethics. They take the view that, *prima facie*, there are universal ethical values that apply across borders and regardless of nationality.[9] Partialists, by contrast, take the view that nation states have distinct political and moral significance, which means that the interests of citizens are, *prima facie*, more important than those of foreigners. States must have largely unfettered powers to deny foreigners access to the national territory where they deem this contrary to the interests of citizens.

Although the division appears to be sharp, in fact both agree that immigration controls may be necessary and both agree that controls must not be blatantly discriminatory, for example on racial or gender grounds, or serve as tools of deliberate oppression. They have not, however, explored greatly what level of hardship may be imposed on 'outsiders' for the sake of achieving any given level of control over borders. This failure has led to a dangerous gap in liberal thinking which has been filled with both political opportunism by governments and instrumental logic on the part of their bureaucracies.

Impartialist accounts: cosmopolitanism and the equality of persons

The idea that states are morally wrong to restrict migration at all (or in the ways that they do) is usually based upon a cosmopolitan account of international justice which holds *individuals* and not *nations or states* to be the fundamental unit of moral concern.[10] As Buchanan puts it, '[a]t the

6 For an early pioneering work see C. Beitz, *Political Theory and International Relations*, Princeton University Press, 1979.

7 S. Caney, *Justice Beyond Borders: A Global Political Theory*, Oxford University Press, 2005; T. Pogge, *Realizing Rawls*, London and Ithaca: Cornell University Press, 1989.

8 M.J. Gibney, *The Ethics and Politics of Asylum*, Cambridge University Press, 2004, Chs 1 and 2. See also S. Mulhall and A. Swift, *Liberals and Communitarians*, 2nd edn, Oxford: Blackwell, 1992, for a detailed review of the debate.

9 B. Ackerman, *Social Justice in the Liberal State*, New Haven, CT: Yale University Press, 1980, argues that migration should be free up to the point in which it damages the 'liberal democratic conversation'.

10 B. Barry, 'International Society from a Cosmopolitan Perspective', in D. Maple and T. Nardin (eds), *International Society: Diverse Ethical Perspectives*, Princeton University Press, 1998, 146. As Pogge puts it, cosmopolitanism has three elements: Individualism 'the ultimate units of concern are human beings, or persons – rather than say, family lines,

heart of moral cosmopolitanism is the idea that human beings are in some fundamental sense equal'. Therefore, rather than viewing sovereignty as the key value in international law and politics, this idea of the moral equality of persons 'requires us to embrace a cosmopolitan view of international law, rejecting both the idea that states are moral persons and the position that states are merely institutional resources for their own peoples'.[11]

Building on this, Carens argues that opening borders will best promote the key liberal value of individual autonomy. Barriers to free movement impede both individual choice and social, political and economic equality.[12] He likens the creation of national citizenships to a privileged feudal status in medieval times and concludes that this arbitrary fact, when translated into restrictions on cross-border movement, determines key aspects of the destiny of persons. Modern states contradict the liberal principle of equality because they treat 'freedom of movement within a state as a moral imperative and freedom of movement across state borders as merely a matter of political discretion'.[13] Utilitarians, such as Singer, agree that modern migration controls are harmful because, from an empirical view, they probably diminish human welfare. He contends that '[t]he current orthodoxy rests on vague and usually un-argued assumptions about the community's right to determine its membership'. By giving 'equal consideration to all interests' we would support much more open borders that would allow relatively poor people to improve their situations, rather than simply protecting the relatively wealthy.[14]

tribes, ethnic ... nations or states'. Universality – 'the status of ultimate unit of concern attaches to every living human being equally – not merely some subset'. Generality – 'this special status has global force. Persons are the ultimate units of concern for everyone – not only for their compatriots ... ' T. Pogge, 'Cosmopolitanism and Sovereignty' (1992) 103 *Ethics* 48–76 at 48.

11 A. Buchanan, *Justice, Legitimacy and Self-Determination: Moral Foundations of International Law*, Oxford University Press, 2004, 87; C. Beitz, *Political Theory and International Relations*, Princeton University Press, 1999 (with Afterword), 215.

12 J. Carens, 'Migration and Morality: A Liberal Egalitarian Perspective', in B. Barry and R.E. Goodin (eds), *Free Movement: Ethical Issues in the Transnational Migration of People and of Money*, Pennsylvania State University Press, 1992, 26. O. O'Neill, *Bounds of Justice*, Cambridge University Press, 2000 and J.H. Carens, 'Aliens and Citizens: the Case for Open Borders', in R. Cohen (ed.), *Theories of Migration*, Cheltenham: Edward Elgar, 1996.

13 Carens, 'Migration and Morality', 28.

14 P. Singer, *Practical Ethics*, 2nd edn, Cambridge University Press, 1993, 256. See also P. Singer, *One World*, New Haven, CT: Yale University Press, 2002, 169–70. S. Scheffler, 'Immigration and the Significance of Culture' (2007) 35(2) *Philosophy and Public Affairs*, 93.

Other impartialists focus upon the artificial and historically determined nature of borders which cannot be morally justified. This focus upon the earth as a shared and limited resource has a long pedigree.[15] Kant himself identified a right of temporary sojourn based partly upon the 'common possession of the surface of the earth'.[16] Gibney says that '[t]his territorial dimension makes the state fundamentally different from other entities often considered analogous in their right to determine membership and exclude outsiders'.[17] In the end, if people are to lead autonomous lives, they need safe territory to go to, but this territory is now completely policed by the interlocking nation state system. Without reasonable access being granted, individuals may find themselves with no means of pursuing freely chosen lives.

In summary, the impartialist position considers borders to be both morally insignificant or, at the very least, overrated.[18] To the extent that migration controls are based purely upon a preference for citizens over foreigners, they are illiberal. Cosmopolitans argue for an important presumption; the liberal state seeking to restrict migration has a burden

15 This was a kind of natural law right, which, although qualified by the creation of states, revived in times of dire need based upon necessity. As Vattel reasoned: 'Banishment and exile do not take away from a man his human personality, nor consequently his right to live somewhere or other. He holds this right from nature or rather from the Author of nature, who has intended the earth to be man's dwelling place.' See Gibney, *The Ethics and Politics of Asylum*, 38.

16 I. Kant, 'Perpetual Peace', in Lewis White Beck (ed., and trans.), *On History* Indianapolis and New York: Library of Liberal Arts, 1957, 85. See S. Benhabib, *The Rights of Others*, Cambridge University Press, 2004, Ch. 2, who shows how his actual reasoning is ambiguous being perhaps based upon a right to associate with others.

17 Gibney, *The Ethics and Politics of Asylum*, 38. The international law rule that a person must be admitted to their own state provides in principle an answer to this concern. Therefore every person should have at least one state in which to reside. In practice their state of citizenship may be dysfunctional, or it may have denaturalized them, refused to accept them back or may itself wish to harm them. They may have no safe home to go to.

18 See for broader perspectives drawing upon all strands of argument against migration control T. Hayter, *Open Borders: the Case against Immigration Controls*, London: Pluto Press, 2000; also G. Kukthas, 'The Case for Open Immigration', in A. Cohen (ed.), *Contemporary Debates in Applied Ethics*, Oxford: Blackwell, 2005; K.R. Johnson, 'Open Borders' (2003) 51 *UCLA L. Rev.*, 193. Not all cosmopolitans believe that free migration has an important role in securing international justice or welfare, but their concerns are based upon practical issues. For example, Pogge does not think that migration is an efficient way to practise cosmopolitanism when compared to international wealth transfers. T. Pogge, 'Migration and Poverty', in V. Bader (ed.), *Citizenship and Exclusion*, New York: St Martin's Press, 1997. He also is unusual in that he does not think refugees have any greater claim to enter than the poor: 'Being imprisoned for one's beliefs is not, in general, worse than working 16-hour days while being permanently hungry' (16).

of justification based upon cogent reasons which must not derive from discrimination against foreigners. Crucially, however, for present purposes, even impartialists accept that there are legitimate grounds for controlling migration. They usually refer to 'public order' or 'public security' or sometimes the preservation of 'liberal democracy'. These coalesce around a concept of 'security' that has been hugely neglected, forming what Waldron rightly calls 'a disgraceful gap in political philosophy'.[19] This gap is a weakness in the liberal legal order, for as Schmitt points out, at first sight, these exceptions appear to be quite 'indeterminate' concepts which are not readily capable of resolution through the legal process itself.[20] Rather, they appear open to primarily *political* interpretation. The great likelihood is that such political evaluations of what 'security' requires will err towards imposing discriminatory or disproportionate burdens on aliens as 'protection' for citizens.[21]

Partialist accounts: the power to determine membership of the liberal nation

The perspective of modern states in relation to migration policy can be described as essentially partialist; the admission of migrants takes place at the discretion of the receiving state. There is little question of any 'right' of migrants to be on their territory at all, much less an equal right to that possessed by citizens. Policy is set by reference to the interests of the

---

19 J. Waldron, *Terror, Torture and Trade-offs: Philosophy for the White House*, Oxford University Press, 2010, 160.

20 Schmitt noted that increasing use of 'situations' not 'rules' in legislation (for example tests of good morals, cases of necessity, public security and order) rendered obsolete the illusion of a law that would be able *a priori* to regulate all cases: 'Today there are now only "indeterminate" juridical concepts ... The entire application of law thus lies between Scylla and Charybdis. The way forward seems to condemn us to a shoreless sea and to move us even farther from the firm ground of juridical certainty and adherence to the law, which at the same time is still the ground of the judges independence. Yet the way backward, which leads towards the formalistic superstition of law which was recognised as senseless and superseded long ago, is not worthy of consideration.' C Schmitt, *State, Movement, People*, Washington: Plutarch Press, 2001, 43–4.

21 Waldron calls attention to this danger when he says 'we should think in terms of a distributive matrix of liberty or civil liberties, uneven across different people or categories of people ... facing a distributive matrix of security, uneven across different people or categories of people ... we can begin thinking like that – thinking in terms of *whose* liberty, *whose* security is being enhanced or diminished – then we will have made some progress'. Waldron, *Terror, Torture and Trade-offs*, 161.

citizens as perceived by the government. This perspective is consistent with social contract ideas in which government must act as the agent of its own citizens and failure to pursue only their interests breaches the fiduciary duty to them.[22] The democratic variant sees the state as enjoined to carry out the democratic will and this could include, but need not, respect for the interests of outsiders.[23] This clearly suffers from the defect of allowing citizens to use migration control measures to inflict serious harm on non-citizens in their midst.

Walzer attempts to provide a richer justification for border controls that goes beyond majority rule.[24] His broad concern is to move away from abstract justice towards a notion of justice that is based upon concrete institutions[25] and cultures.[26] He argues that communities can only arise and flourish if there is a means of controlling access to them: 'the restraint of entry serves to defend the liberty and welfare, the politics and culture of a group of people committed to their common life'.[27] Without restrictions on access, there could be no just institutions, because

---

22 D. Held, 'Democratic City-states to a Cosmopolitan Order?' (1992) 40 *Polit. Studies* 10, 18.

23 The democratic liberals accept that equality is the guiding principle but that the 'demos' must first be determined. This requires inequality through the creation of citizenship laws which determine who is included.'Democracy is rule by the people, but someone must first decide who the people are.' See B. Jordan and F. Duvell, *Irregular Migration: the Dilemmas of Transnational Mobility*, London: Edward Elgar, 2002.

Some argue that there is too ready access to citizenship such that responsibilities and ties of community are undermined. See P.H. Schuck and R.M. Smith, *Citizenship without Consent: Illegal Aliens in the American Polity*, New Haven, CT: Yale University Press, 1985; D. Jacobson, *Rights without Borders*, Baltimore, MD: Johns Hopkins University Press, 1996.

24 M. Walzer, *Spheres of Justice: A Defence of Pluralism and Equality*, Oxford: Basil Blackwell, 1985.

25 See also Dworkin's view that '[T]he best defence of political legitimacy . . . is to be found not in the hard terrain of contracts or duties of justice or obligations of fair play that might hold among strangers, where philosophers have hoped to find it, but in the more fertile ground of fraternity, community and their attendant obligations. Political association, like family and friendship and other forms of association more local and intimate, is in itself pregnant of obligation.' R. Dworkin, *Law's Empire*, London: Fontana, 1986, 206.

26 In this sense his account of justice is rooted in particular communities and he has been identified as a 'communitarian'. For a discussion of the debates between liberals and communitarians see Mulhall and Swift, *Liberals and Communitarians*, 2nd edn. This does not have migration at its centre but rather focuses upon broader issues dividing Kantian and other ways of thinking about justice.

27 *Ibid.*, 39.

membership choices reflect 'the deepest meaning of self-determination. Without them, there could not be *communities of character*, historically stable, ongoing associations of men and women with some special commitment to one another and some special sense of their common life'.[28,29]

This is a powerful argument, but it is one that has been distorted to support modern immigration controls. Walzer's case is really directed at preserving the political character of a nation and therefore centres on citizenship policy. It says nothing explicit about border control. Acquiring citizenship depends on an assessment of capacity and entitlement to fully participate in the political, economic and social life of the community. A person crossing the border does not become a citizen. Mere presence in a complex modern nation often confers very little in either practical or legal terms. Nevertheless, in much contemporary discussion, border control is viewed as a kind of citizenship control; as if migrants, merely by being able to be at large in the community, become citizens. The nation clearly has a range of rights and privileges it can withhold or bestow upon those on its territory (or wishing to enter). Denial of citizenship is less onerous in its effects than denial of fundamental rights like liberty. One cannot justify denial of basic rights by analogy with an argument developed to support restrictions on access to full political citizenship.

Galloway's important work develops this point and seeks to correct the obvious illiberal potential of *unfettered* control over borders and migrants. Thus he seeks to balance the state's legitimacy to rule – which suggests that the preferences and interests of insiders must determine migration policy – against the state's own professed liberal values.[30] Whilst governments must treat all citizens equally (and outsiders worse), he argues for

---

28 *Ibid.*, 62.
29 Thus, Nagel argues that '(j)ustice is something we owe through our shared institutions only to those with whom we stand in a political relation. It is . . . an *associative* obligation.' T. Nagel, 'The Problem of Global Justice' (2005) 33 *Philosophy and Public Affairs* 113–47 at 121, and R. Dworkin, *Sovereign Virtue: The Theory and Practice of Equality*. Oxford University Press, 2000, 6. See also T. Scanlon, *What We Owe to One Another*, Cambridge, MA: Harvard University Press, 1999.
30 'Immigration law serves as a reminder that the state may owe duties not only to its citizens but also to resident foreigners and to strangers. It also impresses upon us the idea that the very legitimacy of the state may hinge on the nature of its (positive and negative) dealings with these individuals and draws attention to the complex relationship between membership and justice.' D. Galloway, 'Strangers and Members: Equality in an Immigration Setting' (1994) 7 *Can. J. L.& Juris.* 149.

important limits upon the *ways* that liberal states should treat migrants.[31] He advocates an obligation to respect the inherent 'dignity' of foreigners. Thus when racial criteria on migration to the United States and Australia were abandoned in the 1960s, Galloway says this was right not because citizen members of those racial groups were diminished by the racism, but rather '[w]here a government fails to identify strangers as people with needs, aims and ambitions, *all insiders* will be able to experience its disdain for them as humans'.[32,33]

In striking language, he argues that liberal political morality must 'give the highest priority to avoiding attack on individuals which could be construed as attacks on their status as human beings'.[34] This leads him to propose a sliding scale of concern ranging across different types of migrants and potential migrants. So whilst citizens merit the highest respect for their dignity, lawful long residents, illegal residents, refugees, foreign students and even potential entrants merit consideration too. Thus, denial of visas, if taken on grounds of, for example, sex, disability or race, would attack migrants' dignity. Governments have a burden of proof to show 'a clear and present threat' to public policy in order to undermine the dignity of individuals. He concludes by saying that there is 'no reason to suppose that legitimacy should not hinge on the state's treatment of all individuals who are morally significant. The moral universe is not circumscribed by national borders, even though borders are of moral relevance'.[35]

Galloway's account is a powerful attempt to reconcile closed liberal nation states with an open-minded consideration for non-citizens as moral persons, worthy of individual respect.[36] However, like most liberal accounts, in the end it looks only at membership or authorization questions. It does not tell us what measures can legitimately be taken to enforce, perhaps perfectly liberal, expulsion or exclusion choices. Applying his test to enforcement action, it is not clear in the abstract what

31 *Ibid.*, 173.   32 *Ibid.*, 164 (emphasis added).
33 We can contrast this with the citizenship/membership approach which sees the obligation of impartiality towards members as extending to an obligation not to discriminate against potential migrants who are represented amongst citizens. G.M. Rosberg, 'The Protection of Aliens from Discriminatory Treatment by the National Government' (1977) *Sup. Ct. Rev.* 275 at 327 – 'it fixes a badge of opprobrium on citizens of the same ancestry'.
34 Galloway, 'Strangers and Members', 168.   35 *Ibid.*, 169.
36 In fact, modern immigration policy reflects some aspects of this. For example, it avoids racist or sexist visa policies. It is also mirrored in the growing judicialization of immigration practice as regards deportation issues, with individualized scrutiny of 'quasi-membership' claims.

type of measures count as an 'attack on [foreigners'] status as human beings'. Furthermore, there is doubt about when an alien or migration presents a sufficiently 'clear and present danger'. Galloway does, however, put a strong case for requiring that liberal nation states, whilst entitled to maintain robust immigration controls, must ensure that these do not contravene their own basic liberal principles.

Non-liberal accounts: Hobbes, Schmitt and the state of war over borders

The debates above between different perspectives within liberalism fail to capture much that is significant about the actual conduct of modern immigration enforcement. Whilst it is true that most states have now removed the most blatant discrimination from their legal migration criteria, it is in relation to combating illegal immigration, asylum seeking and deportation that we see distinctly illiberal policies. The draconian nature of some of these measures are more suggestive of the state of war than peace. There is little here of the liberal cosmopolitan ideal of the equal worth and dignity of each human being. The links between the aliens and war powers is palpable in this space. This is not, however, a difficulty for non-liberal accounts of political theory which seek to found the legitimacy of the state squarely upon the maintenance of order and security above all other considerations.

The origin of this view stems from Thomas Hobbes' famous argument that citizens give their allegiance to the state in return for physical protection against internal and external threats.[37] This protection generates a political legitimacy for the state that is, however, conditional on the state's continued ability to deliver on this commitment to protect. For Hobbes, this duty of protection suggested and required the state to be 'sovereign' – to hold a monopoly over the use of violence.[38] In this light, migration

---

37 For a detailed discussion of the evolution of the idea of the state see Q. Skinner, 'The State', in T. Ball, J. Farr and R. Hanson (eds), *Political Innovation and Conceptual Change*, Cambridge University Press, 1989.

38 The invention of the doctrine of sovereignty did not invent oppression itself. As Hinsley puts it: 'men have often indulged in the unprincipled use of power, both within and between political societies. Such use or misuse of power would have occurred if the notion of sovereignty had never been formulated, as it did before the notion was formulated. It was earlier justified by absolutist theories, if it was justified at all. But it was increasingly justified by reference to sovereignty once sovereignty had driven those other theories from the field; and in its turn the concept of sovereignty, being made to serve the state of the nation regarded as an absolute end, was interpreted as justifying the use of absolute

control may sometimes be viewed as an imperative matter of national survival. In the words of one author: 'There are instances in human history when the migration of peoples seems indistinguishable from conquest by an invading army.'[39] In such circumstances, it is said that political leadership requires actions that cannot be judged from the perspective of peace and good order. Thus as governments 'exist to maximise the benefits to the population and their role requires them to kill people, both in war and in the distribution and regulation of public expenditure. The politician who will not have blood on his hands, who will not seriously contemplate a Hiroshima, a Dresden or a Belgrano . . . is no use to us.'[40]

This is captured neatly in Schmitt's argument that the liberal legal order cannot itself adjudicate upon the fundamental issue of safeguarding public order in the face of serious threats.[41] Only a sovereign taking executive decisions can decide who is a 'friend' and who an 'enemy' of the state. In this view, the very survival of the nation as a distinct political grouping depends upon being ready to define itself in relation to its enemies. To this extent, war is justified not by reference to 'ideals or norms of justice, but in its being fought against a real enemy'.[42]

This leads Schmitt to conclude that there is a fundamental contradiction between liberalism and the state system for '[u]niversality at any

power or symbolizing the actual possession of it.' F.H. Hinsley, *Sovereignty*, 2nd edn, Cambridge University Press, 1986, 217. However, he notes that critics of sovereignty mistake this moral argument for the real argument: 'the concept maintains no more – if also no less – than that there must be an ultimate authority within the political society if the society is to exist at all, or at least if it is to be able to function effectively', *ibid.*

39 D.C. Hendrikson, 'Migration in Law and Ethics: A Realist Perspective', in Barry and Goodin (eds), *Free Movement*, 217.

40 L. Allison, 'The Utilitarian Ethics of Punishment and Torture' in L. Allison (ed.), *The Utilitarian Response*, London: Sage, 1990, 12. M. Walzer, 'Political Action: The Problem of Dirty Hands' in M. Cohen *et al.*, *War and Moral Responsibility*, Princeton University Press, 1974.

41 Schmitt argues that liberalism fails to acknowledge that the ultimate choice between 'friend' and 'enemy' must be made based upon essentially arbitrary grounds, which is incompatible with liberalism. See C. Schmitt, *Political Theology: Four Chapters on the Concept of Sovereignty*, 2nd edn (trans. G. Schwab) Cambridge, MA: MIT Press, 1985.

42 'For as long as a people exists in the political sphere, this people must, even if only in the most extreme case . . . determine by itself the distinction of friend and enemy. Therein resides the essence of its political existence. When it no longer possesses the capacity or the will to make this distinction, it ceases to exist politically. If it permits this distinction to be made by another, then it is no longer a politically free people and is absorbed into another political system. The justification of war does not reside in its being fought for ideals or norms of justice, but in its being fought against a real enemy.' C. Schmitt, *The Concept of the Political*, 2nd edn (trans. G. Schwab) New Brunswick, NJ: Rutgers University Press, 1976/1929, 49.

price would necessarily have to mean total depoliticalization and with it, particularly, the non-existence of states'.[43] The attack made on liberalism by Schmitt is that it amounts to a denial of politics in favour of legalistic individualism which is unable to produce the stable societies that are pre-requisites for legal order.[44] Thus the essence of politics lies in the power of the sovereign body to take the essential step to protect the security of the state and thereby define the nation. This depends upon values that are not open to justification from within the legal system.

In the end, as we have seen above, all shades of liberalism accept that there must be a measure of partialism towards citizens for liberal states to survive.[45] This is an inherent contradiction arising from the apparent impossibility of using *reason* to ground the insider/outsider distinction. Schmitt, however, went further and argued that the sovereign must have unfettered power to decide on the *measures* necessary to deal with the threat posed by an 'enemy'. Thus both the nature of an exceptional situation and the means to remove it must remain beyond the law.[46] As Hobbes himself put it in identifying the 'enemy' as the foreigner: 'the Infliction of what evill soever, on an Innocent man, that is not a Subject, if it be for the benefit of the Common-wealth, and without violation of any former Covenant, is no breach of the Law of Nature'.[47] This is a crucial step and one that forms a central issue for this book. The increasingly widespread political construction of unauthorized or unwanted immigrants as an 'enemy' (but one whose treatment falls under the aliens powers) has been crucial to supporting draconian enforcement measures.

How far should the constitutional and human rights system apply legal tools of *reason* to analyse the *means* used to enforce border controls? Whilst the *political* is dominant in relation to broad choices about which types of foreigners are to be admitted (who are our 'friends'?), the *legal* has sometimes, even if cautiously, been able to assert itself by scrutinizing

---

43 *Ibid.*, 55.
44 'The negation of the political, which is inherent in every consistent individualism, leads necessarily to a political practice of distrust toward all conceivable political forces and forms of state and government, but never produces on its own a positive theory of state, government, and politics.' *Ibid.*, 70.
45 'For liberal values to triumph, then, liberalism is obliged to accommodate a competing, illiberal conception of community that threatens those values even as it promises to actualize them – albeit for only a limited portion of humanity.' P. Schuck, *Citizens, Strangers and In-betweens: Essays on Immigration and Citizenship*, Boulder, CO: Westview Press, 1998, 79.
46 'Sovereign is he who decides on the exception.' C. Schmitt, *Political Theology*, 5.
47 T. Hobbes, *Leviathan*, New York: Collier Books, 1962, 234.

the means used to keep out our 'enemies'. This may include assessing how serious the threat they pose actually is. In the end, this involves courts being willing to subject the notion of 'security' to closer examination rather than simply accepting a political 'definition'. We return to this in Chapter 7.

Migration, detention and the new politics of security

How far does detention policy in practice reflect the 'war' analogy? Throughout this study, we have certainly seen that there have been close links between security concerns and increased resort to immigration detention. Whilst in the past this was more closely linked with a declared state of war or ongoing national security fears, in modern times this state of fear has taken on a more permanent form. As Castles and Miller put it: 'international migration has never been as pervasive, or as socio-economically and politically significant. Never before have political leaders accorded such a priority to migration concerns.'[48] Whilst much large-scale movement of people has been positively desired by governments '[a]ppearing to crack down on "unwanted immigration" is increasingly regarded by governments as essential for safeguarding social peace'.[49] Thus many commentators argue that migration has become in some respects 'securitized'.

This term is not clearly defined but implies that governments and cultures have come to see migration as representing a variety of threats. As Haddad puts it: 'Immigration of any kind is linked to insecurity, and where this movement is seemingly out of control the insecurity increases.'[50] This

---

48 S. Castles and M.J. Miller, *The Age of Migration*, 4th edn, London: Macmillan, 2009, 299. They note that this is perhaps a return to normality: 'In many respects, the period between 1945 and 1980 was unusual. The horrors of World War II discredited the xenophobia of the extreme right and perceptions of migrants as a security threat. Indeed, international migration was often viewed as an economic phenomenon and a largely beneficial one at that' 207.

49 *Ibid.*, 306. F.B. Adamson, 'Crossing Borders: International Migration and National Security' (2006) 31(1) *Int. Security* 165–99 argues that migration affects sovereign prerogative control over all aspects of public policy and law.

50 E. Haddad, *The Refugee in International Society: Between Two Sovereigns*, Cambridge University Press, 2008, 194. J. Huysmans, 'Migrants as a Security Problem: Dangers of "Securitizing" Societal Issues', in R. Miles and D. Thranhardt (eds), *Migration and European Integration: the Dynamics of Inclusion and Exclusion*, London: Pinter Publishers, 1995, 53. Also J. Huysmans, 'The EU and the Securitization of Migration' (2000) 38(5) *JCMS* 751–77 which argues that European-level policy on migration has moved from an internal market dynamic within the EU to a security stance *vis-à-vis* those outside the EU.

sense of insecurity is protean in its forms and causes but in general it has become an important part of national identity. On rare occasions there have been highly visible large-scale influxes of unauthorized migrants which led to a feeling of panic that borders were being overwhelmed. More common now is a sense that the modern state is experiencing a permanent failure to control borders. Cultural stereotypes also tie migration to crime, drugs, prostitution, exploitation, cheap labour and terrorism. We can explain some of this process through socio-political ideas about how societies construct enemies and perpetuate fear in relation to groups defined as deviant.[51] Some argue that the degree of threat posed by migrants has been exaggerated to secure political advantage.[52]

We can take the massive increase in modern detention of immigrants in the United States as an example, but there are echoes of the same phenomena in a number of countries.[53] Welch argues that, at least initially, a kind of moral panic swept the nation. This kind of phenomenon exists when a group is singled out as being especially dangerous and meriting harsh measures which are either unwarranted or disproportionate to the threat. This had first begun in relation to the *Mariel* Cubans in the early 1990s, for whom 'politicians and the INS publicized their suspicion that Castro had exported Cuba's social outcasts to the United States; as a result, Mariels were stereotyped as predatory and dangerous. Resettlement

---

51 M. Edelman, *Constructing the Political Spectacle*, University of Chicago Press, 1988: 'It is reassuring to assume that only in the exceptional case do people victimize others in order to make them scapegoats for social discontents. But the phenomenon is neither exceptional nor growing rare' (89).

'The belief that others are evil, even if it seems unwarranted to historians, is not to be understood as arbitrary, as accidental, or as a sign of inherent irrationality or immorality. In conducive social situations, anyone can be defined as an enemy or categorize others than way for reasons that have nothing to do with the actions of the people who are labelled' (88–9). Stanley Cohen's classic text, *Folk Devils and Moral Panics*, London: Macgibbon and Kee, 1972, argues that during moral panics '[a] condition, episode, person or groups of persons emerges to become defined as a threat to societal values and interest; its nature is presented in a stylized and stereotypical fashion by the mass media and politicians' (9).

52 N. Linn and S. Lea, 'A Phantom Menace and the New Apartheid: the Social Construction of Asylum-seekers in the United Kingdom' (2003) 14(4) *Discourse and Society* 425–52. J. Simon, 'Refugees in a Carceral Age: The Rebirth of Immigration Prisons in the United States' (1998) 10(3) *Public Culture* 577–607.

53 The most obvious examples are the UK's increased use of mandatory detention for asylum seekers in the late 1980s and again in the late 1990s, the UK's mandatory detention of foreign criminal prisoners in 2006 onwards, the Australian mandatory detention of boat arrivals in 1989 and the extension of this to all unauthorized migrants in 1992. In each of these cases there was a combination of public concern, media coverage suggesting loss of control and a government desire to show firmness in the face of a growing panic.

figures, however, contradicted that wave of disinformation; in fact, less than one-half of one percent of the Mariels were found to have serious criminal history.... criminal activity within the general US population was approximately 17 times greater...'[54] This formed part of a wider new hostility towards immigration in political debate at the time.[55]

By 1995, a US Senate report summed up the mood prior to the enactment of a raft of new mandatory indefinite detention provisions: 'America's immigration system is in disarray and criminal aliens... constitute a particularly vexing part of the problem. Criminal aliens occupy the intersection of two areas of great concern to the American people: crime and the control of our borders.'[56] They estimated 'conservatively' that there were 450,000 'criminal aliens' in the country imprisoned or under supervision. This frightening picture overlooked the non-violent nature of most alien offenders and the propensity to crime in the general population. The Senate recommended mandatory deportation be introduced for all felonies however minor.

This idea immediately highlighted the enforcement gap; a problem for which mandatory detention apparently offered a solution. At this time only 6 per cent of deportation proceedings were completed during detainees' criminal sentence. The INS had only 3,500 beds of its own and criminal deportees were often released at the end of their sentence for lack of bedspace. Many did not report for deportation. The Senate argued if there were greater speed in deportation procedures, better use of detention space and greater cooperation with countries of origin, then enforcement could be more effective.

Another Senate Committee around the same time said 'U.S. immigration law is violated on a massive scale'.[57] They noted the continued

---

54 M. Welch, *Detained: Immigration Laws the Expanding INS Jail Complex*, Philadelphia: Temple University Press, 2002, 96.

55 Citing P. Brimelow, 'Time to Rethink Immigration' (1995) *National Review* 30–46 and *Alien Nation: Common Sense about America's Immigration Disaster*, New York: Random House, 1995 as stoking public unease about the United States being exhausted and full up. See also the nativists like P. Buchanan, *The Death of the West: How Dying Populations and Immigrants Invasions Imperil Our Country and Civilization*, New York: Thomas Dunne Book/St. Martin's Press, 2002. Proposition 187 was passed in California despite its being apparently unconstitutional and was mirrored in federal activity to placate restrictionists.

56 US Senate, Permanent Subcommittee on Invesitgations of the Committee on Governmental Affairs, 'Criminal Aliens in the United States', 1995, 104th Congress 1st Session, 104–48.

57 US Senate, Judiciary Committee, Report 104th Cong., 1995–6, *Report on Immigration Control and Financial Responsibility Act of 1996*, 3.

scale of illegal immigrant arrests at over one million. It disparaged and politically discredited the policy of 'catch and release'. The Chair of the US Commission on Immigration Reform summed up the new ambition towards 'perfection' (or at least 'credibility') in enforcement:

> Credibility in immigration policy can be summed up in one sentence: those who should get in, get in; those who should be kept out, are kept out; and those who should not be here will be required to leave. The top priorities for detention and removal, of course, are criminal aliens. But for the system to be credible, people actually have to be deported at the end of the process.[58]

This is a critical statement which clearly set out the new 'absolutist' paradigm in immigration enforcement, not just in the United States, but in many Western nations. Restoring 'credibility' by completely stopping unlawful migration was always impossible, even if the will do so were present. However, for individual unauthorized migrants, a more limited 'credibility' would entail detention until expulsion and would not be confined just to criminal aliens. By refusing to release persons who had no authorization, the state would demonstrate its 'credibility'. Whilst an understandable, even logical, extension of immigration enforcement efforts, such a policy would, however, necessitate internment on an unprecedented scale.

Thus, whilst declining to tackle US employers (the 'pull factor') all sides agreed that detention should be a centrepiece of enforcement, commissioning a 66 per cent increase in bed-space to 9,000 by 1997. It was assumed that expulsion would occur thirty days after sentence completion (deportation having been ordered during criminal sentence).[59] There was no real analysis of the effect of removing bail on the numbers and length of detention. Again the only solution to the problem of delay was to argue for prisoner transfer treaties to be agreed with countries with high numbers of detainees.[60] The optimistic view was that mandatory detention

---

58 Testimony of Barbara Jordan, Chair US Commission on Immigration Reform, US House of Representatives, Committee on the Judiciary, Sub-Committee on Immigration and Claims, 24 February 1995.

59 Section 164.

60 The Act also allowed for the Attorney General to control the mass influx of illegal aliens during an 'immigration emergency' and to use funds to repatriate illegals and intercepts at sea (s. 171).

and deportation would lead to 'real progress toward ridding our nation of the 450,000 criminal aliens in our jails and on our streets'.[61]

Despite their having strong disagreements about almost every other measure to combat illegal immigration, detention was acceptable to all sides.[62] It demonstrated firmness, whilst being part of a package of 'speedy' bureaucratic procedures to hold, process and expel unwanted migrants. It moved towards abolishing 'catch and release'. This is a pattern since repeated in many countries. But whilst greater speed has been achieved in expulsion proceedings on average, significant numbers are held beyond the 'removal periods' fixed by Congress. Nevertheless, the legislature had created an expectation that detainees would be held until removed. Release appeared politically heterodox for enforcement agents. The right to liberty of unauthorized aliens had been politically discredited.

Welch argues that '[d]ue to the enormous impact that the 1996 legislation has had on immigration control, the INS has grown faster than its ability to handle its booming detainee population. As a result, the agency has lost track of detainees on numerous occasions'.[63] The mandatory detention policy has resulted in an industrialization of detention. The INS budget had grown rapidly after the *Mariel* Cubans were classified as dangerous, because this required large funds to house them. The budget rose over 100 per cent from 1982 to 1988 and later to $4.8 billion in 2001, with $900 million for detention. The INS soon accepted that they could not cope and needed a system of parole, but did not implement one. Non-criminal detainees were often swept up in the new facilities. When public defenders represented some detainees who were not flight risks, 80 per cent of those set free had no criminal history but had been detained sometimes for years.[64]

The development of larger and more detention facilities has tended to create its own logic for many political reasons.[65] Lobbies, both private and public, have developed around detention and these seek to secure

---

61 See n. 56 above, Additional views of Senator Abraham, 40.

62 *Ibid*. Additional views of Senator Abraham, who urged that we 'aim our efforts toward the real problem of criminal activity, and away from measures that do more to hurt Americans and others who play by the rules than the law-flouters we are after', 40.

63 Welch, *Detained*, 91.   64 *Ibid*., 126.

65 M. Welch and L. Schuster, 'Detention of asylum seekers in the US, UK, France, Germany and Italy. A Critical View of the Globalizing Culture of Control' 2005 5(4) *Crim. Just.* 331–55.

further funding for it.[66] Because there is never any complete solution it can always be argued that more money is required. It is also difficult for any politician to resist providing further funds, given the consensus on the threat.[67] Thus, turning to the United States again, despite massive increases in detention spaces to over 30,000 by 2005, there were still concerns about a lack of detention estate.[68] Thousands of nationals from countries deemed to be of 'special interest' on security grounds had to be released soon after arrest at the Mexican border. In a post-9/11 world this was viewed as 'increasing the chances that a potential terrorist could slip through the system'.[69]

Alexseev correctly observes the frankly hopeless direction in which this leads policy-makers: 'Because any migrant may be a terrorist and because so many migrants come illegally, any measure restricting illegal immigration would be an effective anti-terrorism measure. Once this logic is accepted . . . migration can be justifiably interpreted as a perpetual and grave national security threat – unless absolutely all instances of abuse of immigration law are eliminated. That, however, is impossible in the

---

66 C. Bacon, 'The Evolution of Immigration Detention in the UK: the Involvement of Private Prison Companies', Refugee Studies Centre Working Paper No. 27, Oxford: Refugee Studies Centre, 2005, which argues that UK practice followed the United States in this respect and that the interests of private firms in being assured of contracts meant that detention increased despite falls in asylum numbers and lack of evidence of a link between detention and deterrence. In the United States, there were over 961 separate detention places across the country in 2007, of which only a tiny number are run directly by the federal authorities. Most were contracted out to private companies and local and state jails. This provides important revenue to some local economies. See National Immigration Forum, Background Paper, 'The Math of Immigration Detention', 7 July 2009. The budget for detention was $1.7 billion.

67 M. Malloch and E. Stanley, 'The Detention of Asylum Seekers in the UK. Representing Risk, Managing Dangerousness' (2005) 7 Punishment and Society 53–71.

68 See Congressional Research Service Report, 'Border Security: Apprehensions of "Other Than Mexican" Aliens', Washington, DC, Congressional Research Service, 22 Sept. 2005. After the 11 September 2001 attacks, detention spaces were inadequate so that non-Mexican migrants could not be detained under expedited proceedings, but were released with a notice to appear.

69 C.C. Haddal, Y. Kim and M.J. Garcia, 'Border Security: Barriers Along the U.S. International Border', Washington, DC: Congressional Research Service, 2009, which notes that despite fence improvements in some areas, illegal entry apprehensions were 1.2 million in 2004 (the same as in 1992). This suggests the difficulty of such schemes. See now the Secure Fence Act 2006, which required 850 miles of fencing. The estimates for unlawful aliens in the United States in January 2009 was 11.9 million. See A. Bruno, 'Unauthorized Aliens in the United States', Washington, DC: Congressional Research Service, 2010.

real world.'[70] This psychology of fear over migration is partly based upon the fact that illegal migrants can so easily enter and disappear into the community. The cost to government of detecting one illegal migrant is vast compared to the minimal cost of avoiding detection. The task is insurmountable '[b]ut because offering no exclusionist measures would make the government look even weaker, some such measures are likely to be adopted'.[71] The government may set a target for removals, but these will only measure a small fraction of total illegal migrants. The government is always vulnerable to the next scandal. The perception of anarchy is stronger because there is a regular flow of stories suggesting 'borderlessness'.

In this way, securitizing migration can be self-defeating for 'the more migration is feared as a security threat, the more of a security threat it becomes...'.[72] Indeed, public opinion surveys have shown public fear of migration has become unresponsive to the actual levels of migration experienced. Guiraudon and Joppke note that 'policy feedbacks can easily develop into a vicious circle: tight controls bring about more smuggling and illegal activities; amplified by sensational media headlines that feed further popular resentment, increased illegal migration, in turn, drives politicians to institute even stricter migration controls, and so on.'[73] Detention policy has certainly developed partly as a reflection of this syndrome of fear, crisis and response.

Large influxes, foreign criminals and asylum seekers: crisis, legitimacy and visualization

In fact, as Joppke says, the contemporary 'loss of control' rhetoric which drives much enforcement policy is inconsistent with the historical record. This shows that states never had omnipotence over migration.[74] Actually, modern states have more tools to restrict migration than ever before, even

---

70 M.A. Alexseev, *Immigration Phobia and the Security Dilemma*, Cambridge University Press, 2006, 59.

71 *Ibid.*   72 *Ibid.*

73 V. Guiraudon and C. Joppke (eds), *Controlling a New Migration World*, London: Routledge, 2001, 21.

74 C. Joppke, 'Why Liberal States Accept Unwanted Immigration' in A. Messina and G. Lahav (eds), *The Migration Reader: Exploring Politics and Policies*, London: Lynne Rienner Publishers, 2006, 526.

if they do not always choose to use them.[75] He argues that the panoply of border controls and visa restrictions are not put to full use, due largely to domestic political and legal constraints. These stem from interest group politics which militate in favour of organized employer and immigrant groups over diffuse opponents.[76] He also cites the (self-imposed) constraints of constitutional legal orders on government action. These factors suggest that 'unwanted immigration is inherent in the liberalness of liberal states'.[77]

In reality, therefore, despite the rhetoric of restriction, liberal states are both restrained and self-limiting in relation to migration policy. There has been a political consensus on the need to promote fair and balanced legal migration. The quid pro quo has been to get tougher on illegal migration.[78] Even here, however, there has been only modest enforcement of sanctions against employers of irregular migrants for domestic economic and political reasons. In order to counter the public perception of weakness, states seek other ways of showing toughness towards unwanted migrants whilst still letting in desirable migrants.[79] One

75 P. Schuck, 'The Disconnect between Public Attitudes and Policy Outcomes in Immigration' in C. Swain (ed.), Debating Immigration, New York: Cambridge University Press, 2007, 17–31, shows how the public is persistently more anti-immigration than the policies, which remain relatively open. The lobby groups are strong on both NGO and employer sides. This emasculates reforms which are restrictive. R.M. Smith, 'Aliens Rights, Citizens Rights and the Politics of Restriction' in Swain (ed.), Debating Immigration, 114–26. 'The state may have lost control over ideas, but it remains a controller of its borders and the movement of people across them', P. Hirst and G. Thompson 'Globalization and the Future of the Nation-State' (1995) 24 Economy and Society 408–42.

76 For example, a return to guest worker systems in Europe became unacceptable and in the United States there was a strong battle to protect equal citizenship for those migrants born there in the face of some voices calling for an end to jus soli.

77 Joppke, 'Why Liberal States Accept Unwanted Immigration', 547.

78 See M.J. Miller, 'Western European Strategies to Deter Unwanted Migration: Neither Barbarian Invasions Nor Fortress Europa', US Commission on Immigration Reform Research Paper, University of Delaware, 1994. Miller argues that the two contrasting images of European migration policy during the period 1989–94 as either uncontrolled or draconian are both inaccurate.

79 Migration cuts across the traditional left/right groupings; for different reasons, social democrats and conservatives can agree on the need to restrict migration, whilst economic liberals and human rights groups support more open borders. There is little consensus and there are few tools for a reasoned resolution of disagreements. Policy on legal migration routes has emerged from keenly fought interest group politics. For pro-migrant lobbies, understandably, most political effort is expended upon protecting or expanding the opportunities for legal migrants or refugees and resisting employer sanctions. By contrast, policy on enforcement and illegal migration, including expanded detention, has been seen as an issue upon which to give concessions to pro-restriction lobbies.

technique to demonstrate firmness is that of increased '*visibility*' of control at the border, tougher law enforcement and *remote control* in the form of pre-flight checks, visa regimes and interceptions at sea in an effort to push out the border.[80] Detention both represents one of the most visible means of showing control over unauthorized migrants that are caught by the state and serves to recreate the border internally by stopping such migrants from being at large.

In this context, there are three main groups of migrants who have been detained in recent years: those seeking asylum, those convicted of crimes and those arriving in abnormally large influxes (who may include asylum seekers). This may be explained by several factors. These groups have engaged the state by announcing their unauthorized presence in the host nation. Asylum seekers enter the asylum process and are subject to formal decisions and subsequent appeal. Criminals are prosecuted (and sentenced or made subject to supervision) by the courts. Large influxes have typically come by boat routes that are known to coast guards. This means that in all these cases 'the state' (in one or other agency) has been put on notice of the unwanted migrant. This creates public awareness through media images or statistics. These groups are thus 'visible' in the sense the state can be held directly accountable for their remaining in the host country.

Given this visibility, a sense of 'emergency' or 'crisis' is understandable. This is based upon both concerns about sheer numbers, security risks and alleged lack of humanitarian status. This perception of loss of control over borders is unacceptable. States face a legitimacy crisis if they cannot control, repel or expel these groups. Detention became an important aspect of bureaucratic strategies to regain control over these crises; procedures which tracked detainees from detection, through adjudication to expulsion. The state could then set its own targets in terms of time frames from arrival to decision and resolution of appeals. Detention was said to be more efficient, as everything was in one place. These efficiency and processing reasons came to support more mandatory detention.

---

80 One example is the EU's action in Eastern Europe by imposing conditions on accession states. It can also involve financial rewards for the return of irregular migrants. See also G. Neuman, 'Anomalous Zones' (1996) 48(1) *Stan. L. Rev.* 1197–234. Furthermore, the United States, faced with poor governance in neighbours, has gone to war in Haiti to deal with the flow of migrants. C. Mitchell, 'The Political Costs of State Power: US Border Control in South Florida' in P. Andreas and T. Snyder (eds), *The Wall around the West: State Borders and Immigration Controls in North America and Europe*, Lanham, MD: Rowman and Littlefield, 2000, 81–97.

Punishment without trial remained officially anathema. It was, however, often admitted that detention was aimed at deterring others.

In the case of migrants who have come as part of perceived mass influxes, the rationale of 'visible' containment was stronger still. This led to the creation of 'off-shore' processing areas in the case of the US base at Guantanamo Bay or the Australian 'Pacific Solution' cases. These served to show that the state had stopped migrants from even reaching the territory of the nation. Furthermore, it put them beyond constitutional and most practical legal protection. They could then be put through accelerated procedures that did not conform to standard practices recognized by international and national law. In these cases, detention was crucial to securing this heightened degree of control over such groups. It allowed governments to more readily claim 'success'. The use of aggressive tactics against boats run by people smugglers (including detaining their client-migrants) did lead to reductions in 'visible' irregular migration. It remains unclear, however, if the overall volume of irregular or unauthorized migration has actually decreased through these tactics.

Detention conditions, disturbances and containment: the practical politics of modern incarceration

In order to more completely understand and evaluate the modern era of mass administrative detention, it is important to consider the conditions experienced by detainees and their responses to incarceration. This is for two reasons. First, detention conditions have served as an important focus in the emerging political debate over detention. Second, the way that governments have managed detention centres provides important clues about the moral, political and legal status of detainees. The modern growth of administrative detention has, at times, produced a culture of 'impunity' amongst those running detention centres towards their charges. It will be argued that such impunity is reinforced by the politicization of detention, at the expense of legal controls, that has been noted throughout this book.

Whilst there are usually legal minimum standards for detention conditions, there remain serious failures in upholding these. This appears to be caused by a complex set of factors, most unique to immigration detention, others prevalent in prisons more generally. Detainees have usually been declared by the law to be 'unwanted'. Given this status, it is obviously difficult to create 'constructive' detention environments. The goal is not reintegration into society, so central to liberal penology, but rather expulsion from it.[81] There are also psychological problems caused by holding large numbers together who have no certainty about their future. Increasingly it can be said 'that detainees are merely warehoused while their cases crawl through the vast bureaucracy'.[82] This concept of 'warehousing' is a useful way of thinking about much modern immigration detention with its connotations of industrial holding centre rather than juridico-legal institution.

Unrest in detention centres: the instability of control

The high levels of unrest in detention centres is something quite new not seen in earlier periods. The creation of large prison-like facilities with many detainees held indefinitely in challenging conditions has changed the paradigm. It is perhaps not surprising that the problems have been greatest in the United States, United Kingdom and Australia. These are also countries which have embraced indefinite and lengthy administrative detention on a large scale and it would be surprising if there were not a close connection between these two phenomena. The disturbances are important because of what they reveal about how far governments have gone to maintain an appearance of firmness towards unwanted migrants.

In the United Kingdom, large-scale detention began in the 1980s when new groups of asylum seekers started to arrive at airports. The numbers were not especially large in themselves, but there was a perception of loss of control over borders. This stemmed partly from heavy media coverage and the fact that the migrants tended to come in groups as part of a pattern of out-flux from one country. One immediately tangible response available to government was to detain en masse all such migrants whilst their cases were processed.[83] This represented a shift away from individualized detention decisions that had been the policy hitherto. This was the approach taken to successively Tamils, Turkish Kurds and Zaireans. It served both as evidence that the government was seeking control of the border and as a deterrent to others thinking of coming. The limited facilities available at that time led to the use of police stations, prisons and even

---

81 Indeed, some establishments are now explicitly named 'removal centres', which merely makes clear what was implicit before.
82 ACLU, *Indefinite Detention*, New York: ACLU, 2000, 105.
83 Other easy responses were to impose visa restrictions upon the nationalities concerned, which stopped them embarking for the UK. In addition, the refusal rate increased and the language of 'economic migrants' and 'bogus asylum seekers' was used to describe the new groups of asylum seekers. This further reinforced the new policy on detention, which could then be seen as part of the removal process.

a floating ship which broke its moorings in a storm in 1987 with many Sri Lankan asylum seekers on board. Many of these groups of detainees were released on bail after hunger strikes prompted by the length and poor conditions of detention.[84] The lack of appropriate facilities available for detention had increased the sense of chaos with the government caught between humanitarian and control objectives.

The United Kingdom has continued to experience such problems despite the construction of specialist immigration detention centres in the 1990s as asylum numbers rose. Campsfield detention centre has been prone to numerous difficulties, which began with a riot by fifty detainees in August 1997.[85] In June 2005 there was a large-scale hunger strike by Zimbabweans who complained that they should not be held whilst removals to that country were suspended.[86] In March 2007, seven staff and two detainees were hospitalized after a fire in which riot police had to attend.[87] In August 2007, twenty-six detainees broke out of the centre.[88] In June 2008 there was another disturbance and fires were started.[89] In August 2008 there was a hunger strike by Kurdish asylum seekers.[90]

Another detention centre at Harmondsworth has also experienced many problems. In July 2004 there was a major disturbance after the suicide of a detainee.[91] It was affected by the hunger strikes by Zimbabweans in June 2005.[92] In November 2006 there were further disturbances and fires.[93] These followed a very critical inspection report by the independent monitoring body for prisons.[94] The domestic courts required

---

84 M. Ashford, *Detained without Trial*, London: JCWI, 1993, who argued that 'inconsistent and arbitrary detention decisions show that this policy on detention is being used to attempt to deter the arrival of asylum seekers' (74). The mass detentions of particular nationalities at particular times suggested that 'little regard has been paid to individual considerations' *ibid.*

85 http://news.bbc.co.uk/1/hi/uk/6449465.stm. See also HM Inspectorate of Prisons Report on this incident.

86 http://archive.oxfordmail.net/2005/6/28/1975.html.

87 http://news.bbc.co.uk/1/hi/england/oxfordshire/6449069.stm.

88 http://news.bbc.co.uk/1/hi/uk/6449465.stm.

89 http://news.bbc.co.uk/1/hi/england/oxfordshire/7454814.stm.

90 http://www.guardian.co.uk/uk/2008/aug/15/immigration.

91 Sue Mcallister, Head of Security Group HM Prison, *Report on an Investigation into a Disturbance at Harmondsworth 19–20 July 2004*, London: Home Office, 2004.

92 http://news.bbc.co.uk/1/hi/uk/4124814.stm.

93 Robert Whalley CB, *Report into the Investigation of the Disturbances at Campsfield and Harmondsworth Immigration Removal Centres*, London, Home Office, 25 July 2007. This noted population pressures, delays in the progress of immigration cases, long and unexpected periods in detention, and uncertainty about outcomes (C5.31).

94 HM Inspectorate of Prisons, *2006 Report* (four months before riots) found it to be the worst centre ever inspected with 'over-emphasis on physical security – which was more

the government to launch an independent inquiry into allegations that the human rights of detainees were breached when they were left locked in after fire broke out.[95] A new flagship detention centre was virtually destroyed by fire following a mass disturbance in which detainees took over the facility.[96] One recent report said that relations with detainees were so poor that, for example, staff were unaware that they had held one detainee for two years.[97]

In relation to the United States, the thousands of long-term *Mariel* Cuban detainees held after 1980–1 or re-detained after being paroled presented the first serious unrest in detention centres. The indefinite detention regime in their cases led to an uprising in 1987 in which a penitentiary was taken over.[98] More generally, throughout the United States there have been persistent concerns about detention conditions falling short of nationally agreed standards.[99] Litigation has been common in order to

appropriate to a high security prison than a removal centre run under rules that require secure and humane detention under a relaxed regime'. Sometimes this led to denial of basic entitlements, such as the ability to attend religious services, http://inspectorates. homeoffice.gov.uk.

95 *AM and others* v. *SSHD* [2009] EWCA Civ 219. The Court of Appeal ruled that the government has an obligation to conduct an independent investigation where there is credible evidence of a potential breach of Art. 2 or 3: Sedley L.J. at 67: 'In my judgment Mitting J was right to find that the issues raised by the claimants, especially in the context of what was by then known from the report of the Inspector of Prisons, were such as to trigger the state's obligation under art.3 to investigate what had arguably been inhuman or degrading treatment, both reactive and systemic, in a custodial institution.'

96 *Report into the Enquiry into the Disturbance at Yarl's Wood* by Prisons and Probation Ombudsman 2002, www.ppo.gov.uk.

97 They found that relationships with staff had deteriorated, inmates felt unsafe and unable to get advice about immigration status, concluding that '[i]n general, staff were distant and reactive. Neither staff nor managers appeared to take an interest in the individual circumstances and concerns of detainees: for example, they appeared unaware of the fact that they had been holding a Chinese man for nearly two years', http://inspectorates. homeoffice.gov.uk.

98 M.S. Hamm, *The Abandoned Ones: the Imprisonment and Uprising of Mariel Boat People*, Boston: Northeastern University Press, 1995, who describes the takeover of the Atlanta penitentiary by 1,394 *Marielitos* in detail, as part of a broader survey of the issue.

99 National Immigration Law Centre, 'A Broken System: Confidential Reports Reveal Failure in US Detention Centres' 2009, www.nilc.org/immlawpolicy/arrestdet/A-Broken-System-2009–07.pdf. The report says that there were 'substantive and pervasive violations of the government's minimum standards for conditions' and that 'the conditions in which these civil detainees are held are often as bad as or worse than those faced by imprisoned criminals'. See also *Voices From Detention: A Report on Human Rights Violations at the Northwest Detention Center in Tacoma*, Washington: Seattle University School of Law, July 2008, which notes that even the federal government's own Accountability Office (GAO), in a 2006–07 compliance review process observing 23 facilities, documented inadequate medical care, lack of access to legal materials, inadequate facility grievance procedures and overcrowding.

injunct the federal authorities to comply.[100] As we have noted, this became most pronounced after the 1996 legislation which increased mandatory detention for many groups of migrants.[101] The rapid rise in both numbers of detainees and length of detention led to all kinds of ordinary prisons, jails, or private facilities being employed.[102] There is evidence that it is harder to maintain standards due to the sub-contracting of detention to local and private operators.[103] Federal standards on detention conditions have remained legally unenforceable at the suit of detainees.

In 1998, one leading NGO reported on numerous concerns. Detainees were being shackled during asylum interviews. There was a lack of access to the outdoors or recreational facilities. There were also widespread instances of assault and forced sedation and an absence of necessary medical care. Many were housed in jails not suited for long-term detention.[104] There have also been concerns about deaths in custody being linked to abuse or lack of medical care.[105] There are suggestions that there was almost a culture of secret detention during the 1990s with the government unwilling to allow the numbers and identities of detainees to be made public.[106] In the post-11 September 2001 round-up of immigrants,

---

100 *Orantes-Hernandez* v. *Meese* 685 F.Supp. 1988 (C.D. Cal. 1988) aff'd sub nom *Orantes-Hernandez* v. *Tonburgh* 919 F.2d. 549 (9th Cir. 1990), which required fair treatment of Salvadoran asylum seekers in terms of access to lawyers and telephones to pursue their claims. As recently as 2009 federal courts continued to uphold this injunction because of widespread evidence of denial of such rights in detention centres. See *Orantes-Hernandez* v. *Gonzales* 07–9609, 08–55231 (9th Cir. 6 Apr. 2009).

101 Welch argues that detention expansion was 'responding to economic cues from the corrections-industrial complex, an enterprise that commodifies lawbreakers as well as undocumented migrants' and that '[d]ue to its economic and organizational links to the corrections-industrial complex, the INS does not merely mimic recent developments in criminal justice, it has also become a fixture in the sprawling apparatus of social control aimed at exclusion and detention rather than integration and assimilation.' Welch, *Detained*, at 151.

102 ACLU, *The Aftermath of the 1996 Immigration Laws: Real Life Tragedies*, New York: ACLU, 2000.

103 www.cidh.org/Comunicados/English/2009/53–09eng.htm.

104 Human Rights Watch, *Locked Away: Immigration Detainees in Jails in the US*, New York: Human Rights Watch, 1998.

105 D. Priest and A. Goldstein, *Careless Detention, Washington Post*, 11 May 2008.

106 Dow describes the continued efforts throughout the 1990s and again post-9/11 to obtain details of detainees and their numbers. M. Dow, *American Gulag: Inside U.S. Immigration Prisons*, Berkeley: University of California Press, 2004, 19–32. There was litigation against both state and federal authorities in this respect: *ACLU of New Jersey* v. *County of Hudson*, Superior Court of New Jersey, No. A-4100–01T, January 22, 2002. See also Dan Malone, *The Dallas Morning News*, *L.P.* v. *U.S. Department of Justice, Immigration and Naturalization Service*, U.S. District Court, Northern District of Texas,

there were again serious concerns about the conditions under which detainees were held.[107] It was also actually difficult for families to locate detainees who were held incommunicado without access to telephones or money.[108] Congress recently acknowledged the ongoing failures of the detention system by legislating to prohibit federal contracting with repeated violators of the federal detention standards.[109]

Australia has experienced very severe problems in its detention centres based upon its mandatory detention policy and the build-up of long-term detainees in isolated camps. The policy has been the subject of eighteen critical reports to the minister by the Australian Human Rights Commission. These have been prompted by numerous complaints filed by detainees and NGOs. In 1997 the Commission concluded that the policy broke international human rights law and recommended it be abandoned in favour of discretionary detention.[110]

As we saw, in the federal election of November 2001 the government made interception and detention policy towards asylum seekers a central policy issue and achieved electoral success.[111] Detainees held, sometimes for years, staged a mass hunger strike and engaged in widespread self-harm at the Woomera detention centre in 2002.[112] This was the subject

Ft. Worth Division, No. 400-CV-0060-Y, January 25, 2000. Malone, a journalist, was seeking information on the number of detainees held longer than three years. He was told initially fifty-three then, following the litigation, the true figure was shown to be 851 (not including *Mariel* Cubans, who were not counted). Welch reports that the INS was overwhelmed by increasing numbers of detainees and on 'numerous' occasions lost track of where they were held in the system, Welch, *Detained*, 171.

107 Human Rights Watch, 'Presumption of Guilt: Human Rights Abuses of Post-September 11 Detainees', New York, August 2002.

108 See Welch, *Detained*, Epilogue, where he describes secret detentions as steps towards a police state. The haphazard movement of detainees between centres was set out in Department of Homeland Security, Office of Inspector General, *Immigration and Customs Enforcement's Tracking and Transfers of Detainees*, OIG-09–41, March 2009.

109 Department of Homeland Security Appropriations Act 2010 (P.L. 111–83).

110 Australian Human Rights Commission, *Preliminary Report of the Detention of Boat Arrivals*, Report to the Minister No. 5, November 1997. They argued for compliance with the UNHCR Excomm. 30 standards.

111 www.abc.net.au/7.30/content/2001/s357998.htm.

112 Report of Justice P.N. Bhagwati, Regional Advisor for Asia and the Pacific of the United Nations High Commissioner for Human Rights, Mission to Australia 24th May to 2nd June 2002, 20: http://jmm.aaa.net.au/articles/1364.htm.

Justice Bhagwati was considerably distressed by what he saw and heard in Woomera IRPC. He met men, women and children who had been in detention for several months, some of them even for one or two years. They were prisoners without having committed any offence. Their only fault was that they had left their native home of great international concern, inducing the intervention of UNHCR.[113] Regardless of such international pressure, in 2004 the Liberal Party ran for office again, saying that 'mandatory detention plays a significant role in maintaining the integrity of the migration program'.[114] In 2006, $400,000 was paid by the federal government as compensation to an eleven-year-old Iranian boy who suffered psychological harm after being held for years in Australian detention centres.[115] The policy continued despite constant criticism that it was excessive in the face of the relatively small numbers of asylum seekers.[116]

and sought to find refuge or a better life on the Australian soil. In virtual prison-like conditions in the detention centre, they lived initially in the hope that soon their incarceration would come to an end but with the passage of time, the hope gave way to despair. When Justice Bhagwati met the detainees, some of them broke down. He could see despair on their faces. He felt that he was in front of a great human tragedy. He saw young boys and girls, who instead of breathing the fresh air of freedom, were confined behind spiked iron bars with gates barred and locked preventing them from going out and playing and running in the open fields. He saw gloom on their faces instead of the joy of youth. These children were growing up in an environment which affected their physical and mental growth and many of them were traumatized and led to harm themselves in utter despair . . . 45. . . . Furthermore such extended and often seemingly open-ended detention appears to cause great distress and psychological trauma to several persons in detention in Woomera. Justice Bhagwati witnessed several persons who had committed acts of self-harm, such as slicing of wrists as well as stitching of lips . . . 62 . . . As noted above, the International Covenant on Civil and Political Rights (Article 7) and the Convention Against Torture and Other Cruel, Inhuman or Degrading Treatment or Punishment, explicitly prohibit torture and all cruel, inhuman and degrading treatment and punishment. The human rights situation which Justice Bhagwati found in Woomera IRPC could, in many ways, be considered inhuman and degrading.'

113 See also UNHCR Position on Detention, Briefing Note, 25th January 2002:

'UNHCR is concerned about the situation in Australia's Woomera detention centre and we are in daily contact with the Australian government, trying to help in finding a solution. In general, UNHCR opposes detention of asylum seekers, particularly when it is prolonged and when it involves minors, which is the case in Australia.

We do not condone any acts of violence, including acts of self-harm committed by asylum seekers at the Woomera detention centre. However, though deplorable, these acts are a gauge of the degree of desperation of the people who commit them' www.unhcr.org.

114 http://web.archive.org/web/20060918194316;http://www.liberal.org.au/default. cfm?action=plaintext_policy&id=2732.

115 www.smh.com.au.

116 For example, see K. Bem, N. Field, N. Maclellan, S. Meyer and T. Morris, *A Price too High: The Cost of Australia's Approach to Asylum Seekers*, A Just Australia and Oxfam Australia, August 2007, http://pandora.nla.gov.au (accessed 12 June 2010).

Following a change of government in June 2008, the new minister responsible said that 'Labor rejects the notion that dehumanising and punishing unauthorised arrivals with long-term detention is an effective or civilised response.'[117] It was proposed that three groups would be subject to mandatory detention: unauthorized arrivals for the purpose of health, identity and security checks; those who pose an unacceptable risk to the community; and those who have been repeatedly non-compliant with visa conditions or immigration processes.[118] The relevant parliamentary committee set out new guidelines, time scales for security checks, maximum lengths of time in detention, more frequent reviews and judicial review on the merits after twelve months.[119] The proposed change in policy has not yet been finally implemented. Even if implemented, lengthy detention in remote camps away from the mainland with minimal judicial oversight would persist. There has been continued criticism of conditions in these places.[120]

In Europe there is no overall collection of data amongst EU Member States' detention policies. The most comprehensive survey of detention conditions conducted so far paints a portrait of generally grim and sometimes very inhuman conditions.[121] Most closed centres have been set up in pre-existing facilities which have been '*recycled*' to detain migrants, including former army barracks, hangars, deserted warehouses, camps

117 www.abc.net.au/news/stories/2008/07/29/2317303.htm.
118 www.aph.gov.au/house/committee/MIG/detention/subs.htm (forward p. vii).
119 Parliament of Australia Joint Standing Committee on Migration 'Inquiry into Immigration Detention in Australia' 2008, www.aph.gov.au/house/committee.
120 2009 Immigration Detention Report: Summary of observations following visits to Australia's immigration detention facilities. www.hreoc.gov.au/human_rights/immigration/idc2008.html:
    The remoteness, infrequent flights and prohibitive costs make it almost inaccessible to external scrutiny bodies, refugee support groups and non-government organisations working on immigration detention issues. The small size and limited capacity of the local community make it difficult for detainees to access services including health care, mental health care, legal assistance, and cultural and religious support. In addition to these overarching views, the Commission has serious concerns about the immigration detention facilities on Christmas Island, particularly the new detention centre. It is a harsh facility with excessive levels of security. (71)
121 Citizens Rights and Constitutional Affairs, *Report for European Parliament, 2007*, 'The conditions in centres for third country national (detention camps, open centres as well as transit centres and transit zones) with a particular focus on provisions and facilities for persons with special needs in the 25 EU member states' (carried out by research consultancy Steps Consulting), www.libertysecurity.org.

and temporary buildings. Police stations, prisons and former prisons were sometimes used to hold detainees alongside criminals. Cages and containers were used in Italy and a former floating platform in the Netherlands. Although hygiene standards were generally adequate, in some of the centres visited they were described as unacceptable, or even inhumane or degrading.[122] In the vast majority of closed centres prison conditions were employed. These included confinement to small cells, restrictions on exercise times, restrictions on visits and the handcuffing of detainees during transfers. A large number of centres are equipped with cells for solitary confinement.

Facilities were not designed for long-term detention. Detainees experienced isolation, confusion over procedures or the duration of confinement and could not access information on their rights. These difficulties are related to various factors, including difficulties communicating with the outside world, a lack of qualified personnel, difficulties accessing NGOs, and difficulties accessing translators and interpreters. The investigators received a constant stream of reports on the large number of people suffering from psychological disorders held in closed centres. The pathogenic nature of confinement itself was often highlighted, especially in cases of prolonged periods of detention. Detention centres create or aggravate psychological or psychiatric disorders. The care available for detainees with psychological or psychiatric disorders was often insufficient or inappropriate.

Malta has experienced the strongest condemnation for its holding of asylum seekers intercepted at sea in two army barracks. The UN Working Group on Arbitrary Detention said that, whilst the government's target was to limit detention to twelve months, many spent '18 months in custody under appalling conditions'.[123] The physical and mental health of detainees was harmed by the duration and conditions of detention. This limited their ability to understand their rights and to follow the legal proceedings related to them. Medical charities at one point refused to continue working in these facilities because they felt the conditions

---

122 In Cyprus, Malta, Spain, Italy and Greece overcrowding, a lack of privacy and a lack of basic hygiene products were reported. In 2009 the UNHCR called for the immediate closure of the Pagani detention centre in Greece because of terrible overcrowding and insanitary conditions: 200 women and children had access to two toilets and one shower. See www.unhcr.org/4aelaf146.html, accessed 12 June 2010.

123 UN Working Group on Arbitary Detention reports on Malta in Press Release 26 Jan. 2009–08-01, see http://jrsmalta.org; www.unhchr.ch.

undermined their efforts to care for detainees.[124] The Maltese government had justified the policy by reference to the already dense population of Malta and the fact that it was a place where boat arrivals of irregular migrants were common. It was accepted that there was an element of deterrence in the policy.

As noted in Chapter 4, in an extension of the EU 'virtual border' there has been detention 'outsourcing' to North Africa. This is linked to EU policies to encourage neighbouring countries to intercept and process migrants en route to Europe. Italy has even transferred detainees from its own facilities to Libya.[125] In this respect detention conditions in some of these countries on the periphery have given rise to serious concern. Investigation revealed that asylum seekers reported numerous violations during their detention at a variety of facilities in Libya, including beatings, overcrowding, sub-standard conditions, not having access to a lawyer and even sexual violence and rape.[126] The European Committee for the Prevention of Torture condemned the Italian policy of interception at sea and forced return to Libya which led to detention in these facilities.[127] The detention of these migrants, although not subject to extensive monitoring because of difficulties in securing access, appears to be extremely lawless with detainees being held entirely at the discretion of their captors.

International politics and detention conditions: sovereignty or external accountability?

Whilst states have pursued policies aligned to domestic political success, the harsh effects of administrative detention have been subject to criticism from a developing international political society.[128] This modest

---

124 Médecins sans Frontières. A report on their work in Maltese Detention Centres is available at www.msf.org.

125 www.hrw.org. Human Rights Watch, *Pushed Back, Pushed Around; Italy's Forced Return of Boat Migrants and Asylum Seekers, Libya's Mistreatment of Migrants and Asylum Seekers*, 21 Sept., 2009.

126 Human Rights Watch, 'Stemming the Flow: Abuses against migrants, asylum seekers, and refugees', www.hrw.org.

127 Report to the Italian Government on a visit to Italy by the Committee for the Prevention of Torture, 27 to 31 July 2009, CPT/Inf (2010) 14, para. 40.

128 It is this kind of 'externality' affecting outsiders that led Held to argue that globalization has rendered orthodox ideas of democracy redundant. He suggests that, until recently, 'democratic theory has tended to assume a "symmetrical" and "congruent" relationship between political decision-makers and the recipients of political decisions'. In fact, strict

accountability beyond the nation-state is less effective than it should be. As Held argues more generally, democracies are not accountable to all those whose decisions they affect. A global cosmopolitan democracy must entail 'the entrenchment of a cluster of rights, including civil, political, economic and social rights, in order to provide shape and limits to democratic decision-making'.[129] In relation to detention practices, we have seen both the strengths and limits of international accountability as it currently operates.

Because supra-national legal enforcement mechanisms remain weak, most external scrutiny amounts to political pressure. This has been facilitated through the evolution of standards on detention conditions both in terms of case-law and those set by international human rights bodies. Most prominently amongst these is Guideline 10 of the UNHCR Guidelines on Applicable Criteria and Standards Relating to Detention of Asylum Seekers.[130] This requires that detention conditions for asylum seekers should be 'humane with respect shown for the inherent dignity of the person' and that standards be prescribed by law. Perhaps the most important duty is to provide an initial screening to identify trauma or torture victims who should generally not be detained. Other important standards are a requirement to provide separate facilities for children, to keep asylum seekers separate from criminals, to allow regular private contact with visitors, to receive appropriate medical treatment, to have basic necessities like toiletries, to practise their religion, to be able to exercise and take recreation, and to receive education and training.

Whilst there has been no definitive study undertaken, some of the national practices outlined above clearly breach the UNHCR guidelines.[131] In 2002, the Special Rapporteur on the Human Rights of

migration policies affect people who were not involved in their making. D. Held, 'Law of States, Law of Peoples: Three Models of Sovereignty' (2002) 8 *Legal Theory* 33. See also D. Held, *Cosmopolitan Democracy*, London: Polity Press, 2000; D. Held, 'Democratic City-states to a Cosmopolitan Order?' (1992) 40 *Polit. Studies* 10.

129 *Ibid.*, 30.

130 Guidelines on Applicable Criteria and Standards Relating to Detention of Asylum Seekers 29 Feb. 1999, www.unhcr.org. Also see 1988 UN Body of Principles for the Protection of all Persons under any form of Detention or Imprisonment, 1955 UN Standard Minimum Rules for the Treatment of Prisoners and the 1990 UN Rules for the Protection of Juveniles Deprived of their Liberty. For Compendium of International Law, standards and guidelines related to the detention of refugees, asylum seekers and migrants, see http://idc.rfbf.com.au.

131 International Detention Coalition calls for an evaluation of the use of the UNHCR Guidelines by states: see www.idcoalition.org.

Migrants said that 'conditions of administrative detention are well below international standards'.[132] He criticized some of the practices described above, such as holding migrants in ordinary prisons with severe restrictions on their freedom of movement, right of communication and access to outdoors. Some facilities were not suitable for long-term detention such as warehouses, airports or stadiums, because they had poor hygiene, no privacy or exercise facilities. The conditions were overcrowded, with a lack of bedding or medical check-up and external oversight.[133] These also failed to comply with General Comment 15 of the Human Rights Committee that persons must be detained 'with humanity and with respect for the inherent dignity of their person'.[134]

More recently, concern has increased with the Special Rapporteur on the Human Rights of Migrants saying that 'by far the most frequent abuses against this group are discriminatory xenophobic and racist practices that occur during the administrative detention of undocumented migrants'.[135] In a recent report he summed up the tension completely: 'Although it is the sovereign right of all States to safeguard their borders and regulate their migration polices . . . It is the responsibility of the State, regardless of the legal status of the migrant, to ensure that fundamental rights norms are adhered to and that all migrants are treated with dignity.'[136] Drawing the link to the wider cultural environment influencing the treatment of detainees, he said: 'anti-immigrant discourse . . . prompted and legitimatized a notable increase in institutionalized discrimination leading to further violations'.

These practices and the heavy criticism they have attracted have also begun to influence international tribunals. Thus the use of airport terminal transit facilities to hold migrants for periods of over ten days was condemned by the European Court of Human Rights in *Riad and Idiab* v. *Belgium* as a breach of Article 3 ECHR because '[b]y its very nature, it was a place intended to receive people for extremely short periods of time. The transit zone, the nature of which could arouse in detainees a feeling of solitude, had no external area for walking or taking physical exercise, no internal catering facilities, and no radio or television to ensure contact with the outside world; it was in no way adapted to the requirements of a stay of more than ten days'. These conditions 'caused them considerable

---

132 *Annual Report 2002*, E/CN.4/2003/85, para. 55.   133 *Ibid.*, para. 17.
134 4 Nov. 1986, 27th Sess., HRI/GEN/1/Rev.0/Vol.1.
135 Annual Report 2005, 27 Dec. 2004, E/CN.4/2005/85 at 75.
136 Annual Report 2008, 25 Feb. 2008, Bustamante A/HRC/7/12 at 14.

mental suffering, undermining their human dignity and arousing in them feelings of humiliation and debasement'.[137]

But despite such cases, it must be emphasized that this is a rare instance of international judicial censure in relation to detention. This is no doubt partly because few cases are actually brought to tribunals, given the practical obstacles of doing so, but also because the threshold required to be met for detention to breach Article 3 ECHR is high. There have been several cases in which the Strasbourg Court has found no breach, particularly where there are no special factors relating to the vulnerability of the detainee or the extremity in conditions of detention. The mere long duration of detention has generally not breached Article 3 so long as other conditions are adequate, including the possibility of being released by judicial order.[138]

The detention of particularly vulnerable groups: the end of extremity?

The detention of vulnerable groups, particularly children, those with mental health problems and victims of torture or trauma has become a particular source of controversy. The true measure of the logic of 'firmness' in relation to border policy can be seen here; the holding of young children in prison-like facilities for months or even years suggests a policy that has become wholly detached from mainstream ethical moorings in the liberal concern to respect the moral worth of each person. The fact that many countries have continued to follow such practices expresses vividly the level of concern of the state to maintain 'legitimacy' over migration control. If there were truly a fair balance to be struck between

---

137 Application nos 29787/03 and 29810/03, Judgment of 24 Jan. 2008, para. 104. The Court was influenced by numerous adverse reports on the use of such inappropriate facilities by the Committee on the Prevention of Torture.

138 *A and Others* v. *United Kingdom*, Appn. no. 3455/05, Council of Europe, European Court of Human Rights, 19 Feb. 2009. In the national security detention cases in which detainees were held for some three to four years, the Court accepted that 'the uncertainty regarding their position and the fear of indefinite detention must, undoubtedly, have caused the applicants great anxiety and distress, as it would virtually any detainee in their position. Furthermore, it is probable that the stress was sufficiently serious and enduring to affect the mental health of certain of the applicants... It cannot, however, be said that the applicants were without any prospect or hope of release... In particular, they were able to bring proceedings to challenge the legality of the detention scheme under the 2001 Act and were successful before SIAC, on 30 July 2002, and the House of Lords on 16 December 2004.'

migration control and harm to detainees, these groups could rarely be deemed suitable for detention. As we have noted, however, state practice has found it difficult to legitimately release those who are unauthorized, however young or vulnerable. The politics of such practices are, however, now increasingly being challenged both from within and without liberal states. For these groups, it has been easier to build political opposition to detention. This stems from both the clearer international legal framework and that the fact that such groups can be viewed more readily as 'victims' rather than 'enemies'.

Turing to children, Article 37 of the UN Convention on the Rights of the Child requires that any detention 'shall be used only as a measure of last resort and for the shortest appropriate period of time'.[139] Article 3 requires that 'the best interests of the child' be the guiding standard for states parties. The Committee on the Rights of the Child said that unaccompanied children should not in general be detained, but where this was exceptionally necessary 'the underlying approach to such a programme should be "care" and not "detention"'.[140] They emphasized the need to ensure that adequate facilities for visits, play and education are provided. This has been extended by the UN Special Rapporteur on

139 States Parties shall ensure that:

    (a) No child shall be subjected to torture or other cruel, inhuman or degrading treatment or punishment. Neither capital punishment nor life imprisonment without possibility of release shall be imposed for offences committed by persons below eighteen years of age;

    (b) No child shall be deprived of his or her liberty unlawfully or arbitrarily. The arrest, detention or imprisonment of a child shall be in conformity with the law and shall be used only as a measure of last resort and for the shortest appropriate period of time;

    (c) Every child deprived of liberty shall be treated with humanity and respect for the inherent dignity of the human person, and in a manner which takes into account the needs of persons of his or her age.

In particular, every child deprived of liberty shall be separated from adults unless it is considered in the child's best interest not to do so and shall have the right to maintain contact with his or her family through correspondence and visits, save in exceptional circumstances;

    (d) Every child deprived of his or her liberty shall have the right to prompt access to legal and other appropriate assistance, as well as the right to challenge the legality of the deprivation of his or her liberty before a court or other competent, independent and impartial authority, and to a prompt decision on any such action.

140 General Comment No. 6, Treatment of Unaccompanied and Separated Children Outside their Country of Origin, 1 September 2005, CRC/GC/2005/6, para. 63.

the Human Rights of Migrants, who said in 2009 that children should not be deprived of liberty as a sole consequence of their migratory status and that unaccompanied migrant children should not be detained at all.[141] Where, in exceptional cases, families with children must be detained, this should be in places promoting the best interests of children. Despite these provisions, lengthy detention of child migrants both with and without their parents is reported as quite widespread in many countries. In the United Kingdom there have been a number of reports highlighting the problem.[142] These have shown that detention in breach of Article 37 is not uncommon.[143]

The European Court of Human Rights took into account Article 37 and Article 3 of the Convention on the Rights of the Child in two important decisions that have limited, but not eliminated, the possibility of detaining migrant children. In *Mubilanzila Mayeka and Kaniki Mitunga v. Belgium*,[144] a five-year-old unaccompanied minor was detained for two months in a centre designed for adults. She was not assigned any specialist care, counselling or education. The Court noted that the state had an obligation 'to enable effective protection to be provided, particularly to children and other vulnerable members of society, and should include reasonable measures to prevent ill-treatment of which the authorities have or ought to have knowledge'.[145] The position of a very young unaccompanied child, with no status in a foreign land, meant that the obligation to offer protection 'takes precedence over considerations

---

141 *Annual Report of the Special Rapporteur for the Human Rights of Migrants*, Jorge Busta-
    mante, 14 May 2009, A/HRC/11/7, at para.106.

142 http://inspectorates.homeoffice.gov.uk.

    'The plight of detained children remained of great concern. While child welfare
    services had improved, an immigration removal centre can never be a suitable place
    for children and we were dismayed to find cases of disabled children being detained
    and some children spending large amounts of time incarcerated. We were concerned
    about ineffective and inaccurate monitoring of length of detention in this extremely
    important area. Any period of detention can be detrimental to children and their
    families, but the impact of lengthy detention is particularly extreme.'

143 'The Arrest and Detention of Children Subject to Immigration Control: A report fol-
    lowing the Children's Commisioner for England's visit to Yarl's Wood Immigration
    Removal Centre', April 2009, which showed that the average time had increased from
    eight to fifteen days. Some were held longer than twenty-eight days and the longest
    recorded is 103 days. In 2010, the new UK coalition government announced its inten-
    tion to cease holding children in detention. It was not clear at the time of writing that
    this commitment had been achieved.

144 *Mubilanzila Mayeka and Kaniki Mitunga v. Belgium*, 13178/03, 12 Oct. 2006.

145 Paragraph 53.

relating to [her] *status as an illegal immigrant*.[146] There was a breach of Article 3 in detaining her under these conditions.[147]

The Court went further in the more recent case of *Muskhadziyeva* v. *Belgium*,[148] in which a family, including four children aged between seven months and seven years, were held together for one month in a closed detention centre designed for adults. In this case, the Court found a violation of Article 3 in respect of the children despite the presence of their parents. This was because of the duration of detention, the age of the children, the medical evidence of psychological damage to one of them caused by ongoing detention and because of persistent adverse reports on the centre by independent monitors.[149] The court also found a violation of Article 5(1)(f) in the case of the children because the means used, including the place and conditions of detention, were not closely linked to the objective.[150] These cases do not make all detention of children illegal, but clearly require the conditions of detention to be completely different to those of adults. Such 'detention' would have to be experienced more like 'care', with more open centres permitting access to outside trips and recreation, play and education.

In the United States the use of detention for children has been the subject of ongoing litigation because of failures to adhere to agreed standards of care. The Supreme Court had established that children could be held in caring environments where no relative with custody was available.[151] Comprehensive standards were agreed to implement this ruling giving.[152] In *Re Hutto*, a federal law suit challenging family conditions at the Hutto detention centre was successful.[153] The investigations revealed the conditions inside the detention centre systematically breached the legal standards by confining children to a threatening medium secure prison with very limited access to recreation, play, education and outside space.[154]

---

146 Paragraph 56 (emphasis added).
147 Importantly, the Court also found a breach of Art. 5, the right to liberty. This is confusing because Art. 5 seems to turn upon the *reason and procedure* for authorizing detention, not the conditions thereof. However, for several years the European Court has looked at the detention regime as applied to the individual detainee to assess whether it is an acceptable means of pursuing the goal of detention.
148 Application 41442/07, Judgment of 19 Jan. 2010.
149 Paragraphs 57–63.   150 Paragraphs 73–5.
151 *Reno* v. *Flores* 507 U.S. 292 (1993).   152 *Flores* v. *Meese* No. 85–4544 (C.D. Cal. 1997).
153 *In re Hutto Family Detention Centre* No. 07–164 (W.D. Tex. 2007). In 2009 the government eventually agreed to stop holding families at the facility.
154 S. Gupta and J. Graybill, *Justice Denied: Immigration Families Detained At Hutto*, New York: ACLU, 2008.

The position of children in Australian detention centres has also been the subject of a number of critical reports by monitoring organizations in relation to international standards. In *Bakhtiyari v. Australia*,[155] the Human Rights Committee found violations of Articles 9 and 24(1) of the ICCPR when a mother and two children were detained for over two years, where there was evidence that the children were self-harming. In relation to the International Convention on the Rights of the Child ('ICRC') these violations arguably include discrimination on the basis of immigration status (Art. 2), failure to act in the best interests of the child as a primary consideration in all actions concerning children (Art. 3), and, *inter alia*, rights to development, healthcare and education.[156]

The conclusion of the Australian Human Rights Commission was that the mandatory detention policy was 'fundamentally inconsistent' with the ICRC. The policy failed to ensure that detention was a measure of last resort, for the shortest appropriate period of time and subject to effective independent review as required by Article 37. The Commission found in 2003 that detention of children averaged one year and eight months. Some sixty-two children (51%) had been in detention for more than two years. The longest period of detention of a child was over five years. Children in immigration detention suffered from anxiety, distress, bed-wetting, suicidal ideation and self-destructive behaviour, including attempted and actual self-harm. The methods used by children to self-harm included hunger strikes, attempted hanging, slashing, swallowing shampoo or detergents and lip-sewing. Some children were also diagnosed with specific psychiatric illnesses such as depression and post-traumatic stress disorder. The government rejected the report, arguing that allowing children out of detention would 'send a message to people smugglers' encouraging them to bring more'.[157] In the face of such criticism, and following a change of government, mandatory detention of children was finally rescinded in 2008.

---

155 UN Doc. CCPR/C/79/D/1069/2002 (29 Oct. 2003).
156 Submission to the National Inquiry into Children in Immigration Detention from the Organising Committee for Seminar on Children and Families in Immigration and Detention Centres (Social Justice and Social Change Research, University of Western Sydney) May 2002, www.hreoc.gov.au. Also 'A Last Resort?', Australian Human Rights Commission National Enquiry into Children in Detention, April 2004, www.hreoc.gov. au.
157 A. Vanstone (Minister for Immigration and Multicultural and Indigenous Affairs), *HREOC Inquiry into children in immigration detention report tabled*, media release, Canberra, 13 May 2004, viewed 22 May 2009, http://parlinfo.aph.gov.au.

Whilst there has been increasing pressure to severely limit the detention of children, who present a relatively easily defined group, the position of other vulnerable groups is more uncertain. UNHCR Guideline 7 says that given the very negative effects of detention on the psychological well-being of those detained, active consideration of possible alternatives should precede any order to detain asylum seekers who are unaccompanied elderly persons, torture or trauma victims or persons with a mental or physical disability.[158] It concludes that detention in such cases should only occur if a medical practitioner agrees it will not 'adversely affect their health and well being'.

Despite this recommendation there remains widespread detention of such persons.[159] Detainees, particularly women, also appear to find it difficult to get appropriate healthcare in detention.[160] This is partly because states do not have effective methods of identifying vulnerable people. In addition, there is a reluctance to accept that the vulnerability is genuine or severe enough to outweigh immigration control interests. The Australian experience is the most revealing. For example, in *Madafferi*

---

158 UNHCR Guidelines on Applicable Criteria and Guidelines relating to Detention of Asylum Seekers 29 Feb. 1999.

159 Institute for Race Relations, 'Driven to Desperate Measures', Sept. 2006, which highlights six suicides since 1989 in one UK detention centre at Harmondsworth. *HMIP Inquiry into the Quality of Healthcare at Yarl's Wood*, 4 Oct. 2006, which said that there was 'a growing concern among medical and other commentators that the increased use of immigration detention raises serious concerns about the mental health of detainees, particularly in cases of prolonged detention of uncertain duration and where detainees arrive with underlying health problems' (1.7). HMIP Inspection of Five Immigration Service Custodial Establishments, April 2003, said that 'healthcare, and particularly mental health care, was an issue in most centres ... arrangements were in place to provide in-patient psychiatric care in the community for those who were seriously mentally ill, but those who were disturbed but not sectionable and arguably not fit for detention remained in a custodial rather than a therapeutic environment. The provision of a psychology service was helpful in assisting with the assessment of stress disorders but it was inappropriate to provide treatment in a custodial environment and their assessments were not routinely used to inform an alternative disposal' (3.3). See also Bail for Immigration Detainees, *Fit to be detained? Challenging the detention of asylum seekers and migrants with mental health needs*, London, 2005 using data compiled by Médecins sans Frontières to show a lack of proper care.

160 Human Rights Watch, 'Detained and Dismissed: Women's Struggles to Obtain Health Care in United States Immigration Detention', HRW, New York, 17 Mar. 2009: 'Most immigration detainees in the United States are held as a result of administrative, rather than criminal, infractions, but the medical treatment they receive can be worse than that of convicted criminals in the US prison system. The inspector general's office at the Department of Homeland Security (DHS) has issued two reports in the past three years criticizing medical treatment at immigration detention facilities.'

v. *Australia*,[161] a detainee was returned to detention despite serious mental health problems. This was found to be a violation of the right to be treated with humanity and have his dignity respected under Article 10(1) ICCPR. In *C* v. *Australia*,[162] it was held to be a violation of Article 7 ICCPR to detain when it was clear that detention was causing mental illness. Despite increasingly serious medical assessments about the detainee's condition and a suicide attempt, it was only after several months that the minister exercised his exceptional power to release him.

The limits of a global politics of migration: immigration detainees as outlaws from international society

Despite the cases discussed above, the international human rights system has been only a residual and relatively weak tool to control detention practices. There is little real appetite on the part of states to accept external constraints on their treatment of detainees. This is largely because they view the political benefits of maximal discretion highly and do not see any great cost in adopting harsh measures. Detainees have little status in international society. The contrast with the example of the laws of war is a telling one. In the nineteenth century sovereign states developed customary practices of agreed welfare standards for war prisoners and protection of their legal rights. This derived from the sovereign equality of states in Europe, so that as Schmitt puts it: '[T]he opponent in war was recognized as a *justus hostis* and was distinguished from rebels, criminals, and pirates... In this way, war was transformed into a relation between mutually equal and sovereign states... it became possible to establish numerous legal institutions. In particular, it became possible to view prisoners of war and the vanquished no longer as objects of punishment or vengeance, or as hostages...'[163] This 'civilization' of war meant depoliticizing the treatment of prisoners in favour of objective standards.

We have not seen similar agreed practices on the treatment of migrants held by states. Diplomatic negotiations in relation to the problem of detainees have been piecemeal and faltering. Detainees are often failed asylum seekers who have impugned their own governments by fleeing. Having failed to secure refugee status, their governments refuse to accept them back, or deny that they are citizens. Some detainees are undeportable

---

161 UN Doc. CCPR/C/81/D/1011/2001 (26 Aug. 2004).
162 UN Doc. CCPR/C/76/D/900/1999 (13 Nov. 2002).
163 Schmitt, *The Nomos of the Earth*, 309–11.

on legal grounds because they face torture in their home country. In all these instances there is a denial of protection by sovereign states of their own citizens. This leads to a kind of *de facto* statelessness.[164] Where it is politically unpopular to take such detainees in, detaining states have sought to induce alternative states to take them off their hands.[165]

This is a marked change from nineteenth-century practice, when, as Simpson notes, '[d]iplomats, soldiers and aliens, for example, were subject to forms of legal protection or punishment but their legal personality was subordinate to or derived from the personality of the state'.[166] Thus harm to aliens was an injury to their state, just as harm they committed during war was their state's responsibility; '[i]n these cases, individual harm or deviance was assimilated to interstate relations'.[167] Nowadays, detained migrants, mainly from less powerful countries, find little diplomatic pressure can be, or is, exerted on their behalf.

Unlike prisoners of war, irregular migrants and those ordered deported now usually stand alone, shorn of this crucial protection by a sovereign government. Given that irregular migration is considered a threat to international order and subject to many initiatives to combat it, we begin to see the immigration detainee as a kind of modern-day pirate.[168] Pirates were defined by their lack of state authority and in acting for private gain.[169] Irregular migrants do not represent their governments. They usually act alone or with private agents out of private motives. Controlling such migrants is part of the 'pest control' of modern life rather than a

---

164 Whilst a number are *de jure* stateless, it is hard to put a figure on this. The most obvious group are stateless Palestinians.

165 In the case of the United States, this is most obvious in relation to national security detainees at Guantanamo Bay who have been declared not possible to prosecute, but whom the government will not allow to enter US territory. In the case of Australian policy under the 'Pacific Solution', detainees were not even alleged to be national security risks, yet the government detained them and then persuaded neighbouring countries to process their asylum claims. In a further twist, the government even refused to accept into Australia detainees it had recognized as refugees at its offshore processing centres. These were also then offered to neighbouring nations in return for funds.

166 G. Simpson, *Law, War and Crime*, Cambridge: Polity Press, 2007, 162.   167 *Ibid.*

168 The United Nations Convention against Transnational Organized Crime, adopted by General Assembly Resolution 55/25 of 15 Nov. 2000. The convention is further supplemented by three protocols, which target three specific areas and manifestations of organized crime including: the Protocol to Prevent, Suppress and Punish Trafficking in Persons, Especially Women and Children and the Protocol against the Smuggling of Migrants by Land, Sea and Air.

169 Simpson, *Law, War and Crime*, concluding that international terrorists are also now treated as pirates, says they 'are characterized as an enemy of mankind . . . operating outside the bounds of law and outside the jurisdiction of national law' 177.

matter of inter-state politics.[170] The old statuses of alien friend and alien enemy which arose from the mutual recognition of sovereign states and conferred diplomatic protection upon foreigners have largely gone from international society.

This is part of a more general failure of any inter-state migration politics to develop.[171] Outside the European Union there is no international consensus on what to do with unauthorized migrants. The 1951 Refugee Convention was the last major treaty signed by Western nations directly conferring rights upon such individuals. This took place only in the specific political climate of the aftermath of World War Two and the Cold War, when it was considered essential to restore international stability in Europe.[172] Since then, destination countries have felt no general sense of mutual interest with sending countries.[173] Countries of emigration and immigration are often widely different in power and influence. Long-term relationships between wealthy host and poorer sending states, leading to mutual diplomatic and political influence over migration policy, have been rare.[174]

170 Schmitt speaks of international 'pest control' arising in the post-World War One period when states no longer recognized each other (and by extension each others' nationals) as equals with mutual and reciprocal rights and obligations. Schmitt, *The Nomos of the Earth*, 309–11.

171 '[T]he framework for immigration policy... is rooted in the past: immigration policy has yet to address the changed role of borders and governments in economic integration as we move into the twenty-first century. Border control remains the basic mechanism for regulating immigration... The receiving country is represented as a passive agent... immigration policy becomes a decision to be more or less benevolent in admitting immigrants.' S. Sassen, *Guests and Aliens*, New York: New Press, 1999, 151.

172 The EEC Treaty concluded in very different economic circumstances provides the basic template for free migration with the EU. The much more difficult task of agreeing policies in relation to third-country nationals in the 1990s and beyond shows how hard such questions have become. Beyond the EU, in modern times the only general treaty specifically conferring rights on migrants is the 1990 UN Treaty on the Rights of Migrant Workers, but this has not achieved acceptance by developed states.

173 This is despite arguments that coordination of the global labour markets would benefit all nations. Nayyar suggests that 'sooner rather than later, therefore, it is worth contemplating a multilateral framework for immigration laws and consular practices that govern the cross-border movement of people, similar to the multilateral frameworks that exist, or are sought to be created, for the governance of national law, or rules about the movement of goods, services, technology, investment, finance, and information across national boundaries'. D. Nayyar, 'Cross-border Movements of People', in D. Nayyar (ed.), *Governing Globalization*, Oxford University Press, 2002, 170.

174 The United States and Mexico is an exceptional case where there has been clear mutual interdependence in relation to migration over many years. This is partly a function also of the political influence of a large citizenry of Hispanic origin in the United States.

More coordination to regulate migration might provide mutual benefits, but there is no consensus to achieve it.[175] The Special Rapporteur for the Human Rights of Migrants has thus argued that 'the phenomenon of irregular migration should be addressed through a new concept of migration management with human rights as an integral part. Migration management is in fact an extremely complex series of processes which go well beyond unilateral punitive measures and control'.[176] The failure to achieve this coordination means that illegal entry is in effect 'created', because unilateral action is taken in the knowledge that migrants will continue to cross borders. This creation of illegality leads to greater incidence of detention. Furthermore, the duration of detention is greater because of a failure to achieve consensus on issues like the issue of travel documents and recognition of nationality of detainees. For decades there have been efforts to broker bilateral readmission agreements between Western nations and migrants' countries of origin.[177] However, given that many detainees are unwanted by any country, including their own, these have limited effectiveness. In short, many immigration detainees have become a nuisance to international society because they do not fit anywhere. They have come to rely upon the relatively weak protection offered by the political exhortations of general international human rights law.

Are detention camps exceptional political spaces beyond all law?

Some have been led to propose that detention centres are a new form of exceptional legal space that is not within the normal legal order. First, although detainees are not being officially punished for any crime, detention is often in prison-like facilities. Second, there are many difficulties in detainees securing access to legal rights. Third, there are clearly instances of serious hardship, neglect and abuse in centres perpetrated against

---

175 In a realist approach, Keohane explains that only where an 'accountability relationship' exists can we expect actors to take account of the impact of their decisions. This kind of relationship depends upon the ability of those affected to impose costs on the decision-maker. He draws the distinction between 'internal' and 'external' accountability; the former denotes accountability to democratic electorates within states, the latter, responsibility to outsiders affected by their decisions. He says that 'internal democracy will not assure accountability to outsiders whom the powerful democracy affects'. R. Keohane, 'Global Governance and Democratic Accountability', in D. Held and M. Koenig-Archibugi (eds), *Taming Globalization*, Cambridge: Polity Press, 2003.

176 *Annual Report 2002*, E/CN.4/2003/85, para. 65.

177 These efforts should not compromise safeguards against *refoulement* of refugees and those facing torture or other breaches of human rights in principle.

detainees. Finally, detainees are held for often long periods by executive order without clear reasons and without clear end points. By extension, detainees are not regulated by regular law but remain at the mercy of executive decisions in a kind of non-legal space.

This perspective draws upon Schmitt's idea that truly 'political' decisions on fundamental questions relating to the foundation and security of the state are 'exceptions' for which the law cannot provide. Thus for Agamben, '[t]he camps are thus born not out of ordinary law ... but out of a state of exception and martial law'.[178] He traces their origins back to older European executive devices to suspend the constitution in order to protect state security. But he contends that, far from being limited to emergency situations, the modern detention camp has become normalized as 'a new juridico-political paradigm in which the norm becomes indistinguishable from the exception'.[179] He draws a connection between concentration camps from the time of Weimar Germany through Vichy France and on to modern immigration holding areas, concluding that '[i]n all these cases an apparently innocuous space ... actually delimits a space in which the normal order is de facto suspended and in which whether or not atrocities are committed depends not on law, but on the civility and ethical sense of the police who temporarily act as sovereign'.[180]

Agamben therefore contends that persons entering such camps are stripped of their rights so completely that 'no act permitted against them could appear any longer as a crime'. They are reduced to 'bare life'. Citing Schmitt's idea that the modern state seeks to control by reference to vague non-justiciable factors in immigration cases, he argues that '[j]ust as the early concentration camps invoked a "state of exception" based on considerations of "national security" rather than criminal behaviour, the inmates of *zones d'attente* at airports and certain outskirts of our cities are deemed to have no claim on the nation while paradoxically they are brought more firmly under its control by virtue of their exclusion'.[181] Finally, he concludes that the inmates of camps have been effectively 'banned' from the legal order, but notes the ambiguity of this statement in evocative language: 'He who has been banned is not, in fact, simply set outside the law and made indifferent to it but rather abandoned by it, that is exposed and threatened on the threshold in which life and law, outside and inside, become indistinguishable. It is literally not possible to

---

178 G. Agamben, *Homo Sacer: Sovereign Power and Bare Life* (trans. D. Heller-Roazen), Stanford University Press, 1998, 167.
179 *Ibid.*, 170.   180 *Ibid.*, 174.   181 *Ibid.*, 148.

say whether the one who has been banned is outside or inside the juridical order.'[182]

Arendt, writing about the camps in Europe during the period 1930–50, drew similar conclusions. She argued that immigration camps for displaced persons after World War Two were on a spectrum that included the concentration camps of Stalin and the Nazis. Although the camps for these refugees and stateless persons were 'relatively mild forms', all the camps had one thing in common: 'the human masses sealed off in them are treated as if they no longer existed, as if what happened in them were no longer of any interest to anybody, as if they were already dead and some evil spirit gone mad were amusing himself by stopping them for a while between life and death before admitting them to eternal peace'.[183] Other writers have reached similar conclusions about modern-day immigration detention centres in Australia,[184] the United States[185] and Europe.[186]

This alarming portrait of modern immigration detention centres as lawless environments where detainees are at the mercy of both their guards and their government masters must, however, be qualified in important respects. The first is that in all democracies detainees have remained, as a matter of law, protected by civil and criminal sanctions. Thus the authorities would in principle face prosecution or civil damages claims if they assaulted or starved detainees. Guards have a basic duty of care for those held in detention. Where they have suffered serious breaches of their civil rights, by being detained without lawful authority, they have not been denied access to justice to sue for damages or to challenge the legality of detention. In this sense they retain legal personality. Civil damages have also been awarded where detainees have suffered serious

---

182 *Ibid.*, 29.   183 *Origins of Totalitarianism*, 445.

184 For exceptional states see J. Webber, 'National Sovereignty, Migration and the Tenuous Hold of Legality' in O. Schmidtke and S. Ozcurumez (eds), *Of States, Rights, and Social Closure: Governing Migration and Citizenship*, New York: Palgrave Macmillan, 2008, 61–90.

185 Simon J., 'Refugees in a Carceral Age: The Rebirth of Immigration Prisons in the United States' (1998) 10(3) *Public Culture* 577–607, who argues that unlike Enlightenment notions of prison as a site of reformation and education, immigration detention 'invokes the earlier tradition of monarchical use of imprisonment as a site for enforcing undemocratic and unaccountable political orders' and 'belongs to a facet of governmental power largely unconstrained by the precedents of twentieth-century constitutional law' 585.

186 S. Perera, 'What is a Camp . . . ?' [2002] 1 *Borderlands e-journal*; M. Gibney, 'A Thousand Little Guantanmos: Western States Measures to Prevent the Arrival of Refugees', in K.T. Tunsall (ed.), *Displacement, Asylum and Migration*, Oxford University Press, 2006, 139–68.

harm by reason of the conditions of detention. There is little evidence of formal immunity from suit for the state. From the perspective of law, detention has generally been based upon a clear legal power based on (a) their unauthorized immigration status; and (b) effecting expulsion or exclusion. Additionally, there is a developing national and international network of organizations scrutinizing detention practices and partially holding governments to account.

Nevertheless, the record shows that conditions in detention centres are troubling. Detainees' legal status, whilst not an exhaustive cause, is a contributing factor to this. They have been deemed unwanted by the state. At best, they should not be present any longer. At worst, they are represented, individually or collectively, as part of a threat to the detaining nation. It is perhaps not surprising that there have been abuses committed towards them. Furthermore, immigration detainees are often likely to be exceptionally vulnerable, lacking contact with the outside world, funds, language skills and lawyers. They find it difficult to secure the civil rights available to them and this may have encouraged a sense of impunity. Where detainees have been held in offshore processing camps their legal position is weaker still. The US base at Guantanamo Bay and the Australian asylum camps in Nauru, Maunus Islands and Papua New Guinea were all outside the territorial jurisdiction of the courts. In these cases, detainees have struggled to even establish the power of domestic courts to review the legality of their detention, much less call upon any of their other civil rights.

Most importantly, detention is not usually authorized or reviewed by courts and is often quite open-ended. Detainees' liberty depends upon a range of factors; processing claims and appeals, reviewing travel document applications, assessing transport arrangements to and security in a country of proposed return. Many of these are in the hands of officials and depend on their discretion, efficiency, good will or resources.

Whilst detainees may withdraw applications or appeals and volunteer to be returned, this will not necessarily end their detention. If they cannot be expelled, detention can often continue indefinitely. It is clear that these features render them vulnerable to arbitrariness. Some states appear to have come to view detention as a contest of wills, to see if they can induce migrants to go home or not migrate in the first place. Mandatory detention provisions further erode detainees' individuality in this battle of wills. Such a detainee is simply part of a problem group rather than a person, with all the complexity and frailty this implies. Where this attitude is transmitted to the detention centres, the dangers of abuse are greater still. Detentions lasting years at a time, seen in Australia and the United States, clearly evoke Arendt's image of detainees being held in a kind of purgatory. Whilst modern administrative detention is not outside the law, current practices erode the dignity of both governments and detainees by inviting abuse of power and arbitrariness.

Imperfect borders and imperfect membership: liberalism, security and imperfection

As we noted above, liberal political theory has not said much about the *administration* of border controls. The problem has been largely assumed away in favour of asking questions about *membership* – which migrants should be admitted or expelled, on what criteria and with how much due process? These amount to questions of abstract justice. Even for illegal immigrants, debates have focused upon trying to resolve membership issues in a more inclusive or fair manner. Thus Benhabib argues for a scheme of *just membership* of a political community for all *persons*, not simply *just distribution* between *citizens*. This should entail, *inter alia*, 'the vindication of the right of every human being "to have rights," that is to be a *legal* person, entitled to certain inalienable rights, regardless of the status of their political membership. The status of alienage ought not to denude one of fundamental rights.'[187]

There may indeed be a set of fundamental moral rights owed to all persons, perhaps derived from international human rights law. However, these rights cannot exist without any regard to border controls. We need to explore how far 'fundamental' rights may be constrained to promote border security. It is not possible *a priori* to decide upon a catalogue of 'rights' for unauthorized persons – this would effectively amount to

---

187 S. Benhabib, *The Rights of Others*, Cambridge University Press, 2004, 3. Benhabib draws upon Arendt's work on the problem of statelessness during the period up to World War Two. Addressing the problem of minorities who were stripped of basic rights (including citizenship) by totalitarian governments, Arendt spoke of this 'right to have rights'. She noted that such practices meant that 'belonging to a community into which one is born is no longer a matter of course and not belonging no longer a matter of choice . . . his treatment by others does not depend on what he does or does not do. This extremity, and nothing else, is the situation of people deprived of human rights.' Arendt, *The Origins of Totalitarianism*, 177. Benhabib argues that the problem faced by modern migrants is similar because they find they have no legal status in their host countries. Their individual qualities, actions and life-plans are subsumed under their unlawful status. Of course, as has been noted, migrants without lawful immigration status do have some rights (for example, the general protection of the criminal law against violence).

their 'reauthorization'. In the end, national and international politics must largely determine, through diplomacy, campaigning, regularization programmes and legislative debate, the position of migrants.

What does liberal political morality dictate can or should be done to unauthorized persons? These 'outsiders' are actually physically present and subject to the power of the state.[188] As Schuck notes, 'these brute facts present liberalism with a poignant predicament'.[189] This book argues that we need to move away from our concentration on *ends* (who shall we allow to be members?) and look instead at *means* (what actions can we legitimately take to uphold our membership rules?). Evaluating which means of control are both effective and legitimate is a key question for contemporary migration politics. In practice, migrants arrive or enter without permission. Others stay beyond their permission or are ordered to leave. Migration controls are imperfect. What steps to prevent entry or secure removal can liberals endorse? The political morality of controlling borders extends to all those arriving or present, not just potential arrivals.[190]

From the use of naval interceptions and extra-legal forced returns, to long-term detention or the denial of rights to work or marry, a failure to engage here with the concept of what 'security' means and requires has allowed inward-looking non-liberal approaches to flourish in this space. Whilst a comprehensive code of rights, a final 'just' cosmopolitan constitution, cannot exist without a global government, practical reason, history and experience can guide such an enquiry. This amounts to

188 J. Fishkin, *The Limits of Obligation*, New Haven, CT: Yale University Press, 1982, who emphasizes the tension between liberalism's dual commitments to equality and to limits on individual moral sacrifice so that the commitment to impartiality and individuality are in unresolvable conflict. In the absence of justice standards that cross borders, liberalism 'moves in two directions: first, to emphasize the pragmatic value of humanitarianism, and second, to the development of "internal" justice standards' 67.

189 'These brute facts present liberalism with a poignant predicament. Committed to the rule of law but confronted by individuals who . . . have found community in America only after flouting that law, liberalism cannot legitimate their presence. Committed to the moral primacy of consent, liberalism cannot embrace those who enter by stealth. Committed to universal human rights, liberalism cannot secure those rights in the real world without rooting itself in political institutions that are actually capable of instantiating its values. Today, and for the foreseeable future, those political institutions are the institutions of the *nation*.' P. Schuck, *Citizens, Strangers and In-betweens*, Boulder, CO: Westview Press, 1998, 78.

190 As Bosniak puts it: 'Under real world conditions, border and interior are inevitably imbricated, most directly and graphically in the person of the alien.' L. Bosniak, *The Citizen and the Alien*, Princeton and Oxford, Princeton University Press, 2006, 124.

adopting what Amartya Sen has recently called, in an attack on social contract approaches to justice, 'open impartiality' towards persons over whom states have 'effective power'.[191]

Beyond membership and constraining the techniques of migration control: interrogating the border 'war'

Although the rhetoric of immigration control has exhibited war-like tones, it seems unlikely that any Western nation is facing an existential threat from migration. Lawful migration has in fact been welcomed and encouraged. The goals of migration policy are usually social and economic, not to achieve 'security' against crime or war. Borders will always remain porous. States will never have the means or even the desire to select and 'approve' every immigrant who enters or remains. This is true even of the millions of 'authorized' workers, tourists or students who are not subject to any real risk assessment. The benefits of current extensive migration are adjudged to outweigh any burdens. Whilst in rare situations, the migration of peoples may have seemed 'indistinguishable from conquest by an invading army',[192] this is wholly misleading. These odd large influxes have not been directed by foreign powers as agents of conquest. In any event, Western governments have usually prevented such large-scale mass movements from taking hold by visa restrictions and other extra-territorial measures.

Where there is no invasion by a foreign power, the 'security' that is in issue is less pressing. It may be economic, cultural or psychological in nature. Even if it relates to crime, as Waldron points out, '[a] legitimate state takes care in regard to the safety of those in the territory it dominates, whereas an illegitimate regime is either careless of the safety of those who are at its mercy or solicitous of the safety of some of them but not of others'.[193] Therefore, whilst managing the process of migration is vitally important, it is becoming increasingly clear that there can and must in fact be limits on what measures can be taken in the name of immigration control: 'popular sovereignty does not mean unlimited sovereignty'.[194]

---

191 A. Sen, *The Idea of Justice*, London: Penguin, 2010, 206.
192 D.C. Hendrikson, 'Migration in Law and Ethics: A Realist Perspective', in B. Barry and R.E. Goodin (eds), *Free Movement: Ethical Issues in the Transnational Migration of People and of Money*, Pennsylvania State University Press, 1992, 217.
193 Waldron, *Torture, Terror, and Trade-offs*, 148.
194 Buchanan, *Justice, Legitimacy and Self-determination*, 102.

We can observe a common concern amongst all liberal theorists that immigration policy should not become despotic or oppressive in ways which are wholly incompatible with liberalism.[195] Rubio-Marín puts it well when she says that, rather than resolve membership issues, we are engaged in 'the more limited task of setting the legitimate constraints within which the state can adopt what it perceives as necessary exclusions'.[196]

Whilst some of the laws and jurisprudence we have seen deny it, all liberal moral theorists agree that 'some conditions of justice do not depend on associative obligations. The protection, under sovereign power, of negative rights like bodily inviolability, freedom of expression, and freedom of religion is morally unmysterious. Those rights, if they exist, set universal and pre-political limits to the legitimate use of power, independent of special forms of association'.[197,198] Whilst not seeking to catalogue such rights, we can see that moral theorists accept that all *persons* have a basic right to liberty. The real issue is how far the scope of this right can be compromised to control borders.[199]

---

195 Walzer himself argued against one form of discriminatory immigration policy – that of 'guest workers' who are permanently denied citizenship and vulnerable to summary expulsion. He concluded that this is 'a form of tyranny. Indeed, the rule of citizens over non-citizens, of members over strangers, is probably the most common form of tyranny in human history'. M. Walzer, *Spheres of Justice: A Defence of Pluralism and Equality*, Oxford: Basil Blackwell, 1985, 62.

196 R. Rubio-Marín, *Immigration as a Democratic Challenge: Citizenship and Inclusion in Germany and the United States*, Cambridge University Press, 2000. She argues that there should be virtually automatic naturalization of long-term residents (both illegal and legally present) leading to equality of rights to citizens. Schuck and Neumann have provided powerful contrasting American perspectives on the interaction between constitutional law and citizenship. Schuck, *Citizens, Strangers and In-betweens*. G. Neuman, *Strangers to the Constitution: Immigrants, Borders and Fundamental Law*, Princeton University Press, 1996.

197 T. Nagel, 'The Problem of Global Justice' (2005) 33 *Philosophy and Public Affairs* 113–47 at 127.

198 In contrast to socio-economic justice, which is a relational concept, Nagel argues that respecting negative rights does not require the same sacrifices so that '[t]he normative force of the most basic human rights against violence, enslavement, and coercion and of the most basic humanitarian duties of rescue from immediate danger depends only on our capacity to put ourselves in other peoples' shoes. The interests protected by such moral requirements are so fundamental, and the burdens they impose, considered statistically, so much slighter, that a criterion of universalizability of the Kantian type clearly supports them.' Nagel, 'The Problem of Global Justice', 132.

199 'Some rights, such as the right not to be tortured, killed, *refouled*, enslaved or arbitrarily deprived of liberty are so fundamental that it seems wrong to put them up for grabs ... By contrast, the right to choose one's country of asylum, or being allowed to reside permanently in a country of asylum is qualitatively different. These rights

States argue that they detain migrants *as a means* of securing borders. The 'security' of citizens is said to be advanced by the restriction of liberty of aliens. More specific reasons include: protecting borders, maintaining the 'credibility' of the system, deterring fraudulent claimants, crime or terrorism prevention or prevention of absconding and queue-jumping.[200] These justifications all appear plausible in the abstract. In the absence of experience they might be thought likely to have only modest effects on liberty. This was certainly arguable during earlier periods of migration control. In practice, during the modern era, we have seen hugely arbitrary and unaccountable detention on a vast scale. Furthermore, the benefits of such practices in terms of securing borders have not been well established. The burden borne by individual foreigners to provide an elusive and ill-defined level of 'security' for citizens and lawful residents is often unnecessary or disproportionate.

We can agree that '[w]hen the right in question is a more significant one ... such as the right to liberty, the standards required for showing that the benefits override the costs are going to be much more difficult to meet'. This is made more so by the lack of judicial oversight so that detention is 'limited only by the availability of detention spaces and the political will to fill them'.[201] The evidence we have reviewed in relation to modern detention suggests clearly that this is correct. We can refer to Galloway's important emphasis upon the fact that a nation may seek to police its borders, but it should not do so by attacks on human dignity without very good reasons. There is little doubt that the human dignity of detained migrants has been undermined by some of these practices of open-ended, extra-judicial detention and the conditions this may entail.

Conclusions

Detention of immigrants has been considered from a political perspective. There is no doubt that migration presents a challenge to liberal political ideas. Many theorists see liberal societies as necessarily quite closed and

certainly touch upon important interests, but failing to respect them is unlikely to inflict *existential damage* [emphasis added] on the individuals concerned.' M.J. Gibney, *The Ethics and Politics of Asylum*, Cambridge University Press, 2004, 252.

200 *Ibid.* These reasons also constitute a type of Catholic double-effect argument that suggests that doing an evil is not unacceptable if it is merely a side-effect of attempting to achieve a good. The problem, as ever, is that it is impossible to define when something is a side-effect. Detention is a deliberate act and hard to characterize as a side-effect when it is the very means of achieving the goal of removal.

201 *Ibid.*

endorse broad discretionary powers over migration. Other liberals argue for more open borders subject only to migration presenting grave threats to liberal democracy. Both agree that there must be limits on migration but that these should not be carried out in illiberal or oppressive ways. This led to the conclusion that there was nothing incompatible with liberal political theory in suggesting limits upon gravely intrusive mechanisms of control such as uncontrolled detention. In fact, the consensus appeared to suggest that any migration policy should always respect basic civil liberties, including freedom from arbitrary detention. This suggested appropriate judicial controls to prevent administrative detention becoming disproportionate or unconnected to measurable goals.

The liberal position is, however, problematic in that it has not engaged closely with the politics of security that have come to surround border control. Non-liberal theorists and many contemporary political actors contend that the fundamental role of the state and of politics is to maintain security. This depends upon defining 'enemies' and 'friends'. The increasing use of detention against unauthorized or deportable aliens suggests that they have become identified as a security threat, as an enemy. In extreme cases, like the Australian example, 'security' has been so distorted as to become synonymous with incarcerating non-dangerous asylum seekers for life. This has been the result of a complex cultural and political process linking migration to economic, social and public order threats along with objective factors such as periodic increases in irregular migration. This has created a nearly permanent atmosphere of crisis for governments scared to 'lose the border'. Paradoxically, the same governments have also sought to maintain inward migration for economic reasons. Strict policies like detention have been politically important in demonstrating firmness over migration.

We have seen this policy of firmness played out in the way that detention centres have become more unstable. As detainees, including children and families, have been held for longer in conditions that are often unsuitable, there have been disturbances. There has been increasing condemnation of the lack of care shown for detainees by national and international human rights bodies. For governments, however, detention has become a matter of political legitimacy at home. The limits of international law and society to constrain the detention and treatment of unwanted foreigners has been clear; apparently 'fundamental' rights derived from human rights instruments have been denied.

The 'non-status' of detainees in international society was highlighted. Whilst in the past states protected their nationals abroad, modern unauthorized immigrants stand largely alone, unable to call upon serious diplomatic protection. They may have fled as refugees or simply find that their government does not care to assist them. As a result, they fall between legal systems; rejected by one state but not accepted by any other. This may amount to *de facto* or *de jure* statelessness. Detention for long periods follows, whilst uncertain and sporadic diplomatic efforts attempts are made to find a 'home' for detainees. There are few signs of reciprocal obligations being accepted between nations in relation to unwanted migrants. This contrasts with the status of enemy aliens in the state of war, who are subject to mutual obligations regarding their treatment and repatriation. The unwanted alien has the assumed the role of a pirate, an outcast from international society.

We considered the argument that detention centres are extraordinary spaces beyond the control of regular domestic law. This is said to result from the non-liberal security perspective that views aliens as an 'enemy' subject to emergency powers. Whilst there are aspects of immigration detention that do encourage a culture of impunity, particularly the lack of judicial oversight, detainees are protected by civil and criminal law in principle. They are legal persons in that sense and are owed a duty of care whilst in confinement. The practical problems of enforcing these duties given their isolation are, however, serious, particularly in the case of detention in off-shore or remote centres. The uncertain nature of the aliens power has meant that the executive has been able to practice 'political' detention whenever a perception of crisis has arisen.

Whilst liberals have debated the ethics of membership, they have neglected its interactions with 'security' and the mechanics of enforcement. We argued that there is no need to finally determine the scope and content of the fundamental rights owed to all humans regardless of immigration authorization. Rather, it was suggested that all moral theorists accept that there is a right to liberty in the abstract. The real issue is what limits to place on this to protect borders. We argued that liberal legal ideas do have a role to play in scrutinizing immigration enforcement policies. There appears to be no real 'security' threat to the survival of Western societies posed by migration. In fact, most countries have actively chosen to maintain relatively open borders. Whilst individual migrants may be as dangerous as some citizens, migration policy is usually concerned with economic, cultural or psychological security. The language and practice of war are not generally appropriate in peacetime. There is room for reasoned moral and legal debate as to what kind of 'security' we mean and what hardships we can legitimately impose to achieve it.

7

Restoring the rule of law and influencing politics: placing boundaries around detention

Introduction

Over one hundred years ago states began to assert a legal power to select amongst arriving immigrants prior to admission. Engaging the rights of friendly aliens to enter or remain was viewed as an aspect of the foreign relations power. This brief process first took place on ships or docksides, and involved care, as well as control. The conflict with the habeas corpus tradition could be papered over; these modest interferences with liberty were seen as ancillary to migration management. Longer detentions only occurred during discrete war or national security crises when the state's prerogative powers over defence again largely eclipsed the rule of law. Detention remained a relatively contained phenomenon for the most part.

Deeper consideration of the relationship between liberty of the person and restrictions on free movement has only come about in the last thirty years. As the politics of border control have become more inflamed, the scale and periods of detention have increased. Inland prisons and detention centres holding thousands have emerged. No longer simply a tool of selection at the border or for the expulsion of small numbers of dangerous persons, immigration powers have come to be employed to incarcerate 'unauthorized' aliens in unaccountable ways. Nor has this been confined to national security or emergency situations. Government practices have called into question the existence of a fundamental right to liberty for *any* unauthorized aliens. This is part of a wider political trend which seeks to deny entitlements to persons lacking immigration status, a trend presenting a fundamental threat to the post-war ideal of 'universal' human rights. Liberal legal systems have become compromised; to reaffirm the importance of individual liberty for all *persons* challenges the modern political tendency to portray unauthorized migrants as an 'enemy' to be segregated and repelled.

This chapter seeks to draw together the material in this study to discuss the relationship between immigration detention, law and politics more broadly. It argues that treating unauthorized persons as hostile 'invaders' and employing arbitrary conceptions of 'security' has led to practices that are inconsistent with orthodox ideas of the rule of law. It is argued that a reaffirmation of the fundamental right to liberty, regardless of immigration status, is necessary. It then elaborates a defensible legal framework for detention based upon the principles of judicial control and proportionality.

Security, reason and authorization

In the previous chapter we noted that most liberal political theorists of migration accept border controls in some circumstances. This legitimates enforcement action of some kind, most effectively by visa restrictions, but also through internal policing. The extent and nature of the danger, if any, posed by unauthorized migration is, however, contested. For 'open borders' theorists, only extreme influxes amounting to public order threats are of serious concern. Generous immigration policies promote individual autonomy, economic development and human flourishing. For 'closed border' liberals, nations must have a broad discretion to shape the nature of their populations to meet wide cultural, economic, social or even psychological goals. Unwanted migration threatens this project. More intrusive enforcement may be necessary to promote a concept of 'security' suggested by closed border liberals. There was also, however, consensus that immigration rules must not operate in ways that amount to oppression or assaults on human dignity.

As we have seen, governments too have also endorsed widely differing conceptions of 'security' in relation to borders. The earliest migration controls were largely targeted at demonized racial and religious groups such as Asians or Jews. Sometimes politically deviant foreigners such as Communists or anarchists were subject to enforcement action in the name of broader concepts of security. During wartime we saw aliens interned under a hybrid of war and immigration powers. This was repeated in more recent anti-terrorism measures. Modern politics has, however, come to suggest that unauthorized migrants *per se* are synonymous with a threat to national security. The creation of large-scale and permanent non-penitentiary detention facilities, unprecedented in peacetime, cannot otherwise be explained.

Governments' increasing assertion that broad 'security' measures must be used against immigrants does not in itself justify such practices. Courts have increasingly been called upon to assess when detention is really necessary. How far are judges able to make such judgments? It is clear that, barring crude discrimination, high-level policy on migrant categories and quotas is a political question for which courts are ill-suited.[1] By contrast, individual decisions on eligibility have increasingly benefited from appeal rights and due process. Enforcement techniques sit at the interface of these two; they reflect large-scale government priorities but they are directed at concrete individuals under the courts' jurisdiction. As the political branches have adopted increasingly arbitrary or disproportionate enforcement measures, courts have been asked to reassert the rule of law with its underlying promise of reasoned, independent judgment.

This necessitates a willingness to subject governments' security claims to closer scrutiny. In particular, what is the nature and extent of the 'security' enforcement policy seeks to protect? Across the security 'spectrum' we move from classical threats to the nation during wartime, through to mass murder by terrorist outrages; next would be ordinary criminal threats and risks to public order, whilst at the softer end would be economic security and welfare. Finally, there is psychological security linked to national identity or morale-boosting measures. As we move along this continuum, serious erosions of liberty become harder to defend. At their most extreme, measures become largely symbolic. As Cole notes: 'Symbols are, of course, important... But incarcerating people without any objective evidence of suspicion [of dangerousness] simply to make the public feel better can be justified, if at all, only on the crudest utilitarian grounds.'[2]

One paradox, recently highlighted by the jurisprudence on contemporary global anti-terror operations, is that where the state employs detention to prevent *serious crime*, then criminal procedures, not immigration powers, should be employed. This was stated most powerfully in the *Belmarsh* decision in Britain. The Guantanamo cases also support the idea that due process must be respected where a person, even an unadmitted alien, is alleged to be dangerous. It is significant that the

---

1 Dauvergne summarizes it thus: 'Executive discretion and judicial deference combine to ensure that migration decision-making is closely associated with the exercise of sovereign power in this essential sense: power which does not conform to judicial or legislative modes of exercise. Migration law also engages the exposed core of state power as border policing, detention and deportation are also within its ambit.' C. Dauvergne, 'Sovereigny, Migration and the Rule of Law in Global Times' (2004) 67(4) *MLR* 588–615, 592.

2 D. Cole, 'The Priority of Morality' (2004) 113 *Yale L.J.* 1753, 1798.

recent EU Returns Directive makes clear that its detention power is solely directed at enforcing removal, not crime prevention. These developments bear out the particular strength, in the immigration context, of Jackson J.'s famous admonition, that 'nothing opens the door to arbitrary action so effectively as to allow those officials to pick and choose only a few to whom they will apply legislation and thus to escape the political retribution that might be visited upon them if larger numbers were affected'.[3] Sunstein, too, has highlighted the tendency for 'precautionary' measures to be directed at immigrants, because guarding against even remote risks will be supported by citizens whose rights are not diminished.[4]

Unpacking 'security' in this way permits examination of the measures said to promote it as applied to actual cases. This adds an important dimension to the political debate around migration. As liberal jurisprudence has begun to reassert the classical doctrine of 'no detention without trial' for the small number of aliens alleged to be really dangerous, the argument for long-term detention without judicial supervision of the *non-dangerous* is rendered even weaker. Emerging jurisprudence forms one, if not the only, source of inspiration for governments to review existing practice. Some governments have indeed begun to recognize the soundness of giving temporary 'authorization' rights to migrants who might otherwise be either held indefinitely in costly detention or disappear into the underground world of the unauthorized sector.

But even if the nature of governmental 'security' claims is scrutinized more closely, there remains jurisprudential debate as to whether 'unauthorized' persons have truly *constitutional* rights to liberty. To free such persons would see judges partially 'authorizing' them contrary to governments' border policies. This may be seen as legitimating those who are often seen, in political terms, as illegitimate 'enemies' of the state.[5] To

---

3 *Railway Express Agency, Inc.* v. *New York* 336 U.S. at 112 (Jackson J., concurring). He was here talking about the arbitrary choices of officials within a legislative framework defined by the generality of its application. The position of aliens has clearly been marked out as distinct in legislation itself, but the point remains valid in relation to 'politicians' rather than officials.

4 C. Sunstein, *Laws of Fear*, Cambridge University Press, 2007. Ch. 9.

5 This binary categorization has sometimes been nuanced by drawing a further distinction between those seeking entry at a port and those who have already entered. In the United States, for example, only the latter have been accorded quasi-constitutional rights. The courts have been steadfast in refusing to force the government to admit persons stopped at the border, or even to confer due process on them. The rationale is not clear, but may stem from the 'invasion' fears that motivated 'plenary power' doctrine. Clearly this is senseless in individual cases, but rather suggests a fear of mass influxes seeking to assert constitutional claims at the border.

deny that there is such a constitutional right provides a neat jurisprudential solution to two problems. It avoids law having to engage at all with
the nature of 'security' in relation to migration, all aliens, even the non-
dangerous, are beyond judicial protection. It also leaves 'authorization'
entirely to the political branches. Courts have no role in interrogating
what rights and obligations unauthorized migrants should have. Under
this circular reasoning, all foreigners are either authorized or not. The
detention centre thereby becomes the 'normal' place to hold them until
their status is resolved in the political sphere and they are admitted or
expelled. The Australian experience is only the most powerful example
of the danger of courts too readily abandoning the cause of individual
liberty to the vicissitudes of politics.

Whilst conceptually clear, this approach raises James Madison's dis-
comfiting question again. As a form of contractarian logic, it opens unauthorized persons up to action without clear legal limits. Governments only
need pass a threshold of showing a measure engages the 'aliens power'.
In this way indefinite detention for life of non-dangerous aliens becomes
possible. In fact, even the relative humanity of being held in a detention
centre is not mandated. Sinking migrant-carrying vessels at sea, before
they arrive, is not obviously ruled out.[6] Perhaps gratuitous cruelty and
torture are excluded, although even these might be advocated as having
deterrent effects. Endorsing such political discretion puts unauthorized
foreigners into Hobbes' state of nature.[7] A kind of state of war against
unauthorized migration then prevails, but one in which even the basic
rules of humanitarian law do not apply. In this respect international terrorism and unauthorized migration present similar issues for law and
government. The physical treatment of aliens, away from traditional bat-
tlefields, has become increasingly 'extra-legal', occurring in places deemed
to be 'outside' legal jurisdiction or subject only to minimal, politically
determined priorities.

This calls to mind again the challenge posed by Carl Schmitt's political
theory to the effect that '[o]rder must be established for juridical order
to make sense. A regular situation must be created, and sovereign is
he who decides if this situation is actually effective'.[8] The fundamental

---

6 We can recall here Marshall J.'s observation that broad powers of enforcement might
   condone mass starvation as immigration control. See *Jean v. Nelson* 472 U.S. 846, 875.
7 See D. Dyzenhaus, 'The Rule of (Administrative) Law in International Law' (2004–5) 68
   Law and Contemp. Probs. 127, 132.
8 See C. Schmitt, *Political Theology: Four Chapters on the Concept of Sovereignty*, 2nd edn
   trans. (G Schwab) Cambridge, MA: MIT Press, 1985, 19.

role of politics (as opposed to law) is to resolve this question.[9] Schmitt saw this sovereign power at its most political (and hence lawless) at 'the most extreme point, that of the friend-enemy grouping'.[10] The border has increasingly been identified as a security barrier, and the unauthorized foreigner as an enemy, in the politics of many Western nations. The nature of this 'barrier' is in fact more symbolic and political than real, given that borders have remained open and appear impossible to seal in any event.

In fact, the material surveyed in this book has illustrated that, whilst sometimes employed in wartime or true national security situations, most immigration detention is now a routine, even banal, adjunct to migration policy. Whilst the rhetoric of war or invasion may endure, there is no reason to suppose that after decades of unauthorized migration, accompanied by continued economic growth and peace, an 'exceptional' situation calling for measures beyond judicial control generally prevails. Most immigration enforcement action can safely be removed from the 'emergency' category and scrutinized more soberly. As Neuman puts it more broadly, whilst:

> *Some* power to control access to membership would appear necessary if a democratic community wishes to maintain its independence and continuity. *Some* power to control the long-term settlement of aliens would also appear necessary... These considerations do not yet justify an absolute power over exclusion and expulsion. One might continue to investigate whether a national identity could be so fragile, or whether its symbolic boundaries could be so essential, that every uninvited alien would threaten the national identity in the tautological way in which the obligation to admit an uninvited alien contradicts absolute sovereignty.[11]

Even if immigration does on occasion present a genuine emergency situation, Schmitt was wrong to contend that legal reasoning cannot evaluate government decisions taken to safeguard the state.[12] As Dyzenhaus argues,

---

9 'To create tranquillity, security, and order and thereby establish the normal situation is the prerequisite for legal norms to be valid. Every norm presupposes a normal situation, and no norm can be valid in an entirely abnormal situation.' C. Schmitt, *The Concept of the Political*, 2nd edn (trans. G. Schwab), New Brunswick, NJ: Rutgers University Press, 1976/1929, 46.

10 *Ibid.*, 29.

11 G. Neuman, *Strangers to the Constitution*, Princeton University Press, 1996, 124.

12 'The precise details of an emergency cannot be anticipated, nor can one spell out what may take place in such a case, especially when it is truly a matter of extreme emergency and of how it is to be eliminated. The precondition as well as the content of jurisdictional competence in such a case must necessarily be unlimited.' Schmitt, *Political Theology*, 6–7.

'it does not follow from the fact that a problem is ungovernable by rules, that is, by highly determinate legal norms, that necessarily a decision about its solution takes place in a legal void'.[13] As we have seen, modern public law has a range of tools such as fairness, rationality, non-discrimination and proportionality to scrutinize the exercise of state power, even in the emergency situations that particularly concerned Schmitt. It will be argued that a richer version of the rule of law doctrine may underlie these ideas. Legal reasoning has only recently begun to grapple with this problem in the context of aliens. However, in navigating through this liberal jurisprudential path, it is clear that borders and immigration status will remain crucial determinates of legal entitlements. Developing the rule of law in relation to aliens would nevertheless mark an important, if modest, form of 'global citizenship'.

International human rights standards and the limits of 'post-national' citizenship

The persistent identification by states of a zone of special power over migrants and borders poses a challenge to arguments that international human rights law is displacing national citizenship as the guarantor of individual rights.[14] There is, however, no doubt that traditional contractarian approaches tied to citizenship are being scrutinized in the light of human rights norms. Sassen argues that increased migration is coexisting with a more modest supra-nationalism in relation to governance.[15] She concludes that whilst '[n]ational governments still have sovereignty over many matters . . . they are increasingly part of a web of rights and regulations that are embedded in other entities – from EC institutions to courts defending the human rights of refugees'.[16]

---

13 D. Dyzenhaus, *The Constitution of Law: Legality in a Time of Emergency*, Cambridge University Press, 2006, 61.

14 Soysal argued that there might be evolving a 'post-national' age in which rights traditionally reserved solely for citizens would be extended to all on the basis of universal personhood. Y. Soysal, *Limits of Citizenship: Migrants and Postnational Membership in Europe*, University of Chicago Press, 1994.

15 'Both the global linking of economies on the one hand, and, on the other, the growth of a broad network of rights and court decisions along with the emergence of immigrants as political actors, have reduced the autonomy of the state in immigration (and refugee) policy making. This should not be surprising given the trends towards trans-nationalization in economies, in culture, and in the battle around human rights.' S. Sassen, *Guests and Aliens*, New York: New Press, 1999, 156.

16 *Ibid.*, 151.

As we have seen, there is some evidence to support this. The European Union (including the case-law of its court) has moved towards creating something approaching an equal social and economic status for EU citizens who migrate. This project has, however, revealed itself to be an exceptional and anomalous one in its return to the 'open' borders of ninteenth-century globalization. Perhaps most strikingly we should note the European Court of Human Rights' ban on expulsion, even in national security cases, for those facing torture on return. However, any trend towards increased supra-national protection of migrant rights must not be exaggerated. The Refugee Convention, created as long ago as 1951, remains by far the most important treaty specifically giving rights to unauthorized persons. Even in this instance, detention practice has exceeded the ability of the convention to constrain it. Outside Europe, more general international human rights norms remain limited in their enforceability.[17]

In most respects, unauthorized migrants remain without effective protection in international law. Whilst competition for *lawful* migrants has pushed states to improve their status under national law, for irregular migrants, however, the gap between citizens and aliens has remained profound.[18] As Hill Maher cautiously notes: 'even in Western states that are vocal champions of human rights, policymakers debate the extent to which they are responsible for protecting the full range of human rights for non-citizen migrants, particularly migrants lacking state authorization'.[19] Benhabib claims that rather than a new form of supra-national citizenship, 'growing normative incongruities between international human rights

---

17 The Inter-American Human Rights system is one example, but even here there are not the same remedies as the European systems possess.

18 We can recall the comment of Arendt upon the inter-war period that '[t]he Rights of Man, after all, had been defined as "inalienable" because they were supposed to be independent of all governments; but it turned out that the moment human beings lacked their own government and had to fall back upon their minimum rights, no authority was left to them and no institution was willing to guarantee them'. H. Arendt, *The Origins of Totalitarianism*, 3rd edn, New York: Harcourt, Brace and Jovanovich Inc., 1966, 292. Arendt mocked the efforts of early advocates for international human rights saying they were put forward 'by a few international jurists without political experience or professional philanthropists supported by uncertain sentiments of professional idealists. The groups they formed, the declarations they issued, showed an uncanny similarity in language and composition to that of societies for the prevention of cruelty to animals. No statesman, no political figure of any importance could possibly take them seriously' *ibid.*

19 K. Hill Maher, 'Who has a Right to Rights? Citizenship's Exclusions in an Age of Migration', in A. Brysk (ed.), *Globalization and Human Rights*, Berkeley: University of California Press, 2002, 9.

norms, particularly as they pertain to the "rights of others" – immigrants, refugees, and asylum seekers – and assertions of territorial sovereignty are the novel features of this new landscape'.[20] In fact, as Dauvergne argues, the very demise of traditional 'sovereignty' in this new globalized world of trade and communication encourages resort to more aggressive migration enforcement measures:

> As nations have seen their powers to control the flows of money or ideas and to set economic or cultural policies slip away, they seek to assert themselves as nations through migration laws and policies which assert their 'nation-ness' and exemplify their sovereign control and capacity.[21]

Faced with these strong assertions of sovereignty over migration, international human rights norms have provided a constant reminder that national immigration policies should not become too parochial. This has, however, fallen far short of amounting to an enforceable cosmopolitan charter of legal entitlements. The growth and expansion in administrative detention is perhaps the clearest illustration of this.

Detention and international human rights: between borders and protection gaps

The lack of effectiveness of international human rights law to constrain immigration detention is particularly significant in that it has principally occurred in nations where the rule of law is generally upheld, not totalitarian or dysfunctional states. Why specifically has supra-nationalism had only modest effects on the treatment of migrants within such democracies? It has now become clear that the main problem is the disconnection between national and international politics. For some time, however, even the international standard was not clear. Ambiguous and conflicting norms emerged from institutions like the UNHCR, the EU, the Council of Europe and the UN Working Group on Arbitrary Detention.[22] The explosion in peacetime administrative detention and this uncertain response to it threw into sharp relief the doubtful legal and moral status of unauthorized persons.

---

20 S. Benhabib, *The Rights of Others*, Cambridge University Press, 2004, 7.
21 Dauvergne, 'Sovereignty, Migration and the Rule of Law in Global Times', 595. She suggests that this may be why EU cooperation in migration for third-country nationals was so slow – 'the capacity to crack down is relation to migration is the new last bastion of sovereignty, and is therefore the hardest to surrender', 600–1. See also C. Dauvergne, *Making People Illegal: Migration Laws for Global Times*, Cambridge University Press, 2008.
22 See Ch. 3 above.

Of the supra-national judicial bodies, only the Human Rights Committee started from the premise that the *universal right to liberty and security of the person should not be inherently limited by lack of immigration status.* This meant that movement across borders, if not a right in itself, should not be policed by unaccountable detention. Unauthorized migrants might be arrested to assess their status, but there must be consideration of issues such as judicial approval, absconding risks, alternatives to incarceration, duration of detention, health impacts and prospects for removal. In short, all states had a duty to put in place demanding *due process procedures* to justify the curtailment of aliens' liberty. By contrast, the European Court of Human Rights initially rejected the idea that there was a basic right to be at liberty for aliens without immigration status. Detention was an inherent aspect of enforcement so long as the state had reasonable *administrative removal procedures* to ensure detainees' expulsion or entry decisions were resolved. There was thus no need for a separate system of due process to guarantee that liberty was not unnecessarily restricted.

The Strasbourg Court's earlier case-law thus saw the doctrine of territorial sovereignty alone as justifying extended detention without significant limits.[23] This reflected the traditional view that the international legal system (and the treaties regulating it) is maintained by sovereign states and that the return of detainees was largely a matter for diplomatic discussion, not legal regulation. It is also significant that Strasbourg developed its principles in the context of national security deportation and extradition cases which were complex and raised hard-core public safety issues.[24,25]

---

23 (Appn. 13229/03) *Saadi* v. *UK* (Judgment of 29 Jan. 2008) may represent the first step in a shift towards closer scrutiny of detention practices but the judgment itself does not completely modify the principles laid down in the earlier case-law. On the facts, however, the Court did suggest that there might be limits on the manner and duration of detention that was imposed purely as part of processing of applicants (when it was accepted that they did not present any absconding risk).

24 The Strasbourg Court had already been very radical in implying rights of migration into the European Convention on Human Rights through Arts 3 and 8. The signatories had probably expected to retain their rights to expel aliens (subject only to the impending Refugee Convention of 1951). With the prohibition on expulsion applied even to foreigners who threatened national security in *Chahal*, the Strasbourg Court was at the outer limits of the politically feasible. For a detailed discussion of the way in which the Strasbourg Court has taken account of political 'reactions' from national courts see N. Krisch, 'The Open Architecture of European Human Rights Law' (2008) 71(2) *MLR* 183. He argues for a pluralist view of human rights protection in Europe, rather than a top-down perspective that sees the Strasbourg Court as sovereign in a traditional sense.

25 The more recent decision in (Appn. 37201/06) *Saadi* v. *Italy* (Judgment of 28 Feb. 2008) is significant in reconfirming the *Chahal* rule. This was despite the demand by some states that the absolute prohibition on expulsion should be relaxed in favour of a balancing

Here the Court stressed the need for procedural rights for detainees to challenge the security findings supporting *de facto* preventive internment.

The 1990s was a politically challenging era with large volumes of asylum-seekers entering Europe without permission and also of increased concern over terrorist threats. Allowing states a broad discretion over detention, if not expulsion, was perhaps considered the lesser of two evils in the light of the Strasbourg decision in *Chahal*[26] to absolutely prohibit expulsion of persons facing torture, even if dangerous. More recently, however, the growth in lengthy and purely administrative detention of asylum seekers and stateless persons has become politically troubling for the Council of Europe. Human rights bodies have become more outspoken in attacking conditions in detention centres. The Strasbourg Court has begun to suggest that time limits and judicial control are as important as bona fide administrative efforts to expel migrants.

The Human Rights Committee went further, largely because it was faced by more obviously draconian measures than European states had contemplated. The Australian policy of mandatory, indefinite detention of non-dangerous asylum seekers for years without even a possibility of bail was something that could not be reconciled with substantive ideas of the rule of law at the heart of Article 9 ICCPR and habeas corpus more generally. As we saw, similar fact scenarios have arisen in the United States, through mandatory indefinite detention, or Hong Kong, as a result of statelessness. These cases were so extreme that they demanded a restatement that, from a global perspective anyway, the right to liberty, that most 'basic' of rights, had not been erased by modern states' assertions of absolute prerogatives over border control. The international human rights mechanism thereby vindicated a tentative new cross-border cosmopolitan civil status.

The Human Rights Committee's views were not overtly accepted by governments with the most extreme practices.[27] This does not mean that

---

of risks where a migrant is found to pose a threat to public safety through terrorist activity.

26 (Appn. 13229/03) *Saadi* v. *UK*, makes the link clearer: 'In conclusion, therefore, the Court finds that, given the difficult administrative problems with which the United Kingdom was confronted during the period in question, with an escalating flow of huge numbers of asylum-seekers', it was permissible to practise administrative detention for processing of applications for asylum without any need to show this was necessary in each individual case.

27 Even some courts did not accept the doctrinal soundness of the Committee's arguments. For example, in the Australian case on mandatory indefinite detention, *Al Kateb* v. *Godwin* [2004] HCA 20, Hayne J., para. 238, refers to Art. 9 ICCPR. He implicitly disagreed with the opinions of the Human Rights Committee against Australia on mandatory detention

they were without political influence. The problem of non-compliance with international law has been considered by political scientists.[28] In principle, independent adjudication, as under the ICCPR, should lead to greater compliance.[29] However, the decision to comply with international rulings depends on a mixture of pragmatism and principle, including '[c]oncern about reciprocity, reputation, and damage to valuable state institutions, as well as other normative and material considerations . . . Yet it is reasonable to assume that most of the time, legal and political considerations combine to influence behaviour'.[30] In relation to detention practice, there has been little reciprocal harm that sending states can or wish to inflict on receiving states. However, reputational damage should not be overlooked. International condemnation over extreme detention practices has also provided domestic political groups with external support for their arguments against detention. Over time, this may be influential in changing the orthodoxy, particularly if several larger nations take a lead.[31]

Governmental power over migration and the domestic courts: between deference and law

In the end, whilst sometimes influenced by international standards, national legal and political systems have reached their own preferred

of immigrants, saying there must be 'doubt about whether the mandatory detention of those who do not have permission to enter and remain in Australia contravenes Article 9'. The Court did not have direct access to Art. 9 as a source of law, so the decision did not have to resolve the question.

28 T. Risse, S.C. Ropp and K. Sikkink (eds), *The Power of Human Rights: International Norms and Domestic Change*, Cambridge University Press, 1999; P. Alston and J. Crawford, *The Future of UN Human Rights Treaty Monitoring*, Cambridge University Press, 2000. See E. Weisband, 'Verdictive Discourses, Shame and Judicialization in Pursuit of Freedom of Association Rights', in S. Mekled-Garcia and B. Cali, *The Legalization of Human Rights: Multidisciplinary Perspectives on Human Rights and Human Rights Law*, London: Routledge 2005.

29 'Highly legalized institutions are those in which rules are obligatory on parties through links to the established rules and principle of international law, in which rules are precise and in which authority to interpret and apply the rules has been delegated to third parties acting under the constraint of rules.' K.W. Abbott, R.O. Keohane, A. Moravcsik, A. Slaughter and D. Snidal, 'The Concept of Legalization' [2000] 54(3) *Int. Org.* 401–19, 418. This would follow Hart's view of law with the rule of recognition for the courts being essentially domestic in focus. The enforcement of the decisions of international tribunals (or lack thereof) would not imperil the validity of the rulings as law.

30 *Ibid.*, 419.

31 The new Australian government's decision to review detention policy in 2008 was clearly influenced by the sheer volume of international condemnation it had suffered over the previous twenty years.

'balance' between border policy and individual rights. We therefore consider how far broader domestic constitutional ideas of the rule of law have responded to the challenge of immigration detention. This will return us to the question of how courts have found ways of reconciling the habeas corpus tradition with migration controls. Certainly for Anglo-American jurisprudence as Galloway puts it:

> By and large, courts have confirmed that a deep Teflon coating protects a government's sovereign powers in relation to borders and nationality, a coating that is usually sufficiently impermeable to ward off most challenges, even those founded on human dignity.[32]

As a result '[t]he rule of law is subordinated to the determination of a government that holds itself as representing the interests of the citizenry'.[33] In other words, courts have often accepted that decisions relating to border control were beyond judicial resolution. As Dyzenhaus argues, this stemmed from the idea that there must be unfettered government discretion over the lawless state of nature in international affairs:

> National security as a matter for the prerogative is connected to the idea that those who threaten the very existence of the state have put themselves into a state of nature with regard to that sovereign. Control over immigration or aliens is thus control over those who wish to enter a civil society from either a state of nature or from another civil society with whom relationship with the first is itself in a state of nature.[34]

This 'traditional' view contrasts with the more modern perspective on judicial review which argues that wide and arbitrary prerogative powers should be brought within the normal legal order in order to fully realize the republican ideal of democracy.[35] This pattern is mirrored in relation to migration decisions which are generally now rooted in detailed statutory provisions. In fact, it has become routine for courts and tribunals to

---

32 D. Galloway, 'Noncitizens and Discrimination: Redefining Human Rights in the Face of Complexity' in O. Schmidtke and S. Ozcurumez (eds), *Of States, Rights, and Social Closure: Governing Migration and Citizenship*, New York: Palgrave Macmillan, 2008, 37–59 at 40.

33 *Ibid.*

34 Dyzenhaus, 'The Rule of (Administrative) Law in International Law', 132.

35 For a defence of judicial review along these lines see T.R.S. Allan, *Constitutional Justice: A Liberal Theory of the Rule of Law*, Oxford University Press, 2003.

review decisions on who qualifies to enter or remain under immigration law. There is no longer any suggestion that this threatens the security of the state.[36] However, as we have noted, the *constitutional* status of aliens remains unclear.

Across the world, constitutional law is in a state of flux in addressing its relationship with migration and aliens. It is not certain which substantive ideas will emerge intact as a result of these changes. We have seen governments take the aliens power in new directions. The courts have begun to modify their traditional deference and contractarian perspectives. We have seen the beginnings of a new cosmopolitan perspective linked to the rule of law as a check on arbitrary state action. There is a struggle about which are the bedrock principles of liberal legal orders in a world of cross-border migration.

This brings us to consider Dworkin's argument that substantive moral principles should guide judicial reasoning:

> Law as integrity asks judges to assume, so far as this is possible, that the law is structured by a coherent set of principles about justice and fairness and procedural due process, and it asks them to enforce these in the fresh cases that come before them, so that each person's situation is fair and just according to the same standards. That style of adjudication respects the ambition integrity assumes, the ambition to be a community of principle.[37]

---

36 Neuman, for example, has argued that, although not settled, there are several readings of more recent US Supreme Court case-law that confer a degree of constitutional protection upon aliens in the immigration context. A balanced form of cosmopolitanism can be seen here in a 'global due process' approach through which courts start with a universalist perspective but then limit this to take account of national interests. Even in relation to exclusion decisions, previously held to be beyond judicial review in *Mezei*, the government was subjected to the 'facially legitimate and bona fide reason' test laid down in *Kleindienst v. Mandel*. G. Neuman, *Strangers to the Constitution*, Princeton University Press, 1996.

37 R. Dworkin, *Law's Empire*, London: Fontana Press, 1986, 243. Dworkin's formulation of his theory of justice does not consider the position of migrants, but seems to see citizenship as the precondition for equality: 'No government is legitimate that does not show equal concern for the fate of all those citizens over whom it claims dominion and from whom it claims allegiance. Equal concern is the sovereign virtue of political community – without it government is only tyranny.' R. Dworkin, *Sovereign Virtue: The Theory and Practice of Equality*, Cambridge, MA: Harvard University Press, 2000, 1–2. His position has hitherto been one which argues that obligations of justice apply within a closed society. His more recent work on anti-terrorism begins to sketch out what obligations may be owed to all who fall under the power of a state, regardless of citizenship. See Ch. 5 above for the discussion there.

Dworkin's characterization of what judges do (or should do) yields contradictory results in relation to migration.[38] We can see at once that the
earliest ideas developed in the court decisions of the nineteenth and early
twentieth century were based upon a deeply partialist and contractarian
political theory of the liberal constitution. Policy should be determined
almost exclusively by reference to the needs of citizens; aliens were not
parties to the constitution.

Faced with new enforcement techniques, jurisprudence has struggled
to find a principled method of both retaining these partialist ideas whilst
upholding important aspects of the rule of law. Previously, legislative or
executive consent to admission or residence in the nation was a precondition for constitutional protection. The extent of the harsh treatment of
unauthorized aliens has, however, tested this constitutional model to the
limit. A new account of constitutionalism is required as national border
control policies collide more violently with the reality of global migration.

Nevertheless, the landmark Australian High Court decision in *Al Kateb*,
holding mandatory indefinite detention constitutional, illustrates the
enduring power of the old ideas.[39] On a jurisprudential level, the position of the majority judges embodied an extreme deference to the other
branches of government. As we saw, the Court accepted the government's very broad view of 'security', stretching it to cover unauthorized
migration.[40] By eliding migration and security, judicial deference was
made to appear as a more orthodox step in the face of an 'enemy'. On
a political level, the decision took a narrow contractarian view of the
Australian Constitution. The unlawful non-citizen is not part of the
community and therefore can make no meaningful claim to constitutional protection from the courts.[41] The rule of law and the principle of
legality only extended as far as requiring judicial review of the citizen/

---

38 For a detailed summary of the arguments against Dworkin's position, see D. Beatty, *The
Ultimate Rule of Law*, Oxford University Press, 2004, Ch. 1. Also M.W. McConnell, 'The
Importance of Humility in Judicial Review: A Comment on 'Ronald Dworkin's "Moral
Reading" of the Constitution' (1997) 65 *Ford. L. Rev.* 1269.

39 *Al Kateb* v. *Godwin* [2004] HCA 20.

40 'Under the aliens power, the Parliament is entitled to protect the nation against unwanted
entrants by detaining them in custody. As long as the detention is for the purpose of
deportation or preventing aliens from entering Australia or the *Australian community*
[emphasis added], the justice or wisdom of the course taken by Parliament is not examinable in this or any other domestic court' *ibid.*, para. 74.

41 The US Supreme Court appears to accept this contractarian approach too, at least for
aliens who have not actually entered the United States (see *Mezei*). Congress has plenary
power under the constitution to determine who may enter the United States. The *Zadvydas*
case, however, appeared to tentatively confirm that where an alien has entered, even
illegally, then they do have constitutional liberty rights to substantive due process.

unauthorized alien boundary. Once a person was correctly found to be an unlawful non-citizen, the detainee could claim no further constitutional right to be released into the community. This was also a view shared by two of the Supreme Court justices in *Zadvydas*.[42]

This rigid application of contractarianism goes beyond the perspective even of those liberal political theorists who argue in favour of broad powers over migration. As we saw, these theorists recognize the need for limits on border enforcement policies. However, modern politics in Western countries towards unauthorized migration has become 'securitized', and detention policy reflects this. As a result of this level of sustained political rhetoric, constitutional courts have faced challenges in interrogating how far unauthorized migration is truly a national security threat justifying commensurately firm measures.

Democratic approval of detention and the scope of judicial review

There is a further, more important, type of deference at work in the case-law we have examined – the distinction between legislative and executive immigration detention. There is rightly a tendency amongst constitutional courts to pay greater deference to legislative measures than to executive action. Executive abuse of power is more clearly a focal point for judicial review. Legislation, by contrast, bears democratic hallmarks. In the United States and Australia, their policies of mandatory detention derived from primary immigration legislation. This reflected particularly shrill politics surrounding migration emerging in the 1990s. By contrast, in France, the pre-legislative scrutiny of the Constitutional Council was able to prevent legislation passing altogether. In the United Kingdom, detention has generally been left to executive policy and the courts have been able to exercise judicial review without direct conflict with Parliament.[43]

Should detention which is required by legislation (as opposed to executive order) be entitled to any more 'deference' from courts?[44] There is

---

42 See the Joint Opinion of Scalia and Thomas J.J.

43 The *Belmarsh* case explored the one exception where the power of indefinite detention of suspected foreign terrorists was expressly set out in the legislation. In this case, however, the courts had a specific mandate to review the legislation through the Human Rights Act 1998, which permitted them to declare it incompatible with the European Convention on Human Rights. The effect was not to overturn the legislation, but leave it to government to decide on appropriate amendments.

44 There is no doubt of the potential for tension between the courts and legislature, which may prove unstable in the long term. Scalia rightly argues that Bills of Rights can 'enable judicial invalidation of a particular piece of illiberal legislation adopted in the heat of

some support for the idea that searching judicial review is more legitimate in the case of laws affecting minorities who are likely not to have had a 'fair' hearing in the democratic process.[45] This again raises the question of whether migrants are viewed as having truly *constitutional* entitlements to liberty. If they do, then under orthodox principle, these should be protected unless the constitution itself is amended. However, if aliens' entitlements are considered to be 'sub-constitutional', then the position is less obvious.[46] In this case, then, where the legislature has made clear that detention should be for life, the courts would have to defer. The mandatory indefinite detention statutes from the United States and Australia did not state clearly what should happen if removal efforts broke down. There remained statutory ambiguity in such cases. This left room for judges, if they so chose, to read the provisions in a way which did not lead to internment.

The *Zadydas* majority opinion in the Supreme Court oscillates on whether constitutional rights were at stake, at first saying that indefinite detention would 'raise a serious constitutional problem' and that plenary power was subject to 'important limitations', but later that, if Congress made its intention clear, then the courts would be powerless to intervene. Similarly, in *Martinez* the Court noted that Congress could amend the statute to provide for indefinite detention of excluded persons should it wish to achieve this. As Kanstroom notes, '[i]t is hard to see how both of these ideas can simultaneously be true'.[47]

passion or under the stress of a supposed emergency. But in the nature of things a Bill of Rights cannot – assuming a well-functioning democracy – permanently prevent the people from doing what they continuously and earnestly desire to do. A long-term fundamental misalignment between a society's beliefs and its Bill of Rights must produce either an amendment of the constitution to permit what the people wish, or the appointment of judges who disregard or distort the Bill of Rights.' See A. Scalia, 'Federal Constitutional Guarantees of Individual Rights in the United States of America' in D. Beatty (ed.), *Human Rights and Judicial Review*, Amsterdam: Kluwer Academic Publishers, 1994, 91. See M. Walzer, 'Philosophy and Democracy' (1981) 9 *Polit. Theory* 379 for a democratic alternative to judicial review.

45 For process theorists see J.H. Ely, *Democracy and Distrust*, Cambridge, MA: Harvard University Press, 1980; C. Sunstein, *Designing Democracy: What Constitutions Do*, New York: Oxford University Press, 2001.

46 It is hard to understand a constitutional right that can be overridden by ordinary legislation in democracies that have binding Bills of Rights. It makes perfect sense only in non-constitutional democracies like the UK. See P. Craig, 'Constitutional and Non-constitutional Judicial Review' (2001) 54 *CLP* 147, for the difference and similarity between the two types of judicial review.

47 D. Kanstroom, *Deportation Nation*, Cambridge, MA: Harvard University Press, 2007, 129.

Perhaps the best interpretation is that the Supreme Court sought a dialogue with the elected branches of government. This suggests a less 'absolutist' approach to the constitutional entitlements of aliens. We can see this same process in the gradual development of due process standards in the Guantanamo cases, which both shaped and responded to Congressional measures. In this sense, plenary power doctrine is simply modified (by a rule of statutory interpretation that presumes against indefinite detention) not jettisoned altogether.[48] Even the UK *Belmarsh* decision only required the government to rethink its policy, but did not of itself mandate the detainees' release.[49] To this extent, the detention of unauthorized aliens remains ultimately a political question, but one in which the courts test the limits of politicians' resolve to pursue policies that lead to indefinite incarceration without trial.[50]

It is clear, however, that this is a modest principle, based upon the extreme limiting case of detentions which have no prospect of ending. At this point, the apparent statutory purpose, that of removal, has obviously fallen away. By contrast, where removal remains a realistic option, the position appears to be different. Thus, for example in *Kim* v. *Demore*, the Supreme Court did not require *individualized* detention decisions, even for lawful residents who were only potentially deportable. It merely asked whether the enforcement policy *as a whole* was rational. This required only that there be general risks amongst the deportable alien population. The British cases on habeas corpus also start with the assumption that the state should be allowed a 'reasonable' period of detention. This suggests again a reluctance to recognize an individual 'right' to due process in relation to the liberty of immigrants against whom the state has commenced enforcement action.

---

48 This idea of constitutionalism suggests a dialogue between courts and the other branches of government as to what fundamental rights are owed to aliens. We can see this in the US Supreme Court cases on Guantanamo Bay. More generally see N. Devins and L. Fisher, *The Democratic Constitution*, Oxford University Press, 2004.

49 The government could have ignored the judgment or passed new legislation repealing the Human Rights Act to the extent necessary.

50 There is also an important practical reason for such constitutional dialogue based upon the limits of the judicial function. To the extent that detainees are simply ordered to be released, their 'reauthorization' to be in the community is only a bare licence to be at liberty. In order for them to both function socially and economically and for the authorities to maintain contact with them, ex-detainees require a set of rules and entitlements. Courts are ill-suited to determine these questions in the abstract. Governments must devise such packages of rights and obligations in a conversation with judicial rulings.

The ambiguity of an individual migrant liberty 'right' reflects both doctrinal and political factors. Courts have not been sure if a 'right of release' is simply incoherent for persons who have (or who may turn out to have) no right to be present at all. Also, it is not clear if such release amounts to an infringement of democratic choices over migration policy, particularly where release itself has been prohibited by law. In the end, some fundamental choices have to be made about whether any liberal state respecting the rule of law can tolerate administrative detention which is not attended by strong safeguards against abuse or hardship. It is to this topic that we turn now.

Migration and the idea of a global rule of law

Across the world, judges have thus struggled to reconcile this tradition of partialism and deference over migration with evolving ideas of the rule of law and equality before the law as checks on arbitrary government.[51] It remains unclear what a Dworkinian 'best reading' of liberal constitutions looks like.[52] Nevertheless, these cases test the very limits of what we mean by a system of *laws*. As one English judge posed the issue '... an illegal immigrant is not an outlaw, deprived of all benefit and all protection which the law affords'.[53] The process of rendering this abstract ideal concrete is entailing a case-by-case assessment of which restrictions on migrants pass muster. Whilst each jurisdiction must reach its own conclusions in light of its own legal traditions, history and politics, there are clearly common philosophical and human rights issues. A comparative approach is beginning to emerge, with courts looking to draw upon a stock of principles developed across jurisdictions.

The problem is made difficult by the fact that immigration measures are generally taken with express legal authority – the rule of law in a formal sense is adhered to.[54] Certainly courts in the past saw the habeas

---

51 Indeed Dworkin himself generally assumes membership in his discussion of law as integrity which 'insists that people are members of a genuine political community only when they accept that their fates are linked in the following strong way: they accept that they are governed by common principles, not just rules hammered out in political compromise', *Law's Empire*, 211.

52 D. Kennedy, 'Form and Substance in Private Law Adjudication' (1976) *Harv. L. Rev.* 1685–778, for a study that illustrates that conflicting principles may persist in case-law alongside each other without either attaining the status of a governing principle.

53 Staughton L.J. in *Castelli* v. *City of Westminster* [1996] *EWJ* 4254 (CA), para. 68.

54 See J. Raz, 'The Rule of Law and its Virtue' (1977) 93 *LQR* 195, who argues, using a positivist approach to its definition, that the rule of law may be largely neutral in moral terms.

corpus jurisdiction as confined to establishing a legal power to detain existed.[55] Modern ideas of administrative law have, however, gradually imposed procedural obligations on government to show that decisions are taken in ways that allow migrants a fair opportunity to be heard.[56] This jurisprudence brings migrants 'within the constitution' to the limited extent that some of the standards developed by the courts in relation to procedural due process extend to them.[57]

Common law courts have thus drawn upon both traditional domestic norms and international sources to engage in this analysis. As we have seen, although not always reaching the same conclusions, there has been an ongoing discussion between courts about appropriate principles. We can agree with Dyzenhaus,[58] who argues that courts must look to 'the substantive values that the separation of powers is supposed to protect which go beyond the positivist values of certainty and stability'. He argues that the '[g]enerality of law, equality before the law, fairness... and the liberty and dignity of the legal subject are all very strong candidates for the common law's stock of legal values'.[59]

This expanded idea of the rule of law is one that aspires to provide an important level of global governance over migration. For Dauvergne the rule of law provides a way of 'unhinging of law and nation' so that law is no longer a limiting factor based upon membership of a contractarian community.[60] This may go further, in some respects, than international human rights law, which accepts that some 'rights' are compromised by lack of immigration status. The rule of law can be seen as 'embodying standards of treatment for those who come before it that are distinct

---

55 See Ch. 1 above for the discussion of the World War One internment cases for a good example.

56 See Dauvergme, 'Sovereignty, Migration and the Rule of Law in Global Times' for detailed discussion of some recent case-law in common law jurisdictions, and the discussion in Ch. 2 above. The development of legitimate expectation has also been used to limit executive action denying fairness to aliens. See *A-G Hong Kong* v. *Ng Yuen Shiu* [1983] AC 629 for a British example.

57 There are still exceptions, particularly in the national security deportation context. See *R* v. *SSHD ex parte Cheblak* [1991] 2 All ER 319, for an example.

58 Dyzenhaus, 'The Rule of (Administrative) Law in International Law', 132.

59 *Ibid.*, 161. He cites *Minister of State for Immigration and Ethnic Affairs* v. *Teoh* [1995] 183 CLR 273 in the Australia High Court, *Baker* v. *Canada (Minister of Citizenship and Immigration)* [1999] 2 SCR 817. See also L. Fuller, *The Morality of Law*, New Haven, CT: Yale University Press, 1965 for eight principles of the rule of law. Also N. Simmonds, *Law as a Moral Idea*, Cambridge University Press, 2007 which argues for deep principles being inherent in the meaning of law, including freedom.

60 C. Dauvergne, *Making People Illegal: What Globalization Means for Migration and Law*, Cambridge University Press, 2008, 46.

from rights claims but that protect individual interests'.[61] A thick version of the rule of law would provide a form of 'international common law' governing the treatment of aliens, in the absence of a definitive treaty fixing their status, thereby '[s]eparating migration law from nation [and] re-imagining the domain of this law in a completely innovative way'.[62]

Reaffirming the rule of law: no immigration detention without judicial approval

In the famous *Mezei* decision, Mr Justice Jackson in US context noted, in 1953 at least, that it was 'still startling, in this country, to find a person held indefinitely in executive custody without accusation of crime or judicial trial'.[63] The years since then have produced a political and legal sea-change. Looking at the United States and most countries now, lengthy or indefinite detention without judicial scrutiny is no longer startling – it is commonplace in the immigration field. This is the root cause of much that is inhumane, costly and arbitrary. Detention without strong judicial control needs to be no longer 'banal', but rather become 'startling' once again. To detain anyone based upon the word of officials alone is to fundamentally deny the worth of the individual person and to invite oppressive conduct.

Jackson J. relied upon constitutional due process norms to underpin migrants' right to challenge the evidential basis for deportation and associated detention. The rule of law in this more demanding sense provides important safeguards for migrants. The recent Guantanamo cases appear to endorse the same principle for persons who have not been admitted to the United States. The case-law from Strasbourg has also endorsed strong judicial review in national security cases where *de facto* internment is occurring.[64] The same level of due process can and should be available in habeas corpus to scrutinize detention based upon alleged flight risk, which is far more common than dangerousness, as a justification.

Beyond this, however, practice has shown that, even where habeas corpus is available, immigration detainees are often held for long periods without any independent review. Such review should therefore

---

61 *Ibid.*, 182–3.   62 *Ibid.*, 183.
63 He concluded that: 'Executive imprisonment has been considered oppressive and lawless since John, at Runnymede, pledged that no free man should be imprisoned, dispossessed, outlawed, or exiled save by the judgment of his peers or by the law of the land' (per Jackson J., *Shaughnessy* v. *United States ex rel. Mezei* 345 U.S. 206 (1953)).
64 See *Chahal* v. *United Kingdom* (1996) 23 EHRR 413.

be *automatic*, not left to the vagaries of individual financial or practical circumstances. The state itself must ensure that its detention decisions are subject to proper scrutiny to avoid abuse and arbitrariness. International standards are moving in this direction. The European Court of Human Rights in *Shamsa* v. *Poland* suggested that this was required by Article 5 ECHR.[65] This mirrors some national jurisdictions which require early judicial authorization.[66] Soft legal standards emerging from the United Nations and Council of Europe also suggest judicial approval is an important element.[67] This would move regulation of detention closer towards that pertaining in relation to police powers, rather than relying upon detainees to activate habeas corpus. These emerging standards suggest basic entitlements to judicial approval at a relatively early stage. However, devising such a scheme and resourcing it is an essentially *legislative* task which is explored below in more detail.

Proportionality: balancing individual interests and enforcement efforts

A right to procedural due process, important as it is, does not solve all the problems of excessive or mandatory detention. A few governments have legislated to detain whole *classes*, or even *all*, unauthorized persons. In these cases only *substantive* rights to liberty, not just procedural safeguards, can help. What legal and moral tools can evaluate the appropriateness of such steps? David Beatty[68] has argued persuasively that proportionality provides a basis for judicial review that both accords with the practice of many constitutional and international courts and is politically neutral:

---

65 Applications nos. 45355/99 and 45357/99, Judgment of 27 Nov. 2003.
66 This book has looked at France, but there are several others, including Canada and Germany.
67 See Ch. 3, above. Recommendation 1327 (1997) on the Protection and Reinforcement of the Human Rights of Refugees and Asylum-seekers in Europe, adopted 24 April 1997 (14th Sitting). Recommendation R (99) 12 of Committee of Ministers to member states on the return of rejected asylum seekers (18 May 1999). Recommendation 1547 (2002) Expulsion Procedures in conformity with human rights and Enforced with Respect for Safety and Dignity. Report of the UN Working Group on Arbitrary Detention, 13th Session, A/HRC/13/30, 15 January 2010.
68 D. Beatty, *The Ultimate Rule of Law*, Oxford University Press, 2004, and also D. Beatty, 'Human Rights and the Rules of Law', in D. Beatty (ed.), *Human Rights and Judicial Review: a Comparative Perspective*, Amsterdam: Kluwer Academic Publishers, 1994.

> Regardless of whether the law is attacked under the banner of equality or liberty, its legitimacy and its life depend on whether it can pass a rigorous evaluation of its ends, its means, and its effects against the principle of proportionality that connects all three.[69]

He cites case-law from the United States, the European Court of Human Rights and the European Court of Justice among many jurisdictions to show how this approach is adopted in practice.[70] The benefit of proportionality over other theories of judicial review is that:

> proportionality permits disputes . . . to be settled on the basis of reason and rational argument. It makes it possible to compare and evaluate interests and ideas, values and facts that are radically different, in a way that is both rational and fair.[71]

The pragmatic nature of proportionality is a crucial virtue in a field like immigration detention where the 'right' of states to control borders is set against the 'right' of migrants to liberty.[72] Proportionality provides a tool for scrutinizing the practices of states without having to resort to absolutism of one kind or another. As Beatty concludes, '[p]roportionality transforms the meaning of rights from assertions of eternal truths into . . . "a discourse for the adjudication of conflict".[73]

Cases like the *Belmarsh* decision and *Zadvydas* explicitly recognized a right to be released even for allegedly dangerous persons. The clearest principle that explains these decisions is that of proportionality. 'Immigration' control objectives must only be pursued using proportionate means.[74] Beyond a reasonable period, such detention became internment. The more demanding proportionality test adopted by the Human

---

69 *Ibid.*, 116.
70 For a detailed consideration of the Strasbourg approach see S. Van Drooghenbroeck, *La Proportionalité dans le droit de la Convention Européenne des Droits de L'Homme: Prendre l'idée Simple au Sérieux*, Bruxelles: Bruylant, 2001.
71 *Ibid.*, 169.
72 Legal pragmatism as a jurisprudential theory has deep roots in the United States. See R.A. Posner, 'Pragmatic Adjudication' (1996) 18 *Cardozo L. Rev.* 1, for a detailed exposition. It clearly has close affinities with proportionality in terms of method and relative neutrality.
73 Citing Ignatieff, who argues proportionality ensures 'individuals are deliberative equals whose views are entitled to a respectful hearing in all moral discussions about how universal standards should apply in each instance'. M. Ignatieff, *Human Rights*, Princeton University Press, 2001, 170.
74 This is consistent with Beatty's view that 'the requirement of proportionality renders unconstitutional laws which compromise freedom in a way and to a degree which is out of line with how the balance between individual freedom and the community's well-being has been drawn in the past'. See Beatty, 'Human Rights and the Rules of Law', 44.

Rights Committee in *A* v. *Australia* goes further, in stating unequivocally that the fundamental right is that of individual liberty – not state
sovereignty. By focusing more upon time-limited detention, the Strasbourg Court appears to be moving towards a form of proportionality test
in the recent *Saadi* v. *UK* and *Mikolenko* v. *Estonia* decisions. This moves
towards the Court's more general proportionality approach outside the
immigration context.[75]

This trend should not be seen as confined to jurisprudence. The political branches of government have historically recognized that extreme
detention periods were undesirable. Release on bail or under supervision
used to be the statutory or executive norm. Only during more recent years
have governments resiled from this. There are now signs of a rethink. The
absolute eighteen-month period of detention allowed in relation to the
return of irregular migrants under the EU Returns Directive, whilst still
excessive, was a political attempt to give legal certainty and strike a balance
between enforcement and liberty. The Australian and US governments
have also begun to seriously review policy.

There may now be a convergence on proportionality as a guiding principle. This said, discussion thus far has focused upon extreme cases. We
should now consider whether there is not a case for this principle to
be used more systematically, rather than simply in the limiting case of
indefinite detention. It is important to emphasize, however, that there is
no complete 'right' answer, as this is a flexible concept, compatible with
a range of responses. What follows is an attempt to set out the broad
parameters. These should inform the human rights framework within
which detention policy is set by the democratic branches of government
and administered by courts.

Circumscribing the legitimate goals of detention: removal not segregation

Proportionality analysis, whilst providing a forum for reasoned argument, does not provide a clear answer to a vexing problem: what are
the legitimate goals of detention? The symbolic dimension of policy can
come to dominate as politicians seek to make an impact upon weary electorates. Courts have an important role in ensuring that symbolism does

---

75 Proportionality also forms part of the general principles of EU law. It is, however, uncertain as yet how far this doctrine will influence the European Court of Justice in its case-law
on aliens.

not count as a legitimate goal of policy when it leads to onerous interference with fundamental human interests, including those of migrants.[76] Nevertheless, the goals of detention have become increasingly broad and elusive.

Governments often speak of detention as promoting 'border control' or protecting 'territorial sovereignty'. These claims are, however, extremely abstract. Border controls such as detention and inspections are very costly and do not appear to produce direct benefits to the state.[77] The benefits are largely indirect, to the extent that such controls aid the wider migration policy by removing or excluding some unwanted individuals or groups.[78] They may also work by way of deterring some potential migrants from attempting unauthorized entry.[79] Goals such as public safety, economic growth, social cohesion, an educated workforce and cultural development are the ultimate goods which it is clearly a rational objective to seek.

By contrast, modern migration politics has suggested another view. Rather than seeing detention as a part of the *means* to pursue rational migration policy, some contemporary political rhetoric suggests it is an *end in itself*. The most graphic case is that of the Australian experience. Detected migrants must be either authorized, expelled or segregated. The state must strenuously resist being seen to legitimate 'in-betweens', almost reducing them to non-persons. Political power seeks to ensure that the release of unauthorized persons is put beyond law. There is no 'right' to liberty, for that would mean the unwanted could make legal demands of the state. The main political objective is to deny that the state can be compelled to provide anything to such persons. This is where

---

76 For a wider discussion of the relationship between judicial and legislative organs which emphasizes the ability of the former to develop reasoned arguments to scrutinize political actions see J. Habermas, *Between Facts and Norms*, Cambridge: Polity Press, 1997, Ch. 6.

77 We leave aside the less common issue of dangerous aliens and focus here upon non-dangerous economic migrants.

78 We can, of course, note those theorists who argue that even on economic grounds, border controls are damaging for the states practising them. See P. Legrain, *Immigrants: Your Country Needs Them*, London: Little, Brown, 2007.

79 This issue has not been tackled by any international court, but the Australian High Court has done so in *Chu Kheng Lim and other* v. *Minister for Immigration, Local Government and Ethnic Affairs and another* [1992] 176 CLR 1 FC 92/051. One factor pointing against immigration detention being punitive was said to be its 'voluntary' nature. There is an implicit endorsement of this in the *Amuur* v. *France* decision by the Strasbourg Court, which seemed to conclude that only asylum seekers could be said to be involuntarily detained. Some domestic judges have instead considered voluntariness as part of the assessment of reasonableness of the period of detention, as in the *Hardial Singh* case in the UK.

proportionality analysis does not always provide the neutral theory of judicial review that Beatty hopes for. In order for proportionality to re-enter the picture, we must make some value judgements about the *reasonable* goals of detention policy.

Clearly modern states experience unauthorized migration on a vast scale all the time. This is the result of practical facts of global demand for labour, inequality, internal repression, war and powerful smuggling networks tied to the transport and communications revolutions.[80] In addition, 'unauthorized' persons are inevitable when the demand to migrate exceeds the supply of lawful permits to do so. Such intense levels of migration are one feature of 'globalization'.[81] Nayyar persuasively concludes that 'despite the political reality of immigration laws, the market-driven conditions and institutions being created by globalization, will sustain, perhaps even increase, illegal immigration and the associated cross-border labour flows'.[82] The economic pressure driving migration is so intense that it is unlikely that any degree of regulation can stop it.[83] This has been confirmed by research suggesting that border restrictions can lead to increased illegal migration and trafficking of migrants.[84]

Protection of 'territorial sovereignty' in the absolute sense is thus not a practical reality. It is an abstraction. 'Sovereignty' is already punctured by the hundreds of thousands, even millions, known to be living and working unlawfully outside their countries of nationality. This is certain to continue regardless of detention policy. The issue is really one of the means used to achieve discernible levels of control over migration. Detention must seen as a modest administrative tool, alongside many, designed to influence broad migration trends. The individuals detained

---

80 Bhagwati argues: '[p]aradoxically, the ability to control migration has shrunk as the desire to do so has increased. The reality is that borders are beyond control and little can be done to really cut down immigration.' J. Bhagwati, 'Borders Beyond Control' (2003) 82(1) *Foreign Affairs* 99.

81 S. Sassen, *Losing Control: Sovereignty in an Age of Globalization*, New York: Columbia University Press, 1996.

82 D. Nayyar, 'Cross-border Movements of People', in D. Nayyar (ed.), *Governing Globalization*, Oxford University Press, 2002, 164: 'The factors which make it easier to move goods, services, capital, technology, and information across borders, but for explicit immigration laws and implicit consular practices, also make it easier to move people across borders.'

83 'It would be reasonable to infer that there is a potential conflict between the laws of nations that restrict the movement of people across borders and the economics of globalization that induces the movement of people across borders', *ibid.*, 165.

84 *An Assessment of the Impact of Asylum Policies in Europe, 1990–2000*, Home Office Research Study 259.

pursuant thereto comprise only a tiny, often random, sample when compared to the total number of unauthorized migrants. Jurisprudence, too, has increasingly recognized it as a means to an end, not an end in itself.[85]

This redefinition of the proper goals of detention has ultimately to be driven also by a reassertion of the more ancient prohibition on administrative incarceration. The seclusion of individuals by means of unaccountable detention should be seen as highly anomalous, not as a convenient tool of migration policy. Internment has been considered to be contrary to liberal constitutional principles for centuries. Reconfiguring the legitimate goals of detention in this way permits proportionality to re-enter. Legal reasoning can evaluate the balance struck between respect for individual liberty and overall migration policy.

Individualized detention decisions and necessity

Proceeding on the assumption that the legitimate goal of immigration detention is to provide support to overall migration policy, we can further investigate when detention is appropriate. Detention which is not necessary in the individual case cannot be adjudged acceptable. The Human Rights Committee in *A* v. *Australia* agreed that an initial period of detention might be justified to investigate cases of illegal entry or those without permission to enter.[86] This author sees such detention as consistent with the historical purpose of incarceration – to afford the state a short period to assess immigration status and entitlement. Beyond this, if further investigations or appeals are required, it is clear that the Human Rights Committee in *C* v. *Australia* required that *individualized* evidence of an absconding risk be adduced to support further detention. The burden

---

85 We should note here Finnis's attempt to use double-effect thinking to support immigration detention when he talks about: 'the ambiguity between hardship imposed as a means and hardship resulting as an unintended though forseen side-effect'. J. Finnis, 'Commentary on Dummett and Weithman' in B. Barry and R.E. Goodin (eds), *Free Movement: Ethical Issues in the Transnational Migration of People and of Money*, Pennsylvania State University Press, 1992, 204. Double-effect arguments suffer from many defects but they, too, accept proportionality as an important limit upon any action.
86 The Strasbourg Court endorsed this too in *Saadi*, where it held that a seven-day detention to enable processing of an application was proportionate even when not necessary in the individual case to prevent absconding: (Appn. 13229/03), *Saadi and Others* v. *United Kingdom* (Grand Chamber) Judgment of 29 Jan. 2008.

was clearly upon the detaining authority.[87] This suggests discretion must be exercised in each individual case.

Turning to the issue of alternatives to detention, there have been a number of studies that have shown relatively successful community supervision schemes. The UNHCR conducted a detailed survey of different national approaches to this question.[88] It looked at the effectiveness of the lowest level of intrusion into personal autonomy through measures like reporting requirements and moved on to consider electronic tagging, residence and movement restrictions falling short of detention *per se*. The report notes the 'remarkable scarcity' of statistics on absconding kept by states which renders conclusions difficult. Nevertheless, the available evidence suggested that use of these alternatives, at least for asylum seekers and failed asylum applicants, often produced high levels of compliance at much less cost to taxpayers than detention.[89] The report more tentatively suggests that provision of a lawyer, clear information about reporting obligations and sanctions for non-compliance, along with material support, all increased compliance rates.[90] It is clear that detention decisions, to pass muster as being necessary, must carefully consider evidence about alternatives.

It is important to notice that some migrants do still abscond under such schemes. Does this mean that the schemes are not sufficiently effective to support their wider use? The answer to this depends upon the legitimate goal of detention and the right of liberty discussed above. It was suggested that the goal cannot be the prevention of any breach of immigration law.

87 By contrast, the European Court of Human Rights in *Chahal* held that Art. 5(1)(f) supported detention even without reference to an absconding risk. The most recent decision in *Saadi* suggests, however, that, in the absence of such a risk, detention would have to be relatively short.

88 UNHCR, *Legal and Protection Policy Research Series: Alternatives to Detention of Asylum Seekers and Refugees*, Geneva: UNHCR, POLAS/2006/03, April 2006. See also A.W. Nicholas, 'Protecting Refugees: Alternatives to a Policy of Mandatory Detention' [2002] *Australian J. Human Rts* 6.

89 The report concludes that absconding rates are very low in countries of 'destination' (those migrants are seeking to reach) compared to higher rates in 'transit' countries. For destination countries, see the Toronto Bail Program (91.6% compliance); Bail for Immigration Detainees in the UK (91% compliance); Vera Institute of Justice in the United States (84% compliance); Hotham Mission in Australia (100% compliance of 200 migrants in a small programme) (see paras 79–154). Data on costs of detention was sparse and hard to compare across countries, but figures in the United States and Australia suggested it was three times more expensive per person than community care (see paras 166–72).

90 Paragraphs 155–65.

This is impossible to achieve without elimination of all movement and construction of vast walls around each nation. The goal of detention must only be to achieve, alongside all the other mechanisms of immigration control, a reasonable level of compliance with immigration law which is consistent with more fundamental principles of due process. Recognizing an individual right to individualized due process for immigrants means that groups should not all be detained simply to prevent the risk of some individuals absconding.[91] This requires consideration in each case of the likelihood of absconding based upon past experience and objective evidence.[92]

Fixing endpoints to detention: striking a fairer balance

The second limb of the proportionality approach looks to striking a 'fair balance' between community interests and individual interests. Within all strands of liberal and human rights theory, personal liberty is considered amongst the most basic human interests. The prolonged loss of liberty is self-evidently an interference with personal autonomy, a value prized for its own sake. However, recently there has been considerable research into the medical effects of detention on immigrants. It was only with the introduction of extensive periods of detention during the late 1990s that it became recognized amongst health professionals and researchers that this might be damaging. Steel *et al.* found that 'prolonged detention

---

91 These arguments appealed to the Australian government in its justification for mandatory detention but were rejected in the *A* v. *Australia* Opinion. By contrast, the absconding rate from supervised schemes was considered a relevant factor in support of mandatory detention of criminal aliens by the Supreme Court in *Kim* v. *Demore*. Similarly there is nothing in the Strasbourg case-law that would prohibit mandatory detention and the recent decision in *Saadi* seems to confirm that this might be possible for a short period. These cases all illustrate the rather attenuated form of proportionality test adopted in such cases – the focus is upon the necessity of adopting mandatory detention policies to achieve zero absconding rates amongst immigrants overall. This is quite unlike standard proportionality analysis that starts from a consideration of each individual and the necessity of interfering with his or her rights. The reason for the switch is clearly the lack of acceptance that migrants have any right of liberty absent authorization to enter or stay.

92 This is perhaps where the Strasbourg Court became confused in *Saadi*. It decided that detention of whole classes of persons was proportionate, without looking at the necessity of detention in each individual case. To that extent they practised a unique distortion of their own standard proportionality test. The answer may lie in the fact that an initial period of detention for processing even non-absconding immigrants is necessary as a part of the bureaucratic mechanism of immigration control.

exerts a long-term impact on the psychological well-being of refugees'.[93] They noted that around half of those detained for less than six months, and virtually all those detained for longer, experienced symptoms. This expands on the findings of other researchers, who have all established short-term mental health effects of detention.[94]

We can thus see that there is a strong case for temporal limits to detention on humanitarian grounds. This must be so even in the case of those deemed likely to abscond or offend. There will be cases where the effects of detention amount to inhuman or degrading treatment if seriously prolonged.[95] The Strasbourg Court has recently suggested that stricter time-limits are appropriate. Domestic courts have also held that only a reasonable period is allowed.[96] It is beginning to be accepted that an absconding risk does not support very lengthy periods of incarceration.

The period of six months as an upper limit to detention for those properly determined by judicial process to be absconding risks is suggested here as an appropriate benchmark. It represents a balanced period considering various needs. The mental health of detainees appears to be often damaged at or beyond this duration. The period is a substantial one for non-criminal executive detention. This is the level of sentence given for some serious violent or property crimes. Immigration detainees should not routinely be held beyond the time set to punish quite serious criminals. To say they are not being punished is simply semantic. In modern immigration detention centres, as we have seen, the conditions and effects are the same, and sometimes worse, than for serving prisoners.

The authorities are still afforded a substantial period to process applications, obtain documents and liaise with other states. Reasonable levels of enforcement will still be possible, as the French experience, among

---

93 Z. Steel, D. Silove, R. Brooks, S. Momartin, B. Alzuhariri and I. Susljik, 'Impact of Immigration Detention and Temporary Protection on the Mental Health of Refugees' (2006) 188 *Br. J. Psychiatry*, 58–64, 63.

94 D. Silove, Z. Steel and C. Walters, 'Policies of Deterrence and the Mental Health of Asylum Seekers' [2000] 284 *J. Am. Med. Assoc.* 604; A.S. Keller, B. Rosenfeld, C. Trinh-Shevrin *et al.*, 'Mental Health of Detained Asylum Seekers' (2003) 362 *Lancet* 1721–3. See M. Fazel and D. Silove, 'Detention of Refugees' (2006) 332 *BMJ* 251–2. M. Porter and N. Haslam, 'Predisplacement and Postdisplacement Factors Associated with Mental Health of Refugees and Internally Displaced Persons: A Meta-analysis' (2005) 294 *J. Am. Med. Assoc.* 602–12.

95 See the cases relating to Australian mandatory detention in Ch. 3 above.

96 See the decision of Lord Woolf in *R* v. *Secretary of State for the Home Department ex parte Hardial Singh* [1984] WLR 704. See *R(I)* v. *Secretary of State for the Home Department* [2002] EWCA Civ 888, where an absconding risk was not enough to support detention beyond sixteen months.

others, demonstrates. Setting a time limit provides an incentive to have in place adequate administrative procedures and resources to ensure such processing happens swiftly. Even when a person is released at the expiry of this period they may be subject to tagging, residence and reporting rules which would provide some controls, should their removal become possible in the future. Furthermore, they may have their access to social support, housing and education (if any) tied to continued compliance with such conditions. There is no sense in which their release would be equivalent to a grant of substantive immigration status or citizenship. They could still be removed if this became possible.

Proportionality and hard-core public security detention

What about that small percentage of detainees who may be genuinely dangerous? The position here is more complex. There is clearly strong intuitive force in the idea that a community should be able to protect itself for 'longer' against persons found, after due process, to present tangible threats to life and limb. Such detention still aims to ultimately secure expulsion but, pending this, serves to protect the public against harm. This represents the most difficult scenario, because it pits the obligation of the state to protect the nation from the risk of tangible danger presented by non-citizens against the traditional liberal dislike of preventive administrative detention.

Although challenging, the answer found in using a proportionality approach points away from employing what tends to amount to internment in practice. Proportionality requires decisions to be made rationally and without arbitrary discrimination. As the House of Lords and the European Court of Human Rights decided in *A and others*, where the danger to national security is found amongst both nationals and foreigners, it is not rational to single out the latter for internment.[97] It is arbitrary because it leaves nationals free to carry out criminal activities unless and until criminal charges are brought. To decide this, however, it was necessary to conclude that *aliens had the same liberty rights as nationals* save for detention employed to deport them. Outside this situation, detention became preventive internment not ancillary to immigration proceedings.

---

97 The European Court of Human Rights and the Commission had both earlier decided that Art. 5(4) required searching judicial review of detention that was stated to be on security grounds, even if annexed to deportation proceedings. See Ch. 3 above, and the cases of *Caprino* and *Chahal*.

This decision was all the more important because the case concerned a state of emergency. This is a vivid endorsement of Cole's argument for non-discrimination in the design of emergency measures, because to pit the interests of citizens on one side against a 'voiceless and often demonized "alien" minority on the other, is a recipe for overreaction'.[98] When measures are taken against everyone, 'the nation takes notice, and the political process is far more attentive to the rights and liberties at stake in the liberty-security balance'.[99]

Turning to 'ordinary' criminal threats, police forces could assuredly reduce crime by preventively rounding up many citizens who are known to be active criminals. This would, however, be unacceptable in anything other than a police state. Preventive detention is an arbitrary and discriminatory method of avoiding criminal law procedures when targeted only at deportable migrants. This was the approach followed by the US Supreme Court in *Zadvydas*, which held that even a risk of criminal conduct could not justify detention beyond the six-month removal period. The Supreme Court crucially reasserted the basic principle that, in matters relating to criminal conduct, even for deportable foreigners there could be no detention without trial.

Immigration detention must be construed narrowly in order to avoid it spilling over into internment. It must be restated that the power to detain was created only to effect removal, not to practise quasi-internment or segregation of aliens.[100] The law reports and practice suggest that in many cases of long-term detention, repatriation was extremely unlikely from the outset. This is usually because the alleged country of origin is known to only rarely accept back its nationals, or because there are no travel connections. Even when removal is wholly speculative, detention continues due to understandable fears held by executive officers and politicians about public anger at their releasing potentially criminal foreigners into the community. There is always a *chance* (or a 'hope' as the Australian High Court put it in *Al Kateb*) that a way will be found to deport. Any

---

98 D. Cole, *Enemy Aliens*, New York: New Press, 2003, 229.   99 *Ibid.*, 230.

100 See the UK cases *R(I) v Secretary of State for the Home Department*, where the risk of offending would afford 'a substantially longer period of time within which to arrange the detainee's removal abroad' (per Simon Brown L.J., para. 29), and *R(A)* v. *Secretary of State for the Home Department* [2007] EWCA Civ 804, where serious offences in the past supported lengthy ongoing detention. The indeterminacy of the matter was spelled out thus: 'there must come a time when, whatever the magnitude of the risks, the period of detention can no longer be said to be reasonable', *R (Mamki)* v. *Secretary of State for the Home Department* [2008] EWCA Civ 307, per Dyson L.J., para. 14.

'non-cooperation' by detainees or exercise of appeal rights, is taken to support 'longer' detention.[101] This, however, pushes detainees into a largely 'lawless' realm of discretion which is incompatible with fundamental principles. Even convicted criminals have been found guilty of an offence defined by law and know for how long they will be detained.

Governments have a number of other tools available. Long or indeterminate sentences for truly dangerous criminals are now sometimes used. If prosecution is impossible, appropriate interim safeguards, such as tagging and residence restrictions can minimize any danger to the public. Such measures could remain in place for a time, but eventually these, too, would have to be withdrawn and a form of permanent status granted. As the UK experience with control orders showed, in the end, it is both impractical and unacceptable to maintain people in a legal limbo that has no basis in immigration enforcement. This serves only to demonstrate political disdain for them, an unwillingness to use the criminal law or a reluctance to declare a more general emergency that would allow citizens to be detained too.

Immigration detention, as opposed to deportation, is a tool to enforce removal, not to prevent crime itself. To employ it preventively is to invite abuse, because it singles out one group for measures that are politically unacceptable for nationals. The powerful logic of the *Belmarsh* and *Zadvydas* decisions suggests that the risk of serious crime does not justify what are effectively emergency measures being applied to only one group of potential criminals. Recourse to a variable 'reasonable' period in such cases leads to impossible and arbitrary calculations about how much preventive detention can be imposed on aliens to provide an uncertain level of protection for citizens. There are no defensible legal standards upon which to base a decision to end such detention whilst a 'hope' of expulsion remains. This presents a slippery slope toward indefinite detention based essentially upon political discretion, with the attendant danger of creating 'political prisoners'.

Not just extreme cases: extending due process to all deprivations of liberty

As we have seen, most of the key constitutional or human rights cases on detention have been triggered by long-term detainees where the removal

---

101 As held by the European Court of Human Rights in *Mikolenko*, the non-cooperation may make it clear that early removal is going to prove fruitless. See Ch. 3 above.

process has stalled, often after many years. These persons may be considered *de facto* stateless, even if not strictly without a nationality in law. As has been noted already, these 'hard' cases have generally made 'good' law. The obvious exceptions have been the Australian decision in *Al Kateb* and the US Supreme Court decision in *Mezei*. This latter case is now looking more like a Cold War exception. It is hard to reconcile it with the Guantanamo cases, which confer constitutional protection on unadmitted aliens. When asked to choose between the rule of law or continuing to cede government wide prerogatives over aliens that result in indefinite detention without due process, the courts have generally endorsed the former.

What should we do beyond the limiting case of indefinite detention? In these cases, removal was no longer likely to occur soon. The state's purpose for detention had ostensibly failed. Nevertheless, the same arguments apply to cases not having reached this stage. Detaining people who do not need to be detained is harmful, expensive and fails to promote immigration control. It is sensible to introduce due process to all stages of detention decision-making because this ensures that scarce resources are targeted where needed in a rational and effective manner. Finally, without such due process, there will inevitably be arbitrary interferences with the liberty interests of unauthorized migrants. It becomes rapidly incoherent to suggest that aliens may be detained with a certain degree of arbitrariness. Either an individual right of due process exists or it does not. Whilst there can be degrees of due process, there is an irreducible minimum content which, at the moment, is rarely adhered to.

Rendering the rule of law: an outline of a statutory system of review of detention

We can therefore conclude that the above analysis suggests the following broad principles: automatic judicial review of the merits of detention, a prohibition on mandatory incarceration and a proportionality standard in executive and judicial decision-making. Proportionality suggested a maximum time-limit to detention, even in the case of potential absconders. As noted above, however, the broad contours of proportionality do no more than set the framework: the hard work of administering a legally robust system of detention requires resources for efficient executive action and judicial hearings. These can only come through democratic decision-making. To the extent that less detention results, however, the result will be cheaper than current practice. This is, to some extent, the province of administrative law, not general human rights law.

In creating a system of automatic judicial review there are two competing considerations at work: the need for an early check on executive discretion as set against the extra cost imposed by too many hearings. It is not clear how often initial 'errors' are made by executive officers under current discretionary detention systems. Certainly the longer detention proceeds, the more likely bail is to be granted. Very early judicial hearings may lead to only modest levels of detainee release.[102] It is to be expected that different groups of detainees are more likely to be released than others. For example, long-term lawful residents are much more likely to have close family ties and funds sufficient for bail. In this way, it is undesirable to design systems for review of detention in isolation from immigration issues.

This author therefore does not favour a single 'police powers' model requiring judicial approval within, say, two days. Rather, there should be a distinction drawn between two kinds of case. For persons who have no *prima facie* visa or permit, there are less urgent reasons to seek judicial approval for detention. They may have no rights of appeal or basis to stay. The expectation may be that they will be expelled swiftly.[103] Whilst habeas corpus should always be available, to review detention in every such case might serve little purpose. After a period of two weeks, however, detention should automatically be reviewed by a court. By that stage it will have become clear that expulsion will be delayed and there may be an application or appeal pending. By contrast, for those detainees who already had an apparently valid visa and were arrested pursuant to deportation or revocation proceedings, the position is different. This group can legitimately claim that they had a right of free movement within the territory which the state has removed. In these cases there should be judicial review after a short time, perhaps forty-eight hours.

At each hearing the court must start with a presumption in favour of release. The right to liberty entails nothing less. The burden to support detention should be firmly on the government. The court should consider a number of factors. First, whether there is a power to detain at

---

102 The French system releases about a third of detainees, but it is not clear if these detainees are released on bail or due to technical faults in their arrest. The French courts do not consider the immigration aspects of the case as, in principle, this is reserved to the administrative judges.

103 For example, detention in the United States in relation to Mexicans held at the border can often be quite brief, because expedited return procedures exist.

all. Second, whether detention is necessary to enforce removal and what alternative measures might suffice, including bail. Third, any humanitarian factors pointing towards release such as minority, torture or mental health problems. Fourth, whether a migrant's case involves an application or appeal that will take any appreciable time to be processed or not. Fifth, whether persons of the detainee's nationality are removable in the light of transport or other practical factors such as documentation. Courts should have access to current information on this crucial issue. The basic merits of any application to remain should also inform the overall assessment. If removal is unlikely to be possible within a short period of time, this points towards release.

Even if the first hearing maintains detention, there should be monthly reviews. These should consider the same factors above but also the diligence of the authorities in processing substantive immigration applications and attempting to effect removal.[104] Detention that is prolonged through inertia or lack of resources cannot be considered necessary. A failure to show how the removal process is progressing demonstrates a lack of respect for the right to liberty of detainees and lack of effort in terms of immigration control; the longer detention proceeds, its ill-effects on detainees increase. This suggests that the authorities should be required to show more clearly that the removal effort is actually likely to be successful.

A reasonable period of detention to secure removal is justifiable for detainees properly judged to be absconding risks. However, if removal is clearly not going to be possible (either from the outset or it later transpires) or there is a lack of administrative effort by the authorities or real mental or physical hardship arising from detention, supervised release is appropriate. This is so even if the detainee is still felt to be a possible absconding risk. Detention should in any event cease after six months, even if none of the above indicators for release applies. Where a detainee is still believed to present a serious absconding or criminal threat, release should be made subject to appropriately strict conditions. They should be able to be re-detained by executive action if their removal

---

104 A 'right' to good administration is something that is inherent in much modern administrative law relating to due process. It is now spoken of as a distinct right in Art. 41 of the Charter of Fundamental Rights of the European Union. See J. Wakefield, *The Right of Good Administration*, Amsterdam: Kluwer, 2007; Lord Millett, 'The Right of Good Administration in European Law' (2002) 47 *PL* 309. See also the Canadian system, which imposes an obligation upon the authorities to show efficient processing of immigration claims to support further detention.

becomes imminent again. Their re-detention should trigger the same process described above again. Breach of conditions should be dealt with by punishment for defined criminal offences.

Going beyond this scheme of management, bureaucracies and courts also need reliable tools to guide their exercise of discretion.[105] One solution would be to impose rules that structure discretion closely.[106] There is, however, a risk that rigid rules will replace discretion and be seen as hurdles that must be overcome to support release.[107] This author suggests that the problem here is not the existence of the rules, but their failure to predict risks. The grounds currently used to support findings that detention is appropriate in individual cases are often speculative.[108] Thus we find reference to factors like clandestine entry and use of false documents being relied upon to detain when there is no hard evidence to suggest that such persons are more likely to abscond.[109] By contrast, a previous history of absconding or clear criminal dishonesty might suggest detention is appropriate to ensure compliance with immigration decisions.

105 S.H. Legomsky,'The Detention of Aliens: Theories, Rules and Discretion' (1999) 30 *Inter-Am. L. Rev.* 531.

106 This was Davis's solution. See K.C. Davis, *Discretionary Justice,* Louisiana University Press, 1969.

107 As Galligan puts it: 'It is tempting to think of discretion as a space or gap waiting to be filled up with rules; indeed, it is often assumed that, over a course of decisions, standards and policies will emerge so that decision-making naturally progresses towards the adjudicative rule-based model', D.J. Galligan, *Discretionary Powers: A Legal Study of Official Discretion,* Oxford: Clarendon Press, 1986, 173.

108 The attempts to provide useful guidance so far on this by bodies like the UNHCR Executive Committee have been very disappointing. It will be recalled that it suggested detention was appropriate 'to verify identity, to determine the elements of the refugee claim, where a person had destroyed their travel documents or used fraudulent documents to mislead the authorities and to protect national security or public order'. This represents a mixture of substantive reasons for detention and evidential matters going to which persons to detain. As such, it confuses administrative tools with substantive criteria in a way which is not helpful. We have examined the substantive criteria for detention above; to conduct a short interview to determine the reason for a migrant seeking entry or stay and to prevent absconding or the commission of crime. See UNHCR Executive Committee Conclusion No. 44 (1986) Detention of Refugees and Asylum Seekers. See also the discussion setting out the haphazard detention criteria employed in J. Hughes and O. Field, 'Recent Trends in the Detention of Asylum Seekers in Western Europe' in J. Hughes and F. Liebaut (eds), *Detention of Asylum Seekers in Europe: Analysis and Perspectives,* Amsterdam: Martinus Nijhoff Publishers, 1998.

109 See L. Weber and L. Gelsthorpe, *Deciding to Detain: How Decisions to Detain Asylum Seekers are Made at Ports of Entry,* Institute of Criminology, University of Cambridge, 2000. See also L. Weber and T. Landman, *Deciding to Detain: the Organizational Context for Decisions to Detain Asylum Seekers at UK Ports,* Colchester: Human Rights Centre, University of Essex, 2002.

More attention to empirical evidence about absconding rates for different groups in different settings is needed.[110] Experience should be derived from criminal pre-trial proceedings and bail practice. Most importantly, decisions to detain must take into account the effectiveness and relative costs of community-based alternatives. The data on alternatives to detention considered above, suggested that much detention could be avoided without significant absconding. The UNHCR study cited above found that legal representation, social and housing provision and clear advice on obligations to report promote compliance.

Detention and immigration 'emergencies'

As we have seen, states have rarely declared official 'states of emergency' to deal with immigration influxes by extended detention. Ordinary immigration powers usually gave government huge discretion to meet political and other challenges by suddenly increasing the use of detention. Even human rights standards did not stand in the way of responding to particular crises. In Europe, for example, there was never any need to derogate from Article 5 on the basis that the numbers seeking asylum constituted an emergency.[111] The Strasbourg court in *Saadi* read Article 5(1)(f) broadly

---

110 Almost all genuine refugees use false documents, clandestine entry modes or deception to enter, as do a great many persons whose asylum claims are fabricated. The former group are unlikely to abscond, although current policy might suggest detention was appropriate on the basis of such factors.

111 The fairly stringent test laid down by the European Court of Human Rights, for example, requires there to be 'an exceptional situation of crisis or emergency which affects the whole population and constitutes a threat to the organized life of the community of which the State is composed'. *Lawless* v. *Ireland* (1979–80) 1 EHRR 1, 13 and 15, para. 28. The test does not require the threat to be of a criminal nature and the Court has left a wide margin of appreciation to states to decide whether such a situation exists. Perhaps it is arguable that a massive migration of people across a border might threaten the life of a nation if it caused public order to break down. But it is submitted that migration which simply imposes financial burdens on the host state or leads to absconding in a number of cases would not be serious enough. The essence of an emergency is a threat to life and limb from some source, natural or human. Amongst Western states, there have not been such large migrations of this character. See for example *Ireland* v. *United Kingdom* (1979–80) 2 EHRR 25. The provision in ICCPR is Art. 4, which speaks of a 'public emergency which threatens the life of the nation and the existence of which is officially proclaimed, the States Parties . . . may take measures derogating from their obligation under the present Covenant to the extent strictly required by the exigencies of the situation'. Article 15 ECHR says: 'In time of war or other public emergency threatening the life of the nation any High Contracting Party may take measures derogating from its obligations under this Convention to the extent

so as to support a policy of 'detention for processing' that was a response to larger asylum volumes in Europe. Such policies arose from a political crisis, not a national security emergency. The lack of any serious due process requirement and the flexible duration of detention permitted under Article 5 has legitimated such 'crisis' responses.

If the rigorous system of judicial approval advocated above were followed, this discretion would be constrained. Due process is not cheap or easy to administer. This might prove difficult in certain situations of unforeseen mass influx. Resources might become stretched and processing cases would be delayed. The Refugee Convention itself acknowledges this in Article 31, with its provision for detention during mass influxes to allow individuals cases to be recorded. This suggests there may be cases where some elements of the due process safeguards proposed might have to be relaxed. This would not, however, be based upon *economic* grounds, as detention is far more costly than community-based alternatives. There might, however, be short-term difficulties if there were insufficient staff to record, interview and place migrants under supervision in the community. What principles should we impose on detention, during true immigration emergencies, to ensure that the rule of law is not dispensed with?

It is mainly within the context of *anti-terrorism* measures, rather than immigration influxes, that there has been considerable academic debate about the proper role for law in emergencies. Dyzenhaus argues that the rule of law, influenced by international human rights, can apply even in emergency situations.[112] He criticizes those who argue that there should be a system of minimal judicial supervision, because they 'give to official lawlessness the facade of legality'.[113] In this respect, in situations of 'mass influx', the most important rule is to maintain detainees' right to access the courts to challenge their individual detention. This said, the requirement to obtain automatic and speedy judicial approval might have to be relaxed if it turned out to be logistically impossible to process cases quickly enough. The time limit of six months on detention should, however, remain as a matter of legal certainty.

---

strictly required by the exigencies of the situation'. Some rights are non-derogable, such as the prohibition on torture and right to life. See R. Higgins, 'Derogations under Human Rights Treaties' (1976–7) 48 *BYIL* 281. *Lawless* v. *Ireland* (1979–80) 1 EHRR 1 at para. 28. See *Aksoy* v. *Turkey* (1996) 23 EHRR 553, in which the internment of terrorist suspects for fourteen days incommunicado was held to be beyond what was necessary to meet the emergency.

112 D. Dyzenhaus, *The Constitution of Law: Legality in a Time of Emergency*, Cambridge University Press, 2006.

113 *Ibid.*, 59.

Criminal sanctions as a more 'legal' alternative to administrative detention

The early history of migration law reveals that lengthy imprisonment was only imposed following criminal conviction for defined immigration offences. This approach has a number of virtues. The legislature has to rank immigration crimes against other crimes on the statute book. A balance between border control, punishment and deterrence must be calibrated. Independent courts rule on guilt and sentencing, thereby assessing gravity and mitigation. Legal certainty and due process are observed. It is accepted that criminal due process applies as much to aliens as citizens. During sentence arrangements for removal can take place. For all these reasons, the presumption should be that criminal detention is the *main* detention. However, the inexorable move towards administrative detention has destroyed these safeguards. National legislative appraisals of the gravity of immigration offences have been sidelined. The duration of detention is left to executive priorities, degrees of efficiency and fate. Due process is said not to be required because detention is not intended as a punishment. Such detention periods have, however, often far exceeded the standard sentence for any crime associated with border crossing.

Whilst there has been persistent criticism of the 'criminalization' of irregular migration,[114] it is important to be clear about the terminology here. To the extent that administrative imprisonment without trial has become widespread, there has in fact been insufficient use of criminal law. If border controls are considered legitimate at all, then it is certainly defensible to impose criminal penalties on those who knowingly and without duress cross borders. There are important caveats here for persons who have no choice but to infringe border controls. Thus, certain refugees are specifically exempted from criminal punishment by the Refugee Convention.[115] Stateless persons are another group who should benefit from similar concessions in prosecutorial practice. With these exceptions, the period of imprisonment served, after a fair trial, to punish illegal entry or overstaying should not then give rise to long 'extensions' under immigration powers. Efficient use of resources should be employed to process cases to avoid additional post-sentence detention. Certainly governments have constantly set targets to process cases quickly. In practice, however, this has proved difficult.

---

114 See UN High Commissioner for the Human Rights of Migrants, *Annual Report 2002*, E/CN.4/2003/85.
115 See Art. 31 Refugee Convention.

The most significant cause of such extended detention is the lack of documentation upon which to remove detainees. Some detainees clearly fail to cooperate with documentation efforts. This problem prompted criminal penalties being imposed in 1952 in the United States for non-compliance. The United Kingdom introduced such a provision in 2004.[116] However, in the main, governments continue to rely not on criminal law, but administrative discretion to extend detention for 'non-compliance'. This is repeated in the EU Returns Directive which allows a twelve-month extension for this reason. This approach is wrong in principle because it totally undermines the rule of law by leaving an overtly coercive power of imprisonment to the discretion of executive officers. The very concept of 'non-cooperation' is fraught with uncertainty. There have been successful challenges to such executive assessments in the United States and the United Kingdom. The same mistaken appraisals will occur in Europe. Criminal process is preferable because it puts the burden on governments to justify their non-compliance claims before independent forensic examination. Clear and exacting definitions of non-compliance, with notice given to detainees under caution prior to any prosecution, are far more consistent with the rule of law.

Conditional authorization and internal rights

We have argued throughout that the liberty/detention balance is but one part of a wider question of what degree of interference states may legitimately impose on the fundamental interests of unauthorized persons. There are three givens. Border control usually implies *some* capacity to impose such disabilities which may not be imposed on citizens. Such disabilities must, however, be shown to be a necessary and effective part of a wider border strategy. Finally, the effects on individuals of imposing such disabilities must not be arbitrary, disproportionate or undermine their human dignity.

At its most demanding, this approach can rule out such disability altogether. Thus in the US cases on immigration offences, aliens were entitled to the same due process rights as citizens. As Bosniak notes, the Supreme Court 'carved out for all aliens a zone of protected personhood, where

---

116 See s. 35 Asylum and Immigration (Treatment of Claimants) Act 2004. *R* v. *Moud Tabnak* [2007] EWCA Crim 380, where the court ruled a 'reasonable excuse' for non-cooperation did not include a person's fear of removal to Iran given that his asylum claims had been dismissed.

the nation's membership interests are of no consequence at all'.[117] This is, however, exceptional. Equal entitlement is not presumed. In the United States there has been real political and legal debate on how far the border can be extended to the interior to discriminate against unauthorized persons who gain entry.[118] In *Plyer* v. *Doe*, for example, the Supreme Court ruled that a ban on education for children of illegal aliens was discriminatory and the state had not shown that migrants would be deterred from entering by such a measure. Whilst condemning illegal entry, the Court was fearful of creating 'a permanent caste of undocumented resident aliens, encouraged by some to remain here as a source of cheap labor, but nevertheless denied the benefits that our society makes available to citizens and lawful permanent residents'.[119]

In the United Kingdom, too, political efforts to curb irregular migration have repeatedly drawn courts in to review questions of proportionality. For example, immigrants without visas were prevented from marrying in order to discourage applications for leave to remain linked to sham marriages. The British courts ruled that the policy was disproportionate, as it caught genuine marriages, too, and amounted to a discriminatory denial of the right to marry.[120] Similarly, successive British governments have sought to restrict social support for asylum seekers who enter illegally.[121] The courts have generally found a legal basis to prevent enforced destitution in such cases. Denial of social support and the right to work to support oneself in combination amounted to inhuman and degrading treatment in breach of Article 3 ECHR.[122]

These situations illustrate that unauthorized persons' 'rights' emerge from a careful political and legal balancing of the impact on individuals as set against the effectiveness of the enforcement policy in question. There

---

117 L. Bosniak, *The Citizen and the Alien*, Princeton University Press, 2006, 65.

118 Bosniak calls them 'convergence' and 'separationist' schools. Both agree that enforcement may be strict at the border, but they disagree on what happens thereafter. The former see internal restriction post-entry as legitimate, whilst the latter seek to uphold conditions of legal equality for those actually living in the community.

119 *Plyer* v. *Doe* 457 U.S. 202 (1982) per Brennan J., IIIA. But by contrast, in *Mathews* v. *Dias* 424 U.S. 319 (1976) a federal ban on entitlement to Medicare until lawful aliens had completed five years' residence was upheld as linked to immigration and meeting the test of rational basis review.

120 See *R (Baia)* v. *Secretary of State for the Home Department* [2009] 1 AC 287. This was based on the ECHR, Arts 12 and 14.

121 For a full history, see L. Morris, *Asylum, Welfare and the Cosmopolitan Ideal*, London: Routledge, 2010.

122 *R* v. *Secretary of State for the Home Department ex parte Adam and others* [2005] UKHL 66.

is no sense in which the full privileges of citizenship are conferred on those who are at large rather than detained. It is a fallacy to say that 'such persons, by their illegal and unwanted entry, could become de facto . . . citizens'.[123] Living under constrained and highly restricted conditions is clearly far short of citizenship status. Historically speaking, governments adopted a pragmatic approach, accepting that if deportation was delayed, detention should not be extended. Detainees should be released and given conditional rights. This pragmatic approach constituted a form of political reauthorization, falling short of full regularization, which allowed both supervision of deportees but also gave them certain entitlements to support themselves. There is a need to return to this pragmatic approach which has become obscured by modern political rhetoric and bureaucratic logic which views each release as a 'defeat' – and each detainee released as a 'victor' – in the battle over unauthorized migration. Modern nation states are generally strong and stable. They do not need to sacrifice fundamental principles to achieve tolerable levels of control over their borders.

Conclusions

The right to liberty is universal and fundamental. Regulation of migration nevertheless suggests some ancillary power of executive detention not applicable to citizens. This difference, relatively unimportant for many years, has more recently led to open-ended and unaccountable detention of aliens. An absence of clear jurisprudential limits to detention allowed policy to become largely politically driven. National security became entwined with migrants and border control in ways that has led to the use of large-scale prison-like facilities. The supra-national human rights system has begun to question such arbitrary and excessive detention of unauthorized aliens. Whilst there is no unqualified right of free movement across borders, liberty of the person has been reasserted as a basic right. This is an important external check which reminds nation states of the wider context in which they conduct immigration policies. Domestic constitutional cases have also begun to reassert the rule of law and the doctrine of no detention without trial.

Automatic judicial review of detention, presently exceptional, should be seen as essential. The principle of proportionality was suggested as a tool that was able to pragmatically balance liberty interests against the needs

---

123 *Al Kateb* v. *Godwin* [2004] HCA 20, para. 46.

of migration control. This should operate at the broader level of setting absolute time limits as well as structuring decisions in individual cases. Whether we choose to call long-term administrative detention 'punitive' or not; whether it is applied to expulsion of residents or exclusion of new arrivals, the fact is that deprivation of liberty of any person must again be seen as a serious interference with a fundamental interest, requiring careful independent scrutiny and justification in each case to avoid the risk of inhumane, arbitrary or disproportionate practices. Much present immigration detention appears to fail to satisfy this test driven, as it is, largely by political priorities and executive policy aimed at demonstrating effort in the struggle against unauthorized migration.

The establishment of workable systems of judicial control is not impossible. Many countries have already done so. Detention should be based upon useful evidence about which individuals pose real risks of absconding and after careful consideration of alternative tools that militate against these risks. Detention should not be prolonged where this is unnecessary, unlikely to lead to removal or causes hardship. For those detainees who present serious criminal risks, criminal procedures should be used rather than internment under the guise of immigration powers. More broadly, detention should be tied more closely to criminal conviction for actual offences rather than executive discretion. This also applies to detainees who abscond or unreasonably refuse to cooperate with removal. Unauthorized migrants presently occupy a legal space between ordinary criminals and invading enemies. Rather than criminal conviction, they face segregation pursuant to campaigns against unauthorized migration that have no obvious end. In the absence of proper legal safeguards, detention will continue to occur in an arbitrary and disproportionate manner which does little to serve either the interests of immigration control or that of immigrants themselves.

BIBLIOGRAPHY

Abbott, K.W., Keohane, R.O., Moravcsik, A., Slaughter, A. and Snidal, D., 'The Concept of Legalization' (2000) 54(3) *Int. Org.* 401.

Ackerman, B., *Social Justice in the Liberal State*, New Haven, CT: Yale University Press, 1980.

Acosta, D., 'The Good, the Bad and Ugly in EU Migration Law: Is the European Parliament becoming Bad and Ugly? (The Adoption of Directive 2008/115: the Returns Directive)' (2009) 11 *Eur. J. Migration and L.* 19.

ACLU, *America's Disappeared: Seeking International Justice for Immigrants Detained after September 11*, New York: ACLU, 2004.

   How the USA-PATRIOT Act Permits Indefinite Detention of Immigrants Who Are Not Terrorists, New York: ACLU, 2001.

   Indefinite Detention, New York: ACLU, 2000.

   The Aftermath of the 1996 Immigration Laws: Real Life Tragedies, New York, ACLU, 2000.

Adamson, F.B., 'Crossing Borders: International Migration and National Security' (2006) 31(1) *Int. Security* 165.

Agamben, G., *Homo Sacer: Sovereign Power and Bare Life* (trans. D Heller-Roazen), Stanford University Press, 1998.

Akehurst, M., *A Modern Introduction to International Law*, 3rd edn, London: Routledge, 1977.

Aleinikoff, T.A., 'Political Asylum in the Federal Republic of Germany and Republic of France: Lessons for the United States' (1984) 17 *Univ. Mich. J.L. Reform* 183.

   'Detaining Plenary Power: The Meaning and Impact of *Zadvydas v Davis*' (2002) 16 *Geo. Immig. L.J.* 365.

Alexseev, M.A., *Immigration Phobia and the Security Dilemma*, Cambridge University Press, 2006.

Allan, T.R.S., *Constitutional Justice: A Liberal Theory of the Rule of Law*, Oxford University Press, 2003.

Allison, L., 'The Utilitarian Ethics of Punishment and Torture', in L. Allison (ed.), *The Utilitarian Response*, London: Sage, 1990.

Alston, P., *International Human Rights Law*, Oxford University Press, 2000.

Alston, P. and Crawford, J., *The Future of UN Human Rights Treaty Monitoring*, Cambridge University Press, 2000.

Anderson, M., *Policing the European Union*, Oxford: Clarendon Press, 1995.

and Bigo, D., 'What are EU Frontiers For and What Do They Mean?' in K. Groenendijk, E. Guild and P. Minderhound (eds), *In Search of Europe's Borders*, The Hague: Kluwer Law International, 2003.

Arendt, H., *The Origins of Totalitarianism*, New York: Harcourt, Brace and Jovanovich, 1968.

Ashford, M., *Detained without Trial*, London: JCWI, 1993.

Association of Jewish Refugees, *Dispersion and Resettlement: the Story of the Jews from Central Europe*, London: De Vere Press, 1955.

Avery, C., 'Refugee Status Decision-making in Ten Countries' (1984) 17 *Stan. J. Int. L.* 183.

Baker, J., *The Oxford History of the Laws of England 1483–1558, vol. VI*, Oxford University Press, 2003.

Baldaccini, A., 'The European Directive on Returns: Principles and Protests' (2010) 28(4) *Refugee Survey Quarterly* 114.

Barde, R.E., *Immigration at the Golden Gate: Passenger Ships, Exclusion and Angel Island*, Westport, CT, London: Praeger, 2008.

Barde, R. and Bobonis, G.J., 'Detention at Angel Island: First Empirical Evidence' (2006) 30(1) *Social Science History* 103.

Barry, B., 'International Society from a Cosmopolitan Perspective', in D. Maple and T. Nardin (eds), *International Society: Diverse Ethical Perspectives*, Princeton University Press, 1998.

Battjes, H., *European Asylum Law and International Law*, Leiden: Martinus Nijhoff, 2006.

Beatty, D., *The Ultimate Rule of Law*, Oxford University Press, 2004.

'Human Rights and the Rules of Law', in D. Beatty (ed.), *Human Rights and Judicial Review: A Comparative Perspective*, Amsterdam: Kluwer Academic Publishers, 1994.

Beitz, C., *Political Theory and International Relations*, Princeton University Press, 1979.

Bell, J., *French Constitutional Law*, Oxford: Clarendon Press, 1992.

Bellamy, R., *Political Constitutionalism*, Cambridge University Press, 2007.

and Castiglione, D., 'The Communitarian Ghost in the Cosmopolitan Machine: Constitutionalism, Democracy and the Reconfiguration of Politics in the New Europe', in R. Bellamy and D. Castiglione (eds), *Constitutionalism, Democracy and Sovereignty: American and European Perspectives*, Aldershot: Avebury, 1996.

Benhabib, S., *The Rights of Others*, Cambridge University Press, 2004.

Bernadot, M., *Camps d'etrangers*, Paris: Terra, 2008.

'Des Camps en France (1944–1963)' 58 *Plein Droit* Dec. 2003.

'Etre interne au Larzac: la politique d'assignation a residence: la guerre d'Algerie, 1958–1962' (2005) 1 *Politix* 1.

Betts, K., 'Boat People and Public Opinion in Australia' (2001) 9 *People and Place* 4.

Bhagwati, J., 'Borders Beyond Control' (2003) 82(1) *Foreign Affairs* 99.

Bigo, D., 'Migration and Security', in V. Guiraudon and C. Joppke (eds), *Controlling a New Migration World*, London: Routledge, 2002.

Bingham, T., *The Rule of Law*, London: Allen and Lane, 2010.

Bird, J.C., *The Control of Enemy Alien Citizens in Great Britain 1914–18*, New York and London: Garland Publishers, 1986.

Blake, M. and Risse, M., *Is There a Human Right to Free Movement? Immigration and Original Ownership of the Earth*, New York University Working Papers, 2005.

Boeles, P., Brouwer, E., Woltjer, A. and Alfenaar, P., *Border Control and Movement of Persons – Towards Effective Legal Remedies for Individuals in Europe*, Utrecht: Standing Committee of Experts in International Immigration, Refugee and Criminal Law, 2004.

Bonner, D., 'Checking the Executive? Detention without Trial, Control Orders, Due Process and Human Rights' (2006) 12(1) *EPL* 45.

and Cholewinski, R., 'The Response of the United Kingdom's Legal and Constitutional Orders to the 1991 Gulf War and the Post-9/11 "War" on Terrorism', in A. Baldaccini and E. Guild, *Terrorism and the Foreigner*, Amsterdam: Martinus Nijhoff, 2005.

Booth, C. and Du Plessis, M., 'Home Alone? The US Supreme Court and International and Transnational Judicial Learning' (2005) 2 *EHRLR* 127.

Borjas, G., 'Economic Theory and International Migration' (1989) 23 *Int. Migration Rev.* 457.

Friends or Strangers: the Impact of Immigration on the US Economy, New York: Basic Books, 1990.

Bork, R., *The Tempting of America*, New York: Free Press, 1990.

Bork, R.H., *Coercing Virtue: The Worldwide Rule of Judges*, Toronto: Vintage Canada, 2002.

Bosniak, L., *The Citizen and the Alien*, Princeton University Press, 2006.

Bossuyt, M.J., *Guide to the 'Travaux Préparatoires' of the International Covenant on Civil and Political Rights*, Leiden: Martinus Nijhoff Publishers, 1987.

Boswell, C., 'Migration Control in Europe after 9/11' (2007) 45 *JCMS* 589.

Boudin, L.B., 'The Settler Within Our Gates' (pts 1–3) (1951) 26 *N.Y.U. L. Rev.* 266.

Bradley, C., 'The Military Commissions Act, Habeas Corpus and the Geneva Conventions' (2007) *Duke Law School Working Paper Series* 96.

Brimelow, P., 'Time to Rethink Immigration' (1995) *National Review* 30.

Alien Nation: Common Sense about America's Immigration Disaster, New York: Random House, 1995.

Brouwer, E., 'Effective Remedies in Immigration and Asylum Law Procedures: A Matter of General Principles of Law', in A. Baldaccini, E. Guild and H. Toner (eds), *Whose Freedom, Security and Justice? EU Immigration and Asylum Law and Policy*, Oxford: Hart, 2007.

Brownlie, I., *Principles of Public International Law*, Oxford University Press, 2003.
   and Goodwin-Gill, G. (eds), *Basic Documents on Human Rights*, 4th edn, Oxford University Press, 2002.

Brubaker, R., *The Limits of Rationality: An Essay on the Social and Moral Thought of Max Weber*, London: Allen and Unwin, 1984.

Buchanan, A., *Justice, Legitimacy and Self-Determination: Moral Foundations of International Law*, Oxford University Press, 2004.

Buchanan, P., *The Death of the West: How Dying Populations and Immigrants Invasions Imperil Our Country and Civilization*, New York: Thomas Dunne Book/St. Martin's Press, 2002.

Callero, E., 'Popular Sovereignty and the Law of Peoples' (2003) 9 *Legal Theory* 181.

Caney, S., *Justice Beyond Borders: A Global Political Theory*, Oxford University Press, 2005.

Carens, J., 'Migration and Morality: A Liberal Egalitarian Perspective', in B. Barry and R.E. Goodin (eds), *Free Movement: Ethical Issues in the Transnational Migration of People and of Money*, Pennsylvania State University Press, 1992.

Carens, J.H., 'Aliens and Citizens: the Case for Open Borders', in R. Cohen (ed.), *Theories of Migration*, Cheltenham: Edward Elgar, 1996.

Castles, S. and Miller, M.J., *The Age of Migration*, 4th edn, London: Macmillan Press, 2009.

Cesarani, D., 'An Alien Concept? The Continuity of Anti-Alienism in British Society before 1940' in D. Cesarani and T. Kushner (eds), *The Internment of Aliens in Twentieth Century Britain*, London: Frank Cass, 1993.

Chalmers, D. and Tomkins, A., *European Public Law*, Cambridge University Press, 2007.

Cholewinski, R., 'European Union Policy on Irregular Migration', in B. Bogusz, R. Cholewinski, A. Cygan and E. Syszczak (eds), *Irregular Migration and Human Rights: Theoretical, European and International Perspectives*, Leiden: Martinus Nijhoff Publishers, 2004.
   'The Need for Effective Individual Legal Protection in Immigration Matters' (2005) 7 *Eur. J. Migration and L.* 237.

Claghorn, K.H., *The Immigrant's Day in Court*, New York: Arno Press, 1969.

Clapham, A., 'A Human Rights Policy for the European Community' (1990) *YEL* 309.

Clark, D. and G. McCoy, *The Most Fundamental Right*, Oxford: Clarendon, 2000.

Cole, D., *Enemy Aliens: Double Standards and Constitutional Freedoms in the War on Terrorism*, New York: New Press, 2003.

'In Aid of Removal: Due Process Limits on Immigration Detention' (2002) 51 *Emory L.J.* 1003.

'The Priority of Morality' (2004) 113 *Yale L.J.* 1753.

Coolidge, M.R., *Chinese Immigration*, New York: Henry Holt, 1909.

Cooper, R., *The Breaking of Nations*, London: Profile, 2004.

Cornelisse, G., 'Human Rights for Immigration Detainees in Strasbourg: Limited Sovereignty or a Limited Discourse?' (2004) 6 *Eur. J. Migration and L.* 93.

Craies, W.F., 'The Right of Aliens to Enter British Territory' (1890) 6 *LQR* 39.

Craig, P., 'Constitutional and Non-constitutional Judicial Review' (2001) 54 *CLP* 147.

and De Búrca, G., *The Evolution of EU Law*, Oxford University Press, 1999.

Curtin, D., *Postnational Democracy: The European Union in Search of a Political Philosophy*, The Hague: Kluwer, 1997.

and O'Keefe, D. (eds), *Constitutional Adjudication in EC and National Law. Essays in Honour of Justice T.F. O'Higgins*, Dublin: Butterworths, 1992.

Daniels, R., *Guarding the Golden Door: American Immigration Policy since 1882*, New York: Hill and Wang, 2004.

Dauvergne, C., 'Sovereignty, Migration and the Rule of Law in Global Times' (2004) 67(4) *MLR* 588.

Making People Illegal: Migration Laws for Global Times, Cambridge University Press, 2008.

Davis, K.C., *Administrative Law Treatise*, St. Paul: West Publishing, 1958.

Discretionary Justice, Louisiana University Press, 1969.

De Greiff, P. and Cronin, C. (eds), *Global Justice and Transnational Politics: Essays on the Moral and Political Challenges of Globalization*, Cambridge, MA: MIT Press, 2002.

De Guchteneire, P. and Pecoud, A., 'Introduction: the UN ICRMW' in P De Guchteneire, A. Pecoud and R. Cholewinski (eds), *Migration and Human Rights: the United Nations Convention on Migrant Workers' Rights*, Cambridge University Press, 2009.

Davins, N. and Fisher, L., *The Democratic Constitution*, Oxford University Press, 2004.

Dicey, A.V., *Lectures on the Relation Between Law and Public Opinion in England*, London: Macmillan, 1905.

Introduction to the Study of the Law of the Constitution, 10th edn, 1959.

Dickinson, J., *Administrative Justice and the Supremacy of Law in the United States*, Cambridge, MA: Harvard University Press, 1927.

Dickson, B., 'Law Versus Terrorism: Can Law Win?' (2005) 1 *EHLR* 11–28.

Dow, M., *American Gulag: Inside U.S. Immigration Prisons*, Berkeley: University of California Press, 2004.

Duker, W.F., *A Constitutional History of Habeas Corpus*, Westport, CT: Greenwood Press, 1980.

Dummet, A. and Nicol, A., *Citizens, Subjects, Aliens and Others: Nationality and Immigration Law*, London: Weidenfeld and Nicolson, 1990.

Dworkin, R., 'Why It Was a Great Victory' (2008) 55(13) *New York Review of Books*, 5.

'Terror and the Attack on Civil Liberties' (2003) 50(17) *New York Review of Books*.

A Matter of Principle, Cambridge, MA: Harvard University Press, 1985.

Law's Empire, London: Fontana, 1986.

Sovereign Virtue: The Theory and Practice of Equality, Oxford University Press, 2000.

Dyzenhaus, D., 'Now the Machine Runs Itself: Carl Schmitt on Hobbers and Kelsen' (1994–5) 16 *Cardozo L. Rev.* 1–19.

'The Rule of (Administrative) Law in International Law' (2004–5) 68 *L. and Contemp. Probs.* 127.

The Constitution of Law: Legality in a Time of Emergency, Cambridge University Press, 2006.

Edelman, M., *Constructing the Political Spectacle*, University of Chicago Press, 1988.

Eff, C., 'The Detention Centre Maze' (2006) 37 *Vacarme*.

Eisgruber, C., 'Should Constitutional Judges Be Philosophers?', in S. Hershovitz (ed.), *Exploring Law's Empire: The Jurisprudence of Ronald Dworkin*, Oxford University Press, 2006.

Ely, J.H., *Democracy and Distrust*, Cambridge, MA: Harvard University Press, 1980.

Equal Rights Trust, *Unravelling Anomaly: Detention, Discrimination and the Protection Needs of Stateless Persons*, London: Equal Rights Trust, 2010.

Erskine May, T., *The Constitutional History of England Since the Accession of George III*, vol. III, Boston: Corsby and Nichols, 1862.

Evans, P., 'The Eclipse of the State? Reflections on Stateness in an Era of Globalization' (1997) 50 *World Politics* 62.

Ewing, K.D., 'The Futility of the Human Rights Act' (2004) *PL* 829.

Fallon, R.H. and Meltzer, D.J., 'Habeas Corpus Jurisidiction, Substantive Rights, and the War on Terror' (2007) 120 *Harv. L.R.* 2029.

Fazel, M. and Silove, D., 'Detention of Refugees' (2006) 332 *BMJ* 251.

Feldman, D., 'The Importance of Being English', in D. Feldman and G. Stedman-Jones (eds), *Metropolis London: Histories and Representations since 1800*, London: Routledge, 1989.

Feldstein, H.S., 'A Study of Transactions and Political Integration: Transnational Labour Flows within the European Economic Community' (1967) 6 *JCMS* 24.

Finnis, J., 'Commentary on Dummett and Weithman', in B. Barry and R.E. Goodin (eds), *Free Movement: Ethical Issues in the Transnational Migration of People and of Money*, Penusylvania State University Press, 1992.

'Nationality, Alienage and Constitutional Principle' (2007) 123 *LQR* 417.

Fishkin, J., *The Limits of Obligation*, New Haven, CT: Yale University Press, 1982.

Fleck, D. (ed.), *The Handbook of International Humanitarian Law*, Oxford University Press, 2008.

Fletcher, G.P., 'Guantanamo Disentangled? The US Supreme Court Steps In: Citizenship and Personhood in the Jurisprudence of War: Hamdi, Padilla and the Detainees in Guantanamo Bay' (2004) 2(4) *J. Int. Crim. Just.* 953.

Flynn, E.J., 'Counter Terrorism and Human Rights: the View from the United Nations' (2005) 1 *EHRLR* 29.

Forsyth, C., 'Showing the Fly the Way Out of the Flybottle: the Value of Formalism and Conceptual Reasoning in Administrative Law' (2007) *CLJ* 325.

Foucault, M., *Discipline and Punish: the Birth of the Prison* (trans. A. Sheridan), New York: Vintage, 1979.

Forsythe, D.P., 'United States Policy toward Enemy Detainees in the "War on Terrorism"' (2006) 28 *H.R.Q.* 465.

Franck, T.M., 'Case Comment: United States: *Hamdan v Rumsfeld* – Presidential Power in Wartime' (2007) 5 *I.J. Const. L.* 380–8.

Fritz, C.G., 'A Nineteenth Century "Habeas Corpus Mill": The Chinese Before the Federal Courts in California' (1988) 32 *Am. J. Legal Hist.* 347.

Fuller, L., *The Morality of Law*, New Haven, CT: Yale University Press, 1965.

Galligan, D.J., *Discretionary Powers: A Legal Study of Official Discretion*, Oxford: Clarendon Press, 1986.

Galloway, D., 'Liberalism, Globalism, and Immigration' (1993) 18 *Queen's L.J.* 266.

'Strangers and Members: Equality in an Immigration Setting' (1994) 7 *Can. J.L. & Juris.* 149.

'Noncitizens and Discrimination: Redefining Human Rights in the Face of Complexity' in O. Schmidtke and S. Ozcurumez (eds), *Of States, Rights, and Social Closure: Governing Migration and Citizenship*, New York: Palgrave Macmillan, 2008.

Gearty, C., 'Human Rights in an Age of Counter-terrorism: Injurious, Irrelevant or Indispensable?' (2005) 1 *EHRLR* 25.

and Ewing, K., *The Struggle for Civil Liberties: Political Freedom and the Rule of Law in Britain, 1914–1945*, Oxford University Press, 2000.

Geddes, A., *Immigration and European Integration: Towards Fortress Europe?*, Manchester University Press, 2000.

'Europe's Border Relationships and International Migration Relations' (2005) 43 *JCMS* 787.

Gibney, M., 'A Thousand Little Guantanmos: Western States Measures to Prevent the Arrival of Refugees', in K.T. Tunsall (ed.), *Displacement, Asylum and Migration*, Oxford University Press, 2006.

Gibney, M.J., *The Ethics and Politics of Asylum*, Cambridge University Press, 2004.

Gifford, D.J., 'Discretionary Decisionmaking in the Regulatory Agencies: a Conceptual Framework' (1983) *South Carolina L. Rev.* 101.

Gilbert, G., 'Is Europe Living Up to its Obligations to Refugees?' (2004) 14(5) *Eur. J. Int. L.* 963.

Gillman, P. and Gillman, L., *"Collar the Lot": How Britain Interned its Wartime Refugees*, London, New York: Quartet Books, 1982.

Golove, D., 'United States: the Bush Administration's "War on Terrorism" in the Supreme Court' (2005) *3 I.J. Const. L.* 128.

Goodwin-Gill. G., 'The Limits of the Power of Expulsion in Public International Law' (1974–5) *BYIL* 55.

International Law and the Movement of Persons between States, Oxford University Press, 1978.

The Refugee in International Law, Oxford University Press, 1996.

'Article 31 of the 1951 Convention relating to the Status of Refugees: Non-penalization, Detention and Protection', in E. Feller *et al.* (eds), *Refugee Protection in International Law*, Cambridge University Press, 2003.

'International Law and the Detention of Refugees' (1986) 20(2) *Int. Migration Rev.* 193.

Gordenker, L., *Refugees in International Politics*, London: Croom Helm, 1987.

Grahl-Madsen, G., *The Status of Refugees In International Law*, Leiden: Sijthoff, 1966.

Groenendijk, K. 'The Growing Relevance of Article 39 (ex 48) EC Treaty for Third Country Immigrants', in *Thirty Years of Free Movement of Workers in Europe*, Luxembourg: European Communities, 2000.

Gross, O., 'Chaos and Rules: Should Responses to Violent Crises Always be Constitutional?' (2003) 112 *Yale L.J.* 1011.

Guild, E., 'Citizens, Immigrants, Terrorists and Others', in A. Ward and S. Peers (eds), *The EU Charter of Fundamental Rights: Politics, Law and Policy*, Oxford: Hart, 2004.

'Seeking Asylum: Storm Clouds between International Commitments and Legislative Measures' (2004) 29 *E.L. Rev.* 198.

'The Variable Subject of the EU Constitution, Civil Liberties and Human Rights' (2004) 6 *Eur. J. Migration and L.* 381.

(ed.), *Constitutional Challenges to the European Arrest Warrant*, Nijmegen: Wolf Legal Publishers, 2006.

and Peers, S., 'Out of the Ghetto? The Personal Scope of EU Law', in S. Peers and N. Rogers (eds), *EU Immigration and Asylum Law: Text and Commentary*, Leiden: Martinus Nijhoff, 2006.

Guillaume, G., 'Terrorism and International Law' (2004) 52 *ICLQ* 537.

Guiraudon V. and Joppke, C. (eds), *Controlling a New Migration World*, London: Routledge, 2001.

Gupta, S. and Graybill, J., *Justice Denied: Immigration Families Detained At Hutto*, New York: ACLU, 2008.

Haas, E.B., *The Uniting of Europe: Political, Social and Economic Forces 1950–1957*, Stanford University Press, 1958.

Habermas, J., *Between Facts and Norms*, Cambridge: Polity Press, 1997.

Haddad, E., *The Refugee in International Society: Between Two Sovereigns*, Cambridge University Press, 2008.

Hailbronner, K., *Immigration and Asylum Law and Policy of the European Union*, Amsterdam: Kluwer, 2000.

'Asylum Law in the Context of a European Migration Policy', in N. Walker (ed.), *Europe's Area of Freedom Security and Justice*, Oxford University Press, 2004.

'Detention of Asylum Seekers' (2007) 9 *EJML* 159.

Hamm, M.S., *The Abandoned Ones: the Imprisonment and Uprising of Mariel Boat People*, Boston: Northeastern University Press, 1995.

Hanlon, L., 'UK Anti-terrorism Legislation: Still Disproportionate?' (2007) 11(4) *IJHR* 481.

Hansen, R., *Citizenship and Immigration in Post-war Britain*, Oxford University Press, 2000.

Hart, H.M., 'The Power of Congress to Limit the Jurisdiction of Federal Courts: An Exercise in Dialectic' (1953) 66 *Harv. L. Rev.* 1362.

Hassan, P., 'The Word "Arbitrary" as Used in the Universal Declaration of Human Rights: "Illegal or Unjust"?' (1969) 10 *Harv. Int. L.J.* 225.

Hathaway, J.C., *The Rights of Refugees under International Law*, Cambridge University Press, 2005.

'What's in a Label?' (2003) 5 *Eur. J. Migration and L.* 1.

Hayter, T., *Open Borders: the Case against Immigration Controls*, London: Pluto Press, 2000.

Held, D., 'Democratic City-states to a Cosmopolitan Order?' (1992) 40 *Polit. Studies* 10.

'Law of States, Law of Peoples: Three Models of Sovereignty' (2002) 8 *Legal Theory* 33.

Cosmopolitan Democracy, London: Polity Press, 2000.

Hendrikson, D.C., 'Migration in Law and Ethics: A Realist Perspective', in B. Barry and R.E. Goodin (eds), *Free Movement: Ethical Issues in the Transnational Migration of People and of Money*, Pennsylvania State University Press, 1992.

Henkin, L., 'The Constitution and United States Sovereignty: a Century of Chinese Exclusion and its Progeny' (1986–7) 100 *Harv. L. Rev.* 853.

Hickman, T.R., 'Between Human Rights and the Rule of Law: Indefinite Detention and the Derogation Model of Constitutionalism' (2005) 68(4) *MLR* 654–80.

Hiebert, J.L., 'Parliamentary Review of Terrorism Measures' (2005) 68(4) *MLR* 676.

Higgins, R., 'Derogations under Human Rights Treaties' (1976–7) 48 *BYIL* 281.

Hill Maher, K., 'Who has a Right to Rights? Citizenship's Exclusions in an Age of Migration', in A. Brysk (ed.), *Globalization and Human Rights*, Berkeley: University of California Press, 2002.

Hilson, C., 'What's in a Right? The Relationship Between Community, Fundamental and Citizenship Rights in EU Law' (2004) 29 *E.L. Rev.* 636.

Hinsley, F.H., *Sovereignty*, 2nd edn, Cambridge University Press, 1986.

Hirst, P. and Thompson, G., 'Globalization and the Future of the Nation-State' (1995) 24 *Economy and Society* 408.

Hobbes, T., *Leviathan*, New York: Collier Books, 1962.

Hobsbawm, E.J., *Nations and Nationalism Since 1870*, Cambridge University Press, 1991.

Hoffman, P., 'Human Rights and Terrorism' (2004) 26 *H.R.Q.* 932.

Holdsworth, W.S., *A History of English Law*, vol. IX, London: Methuen, 1926.

Hollifield, J., *Immigrants, Markets and States*, Cambridge MA: Harvard University Press, 1992.

Human Rights Watch, *Locked Away: Immigration Detainees in Jails in the US*, New York: Human Rights Watch, 1998.

Hughes, J. and Liebaut, F. (eds), *Detention of Asylum Seekers in Europe: Analysis and Perspectives*, Amsterdam: Martinus Nijhoff Publishers, 1998.

Hughes, J. and Field, O., 'Recent Trends in the Detention of Asylum Seekers in Western Europe', in J. Hughes and F. Liebaut (eds), *Detention of Asylum Seekers in Europe: Analysis and Perspectives*, Amsterdam: Martinus Nijhoff Publishers, 1998.

Hutchinson, E.P., *Legislative History of American Immigration Policy 1798–1965*, Philadelphia: University of Pennsylvania Press, 1981.

Huysmans, J., 'The European Union and the Securitization of Migration' (2000) 38 *JCMS* 751.

   The Politics of Insecurity: Fear, Migration and Asylum in the EU, London: Routledge, 2005.

   'Migrants as a Security Problem: Dangers of "Securitizing" Societal Issues' in R. Miles and D. Thranhardt (eds), *Migration and European Integration: The Dynamics of Inclusion and Exclusion*, London: Pinter Publishers, 1995.

Ignatieff, M., *Human Rights*, Princeton University Press, 2001.

Ignatieff, M., *The Lesser Evil: Political Ethics in an Age of Terror*, Edinburgh University Press, 2005.

Iuda, J., *Targeting Immigrants: Government, Technology and Ethics*, Oxford University Press, 2006.

Jackson, V.C., 'World Habeas Corpus' (2006) 91 *Cornell L. Rev.* 303.

Jacobson, D., *Rights without Borders*, Baltimore, MD: Johns Hopkins University Press, 1996.

Jennings, R. and Watts, A., *Oppenheim's International Law*, 9th edn, London: Longman, 1992.

Jesuit Refugee Service, *Detention in Europe: Administrative Detention of Asylum-seekers and Irregular Migrants*, Brussels: Jesuit Refugee Service, 2004.

Johnson, K.R., 'Open Borders' (2003) 51 *UCLA L. Rev.* 193.

Jones, T.D., 'A Human Rights Tragedy: The Cuban and Haitian Refugee Crises Revisited' (1995) 9(3) *Georgetown Immigr. L.J.* 479.

Joppke C., 'Why Liberal States Accept Unwanted Immigration' in A. Messina and G. Lahav (eds), *The Migration Reader: Exploring Politics and Policies*, London: Lynne Rienner Publishers, 2006.

Jordan, B. and Duvell, F., *Irregular Migration: the Dilemmas of Transnational Mobility*, Cheltenham: Edward Elgar, 2002.

Joseph, S., Schultz, J. and Castan, M. (eds), *The International Covenant on Civil and Political Rights: Cases, Materials and Commentary*, Oxford University Press, 1995.

Judt, T., *Postwar: a History of Europe Since 1945*, London: Penguin, 2007.

Juss, S., 'Free Movement and the World Order' (2004) 16 *Int. J. Refugee L.* 289.

International Migration and Global Justice, Aldershot: Ashgate Publishing, 2006.

Kalhan, A., 'Rethinking Immigration Detention' (2010) 110 *Colum. L. Rev.* 42.

Kalmthout, A., Hofstee-van der Meulen, F. and Dunkel, F. (eds), *Foreigners in European Prisons, vol I*, Nijmegen: Wolf Legal Publishers, 2007.

Kanstroom, D., *Deportation Nation*, Cambridge, MA: Harvard University Press, 2007.

'Developments in the Law of Immigration and Nationality' (1952–53) 66 *Harv. L. Rev.* 643.

Kant, I., 'Perpetual Peace', in Lewis White Beck (ed. and trans.), *On History*, Indianapolis and New York: Library of Liberal Arts, 1957.

Keller, A.S., Rosenfeld, B., Trinh-Shevrin, C. *et al.*, 'Mental Health of Detained Asylum Seekers' (2003) 362 *Lancet* 1721.

Kennedy, D., 'Form and Substance in Private Law Adjudication' (1976) *Harv. L. Rev.* 1685–778.

Keohane, R., 'Global Governance and Democratic Accountability', in D. Held and M. Koenig-Archibugi (eds), *Taming Globalization*, Cambridge: Polity Press, 2003.

Kerwin, D., 'The Use and Misuse of "National Security" Rationale in Crafting U.S. Refugee and Immigration Policies' (2005) 17 *Int. J. Refugee L.* 749.

and Lin, S.Y., *Immigration Detention: Can ICE Meet its Legal Imperatives and Case Management Responsibilities?* Washington, DC: Migration Policy Institute, 2009.

Kessler, A.E. and Freeman, G.P., 'Public Opinion on Immigration from Outside the Community' (2005) 43(4) *JCMS* 825.

Klemme, M., *The Inside Story of the UNRRA: an Experience in Internationalism: a first-hand report on the displaced persons of Europe*, New York: Lifetime, 1949.

Kochan, M., *Britain's Internees in the Second World War*, London: Macmillan, 1983.

Koh, H.H., 'Why do Nations obey International Law?' (1997) 106 *Yale L.J.* 2599.

Koslowski, R., 'Intra-EU Migration, Citizenship and Political Union' (1994) 32 *JCMS* 367–402.

Kostakopoulou, D., 'Ideas, Norms and Citizenship' (2005) 68(2) *MLR* 233.

'European Citizenship and Immigration after Amsterdam: Silences, Openings and Paradoxes' (1998) 24 *J. Ethnic and Migration Studies* 639.

Krammer, A., *Undue Process: the Untold Story of America's German Alien Internees*, London: Rowman and Littlefield, 1997.

Kraut, A.M., *The Huddled Masses: the Immigrant in American Society*, Wheeling, IL: Harlan Davidson Press, 1982.

Krisch, N., 'The Open Architecture of European Human Rights Law' (2008) 71(2) *MLR* 183.

Kuijper, P.J., 'Some Legal Problems Associated with the Communitarization of Policy on Visas, Asylum and Immigration under the Amsterdam Treaty and Incorporation of the Schengen Acquis' (2000) 37 *C.M.L. Rev.* 345.

Kukthas, G., 'The Case for Open Immigration', in A. Cohen (ed.), *Contemporary Debates in Applied Ethics*, Oxford: Blackwell, 2005.

Kumm, M., 'The Legitimacy of International Law: A Constitutionalist Framework of Analysis' (2004) 15 *Eur. J. Int. L.* 907.

Constitutional Democracy Encounters International Law: Terms of Engagement, New York University Public Law and Legal Theory Working Papers, No. 47, 2006.

Lahav, G., *Immigration Politics in the New Europe*, New York: Cambridge University Press, 2004.

and Messina, A.M., 'The Limits of a European Immigration Policy: Elite Opinion and Agendas within the European Parliament' (2005) 43 *JCMS* 851.

Lambert, H., *The Position of Aliens in Relation to the European Convention on Human Rights*, Human Rights Files No. 8 (rev.), Strasbourg: Council of Europe Publishing, 2001.

Lavenex, S. and Wallace, W., 'Justice and Home Affairs, Towards a "European Public Order"?', in H. Wallace, W. Wallace and M. Pollack (eds), *Policy Making in the European Union*, 5th edn, Oxford University Press, 2005.

Lee, E., *At America's Gates: Chinese Immigration during the Exclusion Era 1882–1943*, Chapel Hill: University of North Carolina Press, 2003.

Legomsky, S.H., 'The USA and the Caribbean Interdiction Program' (2006) 18 *Int. J. Refugee L.* 677.

Immigration and the Judiciary: Law and Politics in Britain and America, Oxford: Clarendon Press, 1987.

'The Detention of Aliens: Theories, Rules and Discretion' (1999) 30 *Inter-Am. L. Rev.* 531.

Legrain, P., *Immigrants: Your Country Needs Them*, London: Little, Brown, 2007.

Lenaerts, K., 'Fundamental Rights in the European Union' (2000) 25 *E.L. Rev.* 575.
and De Smiter, E., 'A Bill of Rights for the EU' (2001) 38 *C.M.L. Rev.* 273.

Linn, N. and Lea, S., 'A Phantom Menace and the New Apartheid: the Social Construction of Asylum-seekers in the United Kingdom' (2003) 14(4) *Discourse and Society* 425.

Loescher, G., *The UNHCR and World Politics*, Oxford University Press, 2001.
Beyond Charity: International Co-operation and the Global Refugee Crisis, New York: Oxford University Press, 1993.

Lord Millett, 'The Right of Good Administration in European Law' (2002) 47 *PL* 309.

Lord Steyn, 'Guantanamo Bay: the Legal Black Hole' (2004) 53 *ICLQ* 1.

Luban, D., 'Incommensurable Values, Rational Choice and Moral Absolutes' (1990) 8 *Cleveland St. L. Rev.* 65.

MacCormick, N., *Questioning Sovereignty*, Oxford University Press, 2003.

McConnell, M.W., 'The Importance of Humility in Judicial Review: A Comment on 'Ronald Dworkin's "Moral Reading" of the Constitution' (1997) 65 *Ford. L. Rev.* 1269.

McCrudden, C., 'A Common Law of Human Rights?', in K. O'Donovan and G.R. Rubin (eds), *Human Rights and Legal History: Essays in Honour of Brian Simpson*, Oxford University Press, 2000.

McGoldrick, D., *The Human Rights Committee: its Role in the Development of the International Covenant on Civil and Political Rights*, Oxford: Clarendon Press, 1991.

Malloch, M. and Stanley, E., 'The Detention of Asylum Seekers in the UK. Representing Risk, Managing Dangerousness' (2005) 7 *Punishment and Society* 53.

Mancini, G.F., 'The Free Movement of Workers in the Case-Law of the Court of Justice', in D. Curtin and D. O'Keefe (eds), *Constitutional Adjudication in EC and National Law: Essays in Honour of Justice T.F. O'Higgins*, Dublin: Butterworths, 1992.

Mansilla, M.J.G., 'The United States Supreme Court and the Guantanamo Bay Prisoners' (2006) 80 *Australian L.J.* 232.

Marfleet, P., *Refugees in a Global Era*, Hampshire: Palgrave Macmillan, 2006.

Marks, J.H., '9/11 + 3/11 + \7/7=? What Counts in Counterterrorism' (2006) 37 *Colum. H.R.L. Rev.* 103.

Martin, D., 'Preventive Detention: Immigration Law Lessons for the Enemy Combatant Debate. Testimony Before the National Commission on Terrorists Attacks upon the Untied States, December 8 2003' (2003–4) 18 *Geo. Immig. L.J.* 303.

'Due Process and the Treatment of Aliens' (1983) 44 *Univ. Pittsburgh L.R.* 165.

Mikolic-Torreira, S., 'The Cuba Migration Agreement: Implications of the Clinton–Castro Immigration Policy' (1994) 8 *Geo. Immig. L.J.* 667.

Mincheva, E., 'Case Report on *Kadzoev*, 30 November 2009' (2010) 12 *Eur. J. Migration and L.* 361.

Mitchell, C., 'The Political Costs of State Power: US Border Control in South Florida', in P. Andreas and T. Snyder (eds), *The Wall around the West: State Borders and Immigration Controls in North America and Europe*, Lanham, MD: Rowman and Littlefield, 2000.

Moch, L.P. *Moving Europeans: Migration in Western Europe since 1650*, Bloomington: Indiana University Press, 1992.

Moeckli, D., *Human Rights and Non-discrimination in the 'War on Terror'*, Oxford University Press, 2008.

Montfort, P., *La Contentieux de la Retention Administrative des Etrangers en Instance D'eloignment*, Paris: L'Harmattan, 2003.

Morris, L., *Asylum, Welfare and the Cosmopolitan Ideal*, London, Routledge, 2010.

Morrison, T.W., '*Hamdi*'s Habeas Puzzle: Suspension as Authorization?' (2006) 91 *Cornell L. Rev.* 411.

Motomura, H., 'Immigration Law After a Century of Plenary Power: Phantom Constitutional Norms and Statutory Interpretation' (1990–91) 100 *Yale L.J.* 545.

Mulhall, S. and Swift, A., *Liberals and Communitarians*, 2nd edn, Oxford: Blackwell, 1992.

Nafziger, J.A.R., 'The General Admission of Aliens under International Law' (1983) 77 *Am. J. Int. L.* 804.

Nagel, T., 'The Problem of Global Justice' (2005) 33 *Philosphy and Public Affairs* 113.

Nascimbene, B. (ed.), *Expulsion and Detention of Aliens in EU Countries*, Milan: Guiffre, 2001.

Nayyar, D., 'Cross-border Movements of People', in D Nayyar (ed.), *Governing Globalization*, Oxford University Press, 2002.

Neuman, G., *Strangers to the Constitution: Immigrants, Borders and Fundamental Law*, Princeton University Press, 1996.

'Wong Wing v United States', in D.A. Martin and P.H. Schuck, (eds), *Immigration Stories*, New York: Foundation Press, 2005.

'Comment, Counter-terrorist Operations and the Rule of Law' (2004) 15 *EJIL* 1019.

'Anomalous Zones' (1996) 48(1) *Stan. L.R.* 1197.

'Closing the Guantanamo Loophole' (2004) 50 *Loyola L. Rev.* 1.

Neumayer, E., 'Asylum Recognition Rates in Western Europe' (2005) 49 *J. Conflict Res.* 43.

New Shorter English Dictionary, Oxford: Clarendon Press, 1993.

Nicholas, A.W., 'Protecting Refugees: Alternatives to a Policy of Mandatory Detention' (2002) *Australian J. Human Rts* 6.

Noll, G., 'Visions of the Exceptional: Legal and Theoretical Issues Raised by Transit Processing Centres and Protection Zones' (2003) 5 *Eur. J. Migration and L.* 303.

O'Keefe, D., 'The Schengen Convention: A Suitable Model for European Integration?' (1992) 12 *YEL* 185.

O'Leary, S., *The Evolving Concept of Community Citizenship: From the Free Movement of Persons to Union Citizenship*, The Hague: Kluwer Law International, 1996.

O'Neill, O., *Bounds of Justice*, Cambridge University Press, 2000.

Office of Inspector General, *ICE's Compliance with Detention Limits for Aliens with a Final Order of Removal from the United States*, Washington, DC: Department of Homeland Security, 2007.

Oliver, P., 'Non-community Nationals and the Treaty of Rome' (1985) *YEL* 57.

Orucu, E., *Judicial Comparativism in Human Rights Cases*, London: UK National Committee of Comparative Law, 2003.

Overy, C. and White, R.C.A, *The European Convention on Human Rights*, 4th edn, Oxford University Press, 2006.

Page, E.C., 'Europeanization and the Persistence of Administrative Systems', in J. Hayward and A. Menon (eds), *Governing Europe*, Oxford University Press, 2003.

Panayi, P., *The Enemy in Our Midst: Germans in Britain during the First World War*, Oxford University Press, 1991.

   'An Intolerant Act by an Intolerant Society: The Internment of Germans in Britain During the First World War' in Cesearani and Kushner (eds), *The Internment of Aliens in Twentieth Century Britain*.

Pariseault, J.R., 'Applying the Rule of Law in the War on Terror: an Examination of Guantanamo Bay through the Lens of the US Constitution and the Geneva Conventions' (2005) 28(3) *Hastings Int'l and Comp. L. Rev.* 481.

Peers, S., 'Implementing Equality? The Directive on Long Term Resident Third Country Nationals' (2004) 29(4) *E.L. Rev.* 437.

   and Rogers, N. (eds), *EU Immigration and Asylum Law*, Leiden: Martinus Nijhoff, 2006.

Pellew, J., 'The Home Office and the Aliens Act 1905' (1989) 32(2) *The Historical Journal* 369.

Plender, R., *International Migration Law*, Leiden: Sijthoff, 1972.

Pogge, T., *Realizing Rawls*, London and Ithaca: Cornell University Press, 1989.

   'Cosmopolitanism and Sovereignty' (1992) 103 *Ethics* 48.

   'Migration and Poverty', in V. Bader (ed.), *Citizenship and Exclusion*, New York: St Martin's Press, 1997.

Porter, M. and Haslam, N., 'Predisplacement and Postdisplacement Factors Associated with Mental Health of Refugees and Internally Displaced Persons: A Meta-analysis' (2005) 294 *J. Am. Med. Assoc.* 602.

Posner, R.A., 'Pragmatic Adjudication' (1996) 18 *Cardozo L. Rev.* 1.

Post, L.F., *The Deportations Delirium of the Nineteen-Twenties*, Honolulu: University Press of the Pacific, 2003 (1st pub. New York: Kerr, 1923).

Preston Jr., W., *Aliens and Dissenters: Federal Supression of Radicals: 1903–1933*, Cambridge, MA: Harvard University Press, 1963.

Rawls, J., *A Theory of Justice*, Cambridge, MA: Harvard University Press, 1971.

   The Law of Peoples, Cambridge, MA: Harvard University Press, 1999.

Raz, J., 'The Rule of Law and its Virtue' (1977) 93 *LQR* 195.

Reich, N., 'A European Constitution for Citizens: Reflections on the Rethinking of Union and Community Law' (1997) 3 *ELJ*, 131–64.

Reisman, W.M., '*Rasul v Bush*: a Failure to Apply International Law' (2004) 2(4) *J. Int. Crim. Just.* 973.

Richard, C., and Fischer, N., 'A Legal Disgrace? The Retention of Deported Migrants in Contemporary France' (2010) 47(4) *Social Science Information* 581.

Risse, T., Ropp, S.C. and Sikkink, K. (eds), *The Power of Human Rights: International Norms and Domestic Change*, Cambridge University Press, 1999.

Robinson, N., *Convention Relating to the Status of Refugees: Its History, Contents and Interpretation*, New York: Institute of Jewish Affairs, 1953.

Rosberg, G.M., 'The Protection of Aliens from Discriminatory Treatment by the National Government' (1977) *Sup.Ct. Rev.* 275.

Rosenstiel, F., 'Reflections on the Notion of "Supranationality"' (1963) 2(2) *JCMS* 127.

Rousseau, J.-J., 'A Discourse on Political Economy', in V. Gourevitch (ed.), *The Social Contract and Other Later Political Writings*, Cambridge University Press, 1997.

Rubio-Marín, R., *Immigration as a Democratic Challenge: Citizenship and Inclusion in Germany and the United States*, Cambridge University Press, 2000.

Rudge, P., 'Fortress Europe', in *World Refugee Survey: 1986 in Review*, Washington, DC: US Committee for Refugees, 1987.

Salyer, L., *Laws Harsh as Tigers: Chinese Immigrants and the Shaping of Modern Immigration Law*, Chapel Hill: University of North Carolina Press, 1995.

Samers, M., 'An Emerging Geopolitics of "Illegal" Immigration in the European Union' (2004) 6 *EJML* 27.

Sangiovanni, A., 'Global Justice, Reciprocity and the State' (2007) 35 *Philosophy and Public Affairs* 3.

Sassen, S., *Guests and Aliens*, New York: New Press, 1999.

   Losing Control: Sovereignty in an Age of Globalization, New York: Columbia University Press, 1996.

Scalia, A., 'Federal Constitutional Guarantees of Individual Rights in the United States of America', in D. Beatty (ed.), *Human Rights and Judicial Review*, Amsterdam: Kluwer Academic Publishers, 1994.

Scanlon, T., *What We Owe to One Another*, Cambridge, MA: Harvard University Press, 1999.

Scheffler, S., 'Immigration and the Significance of Culture' (2007) 35(2) *Philosophy and Public Affairs* 93.

'Conceptions of Cosmopolitanism' (1999) 11 *Utilitas* 255.

Schmitt, C., *The Concept of the Political*, 2nd edn (trans. G. Schwab), New Brunswick, NJ: Rutgers University Press, 1976/1929.

Political Theology: Four Chapters on the Concept of Sovereignty, 2nd edn (trans. G. Schwab), Cambridge, MA: MIT Press, 1985.

State, Movement, People, Washington: Plutarch Press, 2001.

The Nomos of the Earth in the International Law of the Jus Publicum Europaeum, New York: Telos Press, 2006.

Schriro, D., *Immigration Detention Overview and Recommendations*, Washington, DC: Homeland Security, Immigration and Customs Enforcement, 2009.

Schuck, P.H., 'The Transformation of Immigration Law' (1984) 84 *Colum. L. Rev.* 1.

Citizens, Strangers and In-betweens: Essays on Immigration and Citizenship, Boulder, CO: Westview Press, 1998.

'The Disconnect between Public Attitudes and Policy Outcomes in Immigration' in C. Swain (ed.), *Debating Immigration*, New York: Cambridge University Press, 2007, 17–31.

and Smith, R.M., *Citizenship without Consent: Illegal Aliens in the American Polity*, New Haven, CT: Yale University Press, 1985.

and Williams, J., 'Removing Criminal Aliens: The Pitfalls of Federalism' (1988) 22 *Harv. J.L. & Pub. Pol.* 367.

Schwarze, J., 'Judicial Review of European Administrative Procedure' (2004) 85 *J.L. and Contemp. Prob.* 65.

Sen, A., *The Idea of Justice*, London: Penguin, 2010.

Sharpe, R.J., *The Law of Habeas Corpus*, 2nd edn, Oxford: Clarendon 1989.

Shue, H., *Basic Rights*, Princeton University Press, 1980.

Sibley, N.W. and Elias, A., *The Aliens Act and the Right of Asylum*, London: William Clowes and Sons, 1906.

Silove, D., Steel, Z. and Walters, C., 'Policies of Deterrence and the Mental Health of Asylum Seekers' (2000) 284 *J. Am. Med. Ass.* 604.

Simmonds, N., *Law as a Moral Idea*, Cambridge University Press, 2007.

Simon, J., 'Refugees in a Carceral Age: The Rebirth of Immigration Prisons in the United States' (1998) 10(3) *Public Culture* 577–607.

Simpson, A.W.B., *Odious in the Highest Degree: Detention Without Trial in Wartime Britain*, Oxford: Clarendon Press, 1992.

Simpson, G., *Law, War and Crime*, Cambridge: Polity Press, 2007.

Singer, P., *Practical Ethics*, 2nd edn, Cambridge University Press, 1993.

One World, New Haven, CT: Yale University Press, 2002.

Sjoberg, T., *The Powers and the Persecuted: The Refugee Problem and the Inter-governmental Committee on Refugees, 1938–47*, Lund University Press, 1991.

Skinner, Q., 'The State', in T. Ball, J. Farr and R. Hanson (eds), *Political Innovation and Conceptual Change*, Cambridge University Press, 1989.

Skowronek, S., *Building a New American State: the Expansion of National Administrative Capacities, 1877–1920*, Cambridge University Press, 1992.

Smith, R.M., 'Aliens Rights, Citizens Rights and the Politics of Restriction', in Swain (ed.), *Debating Immigration*.

Soysal, Y., *Limits of Citizenship: Migrants and Postnational Membership in Europe*, University of Chicago Press, 1994.

Spiro, P.J., 'Explaining the End of Plenary Power' (2002) 16 *Geo. Immig. L.J.* 339.

Spjut, R.J., 'Internment and Detention without Trial in Northern Ireland 1971–75: Ministerial Policy and Practice' (1986) 49 *MLR* 712.

Stafford-Smith, C., 'Getting Your Friends in Trouble' (2006) 3(1) *Muslim World J. Human Rts* 6.

Staples, H., *The Legal Status of Third Country Nationals Resident in the European Union*, The Hague: Kluwer, 1999.

Starmer, K., *European Human Rights Law*, London: Legal Action Group, 1999.

Staubhaar, T., 'International Labour Migration within a Common Market: Some Aspects of EC Experience' (1999) 27 *JCMS* 45.

Steel, Z., Silove, D., Brooks, R., Momartin, S., Alzuhariri, B. and Susljik, I., 'Impact of Immigration Detention and Temporary Protection on the Mental Health of Refugees' (2006) 188 *Br. J. Psychiatry* 58.

Streeck, W. and Schmitter, P.C., 'From National Corporatism to Transnational Pluralism: Organized Interests in the Single European Market' (1991) 19 *Politics and Society* 133.

Sunstein, C., 'Incommensurability and Valuation in Law' (1994) 92 *Mich. L. Rev.* 779.

Designing Democracy: What Constitutions Do, New York: Oxford University Press, 2001.

Laws of Fear, Cambridge University Press, 2007.

Takkenberg, L., 'Detention and Other Restrictions of the Freedom of Movement of Refugees and Asylum-seekers: the European Perspective', in J. Bhabha and G. Noll (eds), *Asylum Law and Practice in Europe and North America*, Washington, DC: Federal Publications Inc., 1992.

Taran, P.A., 'Human Rights of Migrants: Challenges of the New Decade' (2000) 38 (6) *International Migration* 11.

Taylor, M., 'Judicial Deference to Congressional Folly: The Story of *Demore v Kim*', in D.A. Martin and P.H. Schuck (eds), *Immigration Stories*, New York: Foundation Press, 2005.

Tholen, B., 'The Europeanisation of Migration Policy – The Normative Issues' (2004) 4 *Eur. J. Migration and L.* 323.

Thym, D., 'Respect for Private and Family Life under Article 8 ECHR in Immigration Cases: a Human Right to Regularise Illegal Stay?' (2008) *ICLQ* 52, 87–112.

Tichenor, D., *Dividing Lines: the Politics of Immigration Control in America*, Princeton University Press, 2002.

Tomkins, A., 'Legislating Against Terror' (2002) *PL* 205.

'Readings of *A v Secretary of State for the Home Department*' (2005) 3 *PL* 259.

Torpey, J., *The Invention of the Passport*, Cambridge University Press, 2000.

Tribe, L., 'The Puzzling Persistence of Process-Based Constitutional Theories' (1980) 89 *Yale L.J.* 1063.

Tridimas, T., *General Principles of EC Law*, Oxford University Press, 1999.

Tushnet, M., *Red, White and Blue: a Critical Analysis of Constitutional Law*, Cambridge, MA: Harvard University Press, 1988.

UNHCR, *UNHCR Handbook*, Geneva: UNHCR, 1979.

Van Drooghenbroeck, S., *La Proportionalité dans le droit de la Convention Européenne des Droits de l'Homme: Prendre l'idée Simple au Sérieux*, Bruxelles: Bruylant 2001.

Vincenzi, C., 'Deportation in Disarray: The Case of EC Nationals' (1994) *Crim. L. Rev.* 163–75.

Wachs, J., 'The Need to Define the International Legal Status of Cubans Detained at Guantanamo' (1996) 11 *Am. U. J. Int'l. L. and Pol.* 79.

Wakefield, J., *The Right of Good Administration*, Amsterdam: Kluwer, 2007.

Waldron, J., *Law and Disagreement*, Oxford: Clarendon, 1999.

Terror, Torture and Trade-offs: Philosophy for the White House, Oxford University Press, 2010.

Walker, N., 'In Search of the Area of Freedom, Security and Justice: A Constitutional Odyssey', in N. Walker (ed.), *Europe's Area of Freedom, Security and Justice*, Oxford University Press, 2004.

Wallace, W., 'Rescue or Retreat? The Nation State in Western Europe, 1945–1993' (1994) XLII *Political Studies* 52–76.

Walzer, M., 'Political Action: the Problem of Dirty Hands', in M. Cohen *et al.*, *War and Moral Responsibility*, Princeton University Press, 1974.

Spheres of Justice: A Defence of Pluralism and Equality, Oxford: Basil Blackwell, 1985.

'Philosophy and Democracy' (1981) 9 *Polit. Theory* 379.

Warbrick, C., 'The European Response to Terrorism in an Age of Human Rights' (2004) 15 *EJIL* 989.

Webber, J., 'National Sovereignty, Migration and the Tenuous Hold of Legality' in O. Schmidtke and S. Ozcurumez (eds), *Of States, Rights, and Social Closure:*

Governing Migration and Citizenship, New York: Palgrave Macmillan, 2008, 61–90.

Weber, L. and Gelsthorpe, L., *Deciding to Detain: How Decisions to Detain Asylum Seekers are Made at Ports of Entry*, Institute of Criminology, University of Cambridge, 2000.

    and Landman, T., *Deciding to Detain: The Organizational Context for Decisions to Detain Asylum Seekers at UK Ports*, Colchester: Human Rights Centre, University of Essex, 2002.

Weber, M., *Economy and Society* (G. Roth and C. Wittick (eds)), California University Press, 1978.

Weiler, J.H.H., 'Thou Shalt Not Oppress a Stranger: On the Judicial Protection of the Human Rights of Non-EC Nationals – A Critique' (1992) 3 *EJIL*, 65 at 68.

Weiler, J.H., 'To Be a European Citizen – Eros and Civilization' (1997) 4 *J. of Eur. Pub. Pol.* 495.

Weiler, J.P., 'The Community System: the Dual Character of Supranationalism' (1981) 1 *YEL* 267.

Weis, P., *The Refugee Convention, 1951: the Travaux Preparatoires Analysed with a Commentary by the Late Dr Paul Weis*, Cambridge University Press, 1995.

Weisband, E., 'Verdictive Discourses, Shame and Judicialization in Pursuit of Freedom of Association Rights', in S. Mekled-Garcia and B. Cali (eds), *The Legalization of Human Rights: Multidisciplinary Perspectives on Human Rights and Human Rights Law*, London: Routledge, 2005.

Weisberg, R., *Vichy Law and the Holocaust in France*, Amsterdam: Harwood Academic Publishers, 1996.

Weinzierl, R., *The Demands of Human and EU Fundamental Rights for the Protection of the European Union's External Borders*, German Institute for Human Rights, 2007.

Weissbrodt, D. and Bergquist, A., 'Extraordinary Rendition: A Human Rights Analysis' (2006) 19 *Harv. Human Rts J.* 123.

Welch, M., *Detained: Immigration Laws the Expanding INS Jail Complex*, Philadelphia: Temple University Press, 2002.

    and Schuster, L., 'Detention of Asylum Seekers in the US, UK, France, Germany and Italy. A Critical View of the Globalizing Culture of Control' (2005) 5(4) *Crim. Just.* 331.

White, R.C.A., 'Free Movement, Equal Treatment, and Citizenship of the Union' (2005) 54(5) *ICLQ* 885.

Winder, R., *Bloody Foreigners: the Story of Immigration to Britain*, London: Abacus, 2004.

Woodbridge, G., *UNRRA: The History of the United Nations Relief and Rehabilitation Administration*, vol. II, New York: Columbia University Press, 1950.

Wooldridge, F., 'Free Movement of EEC Nationals: the Limitations Based on Public Policy and Public Security' (1977) 2 *E.L. Rev.* 190.

Wray, H., 'The Aliens Act 1905 and the Immigration Dilemma' (2006) 33(2) *J.L. and Soc.*, 302–23.

Zelman, J., 'Recent Developments in International Law: Anti-terrorism Legislation – Part Two: the Impact and Consequences' (2002) 11 *J. Transnat. L. and Pol.* 421.

Zolberg, A., *A Nation By Design: Immigration Policy in the Fashioning of America*, Cambridge, MA: Harvard University Press, 2006.

INDEX